About This Book

Why is this topic important?

The education required over a lifetime cannot be delivered by conventional means. People must learn more efficiently and at the time and place of their choosing. E-learning can deliver that education, but only if it is designed to do so.

Over the past decade, e-learning has moved from an experimental procedure used to teach technical subjects within computer companies to a mainstream staple teaching everything from life-saving medical procedures to spiritual vision. If you are concerned with educating others, you cannot ignore e-learning.

There are lots of books on instructional design and lots on how to operate particular tools to create e-learning, but few on how to apply instructional design to e-learning. This is that book.

What can the reader achieve with this book?

This book provides instructional designers, teachers, faculty, information technologists, subject-matter experts, individual consultants, and others tasked with moving to e-learning a clear path to the goal of effective e-learning.

The pragmatic and practical advice in this book is not limited to any particular tool or system. Most of the techniques here can be implemented with simple tools you already know how to operate.

You can acquire a rapid, yet systematic, design process that covers the hundreds of decisions necessary to create great e-learning.

How is this book organized?

The twelve chapters of this book lead the reader systematically through the decisions necessary to design effective e-learning. It starts with an overview of the design process for e-learning. Then it builds up from small pieces to course-wide issues. There are three chapters on how to use technology to create the learning experiences that really teach. Learning games and simulations, guided tours, virtual labs, storytelling, guided research, and many other kinds of practice and discovery activities are covered. Next follow instructions on how to create tests and other assessments that verify and measure learning progress. The next two chapters tell how to integrate activities and tests into learning objects that completely accomplish learning objectives and how to combine topics and activities into lessons that accomplish more ambitious goals. The next chapter covers strategic issues, such as whether to include real-time meetings or an instructor and what standards to follow. The book ends with chapters on how to design and teach instructor-led e-learning in the virtual classroom, how to design the visual display and navigation scheme within the course.

Where did this book come from?

E-Learning by Design is the logical successor to *Designing Web-Based Training*. This book is more than a second edition, but not an entirely new work. It evolves the ideas started there.

This book, as its title implies, is squarely about design. It is not about development tools or other technologies. Design of e-learning involves instructional design, but goes beyond instructional design to include aspects of media design, software engineering, and economics. The goal is to tell readers how to design e-learning that works as well as the best classroom learning.

This book contains my best advice from my experience creating online learning. Since 1971, I have designed, built, researched, and evaluated what we now call e-learning. I have worked in electronic media most of my career from perspectives of design, management, and technology.

How can you get the most out of this book?

Read actively. Skim, scan, skip. Look at the pictures. Find something that interests you and read it in detail.

Where did the examples come from?

All examples were designed by William and Katherine Horton of William Horton Consulting. Unless otherwise noted, all examples were also built by William or Katherine Horton. Many of them are on exhibit at horton.com/eld/. We want to thank The Alban Institute and Indianapolis Center for Congregations, Brightline Compliance, The Gantt Group, Jones International University, The Office of Surface Mining and Reclamation, the Veterans Administration Office of Research and Development, and Web Courseworks for having us design them and letting us show them.

Where is the CD?

This book has an extensive Web presence with dozens of complete examples and supplementary materials. Check it out at: horton.com/eld/.

Who created this book?

William Horton wrote, typed, and indexed it. Katherine Horton designed the layout and formatted the book. William and Katherine drew the graphics. Rebecca Taff contributed proofreading. William and Katherine Horton suggested the cover design. And Pfeiffer took it from there.

About Pfeiffer

Pfeiffer serves the professional development and hands-on resource needs of training and human resource practitioners and gives them products to do their jobs better. We deliver proven ideas and solutions from experts in HR development and HR management, and we offer effective and customizable tools to improve workplace performance. From novice to seasoned professional, Pfeiffer is the source you can trust to make yourself and your organization more successful.

Essential Knowledge Pfeiffer produces insightful, practical, and comprehensive materials on topics that matter the most to training and HR professionals. Our Essential Knowledge resources translate the expertise of seasoned professionals into practical, how-to guidance on critical workplace issues and problems. These resources are supported by case studies, worksheets, and job aids and are frequently supplemented with CD-ROMs, websites, and other means of making the content easier to read, understand, and use.

Essential Tools Pfeiffer's Essential Tools resources save time and expense by offering proven, ready-to-use materials—including exercises, activities, games, instruments, and assessments—for use during a training or team-learning event. These resources are frequently offered in looseleaf or CD-ROM format to facilitate copying and customization of the material.

Pfeiffer also recognizes the remarkable power of new technologies in expanding the reach and effectiveness of training. While e-hype has often created whizbang solutions in search of a problem, we are dedicated to bringing convenience and enhancements to proven training solutions. All our e-tools comply with rigorous functionality standards. The most appropriate technology wrapped around essential content yields the perfect solution for today's on-the-go trainers and human resource professionals.

Pfeiffer
www.pfeiffer.com

Essential resources for training and HR professionals

E-Learning by Design

By

William Horton

Pfeiffer

A Wiley Imprint

www.pfeiffer.com

Published by Pfeiffer
An Imprint of Wiley
989 Market Street, San Francisco, CA 94103-1741
www.pfeiffer.com

Book design and composition: William Horton Consulting, Inc.

For additional copies/bulk purchases of this book in the U.S. please contact 800-274-4434.

Pfeiffer books and products are available through most bookstores. To contact Pfeiffer directly call our Customer Care Department within the U.S. at 800-274-4434, outside the U.S. at 317-572-3985, fax 317-572-4002, or visit www.pfeiffer.com.

Pfeiffer also publishes its books in a variety of electronic formats. Some content that appears in print may not be available in electronic books.

Library of Congress Cataloging-in-Publication Data
Horton, William K. (William Kendall)
  E-learning by design / by William Horton.
      p. cm.
  Includes index.
  ISBN-13: 978-0-7879-8425-0 (pbk.)
  ISBN-10: 0-7879-8425-6 (pbk.)
  1. Employees—Training of—Computer-assisted instruction. 2. Computer-assisted instruction—Design. I. Title.
  HF5549.5.T7H6357 2006
  658.3'124040285—dc22
                        2006010547

Printed in the United States of America

Printing 10 9 8 7 6 5 4 3

Contents

5 TESTS 215

Ways of organizing lessons 321

8 STRATEGIC DECISIONS 357

9 DESIGN FOR THE VIRTUAL CLASSROOM 415

11 NAVIGATION 531

Designing e-learning

Planning the development of online learning

For tens of thousands of years, human beings have come together to learn and share knowledge. Until now, we have had to come together at the same time and place. But today, the technologies of the Internet have eliminated that requirement. Soon anybody will be able to learn anything anywhere at any time, thanks to a new development called e-learning.

WHAT IS E-LEARNING?

E-learning marshals computer and network technologies to the task of education. Several definitions of e-learning are common. Some people hold that e-learning is limited to what takes place entirely within a Web browser without the need for other software or learning resources. Such a pure definition, though, leaves out many of the truly effective uses of related technologies for learning.

Definition of e-learning

There are a lot of complex definitions of e-learning, so I'll offer you a simple one:

E-learning is the use of information and computer technologies to create learning experiences.

This definition is deliberately open-ended, allowing complete freedom as to how these experiences are formulated, organized, and created. Notice that this definition does not mention "courses," for courses are just one way to package e-learning experiences. It also does not mention any particular authoring tool or management system.

Varieties of e-learning

E-learning comes in many forms. You may have taken one or two forms of e-learning, but have you considered them all?

- ▶ **Standalone courses**. Courses taken by a solo learner. Self-paced without interaction with an instructor or classmates. There are numerous examples of standalone courses cited in this book. Search the index for *Using Gantt Charts*, *GALENA Slope Stability Analysis*, and *Vision and the Church*. You can also go to the Web site for this book (horton.com/eld/) to find links to live examples.

- ▶ **Virtual-classroom courses**. Online class structured much like a classroom course. May or may not include synchronous online meetings. Just such a course is described starting on page 336. Also read Chapter 9, starting on page 415.

- ▶ **Learning games and simulations**. Learning by performing simulated activities that require exploration and lead to discoveries. Read more about games and simulations starting on page 141. Also go to horton.com/eld/ for links to live examples.

- ▶ **Embedded e-learning**. E-learning included in another system, such as a computer program, a diagnostic procedure, or online Help. Learn more about embedded e-learning starting on page 387. Also, view an example at horton.com/eld/.

- ▶ **Blended learning**. Use of various forms of learning to accomplish a single goal. May mix classroom and e-learning or various forms of e-learning. Start reading on page 381.

- ▶ **Mobile learning**. Learning from the world while moving about in the world. Aided by mobile devices such as PDAs and smart phones. Mobile learning examples are shown in Chapters 2, 4, 5, and 10.

- ▶ **Knowledge management**. Broad uses of e-learning, online documents, and conventional media to educate entire populations and organizations rather than just individuals. To learn more about practical knowledge management, go to horton.com/html/whckmt.asp.

And that is just the start. As you read this, clever designers are creating even more forms of e-learning.

WHAT IS E-LEARNING DESIGN?

At its best, e-learning is as good as the best classroom learning. And at its worst, it is as bad as the worst classroom learning. The difference is design.

Creating effective e-learning requires both design and development. Design is not the same as development. Design is decision. Development is doing. Design governs *what* we do; development governs *how* we carry out those decisions. Design involves judgment, compromise, tradeoff, and creativity. Design is the 1001 decisions, big and small, that affect the outcome. This book is about design.

Start with good instructional design

Instructional design requires selecting, organizing, and specifying the learning experiences necessary to teach somebody something. Good instructional design is independent of the technology or personnel used to create those learning experiences.

What is instructional design?

In this chapter I use the term *instructional design* in its broad meaning, which includes pedagogy and androgogy, although my usage is closer to the strict meaning of androgogy (teaching adults) than the limited definition of instructional design popular in some quarters. By instructional design, I definitely do not mean the heavy-handed, Stalinesque distortion of theory required to accompany many ponderous instructional systems design (ISD) methodologies.

Instructional design is a vast subject. This humble chapter cannot cover it all. Here you will find a streamlined, rapid instructional-design method. The process taught here is simple, quick, informal, and pragmatic. Use it as your survival kit when you do not have time or money for more. Or use it as a check on your longer, more formal process.

Before you fast-forward to another chapter with more screen snapshots and fewer diagrams, take a moment to decide whether this chapter might have something to offer you.

Instructional design determines everything else

Instructional design translates the high-level project goals to choices for technology, content, and everything else. The instructional design of e-learning informs decisions on what authoring tools, management systems, and other technologies to buy or license. Instructional design directs the development of content and the selection of media. It orchestrates decisions on budget, schedule, and other aspects of project development. So, design your instruction—at least on paper—before buying any technology or recruiting new staff members.

Please do not skip this chapter

True, not everybody needs to learn about instructional design. To decide whether you need this chapter, ask yourself these questions?

▶ Has your instructional design education and experience been primarily for the classroom?

▶ Is your current instructional design methodology too slow and cumbersome to meet your deadlines? Do you need something more rapid and agile?

▶ Do you like to see an overview of where you are going before you depart on a difficult journey?

▶ Do you lack either education and experience in instructional design? Perhaps you are a subject-matter expert or instructor who has inherited the responsibility for designing e-learning. Or a manager who needs to evaluate the portfolios of instructional designers you might hire.

If the answer to any of these questions is yes, read on.

Consider multiple perspectives

In e-learning, the responsibility to provoke effective learning experiences may be divided. Successful e-learning design is the result of four main influences, each contributing concerns and capabilities. Producing effective e-learning is a large job requiring several different skills: instructional design, media design, software engineering, and economics.

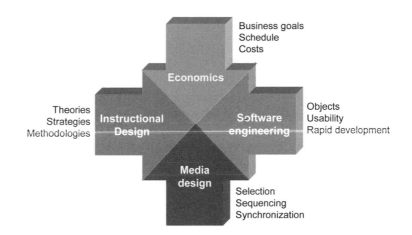

Each of these influences contributes concepts, procedures, and techniques:

► **Instructional design** contributes theories about how human beings learn, strategies for applying these theories, and methodologies to carry out the strategies. The knowledge of how human beings learn can guide selection and specification of new kinds of learning experiences such as simulations, learning games, online meetings, and discussion forums.

► **Software engineering** helps us build reliable computer programs. Like it or not, e-learning is software. It runs on a computer, just as a spreadsheet or word processor does. It has a user-interface and may draw content from a distant database. It transmits media over networks. It thus requires the same careful design and quality control as other forms of software. Software engineering contributes the concepts of object design, usability design, and rapid prototyping.

► **Media design** helps us use digital media well. When the only media were the words on a chalkboard and the instructor's voice, we did not need to "design" media. Today we must select the appropriate mixture of text, graphics, voice, music, sound effects, animation, and video. We must then sequence these various media and synchronize complementary media.

► **Economics** helps e-learning deliver value. E-learning costs money. It may generate revenue. It takes time, people, and other resources to create, offer, and maintain. It must be developed under a budget and on schedule.

In my experience, one of the most common mistakes is equating e-learning design with instructional design. I have worked with instructional designers who refused to consider any of the other factors. They produced designs that were never produced because they could not be realized with available technologies or cost too much.

The day when one person can comfortably perform all these necessary activities is still a way off. Until then, the joint role of e-learning designer must encompass several disciplines. Why? These disciplines are performed by different specialists and teams, especially in complex projects. The goals of one discipline may conflict with those of another. Business goals may call for a sedate, conservative appearance, while the media designer wants to showcase video and animation.

Many people trained in one discipline lack experience in the others. Instructional designers educated over ten years ago may know little about how to select dynamic electronic media. Even recent grads lack extensive training in animation design or game theory.

Some aspects of e-learning production may be outsourced, along with the detail design for that area. On one recent project, a training company outsourced the instructional design to me, had the software engineering done by their in-house information technology department, and outsourced the production of media to a firm in another country.

True designers—and project leaders—will balance all these concerns and be knowledgeable enough to resolve conflicts, make compromises, and spark innovation.

Design all units of e-learning

Design must be applied at all levels of e-learning from whole curricula down to individual media components. It is important to understand these units because they influence what design techniques we use.

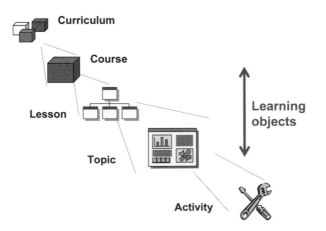

At the top of the pyramid are *curricula*, such as academic programs that include related courses that lead to a degree or certificate in a subject area. A curriculum could also refer to a library of courses on a certain subject.

Curricula are typically composed of *courses*, each of which teaches a broad but specific area of a subject. We might also call such units *books* or *knowledge products.* Course-level design issues are discussed in Chapter 8.

Courses are composed of clusters of smaller components called *lessons*. Each lesson is organized to accomplish one of the broad objectives of the course or a cluster of related objectives. Chapter 7 will help you design lessons.

At a lower level are the individual *topics*, each designed to accomplish a single low-level learning objective. For help designing topics, turn to Chapter 6.

At the bottom level are *learning activities*, each designed to provoke a specific learning experience. Each activity may answer a specific question or make a point, but they are seldom sufficient to accomplish a learning objective by themselves. Activities are the subject of Chapters 2 though 4. Activities used to measure learning are called tests. They are the subject of Chapter 5.

The middle three units (course, lesson, and topic) may all be designed as self-contained *learning objects*.

Let's see how to apply these levels in the real world. Here is a slice down through a single subject area:

Curriculum:	Master's of Business Administration program.
Course:	"Accounting 101."
Lesson:	"Assets and Liabilities."
Topic:	"Evaluating assets."
Activity:	Using a spreadsheet to calculate the values of assets.

DESIGN QUICKLY AND RELIABLY

E-learning benefits most from a rapid, cyclical design process. In this section you will find a minimalist, waste-no-time, results-focused approach to specifying e-learning that actually works. This process omits unnecessary steps and concentrates on the design tasks that really matter.

In the interest of speedy learning, we'll start with a preview, overview, summary, and job aid all rolled into one. Print it out, enlarge it, and pin it to your wall, where you can refer to it throughout your projects. An Adobe PDF version is available at horton.com/eld/.

Ask what matters

Your overall goal tells you what really matters. To clarify your goal, you need to answer two questions.

The first question is "What matters to your organization?" We might phrase the question this way: "For your company, university, department, government, or institution, what is the single most important measure of success?" Try to answer in three words or fewer. That restriction focuses your goal. Three words are plenty. You might say "bottom-line profit" or "return on investment." Or you might say "public service" or "unblemished reputation." On one of our projects, the Gantt Group, a consulting firm specializing in teaching project management, identified their goal as:

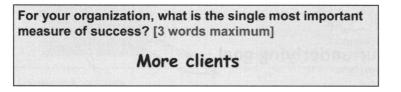

For your organization, what is the single most important measure of success? [3 words maximum]

More clients

They figured if they attracted enough clients, revenues and profits would follow.

The second question asks how your project will help accomplish that goal. How will the e-learning you design contribute to that goal? I am not saying your e-learning will accomplish the goal by itself, but you certainly should be able to state how it will contribute. If you cannot convincingly and honestly argue that your project contributes to the goal, consider canceling the project now. Without such alignment with organizational goals, your project may run out of money, time, and management support. Better to stop now before antagonizing the management of your organization by wasting organizational resources on an endeavor that does not matter to the organization.

Let's look at how this question was answered for the Gantt Group:

How will your project help accomplish that goal?

Convince potential clients that understanding Gantt charts can make them more successful project managers (and that the Gantt Group is the source for that understanding).

The proposed project was aimed at garnering more clients by convincing potential clients that understanding Gantt charts, which are a common tool of project management, could make them more successful and that the Gantt Group was the source for that understanding.

Make your organization's goal your goal

Create a bridge connecting a high-priority goal of your organization and the learning objectives of your e-learning so both business managers and instructional designers see the value of e-learning to the organization. Notice how this statement provides just such a bridge:

> Most misdiagnoses of battery problems are caused by lack of knowledge among customer-support technicians about the modes of battery failure and the symptoms they can produce. By training customer-support technicians, we can reduce the rate of misdiagnosis by at least 90%.

About half of the designers I have worked with stubbornly refuse to consider the underlying organizational goal when designing instruction. They do not feel that organizational goals are their responsibility. They design courses that accomplish little— or that die for lack of organizational support. This is tragic because it only takes two questions to align learning objectives to organizational goals.

Consider a wide range of goals

Organizational goals are not limited to profit or return-on-investment. Peruse your organization's annual report or replay speeches by your organization's leaders. Observe what your leaders emphasize as the values and goal of the organization.

Type goal	Description	Measures
Financial	Monetary success of a for-profit or not-for-profit enterprise.	▶ Profit. ▶ Cash flow. ▶ Margin. ▶ Stock price. ▶ Venture capital.
Intellectual capital	Knowledge the organization controls.	▶ Education level of staff. ▶ Professional experience of staff. ▶ Rates of attracting and retaining talent. ▶ Patents and inventions.

Type goal	Description	Measures
Customers	Consumers of the organization's services or products.	▶ Students. ▶ Accounts, clients, sponsors. ▶ Market share.
Operations	Efficiency and speed with which the organization performs its mission.	▶ Time to market. ▶ Cost per unit.
Reputation	Public image of an organization.	▶ Industry awards. ▶ Rankings and ratings. ▶ Community-service awards.

Set learning objectives

Good objectives are a mission-critical, sin qua non, must-have, make-or-break requirement for effective e-learning. Forgive me for stacking up so many adjectives, but without exception clear objectives make everything go better. In my experience, well over half the failures of e-learning projects would have been prevented by clear objectives.

Everything stems from the objectives. From the objectives, we identify prerequisites, select learning activities, and design tests. Good objectives focus efforts, reduce false starts, and cut waste enormously.

Write your learning objectives

Once you have clarified the goal of your project, you can write the primary learning objective for your course. This objective states what the course will accomplish.

There are many opinions on how to write objectives and complete methodologies on just how to phrase objectives. Search amazon.com for books by Robert Mager or Robert Gagné and you will find some examples. For quick instructional design, however, I use a single, simple formula that works well almost all the time. It states learning objectives in three parts. First, the objective states the intent, that is, what will be taught. Second, it identifies the target learner. Third, it identifies starting requirements.

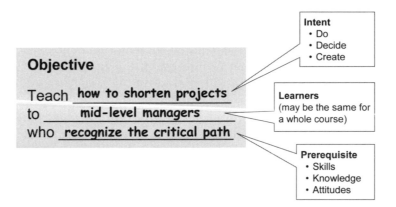

For the example of the course *Using Gantt Charts*, the top-level objective of the course was to teach how to shorten projects. It was to teach this subject to mid-level managers. But those managers had to know how to recognize the critical path in a Gantt chart.

For our quick objective, the first slot records what we want to teach. Usually it is to do something, make a decision, or create something.

The second slot records the group of people we want to accomplish this objective. If an entire course is aimed at a single group of people, this slot may have the same answer for every objective in the course.

The final slot records the prerequisites necessary to make accomplishing the objective practical. Prerequisites are usually stated as the skills, knowledge, and attitudes learners must possess. The prerequisites slot can have multiple answers, but the teach slot has only a single skill, item of knowledge, or attitude.

What makes a good objective?

Good learning objectives are clear, precise, and worthy. Let's look at each of these requirements.

Clear

A learning objective should be clear to everyone involved with it. The objective must tell the project's management team what you intend to accomplish. It must give the media designer specific marching orders. And it must communicate the "what's in it for me" to the learner.

Precise

The learning objective must specify the required learning in enough detail that we can measure its accomplishment. You may be thinking that what we have listed as an objective is not complete or precise enough. Correct. Right now, it is more of a goal. But don't worry; we will tighten it up considerably.

My advice is don't get too precise too soon. Early in a project, it is more important to write down all your objectives briefly than to specify them in excruciating detail. Once you have all your learning "goals" spread out in front of you and have eliminated unnecessary ones, you can flesh them out one at a time.

Worthy

Your learning objective must directly contribute to accomplishing the underlying organizational goal. Responsible developers continually check their objectives against the organizational goal.

Types of objectives

Some complex methodologies for writing objectives list hundreds of different types of objectives. I list six types of objectives—three primary and three secondary. Applied with sensitivity and common sense, they suffice 95% of the time.

Instructional intent can be expressed in the following format. This format consists of a standard preamble and one of six possible completions.

By experiencing this lesson or topic, the learner will be able to:

Primary objectives

- **Do** procedure X to accomplish Y.
- **Create** or design an X that does Y.
- **Decide** X, given Y.

Secondary objectives

- **Believe** X.
- **Feel** X about Y.
- **Know** X about Y.

Primary and secondary objectives

Objectives can be primary or secondary. Primary objectives are the ultimate reasons for learning while secondary objectives enable accomplishment of the primary objective, even though they are seldom the targeted result.

Both are important, but the primary objectives are the ones you must teach to accomplish your overall objective. Primary objectives are *performance* objectives in that they prescribe things people will be able to do as a result of your e-learning. As such they are sometimes called *terminal* objectives. But they can also be *enabling* objectives, that is, things you teach so that learners can learn the terminal objectives. Secondary objectives are always enabling objectives. They are not the main goal, but may be essential nonetheless to accomplish the primary objectives.

So, if you write the overall objective for your e-learning and it looks like one of the secondary objectives here, reconsider. Ask yourself, why do you want someone to believe, feel, or know something? What will meeting such an objective accomplish? The answer to these questions pinpoints your primary objective.

I have not made a big deal about separating cognitive, affective, and psychomotor objectives. Most real-world tasks involve components of all three. For example to perform CPR, you must know the steps of the procedure (cognitive), know how the procedure varies for infants (cognitive), have courage (affective), remain calm (affective), perform coordinated movements (psychomotor), and adjust the procedure based on sounds and tactile sensations (psychomotor).

Primary objectives state your goals

Primary objectives are the goals your e-learning should accomplish. Primary objectives are stated in terms of performance, that is, what the learner will be able to do.

The following table lists the various forms of primary instructional objectives and provides examples of statements of each form.

Type objective	When situation Z occurs, the learner will ...	Examples
Do	Do X to accomplish Y.	...once a month, complete the cleanup procedure to remove invalid e-mail addresses from the mailing list.
		... mix base and tint colors to match a sample provided by the buyer.
		... use the Explorer view to set up the file structure for a complex Web site.
		... lift heavy packages by flexing the knees rather than bending the back.
		... apply principles learned in Calculus 101 to problems encountered in Calculus 201.

Type objective	When situation Z occurs, the learner will …	Examples
Decide	Decide Y.	… pick a course of treatment based on a physical examination of the patient and standard blood tests.
		… select which looping construct is most efficient for each type of iterative procedure.
		… decide a strategy for dealing with a difficult co-worker based on the past behavior of the co-worker.
		… order a salad rather than a double cheeseburger.
		… pick team members based on what they can contribute rather than on familiarity, friendship, or superficial characteristics.
		… use leveraged investments moderately in a rational fashion rather than as a form of gambling.
Create	Design or build an X that does Y.	… plan the development effort for complex XML projects.
		… specify the layout of a city park that meets environmental, aesthetic, and logistical requirements.
		… write a program to export information from a common database to an XML format containing just the information specified.
		… build a 1/24 scale model of the proposed dwelling.

You may be accustomed to writing objectives in terms of skills, knowledge, and attitudes. If so, just remember that skills typically require *do* or *create* objectives. Attitudes use *decide* objectives to ask whether the learner consistently makes choices indicated by the attitude.

Do not fret if your objectives are not 100% clear at this point. You will further clarify your objectives when you design tests to measure accomplishment of the objective.

Secondary objectives help accomplish goals

Secondary objectives teach something necessary to accomplish a primary objective. They state what the learner will know, believe, or feel.

Type objective	When situation Z occurs, the learner will …	Examples
Know	Know X about Y.	… be able to recall the country codes for 99% of our international shipments. … know calming words to use during disputes. … identify all bones in the human hand by name.
Believe	Believe X.	… believe that our company is the most reliable supplier in our market. … believe that they can accomplish their financial objectives by working with us. … deem mutual funds worthy of a place in their portfolios.
Feel	Feel X about Y.	… feel positively about our company's entire product line. … remain calm when confronted by an angry stranger. … have confidence that they can use our products to solve their own problems. … feel sympathy (rather than pity) for co-workers with disabilities.

Spell out the situation

We teach so that learners can apply what they learn, not merely accumulate knowledge. People apply knowledge, skills, and attitudes in real-world situations. As part of the objective, we need to specify what those situations are. That way, designers can tailor the

1

Designing e-learning

design to accomplishing results in these situations. *Situation* is a pretty broad term. It can include three main factors: events that trigger application of learning, conditions under which the learner must act, and resources the learner will need in order to apply learning.

Trigger

What events will trigger application of the learning? What must the learner recognize as a cue to act? Will the learner receive explicit prompts to apply learning? Or will the learner need to infer the need for action from subtle cues in the environment? Is this an action that is applied periodically to a schedule?

Conditions

Under what conditions does the learner perform the action? In what environment does the learner act? Where does the action take place? How noisy is the environment? Is it especially hot or cold? How much room does the learner have? Is lighting adequate? Is the learner subject to frequent interruptions?

Resources

What resources can the learner draw on? Books? Calculators? Access to the Web? Memory only? What assistance will the learner have? A supervisor to guide the learner? Peers with whom to discuss problems?

Set criteria for success

What degree of success will learners accomplish? We like to think that all learners will be perfectly successful in accomplishing the intended results. Ironically, though, designing for a goal of perfect performance often leads to worse, not better, results. Thus, for each objective, we should state realistically how successful learners should be in applying what they learn.

Quantifying the degree of success is not easy, but we can at least set metrics such as these:

▶ Percent of learners who will accomplish the objective perfectly.

▶ Average error rate.

▶ Time required to perform the task.

▶ Results produced in a specified period of time.

▶ Reduction in frequency of problems or increase in rate of favorable incidents.

Examples of complete learning objectives

Here are some examples of learning objectives from different courses:

Learners	Situation	Action	Criteria
Full-time foresters with fewer than five years' experience.	When asked to recommend a policy. They will have access to Web-based resources.	Objectively consider controlled burns as a means of forest management.	Novice foresters will recommend controlled burning with the same frequency as more experienced foresters.
Visual Basic programmers working on database projects.	When the need arises. Access to all online documentation and other Web-based resources.	Write routines to retrieve, alter, and rewrite data using ADO and RDS.	Within 10 minutes, at least 85% will be able to write the routines.
Customer support technicians.	When answering customer complaints over the phone. Using a diagnostic procedure recalled from memory.	Correctly identify the cause of battery failures.	Reduce the current rate of misdiagnosis by 90%.
Individual investors.	Using Web-based resources during the course.	Develop a balanced financial plan to accomplish their individual objectives.	Over 90% will complete their plans.

Analyze learners' needs and abilities

Whose knowledge, skills, and attitudes are you trying to alter? Research the groups of potential learners until you can answer these questions:

▶ What are the learners' current levels of knowledge, biases, skills, and attitudes?

▶ What are their expectations and attitudes toward learning?

▶ What motivates them to learn?

▶ How well prepared are they to use e-learning technologies?

Such intimate knowledge may require conducting surveys, interviews, and testing. I use a form like this to summarize the characteristics of each group of learners who will take my e-learning:

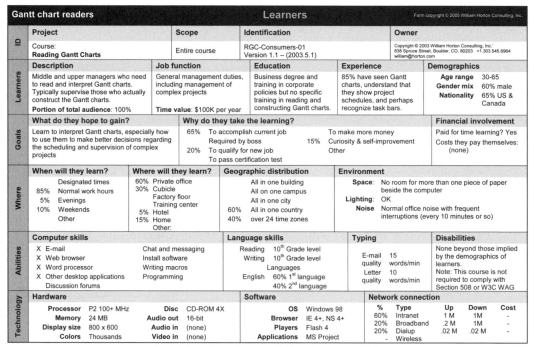

An Adobe PDF version is available at horton.com/eld/.

Consider defined curricula

When setting objectives for a course or curricula, consider whether someone has already defined the required body of knowledge or skills to be taught. For the area of your course or curriculum, are requirements defined by:

▶ Government regulations?

▶ Certification or licensing procedures?

▶ Standard reference works?

▶ Professional associations?

▶ Standardized academic curricula?

Such definitions can save you months of research and debate in defining learning objectives of your project.

Teach essential skills

Instruction is only effective if it teaches the right things. One common problem occurs when we teach low-level, explicit knowledge that learners already know, could figure out on their own, or will never apply. For instance, many courses on computer operations teach typing rather than the skills really needed to use the computer successfully.

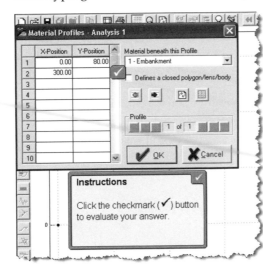

For example, this portion of a simulation requires learners to type numbers into the cells of a grid.

The problem with this approach is that it focuses attention on the task of typing in numbers. It encourages tunnel vision that distracts from the more important task of teaching what goes into the grid.

Typing skills are not the critical skill. The critical skill is entering the right pattern of data. This revision of the activity focuses attention on the relationships among values rather than merely typing numerals.

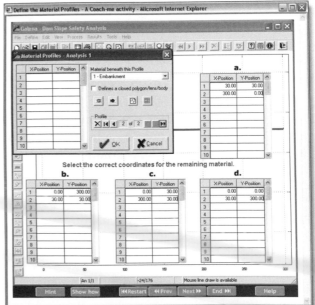

Created with Adobe Captivate.

Identify prerequisites

No project of any complexity will have just a single, simple learning objective. Whatever the top-level learning objective, it has prerequisites that you must identify. Such prerequisites specify the skills and knowledge learners must possess before they can begin to accomplish the main objective.

Spot related objectives

Starting with the top objective, the design identifies a cascade of prerequisite objectives. As an example, let's look at the top objective for the course *Using Gantt Charts*. It is to teach how to shorten projects to mid-level managers who can interpret the critical path. Fine, but not all mid-level managers will already know how to interpret the critical path.

That means we need another lower-level objective to meet that prerequisite. This objective would require teaching how to interpret the critical path. It would be aimed at the same mid-level managers as before. This new objective has its own prerequisite, namely, the ability to interpret Gantt charts in general.

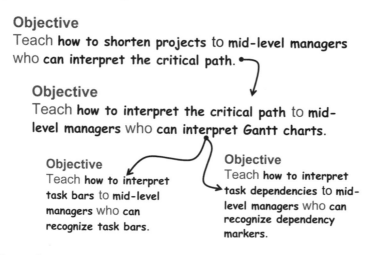

Objective
Teach **how to shorten projects** to **mid-level managers** who **can interpret the critical path.**

Objective
Teach **how to interpret the critical path** to **mid-level managers** who **can interpret Gantt charts.**

Objective
Teach **how to interpret task bars** to **mid-level managers** who **can recognize task bars.**

Objective
Teach **how to interpret task dependencies** to **mid-level managers** who **can recognize dependency markers.**

Interpreting Gantt charts in turn requires objectives on how to interpret task bars and how to interpret task dependencies. Both of these two new objectives are prerequisites of the prior objective.

Thus, objectives develop in a cascade downward from the top-level learning objective as we repeatedly ask what the learner must know before beginning an objective.

State objectives in shorthand

My formula for writing objectives is simple, but writing dozens of objectives can become tedious. Perhaps that is why many designers skip all that work and just begin developing content. Resist that urge. If you want to, you can streamline the process by writing objectives in a shorthand fashion.

To streamline the statement of an objective, state just what the learner will be able to do after accomplishing the objective. "Teach how to shorten projects to mid-level managers who can interpret the critical path" becomes just "shorten projects." Our next objective becomes just "interpret the critical path." And our final two objectives become just "interpret task bars" and "interpret task dependencies."

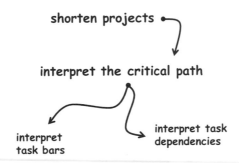

We can streamline the statement of objectives because the learners are typically similar throughout an entire course and because the prerequisite for a higher-level objective becomes the subject for the next objective down the cascade.

This shorthand works best when the objective is stated in the grammatical form that expresses it as a task the learner will be able to accomplish. The first part of this grammatical form is an active verb, such as "interpret" or "shorten." The second part is a phrase representing the direct object of the verb, that is, what the verb acts on. This format keeps the focus on performance.

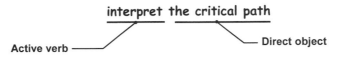

Here's a best practice for you. The best tools for cataloging your streamlined learning objectives are a whiteboard or Post-it® notes because they make it easy for you to change your mind.

Example: Bottom-up sequencing

The course *Good Clinical Practice* had a bottom-up structure. This course dealt with a critical subject with life-or-death consequences. Its goal was to teach experienced medical researchers to follow regulations and ethical practices in conducting tests on human subjects, some of whom had died due to lapses by researchers.

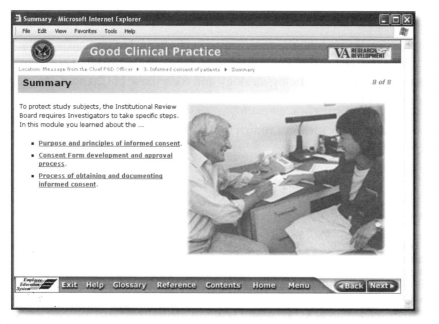

The structure of the course is made evident by the **Next** button in the lower right, suggesting a strongly recommended path through the course.

Built using Adobe Dreamweaver.

The legal concerns were great. The course was mandatory. Every learner was required to complete every page of the course. A sequential structure aided that goal.

Let's look at the sequence of topics within a lesson on obtaining the informed consent of test subjects before conducting experiments on them. The lesson starts with a definition of informed consent as this is the basis of the whole lesson. Next, the lesson introduces the general principles of informed consent that will guide the researcher. Next are spelled out the specific elements of the document used to record informed consent. After that come details of the process through which the document goes to fully secure and document informed consent.

With all the background established, the lesson now provides specific details about obtaining consent from the test subject. Finally, it specifies the requirements the researcher must follow to document informed consent. The following pages provide a practice activity and a summary.

Did you notice how the lesson carefully begins with definitions, fundamental concepts, and contextual background before presenting the exact procedure the researcher must follow. That order is a classic example of the bottom-up sequence.

Example: Top-down sequencing

Let's look at an example of a top-down sequence. This example teaches operation of the *GALENA* Slope Stability Analysis computer program which is used to analyze the stability of earthen dams, road cuts, surface mines, and other slopes.

After an introduction, the course starts with a preview of the entire process of using the program. As part of this preview, the learner can select a show-me demonstration (p. 54). The demonstration provides a narrated, over-the-shoulder look at the use of the program to analyze an earthen dam. The demonstration is complete. If that is all the learner needs, the learner can quit the training and begin using the program.

If not, the learner can continue for more detailed instruction on how to perform each of the steps shown in the overview.

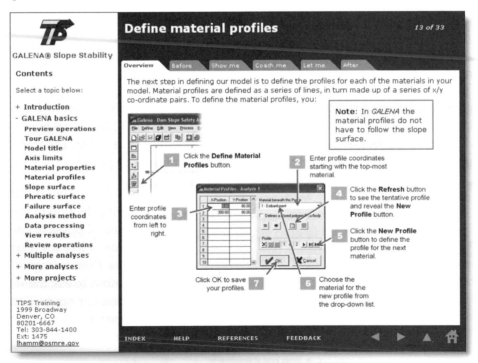

Tabbed interface built using Adobe Dreamweaver and custom JavaScript. Screens captured with TechSmith SnagIt. Illustrations created in Microsoft PowerPoint.

For example, if the learner selects the Material profiles step, the lesson on how to define the cross section of a slope model appears. Note that this lesson also has a top down

Create objects to accomplish objectives

Now that we have identified our prerequisites and narrowed them to the ones the course will directly accomplish, it is time to plan how we will accomplish those objectives. It is time to start specifying modules of learning for each objective. And that leads us to learning objects.

What is a learning object?

What do we mean by the term *learning object*? Let's start with a simple definition:

> **A learning object is a chunk of electronic content that can be accessed individually and completely accomplishes a single learning goal and can prove it.**

That's a mouthful, so let's look it a bit at a time:

chunk of electronic content	A learning object is not an ephemeral concept but a concrete collection of electronic media. It contains text and graphics and perhaps animation, video, voice, music, and other media.
can be accessed individually	Through a menu, search engine, or just a Next button, the learner can get to just this piece of content apart from other pieces. That is, this piece appears to the learner to be separate from other objects.
completely accomplishes a single learning goal	The key characteristic of a learning object is that it accomplishes a learning objective. The objective may be narrow or broad.
can prove it	The object contains the means to verify that the objective was met. This may be a simple test or a sophisticated simulation. A score may be recorded or not. In the end, though, the learner or the organization offering the object can tell whether the objective was met.

A simpler, although less precise definition is this:

> **A learning object is a micro-course designed to be combined with other micro-courses.**

If a course is a unit of education that can be completed in some number of hours, then an object is a similar unit that can be completed in some number of minutes. An object is smaller, but still complete. An object may teach less than a course, but it teaches it equally well.

What a learning object is not

The term learning object is used quite loosely. The term is applied to many things that are not true learning objects. To understand what we mean by the term, let's focus on some of the things a learning object is not.

A learning object is not a shrink-wrapped product you can buy. Although many vendors use the term in referring to their content and tools, a learning object is much more than a single, simple product. It is more like a philosophy for developing and packaging reusable content.

Likewise, learning objects are not a proprietary tool or technology. They depend on tools and technology but are not the province of any particular vendor.

Some learning objects can contain other learning objects which contain still other learning objects. This hierarchy means that learning objects can be entire courses or just individual components of a course.

Because learning objects can contain a hierarchy of other learning objects, a learning object is not always a single file. At the bottom of this hierarchy each object may be a file or page, but clearly higher-level objects cannot be limited to single files.

The definition of learning objects is not always apparent to the learner. Nor should it be. Learners just want to acquire new skills, understanding, or information. They do not care where one learning object leaves off and another begins. As long as they can navigate and access the knowledge they need, learners are happy. Only designers and builders need be highly concerned with the precise definition of learning objects.

Learning objects can serve multiple purposes. And an object-based development method can work for different kinds of courses. Learning objects can be used for training, for reference information, for quick-reference to facts, for job aids, and even for games and other forms of entertainment.

Common nonsense about objects

The Lego block analogy

A Lego block is a toy made by the Danish Lego company. There seems to be an ISO standard that requires that all speeches, presentations, and documents on learning objects whether in person, on paper, or online, must contain at least one picture and three verbal references to Lego blocks as a metaphor for learning objects.

If what you teach is as simple as a Lego block, you do not need learning objects. You do not need e-learning. You probably do not need any formal learning efforts at all.

Following standards is not enough

Merely following standards does not make content into a learning object. And standards do not make objects reusable … or even usable in the first place.

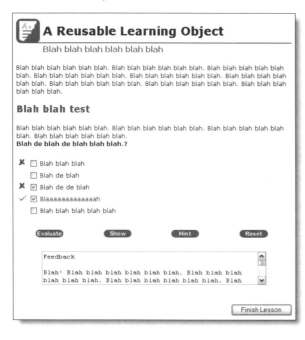

Here is an example of an object that follows SCORM standards. It has a test that reports scores to a SCORM-conformant learning management system.

If you look closely you will see that no one will ever learn anything from this object because it is filled with nonsense. It may be an object—but it is clearly not a learning object.

Yet it meets the SCORM standard (p. 399).

Create tests

Tests gauge accomplishment of the objective. They can range from small tasks that give the learner confidence to move to the next object all the way to formal tests used to legally certify the learner's skills. Chapter 5 will help you design effective tests.

A learning object requires both learning activities and tests. Most people create the learning activities first and then, if time permits, tack on a few multiple-choice test questions. A better approach is to create the tests as soon as you have defined the learning objective. It may seem illogical to create the test before creating the learning that the test measures, but the test is the best guide to designing learning activities. By developing tests first, you save time and money while making your testing and teaching more effective.

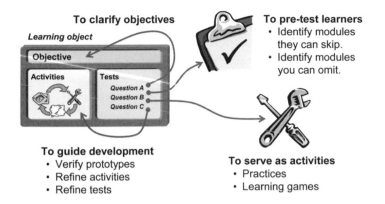

Tests clarify the objective. There is no clearer and less ambiguous statement of a learning objective than a test question that measures whether that objective has been accomplished. If the test is valid, passing the test indicates accomplishing the objective. Rather than struggle through a complex methodology for writing objectives, focus your efforts on writing good test questions.

You can then use the tests to pre-test learners. Such pre-tests will identify objects that learners can skip. More importantly, pre-tests used early in the development process can identify objects you can omit because the tests show learners already can meet the objectives.

Tests can often serve as the learning activities for the object. Tests can be designed as practices, learning games, simulations, or work assignments.

Tests can guide you in the development of content. Tests can verify prototypes for learning experiences. If learners take the prototype and pass the test, the prototype is working. Tests can help refine learning activities by comparing the learning results from different designs or variations. Having tests available early gives time to refine the tests, sharpening the focus and removing ambiguity.

So develop tests first and then the learning activities necessary to prepare for the tests.

Select learning activities

Activities are necessary to provoke learning experiences. Used in combination, learning activities can accomplish difficult learning objectives.

Learning activities exercise basic skills, thought processes, attitudes, and behaviors. But mere action is not a learning activity. People learn little by merely clicking the mouse or chatting about vacation plans. People learn by considering, researching, analyzing, evaluating, organizing, synthesizing, discussing, testing, deciding, and applying ideas. Activities may use mouse clicks and chat sessions, but their goal is to provoke the exact mental experiences that lead to learning.

To accomplish learning objectives, we typically require three types of learning activities: *absorb*, *do*, and *connect* activities. What are they and why do we need them?

What kinds of activities do you need?

With clever design, any kind of activity is possible. If you can do it in a classroom, you can do it in an e-learning course. But do you want to? What kinds of learning activities should you create? To accomplish a learning objective usually requires three distinct types of learning activities.

One type has the learner absorb knowledge, typically by reading text, watching an animation, or listening to narration. In an absorb activity, the learner is physically passive, but mentally active.

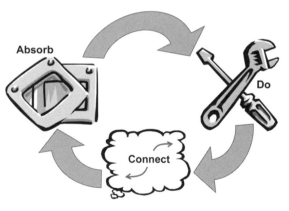

A second type of learning activity has learners do something with what they are learning. It might have the learner practice a procedure, play a game, or answer questions. The learner practices, explores, and discovers.

The final type of learning activity has learners connect what they are learning to their work, their lives, or their prior learning. Connect activities are aimed at making it easier to apply learning when it is needed later.

These three activities are shown as a cycle starting with the absorb activity. This is the most common sequence for cognitive subjects, but it is not a requirement and not always the best sequence. Different types of subjects and different instructional strategies will demand a different sequence.

Proven learning experiences

Consider learning experiences in your life. Can you classify them as absorb, do, or connect activities? Remember that *absorb* activities typically have the learner read, watch, and listen. *Do* activities have the learner do something with knowledge, such as practice, explore, and discover. *Connect* activities lead the learner to connect current learning to life, work, and prior learning.

Common types of learning experiences include discovery activities, field trips, job aids, original work assignments, ponder activities, practice sessions, readings, research, stories told by the teacher, and stories told by the learner. Which are **absorb**, which are **do**, and which are **connect** activities?

Here's how I classify them—which is important only in that that is how they appear in the rest of this book.

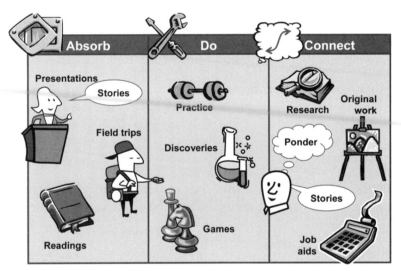

Absorb-type activities

In the absorb column are activities during which the learner reads, listens, and watches.

Presentations lurk at the left edge of the absorb column, as all the learner can do is look and listen. We hope the learner absorbs the information in the presentation actively.

Stories by the teacher are likewise absorbed by the learner.

Readings include activities for which the learner reads from online or paper documents, such as textbooks, research papers, or technical manuals.

Field trips are at the right edge of absorb activities. Although the learner may be physically active on a field trip, the learner learns by absorbing information. In a field trip to an art museum, for example, the learner may learn by looking at paintings, reading their descriptions, and listening to a museum docent lecture about them. A field trip to a hands-on museum, such as the Exploratorium in San Francisco, however, would be more of a do activity, as learning occurs through experiments and discovery.

Do-type activities

In the do column we place activities during which the learner actively exercises, explores, and discovers.

Practice activities fall squarely in this column. They allow learners to apply skills, knowledge, and attitudes and receive feedback on their efforts. They help learners refine and polish learning. Practice activities can range from simple drill-and-practice exercises to sophisticated guided-analysis activities.

Discovery activities are times for experimenting and exploring. Their goal is to lead the learners to discover concepts, principles, and procedures for themselves.

Games and simulations let learners learn by attempting to apply skills in a safe environment. Learners can gain insights and confidence as they solve realistic problems in an entertaining context.

Connect-type activities

Connect activities lead learners to link what they are learning to prior learning and to situations in which they will apply the current learning in subsequent courses or on the job.

Research activities, during which learners must identify learning resources on their own, are connect activities, as they require accessing and interpreting outside resources.

Ponder activities ask the learner to stop and think about the subject more broadly and deeply. They encourage the learner to view the subject from a new perspective. They are typically used for connecting to what the learner already knows.

Stories told by learners require the learners to draw on their own experiences. They require the learner to connect the subject of learning to personal experiences.

Job aids are used on the job at the time when learning must be applied. As such they help connect learning to work.

Performing **original work** is the ultimate final exam. It fully connects learning to the life of the learner.

Can't wait to learn more about these activities? Here are some destinations for you:

Absorb activities (Chapter 2)	Do activities (Chapter 3)	Connect activities (Chapter 4)
Read, watch, and listen.	Exercise, experiment, and discover.	Link to prior learning, to work, and to life.
▶ Presentations and demos (p. 49). ▶ Stories by the teacher (p. 72). ▶ Readings (p. 78). ▶ Field trips (p. 89).	▶ Practice (p. 106). ▶ Discovery (p. 125). ▶ Games (p. 141).	▶ Ponder activities (p. 169). ▶ Stories by the learner (p. 75). ▶ Job aids (p. 183). ▶ Research (p. 194). ▶ Original work (p. 206)

Where did this list come from?

The activities we identified have been essential for learning in different eras, from different cultures, for different learners, on different subjects, and in different media. If the same technique was used three thousand years ago in Asia for face-to-face religious instruction and today in Canada for satellite TV training in business management, then it is a very powerful and versatile technique indeed.

We chose them because they are proven and flexible activities. When well designed and appropriately deployed, they work well. They can be adapted to work with any subject matter. Many can be used with the class as a whole, by small teams, by individuals monitored by the instructor, and by learners working alone.

Specify learning activities to accomplish the objective

It is one thing to know what types of learning experiences we need. It is another to list the exact learning activities we need to accomplish a specific learning objective.

Here's how we go about it. We start with a slot for the objective of our learning object. We consider the three types of essential activities we will need: absorb, do, and connect. For each of these types, we need to describe the actual experience. And we need to specify the order in which each experience occurs. For example, let's specify learning experiences for an objective from the *Using Gantt Charts* course.

Objective	Teach how to interpret a Gantt chart to mid-level managers who recognize the individual symbols.	
Activities		**Type**
Watch a narrated animation of a typical Gantt chart being constructed.		Absorb
Examine Gantt charts at work to see how they were constructed.		Connect
Construct a similar Gantt chart by dragging and dropping pieces into place.		Do

We might start with an absorb activity that has the learners watch a narrated animation of a typical Gantt chart being constructed. Next, we might include a connect activity that guides learners to examine Gantt charts in their environment to see how they were constructed. We could close with a do activity that requires the learners to construct a similar Gantt chart by dragging pieces into place.

Although we have listed the experiences in order by absorb, do, connect, I chose to teach this objective by making the absorb activity first, then the connect activity, and finally the do activity.

Example of essential activities

Let's look at how these essential learning activities were implemented. Here you see the resulting learning object.

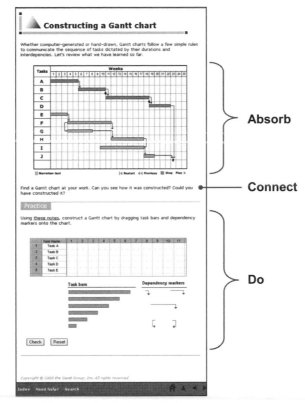

View example at horton.com/eld/.

At the top of the page is an animated presentation with voice-over narration. The animation shows the construction of a simple Gantt chart. Watching the animation is the *absorb* activity.

At the bottom is a practice activity that lets the learner construct a Gantt chart by first popping up a description of the tasks of a project and then dragging symbols into place representing the project. This practice implements the *do* activity.

Above the practice activity is a ponder activity. It invites learners to find a Gantt chart in their work. It then asks whether they can figure out how it was constructed and whether they feel they could have constructed it. Answering this rhetorical question makes up the *connect* activity.

More examples of learning activities

Here are several sample objectives and potential learning activities to accomplish them:

Objective	Learning activities
Decide where to use the chemical element niobium.	Absorb: Presentation on chemical properties. Do: Practice deciding whether to use niobium for specific goals. Connect: Identify some uses for niobium in your work.
Predict consequences of mixing TrueType and PostScript fonts in one document.	Absorb: Presentation on what happens if different types of fonts have the same name. Do: Classify samples of formatting problems as caused by font mismatch or not. Connect: Examine and report on the fonts installed on your computer.
Decide whether a main bank can delegate to an association bank the authority to make loans.	Absorb: Watch and listen to a presentation of legal problems that resulted due to improper delegation. Do: Find rules concerning delegation in online policy manuals. Do: Decide in several scenarios whether the main bank properly delegated authority. Connect: Research policies at your own bank.

THEN REDESIGN AGAIN AND AGAIN

Design of e-learning never follows a smooth and straight path. First you analyze your requirements and design your e-learning. Then you build it and test it. Oops! Better analyze the results and redesign a bit. Then you need to build in a few changes and test again. And so it goes.

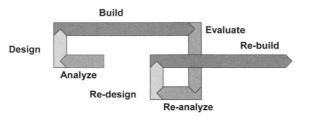

Re-design but do not repeat

The design process proceeds in a cycle of analyze, design, build, and evaluate. The evaluation in one cycle becomes research for the analysis in the next cycle. Thus, design is a series—sometimes a seemingly endless series—of decisions. The design process is essentially cyclical, corkscrewing in from high level to detailed issues while continually revisiting the same requirements over and over again.

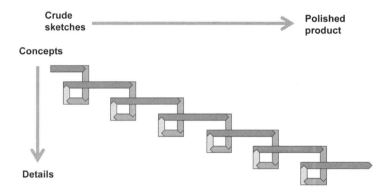

Not your sequential ADDIE process

If you are familiar with the ADDIE (Analyze, Design, Develop, Implement, and Evaluate) process, you may think we left out one of the phases. Not true. We just consolidated Develop and Implement into Build. Two reasons: One, since e-learning is delivered over networks, the implementation is a natural part of development. And two, since the process is iterative—as opposed to sequential, implementation does not lag development but goes on at the same time.

Make steady progress

The design process involves top-down design gated by testing at every level and tempered by a willingness to back up and start over where called for. At the beginning, you deal with high-level issues and work with a crude prototype, perhaps nothing more than a stack of sketches on index cards. At the end of the process, you are fine-tuning individual pixels of the final e-learning.

IN CLOSING ...

Summary

E-learning uses computer and network technologies to create learning experiences. Varieties of e-learning include standalone courses, virtual-classroom courses, mobile learning, embedded e-learning, blended e-learning, simulations, and learning games.

The advantages of e-learning are not automatic nor are the disadvantages inevitable. Good design makes all the difference. Designing e-learning requires more than traditional instructional design. Designers must incorporate ideas from software engineering, select and combine new digital media, and work under tight economic constraints.

Start with clear goals and objectives so you do not waste time and effort or just bores or distracts learners. Systematically identify the prerequisites for each learning objective you must accomplish and decide how learners will achieve each prerequisite. Specify the learning activities to accomplish each objective. Determine what knowledge the learner must absorb, what the leaner must do with the knowledge, and how the learner will connect the knowledge to work and life. Invest in good tests. Tests will (1) tell you how well your design is working, (2) help learners monitor their own progress, (3) show what content learners can skip and what content you can omit, and (4) make your objectives crystal clear.

Build your e-learning using iterative cycles of analysis, design, building, and evaluating. Start with big-picture issues and proceed to low-level details.

For more ...

The rest of this book will guide you in carrying out the steps shown in the overview provided in this chapter. For more on designing learning activities, flip to Chapters 2, 3, and 4. For help creating tests, go to Chapter 5. If you want to start designing learning objects, turn to Chapter 6 on Topics and Chapter 7 on Lessons. For higher-level design issues affecting the course as a whole, turn to Chapter 8.

As far as instructional design is concerned, this chapter was just a crib sheet. For the complete book, pick up *Multimedia-Based Instructional Design* by William Lee and Diana Owens or *Principles of Instructional Design* by Robert Gagné.

Or, search the Web for: *e-learning and "instructional design."*

Absorb-type activities

Presentations, demonstrations, stories, and field trips

Absorb activities inform and inspire. Absorb activities enable motivated learners to obtain crucial, up-to-date information they need to do their jobs or to further their learning. In absorb activities learners read, listen, and watch. These activities may sound passive, but they can be an active component of learning.

ABOUT ABSORB ACTIVITIES

Of the three types of activities (absorb, do, and connect), absorb activities are the ones closest to pure information. Absorb activities usually consist of information and the actions learners take to extract and comprehend knowledge from that information. In absorb activities, the learner may be physically passive yet mentally active—actively perceiving, processing, consolidating, considering, and judging the information.

In absorb activities, it is the content (really the designer or teacher or writer of it) that is in control. The learner absorbs some of the knowledge offered by the content.

Common types of absorb activities

Several types of absorb activities have established themselves in conventional education and have made the leap to online learning.

▶ **Presentations** during which learners watch or listen to a slide show, demonstration, podcast, or some other organized explanation (p. 49).

▶ **Storytelling** during which the teacher tells a story relevant to the subject of learning (p. 70). By inviting the student to tell a story too, we make this into a connect activity as well.

▶ **Readings** for which learners read online or paper documents (p. 78).

▶ **Field trips** for which learners visit museums, historic sites, and other places to examine many relevant examples (p. 89).

When to feature absorb activities

Where would we rely heavily on absorb activities—not to the exclusion of all others—but for what they can offer as part of a complete design?

Because absorb activities provide information efficiently, they are ideal when learners need a little information. They are especially helpful when just updating current knowledge. For example, the learner has used Version 6.0.2 of a software package for months and just needs to learn how to adapt to Version 6.0.3. Or when long-standing regulations have undergone a slight revision.

Absorb activities are also an efficient way to extend current knowledge and skills. Learners who understand the fundamentals of a field can increase their knowledge by absorbing new details that elaborate a theory, concept, or principle. If learners have the trunk and limbs of a field, they can absorb branches and leaves.

Additionally, absorb activities are good partners to other kinds of activities. Often they are used to prepare learners for a do activity. The absorb part of the partnership orients the learner, sets the context, establishes vocabulary, introduces principles, and supplies instructions needed before the learner can engage in a highly interactive do activity. Likewise, absorb activities are a good follow-up to do activities. For instance, a do activity, such as a learning game, may lead learners to discover the main principles of a subject and evoke curiosity to learn more. After the game, learners may be ready to absorb the principles and theories that will help improve their game scores.

Absorb activities are best for highly motivated learners. They are not inherently interesting. However, they are highly efficient for individuals who can focus their attention and are motivated enough to expend the effort to learn from "mere information."

PRESENTATIONS

Presentations supply needed information in a clear, well-organized, logical sequence. They are analogous to a classroom lecture or an explanation by an expert.

Students learn by watching and listening to the presentation. Presentations may be experienced live in an online meeting or may be played back from a recording.

About presentations

Presentations convey information and demonstrate procedures and behavior in a straightforward (literally) flow of experiences.

When to use presentations

Presentations explain and demonstrate things to learners. They are commonly used to convey basic information, to demonstrate well-defined procedures, and to model human behaviors.

Presentations allow the designer to control the sequence of learning experiences. Use them where designers really *do* know the best way to teach certain material. Someone who has taught a course for 10 years may know that certain explanations work better than others and that ideas must be introduced in a particular order to avoid confusion.

How presentations work

Presentations have a sequential structure. Most often they consist of an introduction, the body section, and a summary. The sequence is chosen to clarify the subject. Relatively uniform size segments occur at a regular pace.

Throughout this book I use little diagrams (such as the one that follows) to visually capture the flow of various activities. The little stick figures show what the learner or instructor is doing, and the rectangles more fully describe the type of activity in which they are engaged.

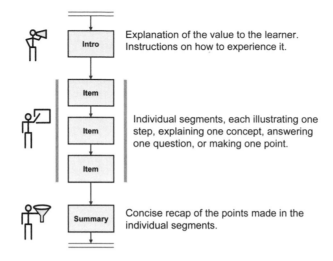

Although presentations may allow some optional topics, the primary pathway is linear—with the designer controlling the order of learning experiences. In recorded presentations learners can control the pace of the presentation. And in live presentations the learner may ask some questions, but the presenter determines the order.

Types of presentations

The types of presentations that are popular and effective in the classroom are popular and effective online. You may also want to model your presentation on one of these familiar forms:

▶ **Slide shows** are based on an effective business or classroom slide show. True, most such presentations are not effective, but they could be. And yours can be too. A good slide show makes each point on a single slide. Slides include informative graphics and just enough text to convey the main point. Many use recorded voice to narrate the slides (p. 51).

▶ **Physical demonstrations** show a person performing a physical procedure such as repairing a leaky faucet or lobbing a tennis ball. Physical demonstrations may be live or recorded as video (p. 52).

▶ **Software demonstrations** are an over-the-shoulders view of an expert performing a complex procedure with a computer program. We hear the expert's words and watch as the mouse clicks and typing appears (p. 54).

▶ **Informational film**s, such as documentary films, have been used to educate, inform, and motivate people since the development of film. Although now the "film" is digital video, the information conveyed uses many of the same cinematic techniques (p. 56).

▶ **Dramas** show people in a fictional scene. You might use dramas to illustrate a successful interview or reveal team dynamics (p. 58).

▶ **Discussions**, such as interviews, debates, and panel presentations, are useful for revealing important information and opinions (p. 59).

▶ **Podcasts** are audio presentation that learners can download over the Web and play on their computers or digital-music devices, such as the Apple iPod, which contributed to the name for this type presentation (p. 60).

If people can learn by watching and listening to something, it can be an effective online presentation. Recorded presentations are thus as varied as designers are clever. You can alter them by your choice and sequencing of topics, by use of different media, and by ways you share control over pacing and branching with the learner.

Slide shows

Classroom slide shows can be converted to online recorded presentations. These are usually a series of linked slides or Web pages through which the learner advances, typically by jack-hammering a **Next** button or hyperlink.

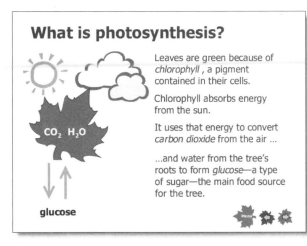

This slide from the middle of a slide presentation about why leaves change color in the fall, explains the process of photosynthesis. Animation shows the basic phases of photosynthesis and is synchronized with the text and voice-over narration.

Created in Microsoft PowerPoint and converted for Web delivery using Impatica for PowerPoint. View example at horton.com/eld/.

Online slide shows may be created by narrating a classroom slide presentation and converting it to Web media. Tools for doing this include Articulate Presenter (www.articulate.com), Breeze Presenter (www.adobe.com), and Impatica for PowerPoint (www.impatica.com). Or you can record an online meeting during which you present slides.

2

Absorb-type activities

Such sequences can be quite concise and graphical, especially when commentary is provided by voice-over narration. If sound is not a practical option, the commentary can be provided in text—after editing to reduce the amount of text, of course.

Slide shows rely primarily on text and graphics to tell their stories. They may also incorporate podcasts, informational films, dramas, demonstrations, and other forms of presentation.

Where to use slide shows

Since recorded presentations are much like a conventional slide show, they work well when presenting logically connected ideas, especially if expressed visually.

They may be the best choice economically and technically when you have proven slide presentations and the tools to quickly convert them for Web delivery.

Best practices for slide shows

- ▶ **Communicate visually**. Make graphics carry the load. Convert paragraphs to pictures, tables, and lists. Where you can, replace wordy bullet lists with illustrations or diagrams.

- ▶ **Narrate clearly**. Move excess text to voice-over narration. Make a transcript available by a button click so none of the text is lost.

- ▶ **Animate graphics**. Use motion and transitions to tell the story. Show how things move and evolve.

- ▶ **Build up the display** one object at a time to avoid overloading learners or creating a cluttered display. Add each item at the time when it is discussed. This will focus attention on the item and control how learners perceive the item.

Physical demonstrations

In a physical demonstration, learners see a person performing a procedure, such as repairing a device, kicking a soccer ball, or performing a dance move. The demonstration shows the right or wrong way to interact with a three-dimensional object. Such demonstrations are almost always conveyed as video.

Here is a physical demonstration from a course about project management. It introduces the task of making coffee, which was used as an example of a simple project that could be shortened with proper attention to the tasks of the project.

Where to use physical demonstrations

Use a physical demonstration to introduce a physical task you are teaching learners to perform. This could be a task they perform as part of their work, such as lifting heavy packages. Or it could be a movement they make in dance, athletics, or performing arts.

Physical demonstrations can also be used to model human behavior, such as how to greet business associates of different cultures. Such demonstrations may involve gestures, body language, facial expressions, and tone of voice.

Best practices for physical demonstrations

▶ **Preview the action**. Start with an establishing shot showing the location of the action. Introduce the actor. State the purpose of the demonstration.

▶ **Use close-ups to show individual actions**. Because the video may have to appear in a small window, do not waste pixels.

▶ **Move smoothly and slowly**. The video may be played at a lower frame rate than conventional television, so actions may appear jerky. And fast motions may be missed altogether. For steps that must be performed quickly, show the individual steps slowly and then combine them at normal speed.

▶ **Keep the demonstration short**. Show a single action or phase of a task. If you have to teach a complex task, divide it into its component actions. Teach them, and then teach how to combine the actions.

▶ **Let learners control the demonstration**. For recorded demonstrations, give learners playback buttons to let them re-start the demo, fast forward it, play it backwards, and play it in slow motion.

Software demonstrations

Software demonstrations of late have become a category in their own right. A software demonstration, or *show-me* activity, lets learners watch a clear sequence of actions. These actions are explained by commentary provided as displayed text, spoken narration, or both. Software demonstrations can be performed live in an online meeting or recorded for playback by learners.

Demonstrations are good for how-to procedures like the one shown in this example—creating a system data source name.

Built in Adobe Captivate. View example at horton.com/eld/.

Software demonstrations are not the same as software simulations (p. 150). In demonstrations, the learner watches and listens as someone else operates the software. In software simulations, the learner performs the operations.

Software demonstrations are created by starting a recording program, performing the demonstration, and editing the recording. Such recordings capture the motions and clicks of the learner's mouse, text entered from the keyboard, and other actions visible on the screen. They record this action to a format that can be edited and then converted for Web delivery. Camtasia (www.techsmith.com) and Captivate (www.adobe.com) are a couple of popular tools for creating software demonstrations.

Software demonstrations are frequently used in standalone e-learning. However, do not forget to make use of live demonstrations in online class meetings.

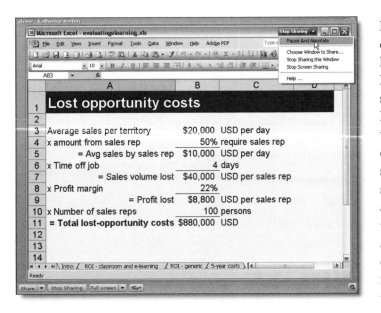

Here, the instructor discusses how to calculate lost opportunity costs. Rather than simply show a static spreadsheet and tell learners how to arrive at the values shown, the instructor demonstrates how the spreadsheet works by sharing the Excel application. The learner sees the spreadsheet just as it appears on the instructor's computer.

Microsoft Excel window shared using Adobe Breeze Meeting.

As learners watch the instructor conduct the demo, they experience an absorb activity. The instructor may then call on a student to perform a similar procedure. For that student, it is now a do activity. For the other students watching, however, it is still an absorb activity.

Where to use software demonstrations

Use software demonstrations to introduce computer procedures. They are effective in introducing the navigation scheme of a Web site, learning portal, or other electronic document to new learners. Software demonstrations are a good first step in teaching people to use an unfamiliar feature in a computer program.

Software demonstrations are seldom sufficient by themselves to teach absolute novices to use the software, but they can prepare the novice for a software simulation (p. 150) during which the novice attempts to perform the procedure demonstrated. For experienced learners, the demo may be adequate to teach a new procedure, especially if the learners follow along in the actual program.

This lack of interactivity is the strength and weakness of a demonstration. It is a strength because it requires little skill or motivation on the part of the learner. Learners who can play a VCR can watch a demonstration.

Best practices for software demonstrations

▶ **Introduce the demonstration**. At the beginning tell learners what they will gain, what software is involved, and what the demonstration will cover. A few words of text and a sentence or two of narration are usually sufficient.

▶ **Keep demonstrations simple and to the point**. In each demonstration, illustrate just one way to perform one task. Do not clutter the demonstration with too many alternatives, shortcuts, and exceptions.

▶ **Make clear this is a demonstration, not a simulation**. If you say "Click the **OK** button," some of your learners will try to do so. Tell learners just to watch.

▶ **Follow the demonstration with a simulation**. After showing learners how to perform the procedure, let them practice it in a simulation (p. 150).

▶ **Invite learners to follow along**. If the procedure is not dangerous, invite learners to start up the software and try to follow along. Remind them to pause the presentation when it is time for them to attempt a step or two.

▶ **Provide a low-bandwidth alternative**. If the video-with-voice format of your demo is too large for all learners, provide an alternative version with still pictures and a transcript of the narration.

Informational films

Since the invention of motion pictures, the documentary film has presented factual information in a visual narrative. In the context of e-learning, the technology of film has been replaced with digital video.

This example of a documentary film shows the aftermath of the 1906 San Francisco earthquake. The film by the Thomas Edison Company shows a panorama from the east side of 4th Street near Natoma, just south of Market. This is just one example of many such historical films available from the U.S. Library of Congress (memory.loc.gov).

It is far beyond the scope of this book to tell you how to design, author, direct, and produce such films. For a starting point, pick up *Communicating Ideas with Film, Video, and Multimedia: A Practical Guide to Information Motion-Media* by Marty Shelton.

Where to use information films

Use the information film to explain a subject in a definite logical order, especially where the subject is visual but may be difficult for the learner to imagine.

Use it to present a logical narrative for which the order of images and experiences is important, for example to convey cause-and-effect relationships or to follow a chronological sequence. You might use it to show the chain of discoveries that led to a particular invention or to walk a chemical engineer through the processes and pipelines of a refinery. Use it when the motion of three-dimensional objects is especially important, such as when explaining how birds fly or fish swim.

Creating an information film from scratch is complex and expensive, so you may want to reserve this form for critical, high-budget projects. Or you may want to reuse an existing documentary film.

Best practices for information films

▶ **Borrow if you can**. Designing, authoring, shooting, editing, and publishing a documentary film is expensive and a lot of work. (I know first-hand. I wrote and edited a short documentary called *Flights of Fantasy* about ultra-light airplanes and the interesting people who fly them.) If possible, re-use an existing documentary film. Supplement it with materials to adapt it to your purposes. You may need to provide a docking module (p. 315) to introduce the film to your learners.

▶ **Get permission.** Before you publish e-learning with someone else's video in it, make sure you have permission in writing.

▶ **Design for the small screen.** To reduce download times and to make the video play smoothly, keep the video window small. To make things clear in such a small window, always start with an establishing shot to give an overview and then proceed through a series of close-ups that reveal details. Periodically zoom back to re-establish the location.

▶ **Beware the bandwidth monster.** Good information films feature motion and present interesting details—just the kind of video that is hard to compress. So try several compression schemes to find the best for your material. Offer several versions so learners can pick one appropriate for their connection speed. For those with slow connections, provide a sequence of still pictures accompanied by the text of the narration or dialog.

Dramas

In a drama, learners watch a fictional scene among people, for example to illustrate a successful interview or reveal team dynamics. Dramas can be conveyed in video, a combination of still pictures and voice, or by just voice alone. They are the fictional counterpart to the information film.

This example from a course on Workplace Ethics by Brightline Compliance (www.brightlinecompliance.com) shows two people discussing whether to use a company credit card for a personal purchase. It demonstrates how ordinary situations can require ethical decisions and how such decisions are seldom clear-cut.

Where to use dramas

Dramas are good to illustrate desirable and undesirable human behaviors and styles of interaction. I have used them for teaching lawful hiring, ethical behavior, and interviewing skills. Dramas can also be used to re-enact historic events, such as scientific discoveries or political discussions. Dramas may be useful to prepare learners for multi-person role-playing activities and simulations.

Best practices for dramas

▶ **Write credible dialog**. The way people speak in successful movies and television series is quite different from the way people talk in the real world and even more different from the way people write. Aim for dialog that is credible and clear. Hire a good fiction writer. At least read your dialog aloud and revise, revise, revise until it sounds right.

▶ **Hire good actors**. Recruit players who can put emotion into their voices and whose body language and gestures reinforce what they are saying. If you cannot afford professional actors, use still photos. Pose your players carefully before you snap the shutter.

▶ **Don't forget the drama**. If the sequence is totally predictable, there is no drama—and hence no curiosity. Keep the learner wondering how things will work out. Avoid stereotypical characters and situations.

▶ **Tell a story**. When we see people interacting, we expect a story with an introduction of characters, a crisis, and a resolution for good or ill. The story can be that simple (p. 70).

Discussion presentations

We watch events wherein people interact, and we learn from what they say and do. The interplay among human beings is inherently interesting and provides a natural contrivance for revealing important information and opinions. People can be shown interacting as part of a live online meeting or can be recorded interacting so learners can play back the recording. Most such events are shown in video, but audio recordings of discussions are sometimes useful as well. To see some examples of discussion-type presentations, search the Web for these words: **panel discussion video**.

Where to use discussion presentations

Use discussions when a speech would be too boring or might challenge the learner's opinions too directly. Many would rather watch a debate and make up their own minds than to listen to an expert state an opinion.

One of the best reasons to use this form is that it helps elicit valuable information and opinions from experts in a form that learners find interesting. In a speech, the expert drones on in a nervous monotone; in an interview, the expert enthusiastically responds to friendly provocation from the interviewer.

Forms of discussion presentations

Here are just a few forms of people interacting in ways that reveal ideas, opinions, and information:

▶ News interviews.

▶ Talk-show interviews.

▶ Debates.

▶ Panel discussions.

▶ Mock trials.

Best practices for discussion presentations

▶ **Record the interaction with multiple cameras.** Then you can cut from person to person without having to swish back and forth across the scene, making viewers seasick.

▶ **Light the scene well**. Use adequate lighting and keep the lighting even throughout the scene (flat lighting) as is done for most TV interview shows.

2

Absorb-type activities

► **Use close-ups of people**. Get in close enough so that the learner can see the emotions of the speaker as illustrated in gestures and facial expressions.

► **Don't use it if it does not work**. Sometimes discussions go flat. Panelists can just say, "I agree." Debates can expose too much rancor and not enough information. If your event flops, throw away the recording and pretend it never happened.

► **Take care with borrowed presentations**. I did not include an example of this type because of two problems you may face. To show the discussion, you may need legal permission from all the individual participants. And such presentations have a relatively short life on the Web. You will need to obtain a copy and make it available to your learners.

Podcasts

Podcast sounds so much more inviting than "lecture" doesn't it? But what are informational podcasts but audio recordings of lectures?

As I write this in February 2006, the term *podcast* refers primarily to audio segments that people can download and play on music-playback devices such as Apple's iPod. Most podcasts appear periodically, say once a week or every few days. Most have adopted the format of a radio program.

Some podcasts are now adding video. They can be played back on desktop and laptop computers and video-capable PDAs, iPods, and other media players. I wish I could be you reading this section several years from now so I would know what we would be calling them then (vidcasts, vodcasts, meTV?).

For our purposes in this book, I will use the term podcast to refer to an audio-only segment. It may be part of a series or may stand alone. Video podcasts fall within the other types of presentations mentioned earlier.

To find a list of podcasts, try podcasts.yahoo.com, or podcastalley.com. Some are pure entertainment, many are self-indulgent, but a whole lot of them are educational. I have subscribed to a half-dozen podcasts as part of my continuing professional education.

Where to use podcasts

Podcasts work well when you can communicate using just audio. It is especially useful for learners who have spare time to listen to the podcast, say when riding on a train or on an airplane. I'm a little concerned about their use while driving an automobile, but they may be just the ticket for ignoring the other riders in your carpool.

Do not use a podcast if your idea could be summarized to a page of text. And stick to factual, procedural information. You are in the education business, not entertainment.

Another argument for using a podcast may be economic. It may be easier and quicker to capture the expertise of authorities by having them talk rather than by requiring them to write it down. Some people are fluent speakers but hesitant writers. So let them talk. If you are worried they will ramble, record an interview during which you choose questions to structure the responses. Then edit out the questions.

Podcasts are a natural for subjects that involve sound, such as music or language. They may prove more difficult if the subject is highly visual. Still, clever podcasters have overcome such difficulties. The winner in the 2005 People's Choice Podcast Awards in the Education category was one on digital photography (www.tipsfromthetopfloor.com). The host, Chris Marquardt, focuses primarily on the procedural aspects of photography and supplements the audio podcast with a Web site and discussion forum.

Forms of podcasts

Podcasts can be lectures that explain a subject directly. But many other forms are possible. Just listen to your radio. What do you hear?

- ▶ Interviews.
- ▶ Tips.
- ▶ Product reviews.
- ▶ Dramatizations of real or imagined events.
- ▶ Reading aloud like "books on tape."
- ▶ Live field activities.
- ▶ Trip reports.

Two of these seem especially useful. One is the live field activity, sometimes called *soundseeing*. Here you listen along as an expert does something important. You might listen as a game biologist approaches a skittish herd of moose or a photographer stalks the perfect exposure.

Another useful podcast is the *trip report*. You might report back from a conference or trade-show you attended. You could summarize developments you noticed and ideas you heard.

Best practices for podcasts

Here are some best practices for better educational podcasts:

- ▶ **Keep everything simple,** especially if learners may listen while driving their cars. No complex follow-along activities please. Ten minutes per segment. Do not require writing anything down.

- ▶ **Make what you say memorable**. Repeat. Give mnemonics. Emphasize key points. Post URLs, names, and other details to a Web location.

- ▶ **Use only words that learners already know**. If you introduce a new term or concept, explain it.

- ▶ **Keep the introduction and close short, especially** if learners will listen to several episodes at once.

- ▶ **Do not mimic radio**. Entertainment podcasts are radio. Informational podcasts are **not**. Downplay the music, reverberating intro, and other radio effects. No advertisements, please.

- ▶ **Select music to please your audience not yourself**, especially if your audience spans several generations.

- ▶ **Keep information current**. Include less information that goes stale. Or publish a reusable, timeless version that does not contain information likely to go out of date.

- ▶ **Make voices clear and pleasant**. Invest in a good microphone. Equalize and normalize voices. In a sound-editing program adjust the frequencies of the voices and adjust volumes to a constant level. Speak in an upbeat, emotional voice. Speak to a simulated studio audience.

- ▶ **Smooth the flow**. Rehearse and rehearse again. Edit out mistakes and long pauses. Include short tips and other pieces to splice together longer segments.

Best practices for presentations

Now here are some suggestions for better presentations, regardless of the form.

Give learners control

Give learners control over how they experience the presentation.

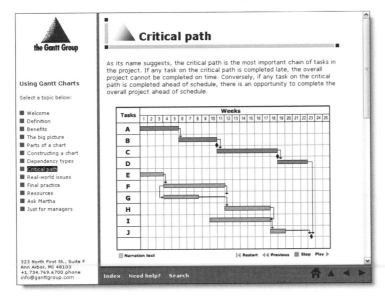

Using Gantt Charts shows learners how to recognize the critical path. An embedded Flash animation with narration demonstrates the characteristics of the critical path. The buttons at the bottom of the animation let learners control the pace of the presentation.

Built using Adobe Dreamweaver, JavaScript, and Flash. View example at horton.com/eld/.

Let learners read the narration as well as listen to it. Some learners may be deaf, dyslexic, or listening in a language other than their first. Reading along while listening will help comprehension. Also, some learners may work in open cubicles, making it difficult to turn up the volume of the computer audio. Sometimes learners just need to check a fact.

Let learners print a transcript of the narration, too. Being able to print the narration makes reviewing the material much easier.

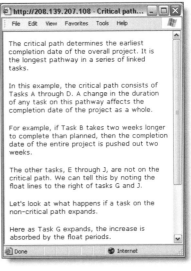

Supply examples, examples, examples

Many lectures have too much theory and not enough concrete, specific, realistic examples. Remember, not everyone can reason from general concepts to particular applications, or at least not without the help of examples that they can understand and apply.

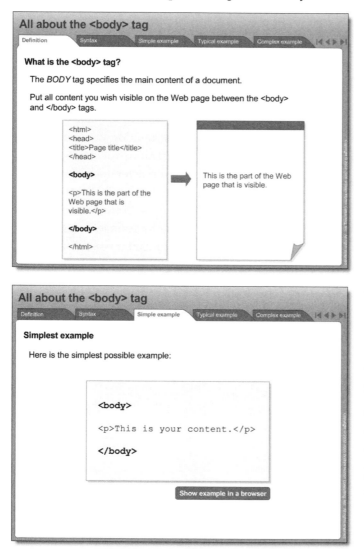

The topic shown here is from a course on HTML. For such practical, but abstract subjects, include at least three examples of key points.

The topic starts with a definition. The Syntax tab contains the abstract format of the tag.

Created in Microsoft PowerPoint and converted for Web delivery using Adobe Breeze Presenter. View example at horton.com/eld/.

The first example is the simplest possible use of the tag. It gives learners something they can easily understand and apply immediately.

The **Show example in a browser** button launches a browser window that shows how this fragment of code displays.

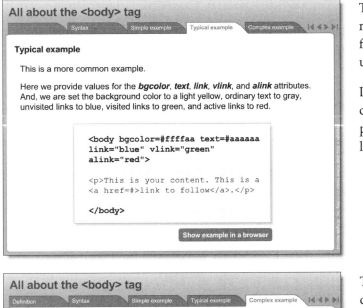

The second example is the most common case. It shows features most learners will use frequently.

Like the simple example, it contains a button to launch a page containing the tag so learners can see its effect.

The final example is a quite complex one. It shows the tag to its full capabilities. It illustrates many features that the advanced learner may find useful.

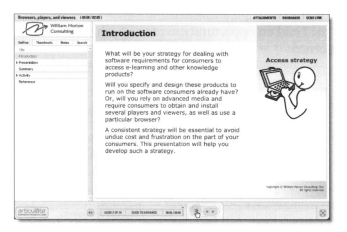

A brief introduction sets the stage for the presentation. The introduction suggests questions that the presentation will answer.

Here we see a single slide from the presentation. The displayed text summarizes the voice narration.

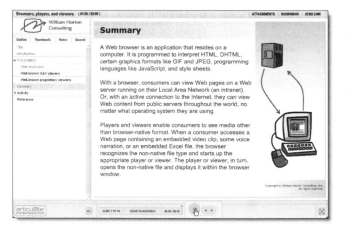

The summary recaps the main points we want the learner to retain from the presentation. Because this summary was created separately from the presentation, it can emphasize things especially important for this particular use of the presentation.

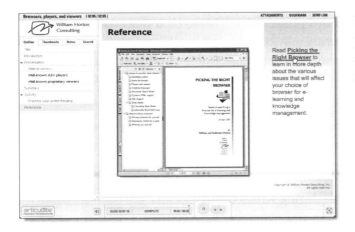

The augmented presentation includes a simple test to help learners gauge their knowledge.

Because the presentation provides only an overview of the subject, it includes a link to a more detailed document.

Created in Microsoft PowerPoint and converted for Web delivery using Articulate Presenter. View example at horton.com/eld/.

Combine presentations with other activities

Like all activities, presentations gain power when combined with complementary activities. Here are some tested combinations:

▶ Follow hardware and software demonstrations with practice activities (p. 106) to let learners apply what you demonstrated.

▶ Use discovery activities (p. 125) to help learners notice principles and slide shows and information films to expand on these principles.

▶ Begin games (p. 141) with a short slide show to teach the rules and user-interface of the game. Make available an information film or slide show to teach concepts needed to win the game.

▶ Supplement presentations with readings (p. 78) to reveal details only hinted at in the presentation and to satisfy curiosity about a subject aroused by the presentation.

Tell stories to learners

Don't just tell stories to learners. Encourage learners to think how the stories apply to them.

Example of a story-telling activity

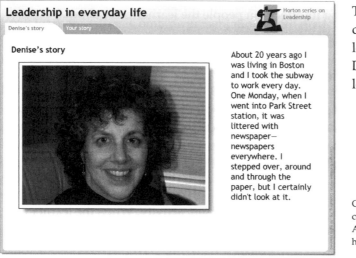

Leadership in everyday life

Horton series on Leadership

Denise's story   Your story

Denise's story

About 20 years ago I was living in Boston and I took the subway to work every day. One Monday, when I went into Park Street station, it was littered with newspaper— newspapers everywhere. I stepped over, around and through the paper, but I certainly didn't look at it.

The example shown here comes from a course on leadership. We see a picture of Denise who tells a story about leading by example.

Created in Microsoft PowerPoint and converted for Web delivery using Articulate Presenter. View example at horton.com/eld/.

Here is what she says:

> About 20 years ago I was living in Boston and I took the subway to work every day.

> One Monday, when I went into Park Street station, it was littered with newspaper— newspapers everywhere. I stepped over, around, and through the paper, but I certainly didn't look at it.

> Standing not too far from me, waiting for his train, was a middle-aged man. He was looking around at the mess and then looked down at his feet. He bent down, picked up some of the newspaper and took it to the trash. He did this a few times until his train arrived.

> After his train was gone and the station had quieted down a bit, a young woman on the platform bent down and picked up some newspaper at her feet and took it to the trash. Then a young man did the same thing. Finally, we were all in the act. By the time my train arrived, the station looked pretty good—and the trashcans were full.

> You know, I wonder if that man had any idea I would be telling this story 20 years later, or that he had had such an effect on my life? But I think it illustrates something about leadership that we tend to forget. That is, leadership is not just what prime ministers and CEOs do, but leadership is how we lead our lives every day and how we affect other people.

Every time I play this story in a classroom, students cease fidgeting and whispering and give it their rapt attention. Such is the power of stories.

Types of stories

Just about any kind of human story can be used effectively in e-learning—provided it is relevant to the subject and appropriate for the learners. Here are some that have proven themselves over the past few millennia:

Hero stories

Hero stories, sometimes called "war stories," tell how an ordinary person with whom the learner can identify overcame obstacles like those facing the learner. The hero triumphed by applying knowledge and behaving correctly. Usually the hero is the story-teller. The story told by Denise is a hero story.

The hero story is as old as story-telling. From prehistoric campfires to the latest scientific conferences, hero stories have been told. Such hero stories follow a familiar pattern: First we meet the hero and learn about the setting. Then the hero encounters a challenge and is stymied by its difficulty. The hero then finds or develops strength that enables the hero to overcome the difficulty. The hero profits from the experience.

The hero story is good for giving learners courage to take on difficult tasks and for suggesting how the subject they are studying will help them overcome difficulties. Such stories are popular in business, politics, religion, warfare, and other complex human endeavors for which learners need encouragement to apply what they are learning.

The hero stories are also good for motivating learning of difficult material. Use them to illustrate how applying the subject of learning saved the day.

Love stories

Love stories concern the wooing and winning and happily thereafter of two people. Love stories might seem an odd thing to include in e-learning. However, love stories are not just the province of Shakespeare and Jane Austin. They are not limited to Hollywood romantic comedies. Love stories can tell how a sales representative won the affections and purchase orders of a reluctant customer. It can tell how a scientific theory won, lost, and then regained favor among the scientific community.

The structure of the love story is amazingly consistent: A meets B. A pursues B, but B resists. A wins B. A and B break up because of a silly mistake by A or the treachery of a rival. A and B get back together and live happily ever after.

Use love stories to illustrate the importance and difficulty of winning loyalty, trust, respect, and commitment. Use them to point out the fragility of human relationships.

In an online meeting where learners can speak, you can invite learners to tell their own stories. If learners cannot communicate by audio in the meeting, do not ask them to type their stories into chat. Unless they are super typists, the process is so painful it will become its own disaster story. Instead, invite them to contribute their stories to a discussion forum (p. 427).

The invitation to tell a story adds the element of reflection and encourages learners to think about what has been said and how it applies to their own situations. The process of composing an analogous story connects the events to the learners' lives. It also verifies learning. If learners tell appropriate stories, you know they got the point of the story you told. And letting learners tell stories is a great way to gather new stories.

Best practices for story-sharing activities

The effectiveness of a story-sharing activity depends on the story and how it is told.

Tell effective stories

What makes a good story for e-learning? There is no magic formula, but effective stories do seem to share some characteristics.

- ▶ **The story is credible**. It may be a composite of several experiences or even a parable, but it sounds and feels true to learners.

- ▶ **The story is important**. It makes a valuable point and is apt to the subject at hand. It directly helps accomplish the learning objective.

- ▶ **The story is short and focused**. Everything in the story contributes to its objective. In e-learning, stories should be about one-third or one-half the length of a story told in the classroom.

- ▶ **The story is dramatic**. The result is not clear until the end. And learners want to know how the story ends.

- ▶ **We care about the characters**. We have a hero we can identify with, a victim we can sympathize with, a villain we can despise, and others who make us feel joy, fear, or anger. The worst reaction to a story is "Who cares?"

- ▶ **The story-teller cares**. The story is told with emotion. The story-teller's feelings for events and characters are not hidden. The voice is well modulated and rhythmical.

- ▶ **The moral is clear**. The learner does not have to ask, "What was the point?" The point of the story is abundantly clear. Or the story-teller states it explicitly. Sometimes both. You can record multiple morals and then reuse the same story for different purposes.

Polish the telling

Tell the story well. Perfection is not the goal, but credibility and clarity are.

- ▶ **Coach story-tellers** to put enthusiasm and emotion into their voices. Rehearse the telling. Remember, the goal is to sound credible, not professional.

- ▶ **Aim for sincerity**. A professional narrator can sound too perfect. Better a few *uhs* and *ahs* in a credible voice than a perfectly polished enunciation.

- ▶ **Require good voice quality**. Record and edit the voice carefully. If emotion is an important component of the story, you will require higher audio quality than if you were just relating facts.

- ▶ **Do not settle for the first take**. To get a good recording from a hesitant story-teller, have the story-teller repeatedly tell the story. Use whatever ruse works, such as "Sorry, I forgot to push the Record button." With each telling the story gets shorter and more to the point. Usually the third version is the best one.

Develop the story

Go beyond a bare-bones telling of a simple story.

- ▶ **Show the face of the story-teller**. Video is not necessary, but a good quality photo will help the listener imagine the person. You might even show a series of three repeating photographs, each dissolving into the next. Many viewers will remember it as video.

- ▶ **Illustrate the story**. Add newspaper clippings and other materials to flesh out the story. The story can thus become part of a larger case study.

- ▶ **Spread a single complex story throughout a lesson**. Tell the story in episodes, arousing curiosity and building suspense.

Combine stories with other activities

Story-telling by itself is seldom sufficient to accomplish an ambitious learning objective. Consider some combinations that ally the story with other activities.

- ▶ Interleave stories with presentations (p. 49) and readings (p. 78) on an abstract subject. The stories remind learners of the practical application and value of the abstract information.

- ▶ Precede any difficult activity with a story that illustrates the value of overcoming obstacles and the value of what will be learned.

- ▶ Use a story to launch a research activity (p. 194) wherein the learner gathers background information about the teller of the story or the event spoken of.

READINGS

Sometimes the best e-learning is a good book ... or a good e-book.

Reading is not dead. Far from it. E-learning can effectively incorporate reading assignments. We can direct learners to individual documents or make entire libraries available to them.

About reading activities

Reading activities direct learners to electronic or paper documents that are well researched, organized, and written. By reading these documents, learners gain important information and inspiration.

Printed documents may seem so very 20th Century. Their displays just sit there. They lack play buttons and offer limited interactivity. Yet it is this stability that gives them their value in this increasingly ultra-dynamic, hyper-interactive world. Written documents do not squirm, shift, twitch, flicker, or misinterpret the reader's subtle intentions. They present information in a precise visual organization and a predictable sequence.

Ironically, reading may be a more active learning experience than some learning games, especially as the learner skims, peruses, reads, imagines, compares, re-reads, jots notes, makes bookmarks, and reflects.

When to use reading activities

Use reading activities to present complex and difficult information in a stable form for careful study by the learner. Use reading activities when:

▶ Learners need deeper knowledge on a subject.

▶ You do not have time to develop more interactive materials and well-written documents are readily available.

▶ Learners are skillful readers and motivated enough to read on their own.

Types of readings

Reading activities for e-learning typically provide access to readings in three ways:

▶ Individual documents.

▶ Libraries of documents to select from.

▶ Predefined searches to find Internet resources.

How reading activities work

The procedure for reading activities is quite simple. First the learner obtains the document and then reads it.

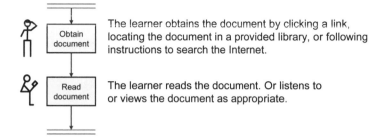

The learner obtains the document by clicking a link, locating the document in a provided library, or following instructions to search the Internet.

The learner reads the document. Or listens to or views the document as appropriate.

Obtaining the document should be simple, swift, and reliable—unless this step is part of a research activity (p. 194).

Assign individual documents

The simplest form of reading activity assigns a single, specific document. The learner typically clicks a link to obtain the document and then reads it either online or after printing it out.

Consider many types of documents

Many different types of documents can be useful in e-learning. Here is a short list to start you thinking.

▶ Textbooks.

▶ Popular books.

▶ Manuals.

▶ Handbooks.

▶ Reports.

▶ Regulations.

▶ Brochures.

▶ Data sheets.

▶ Specifications.

▶ Diaries and journals.

▶ Scholarly papers.

▶ Trade journals.

▶ Magazines.

▶ Newspapers.

▶ Blogs.

Include standard references

Many fields of study have standard reference works that make a valuable addition to your e-learning.

Bible search

Enter a citation in the text box . Then click Find. The passage will appear below. Be sure to format your citations like the examples shown.

| I Corinthians 4-9 | Find | *For example: I Corinthians 4, John 3:18, Amos 5:23-24, Genesis, Matthew-Mark, Luke-John 3:16* |

I Corinthians 4:1 - 9:27

I Corinthians Chapter 4

1   Let a man so account of us, as of ministers of Christ, and stewards of the mysteries of God.

2   Here, moreover, it is required in stewards, that a man be found faithful.

3   But with me it is a very small thing that I should be judged of you, or of man's judgment: yea, I judge not mine own self.

4   For I know nothing against myself; yet am I not hereby justified: but he that judgeth me is the Lord.

5   Wherefore judge nothing before the time, until the Lord come, who will both bring to light the hidden things of darkness, and make manifest the

A project for church congregations provided access to one reference work particularly important to them. Learners could find Biblical passages by typing in the citation in conventional form, including ranges.

Built using Adobe Dreamweaver and Active Server Pages. View example at horton.com/eld/.

Standard reference works include:

▸ Textbooks for conventional courses in the field.

▸ Professional handbooks used by practitioners.

▸ Laws and regulations governing the field.

▸ Classical literature that may be the subject of study.

▸ Scripture that is the basis for values and policies.

▸ Biographies of key figures in a field.

▸ Historical reviews of a field.

▸ Collected works of important researchers or artists.

Pick file formats for documents

If you are making documents available for learners, consider how you will convert conventional documents to Web-accessible media. Several formats are quite common in e-learning.

Format	Advantages	Disadvantages
HTML	Can be displayed in browser with no plug-ins.	Only for simple formats. Otherwise the conversion efforts are complex.
Adobe Acrobat Portable Document Format (PDF)	Faithful to original format, even if complex. Works for any document you can print.	Requires learners to have the Acrobat Reader software.
Adobe FlashPaper	Faithful to the original format. Displays using the Flash player, which also handles animation, graphics, and video.	Requires learners to have the Flash Player.
Microsoft Word or Rich Text Format (RTF)	Can be opened by Word and other word processors for editing.	Requires learners to have a word processor or download a viewer. You cannot control what learners do with your document.

I find Adobe's Acrobat Portable Document Format (PDF) an attractive format for documents and handouts the learner may need to read. PDF provides a high-fidelity image of the original document—as it would appear printed. In fact, this is the strength of PDF: It can be used for any computer document that can be printed. And creating a PDF file is little more difficult than printing a document.

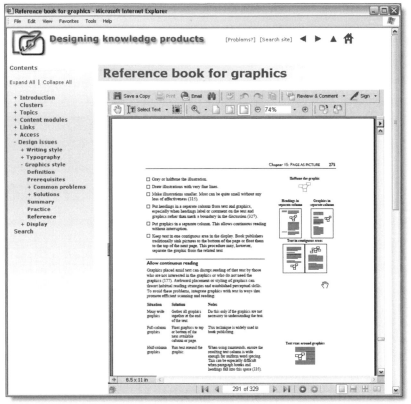

Built using Adobe Dreamweaver and Adobe Acrobat Professional.

PDF does, however, require learners to download and install the free Acrobat Reader. For technically sophisticated learners, this task is not a serious barrier. But not all learners are technically sophisticated … or blessed with an attentive information technology department to install the reader for them.

The advantage of PDF is that documents are 99% faithful to their original format, including graphics. PDF files are not as compact as HTML, but still relatively compact, especially compared to straight, graphical formats.

There is an easy test to determine whether you should use PDF. If the document is long, intricately formatted, and will be read from a printout, use PDF so that the learner gets a legible and precisely formatted copy.

Publish a listen-and-print version

For several projects, I have included a listen-and-print version of the document aimed at readers with less than perfect eyesight.

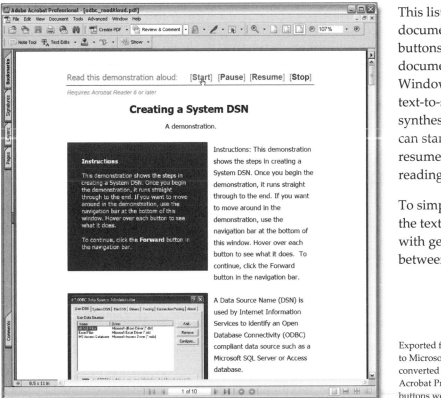

This listen-and-print document contains buttons to read the document aloud using Windows XP's built-in text-to-speech synthesis. The learner can start, pause, resume, and stop the reading.

To simplify reading, the text is extra large with generous spacing between lines.

Exported from Adobe Captivate to Microsoft Word, and then converted to PDF using Adobe Acrobat Professional, where the buttons were added.

At the end of a long day of reading from a computer screen, I must admit I like having the computer read to me.

Create an online library

Sending learners off to the library for a bit of reading is a tradition in education—one that e-learning designers can well capitalize on by integrating libraries into e-learning courses.

We can make reading assignments much quicker, more reliable, and less frustrating by providing learners with a well-organized and cataloged library of learning resources. Rather than assign specific works to read, we can provide a library of relevant material for learners to select from.

One advantage of this approach is that the reading activity does not fail if a single source of information is removed from the Web or an individual server goes down. Another advantage is the ease of combining research and reading activities.

The basic idea of libraries has not changed much since ancient Alexandria. It has not needed to. Libraries make knowledge accessible by collecting the best and most needed works, labeling them, organizing them, cataloging them, and enabling people to find them on their own. And Web-based libraries keep longer hours.

Here is an example of the learner-interface for an online library.

Built using Adobe Dreamweaver and Active Server Pages.

Design your library not as a monumental shrine to dusty books, but as an inviting portal to self-education. Make the library practical, helpful, and fun. Tailor it to the needs and tastes of learners.

Such libraries can be as simple as a page of hyperlinks to valuable resources. Or it can be as rich as a vast database of thousands or millions of resources. The key to a successful virtual library though, is not the breadth of content, but that the content is well organized and easily accessible. What will your library offer that public search engines do not already offer? The one thing you can probably offer is the application of your knowledge in a field, so that learners using your library get better answers to their questions in less time than they can with any search engine.

Be sure to verify the quality of your resources. Include the *best* resources on a subject, not *all* the resources on a subject. Remember, one of the goals of the librarian is to reduce information overload.

Design your libraries to serve multiple purposes. They can be the basis for research activities (p. 194). One library can serve the needs of multiple courses. And a library can be a valuable information source in its own right.

Rely on Internet resources

In a sense, the whole Web is like a library … after an earthquake. The Web contains the equivalent of trillions of pages of information, but finding the one you want requires a lot of rooting around in disorganized piles. You want to spare your learners that effort. So a third way to direct learners to specific Internet readings is to link to them directly or trigger specific Internet searches.

Link to Internet resources

One of the simplest ways to use the Web is to link directly to documents useful to your learners. To see the document, learners just click on the link.

This course on medical ethics and procedures links to regulations and guidelines defining correct behavior for learners of this course. It links to specific parts of the Code of Federal Regulations.

Designed by William Horton Consulting. Built by William Horton Consulting and VA Research and Development.

Trigger a search engine

Provide specific search terms learners can enter into a search engine. Or provide a link that triggers a Web search on a search engine and display the results to your learners. This removes the trouble of typing in the search terms and the risk of typing them wrong.

This example shows a Google search page available from the course table of contents. Learners can click predefined search terms or enter their own terms.

Search built with Adobe Dreamweaver and Flash. Searches are performed by Google under license.

The advantage of this procedure is clear. You do not have to maintain the list of reading materials. The individual providers do that, and the search engine finds them for you. The list never goes stale.

Before you do this, however, make sure you have permission from the search engine to display their results in your course.

Sources of useful documents

Even if 99.999% of the content on the Web were trash, there would still be enough valuable reading material to supply millions of e-learning courses. Here are some places to look for readings for your activities and courses:

scholar.google.com	Searches scholarly literature such as papers, articles, books, abstracts, and journals.
print.google.com	Google Book Search searches the full text of books to find items of interest. It can display images of full pages and links to places where you can buy or borrow the book.
www.gutenberg.org	Project Gutenberg makes available over 17,000 free electronic books you can download.
books24x7.com	For a fee, Referenceware provides access to the complete online versions of popular scientific, technology, and business books.

Best practices for reading activities

Reading activities can be boring and pointless or engaging and enlightening. Opt for the latter.

Grow your library gradually

Grow your library smoothly and surely. Start with a Course Resource page. As it grows to several scrolling zones, put a menu in front of it. As it increases beyond a few hundred resources, incorporate a database to hold the individual records. As you begin offering more and more kinds of resources and services, consider migrating to a true knowledge-management system. Start simple and adopt technology only as you need it.

Publish a usage policy

Make clear what learners can do with the documents you provide them. Specify what rights learners have to read, share, copy, reuse, and modify the documents. Some items may be ones you own, while others are ones you have rights to display only. Still others may be resources you do not possess but provide links to.

One practical solution is to include a blanket rule that is quite restrictive and to flag items for which learners have additional rights.

Simplify obtaining documents

For freely available electronic documents, you can just link to the document. But what about documents not available online or documents that charge a fee?

▶ Link to sales site where learners can order a copy or purchase access.

▶ Link to Amazon (www.amazon.com), Barnes & Noble (bn.com), or some other online bookstore.

▶ Set up your own bookstore and sell the item yourself. This is easier than it sounds. Amazon or another seller will handle the technology and billing for you.

▶ Buy limited electronic rights and make them available to just your learners.

Feature active examples

One of the most valuable forms of online resources is a library of examples that learners can actually manipulate and use.

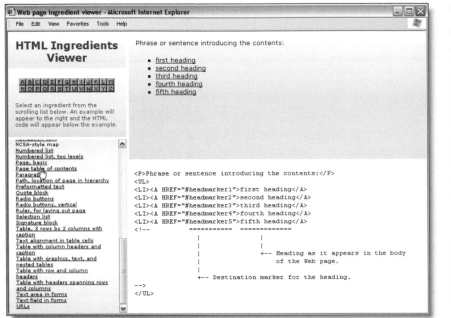

The collection shown here offers HTML ingredients that can be used in Web pages to create tables, headings, bullet lists, and so forth.

Built using Adobe Dreamweaver and JavaScript. View example at horton.com/eld/.

Here's how it works. The learner clicks a letter button to scroll through the list of examples to the ones with names beginning with that letter. The learner then picks an example in the list. The example appears formatted at the upper right and as HTML at the lower right.

The learner can then copy the HTML to an authoring program. Embedded comments guide learners in modifying the example to suit their purposes. Because such examples can be modified and used by learners, we call them active examples.

Use active examples for:

▶ Programming code.

▶ HTML, XML, and other tagging languages.

▶ Templates used to create slides, documents, etc.

▶ Forms to print out and fill in.

Combine readings with other activities

Merge your library and museum

Build and manage a library and a museum (p. 96) as one operation. They are separate institutions in the physical world only because they warehouse different kinds of objects: paintings and sculpture in art museums, books in libraries. Online, all objects are just bits.

The missions of libraries and museums are complementary. Museums contain unique original two- and three-dimensional objects and provide tiny plaques of commentary on them. Libraries provide extensive commentary on everything imaginable but only low-fidelity reproductions of objects of interest. Sounds like an ideal merger.

You may still want to maintain separate learner interfaces for the library and museum—at least until patrons seem ready to accept a merger. Behind the interface, the two institutions can share a common Web server, database, and access mechanisms.

Teach learners to use your library

▶ Create a guided tour (p. 91) of the library to show learners around. Focus on items related to your course.

▶ Conduct scavenger hunts (p. 196) to familiarize learners with the organization and search mechanisms of the library.

▶ Assign guided research activities (p. 199) that get learners in the habit of using library resources.

Integrate readings into other activities

▶ Supplement presentations (p. 49) with readings that provide more depth and detail.

▶ Attach readings to games (p. 141) to provide the principles needed to win the game and to help learners who find the high degree of interactivity required in computer games a bit intimidating.

▶ Use library-based materials throughout e-learning. Get in the habit of beginning each lesson with links to alternative ways of learning the subject and ending it with links to ways of learning more on the subject.

FIELD TRIPS

Online field trips take learners on educational excursions to places where they can observe concrete examples of what they are learning. In conventional education, a geology student might take a hike through a canyon to examine various rock layers, or an art student might visit a museum to see the paintings. In e-learning, the same students might tour an online representation of the canyon or search exhibits in a virtual museum.

About field trips

Field trips take us to educational examples and intriguing displays. The essential aspect of the field trip is not walking from example to example, but in examining the examples and seeing relationships among them. Field trips let us visit museums, parks, battlefields, historic neighborhoods, zoos and greenhouses, archaeological digs, manufacturing plants, and ancient ruins.

When to use field trips

Get learners out of the virtual classroom. Send them on a virtual field trip. Use them whenever you would recommend a real field trip, but schedule and budget say no. Use field trips to:

▶ Show how concepts taught in the course are applied (or misapplied) in the real world.

▶ Provide access to many concrete examples.

▶ Reveal examples in context.

▶ Orient learners in a new environment or system.

▶ Encourage discovery of trends and patterns.

Types of field trips

There are two main types of online field trips:

▶ **Guided tours**, which are perused in a predetermined order. Guided tours take us to physically separated examples. Guided tours can be self-directed or instructor-led and can be conducted live or played back from a recording.

▶ **Museums** (p. 96), in which the learner decides where to go next. Museums collect examples in one place. In museums, learners can compare examples and discover relationships.

Guided tours

The guided tour orients the learner in a virtual or real environment. The guided tour can be used to lead learners through an online representation of a real environment, such as teaching the layout of equipment in the bay of an ambulance, the twists and turns of a river channel, or the sequence of rock strata in a mountain range.

Another popular guided tour introduces an interactive computer system, such as a computer application, a Web site, or an e-learning course. It does not teach how to operate the software, but does give an overview of its structure and a preview of its capabilities.

Example of a guided tour

The following guided tour introduces repository of learning resources. The learner can embark on the tour from any page by clicking a **Tour** button (at the bottom of the main window). Clicking the **Tour** button displays the first stop on the tour and opens a separate tour window that guides the learner through the tour. The learner clicks on the **Next** button to advance to the next stop. Here are the second, third, and forth stops:

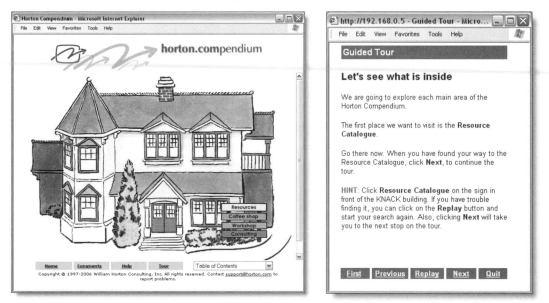

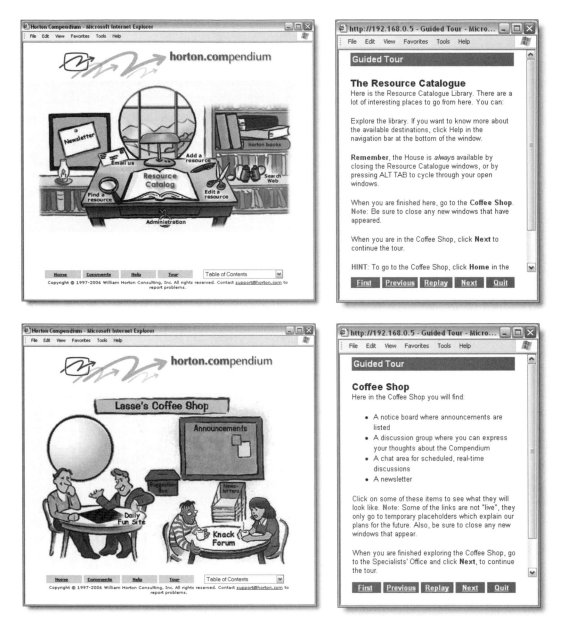

Built using Adobe Dreamweaver and Active Server Pages. Graphics created with Adobe Photoshop.

Notice that the tour describes the stop and suggests exploring it—like going ashore from a cruise ship. The learner can always rejoin the tour by clicking on the **Replay** button, which resets the underlying window to the current stop in the tour. Other buttons also give the learner choices. **Previous** lets the learner return to the previous stop, and **First** restarts the whole tour from the beginning.

At the end of the tour, learners are returned to the point where the tour started and are given a brief summary of what they saw.

How guided tours work

Typically, the learner starts the tour by clicking on a button or link in a Web site, computer program, or e-learning course. This action pops up the tour window.

The learner begins the tour in earnest after a brief introduction, which states the purpose and subject of the tour.

At each stop on the tour, pertinent features of an exhibit, object, or location are pointed out. In some tours advancing to the next stop automatically displays the item discussed at that stop of the tour. In others, the learner receives instructions on how to navigate to find the next stop.

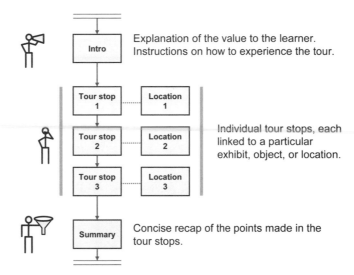

At the end of the tour, the learner sees a summary of the highlights of the tour.

When to use a guided tour

Use guided tours to orient learners in an environment, building, Web site, computer program, or e-learning course. Provide a quick guided tour for those who:

▶ **Need to see the big picture before getting lost in the details**. Use the guided tour to walk learners through a complex procedure before asking them to perform it on their own.

▶ **Just want an overview**. For example, sales representatives need to know enough to demonstrate a product and its advantages, but do not have time to learn to operate it.

▶ **Will be involved with a product but will not be operating it**. These might include managers of the operators, prospective buyers of a product, and product reviewers too lazy to actually use the product.

Use guided tours to help people explore a place they cannot visit in person. The place visited can be a real locale or an imaginary one. Use guided tours when the locale is:

▶ **Too far away**. To travel to the real locale would be expensive and time consuming.

▶ **Too spread out**. A field trip can include stops in Mobile, Moscow, Montreal, Mumbai, Monte Carlo, and Metropolis. The only airfare is a mouse click.

▶ **Too dangerous**. Nuclear radiation, fragmentation grenades, and cosmic rays cannot penetrate the computer screen.

▶ **Imaginary**. How about taking learners to a place where impossible theories are real and alternate realities predominate?

Variations of guided tours

Adapt guided tours to your style of e-learning and your technology.

Personal travel diaries

A simpler form of a guided tour resembles a personal travel diary illustrated with snapshots. Such tours can present an individual's experience of a subject in a direct and interesting way.

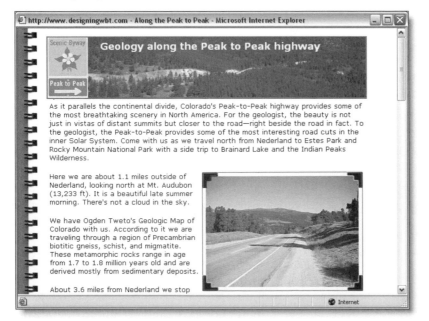

This example introduces learners to the geology of the Rocky Mountain region. It recounts an automobile trip northward along the Peak-to-Peak highway in Colorado. Each stop consists of an annotated photograph of a vista or road cut.

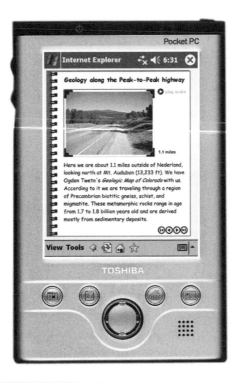

If a tour involves movement through physical locations, you may want to design the guided tour so learners can take it along. That way, learners can recreate the tour and experience it for themselves.

This version of the tour was designed to play on a mobile device. And learners could choose to listen to a recording of the displayed text.

Web-page version built with Adobe Dreamweaver. Mobile version built with Adobe Flash. View examples at horton.com/eld/.

Web tours in an online meeting

In online meetings you can conduct guided tours of Web sites and other electronic media using Web tours (p. 435) or application sharing (p. 436). On such tours learners watch the locations visited by the instructor. In others, the instructor takes learners to a location where they can explore on their own.

Tours of imaginary worlds

Let learners explore virtual locales. Provide tours of imaginary worlds and of physical objects they could not tour in reality. Here are some examples of imaginary tours.

▶ **The human body**. Swim through arteries. Use the diaphragm for a trampoline. Tickle the funny bone.

▶ **An imaginary town** with exactly one example of every architectural style, kind of like Greenfield Village (www.hfmgv.org/village), but more so.

▶ **A cave** through all the major kinds of rocks found on earth.

▶ **The atom**. Scuba dive thorough electron clouds and touch down on the nucleus.

For a menu, create a schematic map or scene containing all the features you need to display.

2

Absorb-type activities

Best practices for guided tours

A good tour leaves learners excited, satisfied, and confident to navigate on their own.

Let learners explore objects of interest. Let learners click on an object to enlarge it or to display commentary about it. Let learners select among various viewpoints at a stop. Clearly flag activities, that is, places where the tourist can do more than just look and read.

Narrate stops well. Tell learners what they should notice on the tour. Otherwise they may flail or become distracted by all the pretty pictures. For each stop, explain what the scene shows. What are the names of the objects shown? From what direction is the scene viewed? What in particular is significant about the objects shown in this stop? If technical conditions permit, consider providing the narration by an authoritative voice as well as in text.

Show spatial relationships. If the spatial relationships among objects on the tour are important, help learners see the relationships. Overlap the stops so that the next stop is visible in the edge of the current stop. Show both on a you-are-here map. And be sure to include an overview map showing all the stops in the guided tour.

Encourage learners to explore on their own. Have learners explore the sights at each stop. Suggest things to click on. Map out a side trip or two. Let learners pick or design their own tours. Provide an overview map and gallery from which learners can pick destinations in any order they choose.

Make side excursions safe. If there is any danger that learners will wander too far afield, include a **Rejoin tour** button to rescue them. Or start digressions away from the tour in a separate window so that the main tour window remains on the screen.

Anchor each stop with a visual. For each stop, display a compelling visual image. It should be attractive, but it is more important that it clearly communicate the main idea of the stop.

Keep the tour focused. A tour is not a tutorial, a Help facility, or an instruction manual. A tour provides a broad overview of how the pieces fit together.

Virtual museums

A museum is an organized collection of exhibits gathered in one place. Exhibits consist of informative objects, such as paintings by van Gogh or the skeleton of a T-Rex, annotated with relevant facts. A virtual museum is much the same, except that the place where objects are gathered is not a building made of granite and marble but an online space viewed through a browser.

A virtual museum is much like a guided tour except that the learner decides how to navigate the museum. Virtual museums are also called *Web-based museums*, *e-museums*, *virtual galleries*, *online museums*, and *online galleries*. Virtual museums have been used to showcase objects as diverse as human organs, paintings by a second-grade class, and airsickness bags.

Example of a museum

Here you see a small museum of minerals. It contains pictures of minerals and information about them. A learner can pick a mineral by appearance or by name to jump to the exhibit of that mineral.

Built using Adobe Dreamweaver and Active Server Pages. View example at horton.com/eld/.

The individual exhibit shows a single mineral. It also provides technical details about the mineral, along with a brief description of it.

The **Next** and **Previous** buttons take the visitor forward and backward through all the minerals in the museum. The **Fast Forward** button starts advancing through the exhibits at a rate of about six seconds per exhibit. This is called *autoscanning* (p. 561). The **Stop** button stops on the current exhibit. Paging through the exhibits is useful if the visitor can recognize a mineral, but does not know what it is called.

![Mineral Museum Search page screenshot showing search form with Color: Green, Hardness: 5-Apatite to 10-Diamond on the Mohs scale, Where found: Arizona, Keywords: crystal, Display matches as Gallery/List, Submit and Reset buttons]

Clicking on the **Search** button lets the visitor search for minerals that meet specified characteristics.

How virtual museums work

Virtual museums let learners create their own tours and displays. The learner specifies what kinds of exhibits are desired, and the museum makes them available.

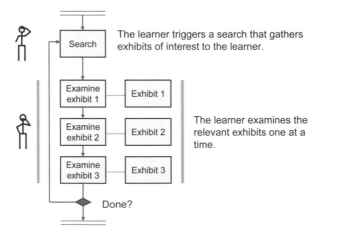

After examining the gathered examples, the learner may quit or continue with another search.

When to create a virtual museum

Museums organize large numbers of separate objects into meaningful collections. Museums are useful to:

▶ **Provide** access to many concrete instances of objects from a field being studied.

▶ **Enable** learners to discover patterns and trends among separate objects and instances.

▶ **Make available** the artifacts of a field of endeavor—or of an organization engaged in that endeavor.

On university campuses, learned professors lecture about subjects that their listeners cannot visualize. Abstractions remain clouds, gently blowing away. A museum of concrete instances of what the professor is talking about would bring the abstractions back to earth.

Every day busy companies with crowded offices and cramped disk drives archive their history with the Delete key. Years later, their leaders wonder why employees have no sense of the tradition or heritage of the great company they work for. A museum is a great way to preserve and organize the artifacts of an organization's formative years and epic struggles. I am not suggesting you exhibit the hairdos worn in 1983 by the current CEO or video clips of embarrassing incidents at last year's Christmas party. No, the best use of the virtual museum will be to display how the organization got where it is today and why certain traditions exist.

Best practices for virtual museums

Think about your last visit to an art museum. Close your eyes and imagine yourself walking through one of the galleries. What do you see? Fine art, for sure, but what about the people you see? Do you see a shushing teacher herding a gaggle of giggling third-graders? Do art students from the local university languidly sketch the exhibits between trips to the espresso bar? Do parents with children in tow sidestep around the perimeter of the room, dutifully reading the plaques of every painting? Museums are places where many different kinds of people can learn many different things in many different ways. Here are a few suggestions to enable just as many kinds of learning in your virtual museums.

Put learners in control. Let learners choose the exhibits they want to see. Guide them through the collection, but let them decide which exhibits to view and which objects to study in detail.

Give private tours. A virtual museum has no fixed floor plan, no permanent arrangement of exhibits, no limitations on available space. The use of search engines and databases makes it possible for learners to have an experience custom-tailored to their individual needs. Here are some ways to custom-tailor the display.

▶ Display just the subset of interest to the individual learner.

▶ Arrange the exhibits to reveal trends and patterns of interest to the learner.

▶ Generate custom maps and menus that reveal what the learner is interested in learning.

Let learners make their own tours. Let learners search the museum for exactly what they want to see right now. Do not force them to plod through the whole Louvre if all they want to see is the Mona Lisa. Here are some ways to make it easier for visitors to find the exhibits they want to see:

▶ **Catalog**. Index the whole museum. Provide a conventional alphabetical index listing each object in the museum by its name and by what it illustrates.

▶ **Menus**. Provide several menus that let learners search by whatever characteristics are important to them. For example, a corporate history museum might contain menus organized by time period, by current product line, by underlying technology or market, and by the person in charge.

▶ **Visual gallery**. Let learners pick objects by scanning thumbnail images of all objects on exhibit. Also let them graze the display by having it automatically advance from item to item at a rate of about one per second until the learner says, "Stop, that's the one I want."

▶ **Linked keywords**. Assign keywords to each exhibited item to describe it. Let learners search for items indexed with a particular keyword. Also display the keywords on each exhibit. Make them links so that clicking on one displays a list of other items indexed with that same keyword.

▶ **Search by characteristics**. Include a search engine that lets learners find exhibits by specifying detailed characteristics of the item sought.

If many paths through the museum are possible, suggest a simple one. Or provide a tour (p. 91) conducted by a docent.

Integrate museums into e-learning

Wandering a virtual museum on your own may be a pleasant way to while away an afternoon, but it is not automatically a learning experience. Here are some tips to increase the learning that takes place in the galleries of your museum and to make the museum a part of your overall e-learning efforts.

▶ **Create a learner's tour of the museum**, pointing out the galleries and exhibits of interest to learners in your course. The guided tour can teach learners to search and navigate the museum on their own.

▶ **Create research activities** that require learners to find information and examples in a museum. Give learners tasks that, for example, require them to search a virtual museum for exhibits of a particular type and discover how they are related. Scavenger hunt activities (p. 196) are especially good ways to motivate searching in a museum.

▶ **Craft guided-research activities** (p. 199) that use the museum's assets as resources.

▶ **Organize specialized tours** through exhibits to reveal patterns and trends you are teaching.

▶ **Assign learners tasks** to find relevant objects of personal interest.

▶ **Combine a museum with a presentation** (p. 49) **or reading** (p. 78) so the museum provides concrete instances of the theory presented in the reading or presentation. Or the presentation or reading provides more background and details about individual museum exhibits.

Best practices for field trips

Whether you are using guided tours, museums, or some other form of field trip, you need to make sure it advances learning. Here are a few suggestions.

Require learning

Require specific learning outcomes. Make the field trip more than a vacation away from the responsibilities of learning. Give learners specific assignments they must accomplish on the field trip—objects they must find, patterns they must notice, or principles they must infer.

Include a variety of media

Enrich your museum with other media as well. Here are some candidates.

▶ **Scanned documents**. Print advertisements, covers of annual reports, articles of incorporation, the first stock certificate, and critical patents.

▶ **Video clips of important events**. Speeches, technical presentations, product demonstrations, experiments, product tests, award presentations, and TV commercials.

▶ **Audio recordings**. Speeches, presentations, and jingles from commercials.

▶ **Virtual reality.** Models of prominent or proposed buildings, walkarounds of important objects, and conceptual models of a field of research.

Tell what is important

Highlight the aspect of the exhibit that is important for the learner to notice. Learners may discover the important point on their own. Or they may not. Why take chances? In our online collection of good examples of e-learning (horton.com/examples), we include a list of important features to notice.

What to notice	
	• **Vast explorable world**. This environment contains a 3D model spanning 64 tombs, some containing many separate chambers linked to dozens of photographs and descriptions. A learner could spend months exploring.
	• **Appropriate media usage**. Animated 3D models are used to show orientations and inclines, not to distract with twirling logos. Videos are short and to the point. Paintings and statues are illustrated with photographs.
	• **Unified design**. The consistent user interface, harmonious color scheme, and clear organization make navigation pleasant and predictable.
	• **Layered information**. Both a fifth grader completing a homework assignment and a post-grad Egyptologist will gain useful knowledge here.
	• **Subject-specific search**. Learners can search for tombs by dynasty, discoverer, or architectural characteristics.

Annotate exhibits thoroughly

Label items you exhibit. Provide concise but thorough details for each item on exhibit. Here is a checklist of the kinds of details people may want to know. No individual item will need all these details, but this checklist will make sure you consider all possibilities.

▶ **Name**. Include both official and unofficial names. Include the formal, legal, scientific name of an object along with its informal common name.

▶ **Description**. What is the object? What does it exemplify? Why is the object on exhibit here? What is important about it?

▶ **ID number**. What is the product number, model number, or serial number of the item?

▶ **Dimensions**. What are the object's height, width, depth, weight, area, and volume?

▶ **Creator**. Who is responsible for creating this object? List the lead designer, artist, and project manager. Link to their biographies, if available.

▶ **Date**. When was the object manufactured, completed, or discovered? If you cannot give a specific date, consider specifying a time span, historic era, or geological period.

▶ **Medium**. Of what materials is the object constructed? What are its important components?

▶ **Owner**. Who owns the actual object? Who holds copyright on its design?

▶ **History**. How and when was the object conceived, created, and modified? What is its provenance?

▶ **Classification**. Does the object fit into a defined taxonomic scheme? Does it fit a standard industry category? Does it illustrate an artistic or design movement?

▶ **Rating**. How does this object compare to comparable objects, as rated by the curator of the museum, by an industrial rating agency, or by museum patrons?

▶ **Sales**. If the object is a product, how many were sold and for how much money?

▶ **Price**. If the object is for sale, what is its price?

▶ **Keywords**. How is the object indexed? Link each keyword to other objects indexed with the same keyword.

▶ **Links to details**. Link the annotation of the object to more complete materials about it.

Let learners choose what to download

Guided tours and museums can contain a lot of large graphics and multimedia. This is appropriate to their mission. What is not appropriate is to fail to warn learners before starting a lengthy download. Here are some common-sense courtesies to practice.

▶ **Preview the object**. Describe the object in words or display a small thumbnail image. Then let the learner decide to download it.

▶ **Specify the size** of the download.

▶ **Consider providing both high- and low-bandwidth versions**. For example, for a photograph, you might provide a large JPEG image optimized for quality, along with a smaller version optimized for maximum compression.

Let learners inspect items in detail

Let learners enlarge photographs to inspect items of interest. Make the image of an exhibit into an image-map with each object linked to its enlargement. Or overlay the illustration with a grid of rectangular areas, each triggering the display of an enlargement of that area.

IN CLOSING ...

Summary

Absorb-type activities provide information to learners. In absorb activities, learners read, listen, and watch. In well-designed absorb activities, learners also consider, select, combine, judge, and process information. Absorb activities come in several forms. Here is where you might use each:

Presentations To provide information or to introduce a subject. Presentations are especially useful where you can organize information in a clear and logical sequence.

Story-telling To show the human dimension of a subject by showing how it affected the life of the instructor, and expert, or someone else respected by the learner. Stories told by the teacher are absorb activities; stories by the learner are connect activities.

Readings To enable learners to pursue subjects in greater detail. Readings make good use of existing documents to broaden the scope of e-learning and to let learners customize learning to their individual interests.

Field trips To let learners experience a variety of real-world examples the way they might on a physical field trip or visit to a well-stocked museum.

For more ...

To learn more about any of the absorb activities described here; search the Web for the name of the activity. If necessary, include words like *online*, *virtual*, and *e-learning* to bias the results toward electronic versions of the activities.

The next two sections suggest even more activities to include in your e-learning. The next chapter on *do* activities will help you find more active partners for your *absorb* activities.

On horton.com, we have made available a wide variety of materials on producing online documents and information. Help yourself.

3 Do-type activities

Practice, discovery, and playing games

If *absorb* activities are the nouns, then *do* activities are the verbs of learning. They put people in action. They elevate learning from passive reading and watching to active seeking, selecting, and creating knowledge. Doing begets learning.

ABOUT DO ACTIVITIES

While absorb activities provide information, do activities transform that information into knowledge and skills. In do activities, learners discover, parse, decode, analyze, verify, combine, organize, discuss, debate, evaluate, condense, refine, elaborate, and, most importantly, apply knowledge.

Common types of do activities

Do activities include a variety of forms that exercise learning.

▶ **Practice activities** (p. 106) give learners experience applying information, knowledge, and skills. They include drill-and-practice, hands-on, guided-analysis, and teamwork activities.

▶ **Discovery activities** (p. 125) lead learners to make discoveries. They include virtual laboratories, case studies, and role playing activities.

▶ **Games and simulations** (p. 141) have learners attempt tasks in safe environments and learn from the feedback they receive. These activities include quiz show games, word puzzles, jigsaw puzzles, adventure games, software simulations, device simulations, personal-response simulations, mathematical simulations, and environmental simulations.

When to feature do activities

Where should we rely most on do activities? Do-type activities require active imagination to concoct and extensive testing to perfect. When is this cost and effort justified? Use do activities to:

▶ Provide safe, encouraging practice to prepare learners to apply learning in the real world.

▶ Motivate learners by activating curiosity for material learners might otherwise consider boring.

▶ Prepare for absorb activities by showing learners how little they know about the subject and making clear the value of information they are to absorb.

▶ Enable learning by exploration and discovery.

As a rule, learners should spend 50% of their time in *do* activities (90% would be better; but 50% will do just fine).

PRACTICE ACTIVITIES

Practice helps learners strengthen and refine skills, knowledge, and attitudes by applying them and receiving feedback. Practice tasks do not teach new information. They give learners an opportunity to exercise newly acquired abilities.

About practice activities

Practice activities are like classroom sessions in which students are encouraged to apply what they have just heard the teacher talk about or what they have just read in a book.

When to use practice activities

You have probably heard that practice makes perfect. Practice certainly does refine skills and streamline performance. Use practice activities in e-learning to:

▶ Prepare learners to apply skills, knowledge, and attitudes in real situations.

▶ Teach learners to adapt general, abstract knowledge to specific, concrete situations.

▶ Automate skills and consolidate separate bits of learning so that application is faster and more fluent.

▶ Build confidence in the ability to apply learning.

▶ Verify the ability to apply low-level skills or knowledge before moving on to more complex items.

Types of practice activities

Practice activities range from simple, mechanical activities to analytical, multi-person activities.

▶ **Drill-and-practice activities** (p. 108) are the repeated application of a series of similar, simple tasks. They help learners automate skills and improve fluidity of application.

▶ **Hands-on activities** (p. 110) allow learners to perform tasks with real tools but with guidance. They teach real tasks and help learners apply theory.

▶ **Guided analysis activities** (p. 113) lead learners through an analysis task with step-by-step instructions. They strengthen a learner's ability to perform a complex cognitive task.

▶ **Teamwork activities** (p. 120) require learners to perform a complex distributed task. They help develop collaborative skills.

How practice activities work

Practice activities have a recurring 3-step sequence. First the instructor or the computer assigns the practice task to the learner, explaining it in adequate detail for the learner to begin the task immediately. The learner performs the task and receives feedback from the instructor or the computer.

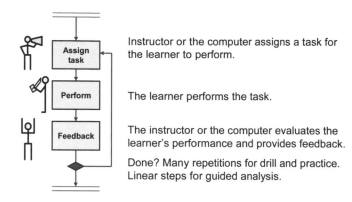

Instructor or the computer assigns a task for the learner to perform.

The learner performs the task.

The instructor or the computer evaluates the learner's performance and provides feedback.

Done? Many repetitions for drill and practice. Linear steps for guided analysis.

The cycle may recur for another step in a procedure or for a slightly more advanced objective.

Drill-and-practice activities

Drill-and-practice activities repeatedly exercise a simple or small area of knowledge. They are like the flash cards used to teach multiplication or a foreign language vocabulary.

A drill-and-practice activity starts with an introduction that welcomes learners and explains how the activity works. Then learners repeatedly solve problems and receive feedback on their solutions. At the end, learners may review what they have learned and try applying it in a more realistic situation.

Practice recognizing nautical flags!

One day you may find yourself sailing in the ocean with no radio or ship-to-shore phone, and a fire is not an option (leaving out smoke signals). What will you do if you need help? Use nautical flags of course!

Using the Drill Sergeant, test your ability to recognize letters. If you have trouble, review the lesson on the All About NauticalFlags.

What letters are displayed?

| bgtah |

Check   Next   Help   Translate

Feedback:
```
Correct. Good.
Click 'New Question' to continue.
```

This drill and practice teaches learners to recognize nautical flags and associate them with letters of the alphabet. Learners view a grouping of flags and then enter the equivalent letters.

Built using Adobe Dreamweaver and JavaScript. View example at horton.com/eld/.

When to use drill and practice

Educational theorists of late have so thoroughly condemned drill and practice that it is easy to believe that this method has no use whatsoever. However, drill and practice is very useful in helping people memorize facts that they must be able to recall reliably without hesitation. Some examples include:

▶ Foreign language vocabulary.

▶ Sign language.

▶ Symbols, emblems, and signs used in a profession.

▶ Spelling, grammar, and punctuation rules.

▶ Syntax of a programming language.

Drill-and-practice activities are also useful to automate procedures learners must perform fluidly without much conscious thought. Basic movements in sports and dance fall into this category, as do all emergency procedures that must be performed under noisy, confusing situations.

Use drill and practice to help people learn the simple rules and procedures that they must apply unconsciously as part of higher-level activities.

Varieties of drill-and-practice activities

Online drill-and-practice activities come in several varieties.

▶ **Auto-generated problems.** Use the computer to generate unique problems for the learner to solve. See page 271 for an example of how this might be done.

▶ **Increasing challenge**. Start with a simple problem to establish a baseline of acceptable performance. Then ratchet up the difficulty of practices. Offer more complex and difficult problems. Give learners less time to solve problems. Add distracters or noise.

▶ **Database of problems**. Draw individual problems from a fully developed repository of problems. Problems can be chosen at random or sequenced by prerequisites and paced by the learner's demonstrated abilities. Such an approach works well for subjects with simple recurring tasks, such as learning the grammar and syntax of a language.

Best practices for drill and practice

When designing a drill-and-practice activity:

- ▶ **Combine drill and practice with other learning activities** to teach how the rote knowledge exercised in the drill and practice can be applied. Drill and practice is seldom sufficient in itself.

- ▶ **Increase the difficulty level as the learner progresses.** Give more complex problems or require faster responses.

- ▶ **Give learners lots of problems to solve.** Let learners decide when to quit. If possible, design the activity so that it can generate an infinite number of new problems. That way the material is always fresh.

Hands-on activities

Hands-on activities give learners a small piece of real work to perform. In a hands-on activity the learner completes a task outside the lesson, such as performing a calculation with an on-screen calculator, filling in a form, or operating a piece of machinery.

The hands-on activity guides learners through the real-life task and provides feedback on their success. The instructor or computer assigns a task and gives detailed instructions. Learners perform the procedure, checking each step as performed. After a review of the procedure, learners repeatedly perform the task on their own.

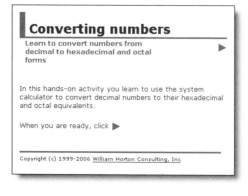

Converting numbers

Learn to convert numbers from decimal to hexadecimal and octal forms

In this hands-on activity you learn to use the system calculator to convert decimal numbers to their hexadecimal and octal equivalents.

When you are ready, click ▶

Copyright (c) 1999-2006 William Horton Consulting, Inc.

This example teaches the use of the Windows system calculator to convert decimal numbers to their hexadecimal and octal equivalents.

The activity begins with an introduction explaining what the learner will accomplish. The window is small so that the rest of the screen is available for performing the hands-on activity.

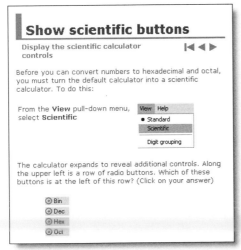

Start calculator

First, start up the calculator program   ◄◄ ◄ ▶

Open the calculator program.

To verify that you have started the calculator correctly, answer the following question:

The menu (just below the word "Calculator") contains three items. Which is the middle one:

> File
> Edit
> View

I do not know. <u>I need help opening the calculator</u>

To start the calculator

Instructions on how to start up   ◄◄ ◄ ▶
the calculator program

Need a little help starting the calculator? No problem. Here's how:

> From the **Start** menu select **Programs >
> Accessories > Calculator**

To verify that you have started the calculator correctly, answer the following question:

The menu (just below the word "Calculator") contains three items. Which is the middle one:

> File
> Edit
> View

Show scientific buttons

Display the scientific calculator   ◄◄ ◄ ▶
controls

Before you can convert numbers to hexadecimal and octal, you must turn the default calculator into a scientific calculator. To do this:

> From the **View** pull-down menu, | View   Help |
> select **Scientific**   • Standard
>   Scientific
>   Digit grouping

The calculator expands to reveal additional controls. Along the upper left is a row of radio buttons. Which of these buttons is at the left of this row? (Click on your answer)

> ⊙ Bin
> ⊙ Dec
> ⊙ Hex
> ⊙ Oct

Learners must perform a step and answer a question. To answer the question, they must successfully complete the step. The answer requires observing something not visible until the step is completed.

Requiring an indicator of success makes this a *gatekeeper* task, that is, one that requires performance of a prerequisite task before the learner can advance. A correct answer reveals the next step in the procedure.

Learners who cannot perform the step successfully can click "I need help opening the calculator" to get more detailed instructions.

If learners make a mistake, they receive help getting back on track. For example, learners who click on **Dec**, rather than the correct answer **Hex**, see the next page.

Need help?

Your answer was not correct. ◄◄ ◄ ►

Would you like to:

▶ Try again
▶ Start again from the previous step
▶ Start again from the beginning

Here, learners have three choices: to try again, to go back a step, or to start from the beginning.

For simple steps, where errors occur almost exclusively from inattention and carelessness, let learners go back and try again.

Summary

How to convert a decimal ◄◄ ◄ ►
number to hexadecimal or octal
form

Use the system calculator to convert decimal numbers:

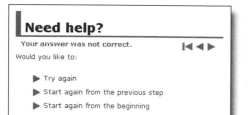

1	Start up the calculator program	
2	Select the scientific mode	
3	Select decimal format	⊕ Dec
4	Enter the number to convert	
5	Select the target format	⊕ Hex or ⊕ Oct

Select ▶ to take the activity test.

After completing the activity, learners see a summary. It serves as a review as well as a job aid. Learners may bookmark or print the summary.

Make sure the summary is compact enough to print to a single page of paper. Or provide a button to jump to a special printable version.

Test — Convert numbers

Demonstrate your ability to ◄◄ ◄
convert numbers to hex and
octal

Convert the decimal numbers in the left column to their hexadecimal and octal equivalents. Enter the converted numbers in the slots provided and select **Submit**.

Decimal	Hexadecimal	Octal
546		
4556		
10,298		

Evaluate   Reset   Show

Finally, learners test their ability to perform the procedure on their own.

This test requires repeated applications to confirm and lock in the skills.

Built using Adobe Dreamweaver and JavaScript. View example at horton.com/eld/.

When to use hands-on activities

Use hands-on activities to teach hands-on tasks. Although not especially effective in teaching abstract knowledge, hands-on activities can provide a pleasant descent from the stratospheric heights of conceptual thought common in many courses. They are powerful stimuli for learning practical skills.

Variations of hands-on activities

If performing the task for real is too dangerous or daunting to the learner, provide a simulation that mimics the look and feel of the real system (p. 151). Application sharing (p. 436) can also be used for hands-on activities. The instructor might start an application and then call on a learner to demonstrate a task for the rest of the class. For the learner performing the task, this is a hands-on activity.

Best practices for hands-on activities

Use gatekeeper tasks. To control advancement to the next step, ask questions about things learners can only observe by successfully performing the current step. Such questions can focus attention on important parts of the task and on those parts of the scene that will be important in subsequent steps.

Print out instructions. If learners must perform the activity away from the computer, let them print out the instructions and any other materials they may need. If they must record data, give them a paper form on which to write the data.

Require evidence. Have learners submit digital photographs of the results of any hands-on activity that produces visible results. One way to monitor learning of computer skills is to require learners to e-mail screen snapshots of the results.

Guided-analysis activities

Many designers limit practice activities to rote procedures and almost manual tasks. Practice is even more important for intellectual tasks that require sensitive application of adaptive procedures.

Guided analysis activities step learners through the process of analyzing a complex situation. Guided analysis answers one of the most important questions ever asked: "So what?" Guided analysis helps learners to separate useful from useless information and to infer general principles and conclusions from separate, confusing, concrete instances. It teaches learners how to turn data into information—and even knowledge.

This example guides forestry professionals in classifying soil textures based on the proportions of sand, loam, and silt in the soil.

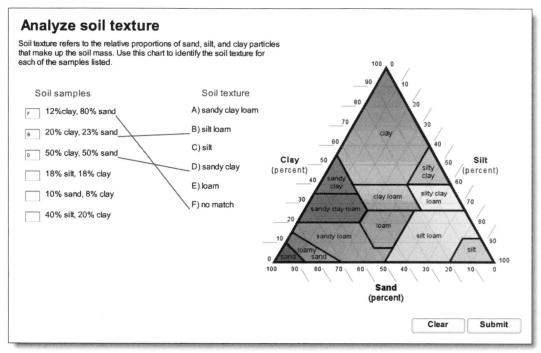

Built with Adobe Captivate. View example at horton.com/eld/.

In guided analysis, the learner follows a procedure to gather and analyze data. After several cycles of gathering and analyzing, the learner may abstract a principle revealed by the analysis and test it by analyzing new data. The learner may have to revise the principle until it reliably predicts results.

When to use guided analysis

The primary use of guided analysis is in teaching formal analysis techniques. The technique may involve calculating or estimating mathematical values. Or it may involve sorting, classifying, or ranking items according to defined procedures.

A secondary use is teaching principles *revealed* by the analysis of data. In this case, guided analysis exposes a trend or pattern that learners might not otherwise notice or believe. If exposing a trend or principle is primary, use a discovery activity instead.

Ways to guide analysis

One way to guide analysis is to have the learner apply a specific formula or procedure. Here are a few more methods of analysis. Each focuses the learner's attention and thought on a different aspect of the data.

Compare and contrast

Evaluating complex data is … well, complex. One way of simplifying it is to guide learners in comparing alternatives. The easiest way to do this in e-learning is to have learners create a side-by-side comparison.

Using the form below, compare the Dow Jones Industrial Average and the Standard and Poors 500. Use the blank lines at the bottom to add some characteristics of your own.

Characteristic	Dow Jones	Standard and Poors
Number of stocks		
Percentage of all New York Stock Exchange stocks		
Average PE ratio		
Total market capitalization		

Submit   Reset

In this example, learners compare two major indexes of the stock markets in the United States.

The form draws attention to critical differences between the two indexes. It requires learners to juxtapose contrasting facts so differences are inescapable.

To encourage independent thought, the form includes blank rows where learners can compare the two indexes according to characteristics learners select.

Classify items

Much learning in science and business involves classifying items into established categories. To classify items, learners assign real-world or net-available objects to established categories.

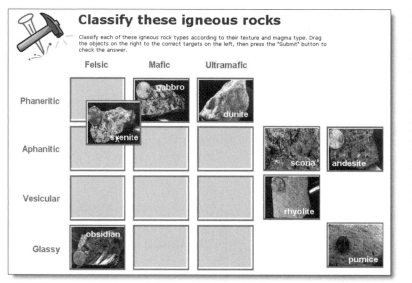

In this example, learners classify igneous rocks by their texture and magma type. To classify the rocks listed to the right, the learner drags each rock into a box in the appropriate row and column.

Built using Adobe Dreamweaver. View example at horton.com/eld/.

There are several ways to have learners assign items to categories. You can have learners:

▶ Pick categories from a drop-down list beside each item to be classified.

▶ Select from a pick-one list of categories the item could belong to.

▶ Select from a pick-multiple list to identify members of a category.

▶ Match items in one list with categories in another.

▶ Drag items to their categories or categories to their members.

Outline items

Most technical and business fields rely on hierarchical organization. Having learners outline items requires them to put individual items into a hierarchical scheme. This kind of guided analysis teaches general organizing skills as well as particular organizational schemes.

✏ Order from chaos

American architectural styles from 1600 to 1940

Organize the listed styles into a hierarchical scheme of three levels (use about five spaces to indent each level). If you do not find the first-level heading you want, add it. The second- and third-level headings or styles do not have to be in any particular order. However, before submitting your outline, make sure the first-level headings or styles are in chronological order.

Styles:

Adams
American Four Square
Art Deco
Arts and Crafts
Beaux Arts
California Bungalow
Cape Cod
Carpenter Gothic
Chalet
Chateauesque
Colonial
Colonial Bungalow
Colonial Revival
Cottage
Cubic
Dutch Colonial

```
Colonial
            Postmedieval English
            Dutch Colonial
            French Colonial
            Spanish Colonial
            Georgian
            Adam
            Saltbox
            Early Classical Revival
            Federal
Vernacular
            I-Style
            Upright-and-Wing
Romantic Houses
            Greek Revival
            Regency
```

This example of guided analysis asks learners to organize the list of architectural styles by categories and sub-categories.

Built using Adobe Dreamweaver. View example at horton.com/eld/.

In a field without clear, well-defined categories, this activity may still be valuable, although quite complex. Allow enough time for learners to change their minds several times. Or make it a team activity. The discussions of the team can provoke a lot of thinking about categories and classification schemes.

Re-create famous examples

Have learners re-create a famous example from the area of study. Examples learners can re-create include:

▶ Paintings and photographs.

▶ Scenes from famous films and plays.

▶ Writings.

▶ Music compositions.

▶ Architectural drawings.

▶ Scientific experiments.

Have learners start by reproducing the example exactly as done originally. Then have them try slight variations. Next they can reproduce the example, but in the style of another example. Finally, they can try to create examples in entirely their own styles.

3

Do-type activities

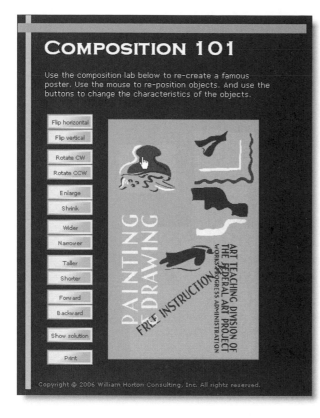

Here learners are challenged to re-create a famous poster they have studied. They have all the pieces and must rearrange them by dragging pieces around, resizing them, and flipping them vertically and horizontally.

Built using Adobe Flash and Adobe Dreamweaver. View example at horton.com/eld/.

To see another example, visit www.wildlifeart.org/Rungius/home.html.

Best practices for guided analysis

Focus on techniques or principles

Do not forget what you are teaching. If you are teaching the analysis technique, emphasize the technique. Lavish attention on each step. If, however, you are using the analysis to reveal principles that are the real subject, then focus attention on the principles and keep the analysis simple. If the principles are primary, consider a discovery activity (p. 125) instead.

Spend time analyzing, not collecting, data

Eliminate unnecessary steps that may distract from what you are teaching. If finding the data is not part of the activity, provide it or link directly to it. If calculations are complex, provide a calculator (p. 189).

If gathering data is part of what you are teaching, combine the guided-analysis activity with a research activity (p. 194).

3

Specify a format for answers

You could let learners submit answers in any format they chose. However, structuring the response can focus attention on the idea being taught and away from irrelevant details. It can also simplify evaluation by the instructor and perhaps permit automatic evaluation and scoring by the computer.

The most direct way to structure an answer is to require the learner to fill in a form.

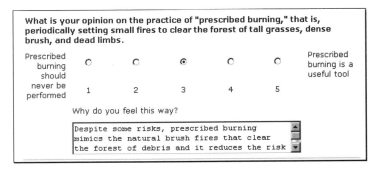

This form requires the learner to express and defend opinions. It simplifies and focuses the process by defining each issue as a scale between two extreme positions.

It simplifies answering by letting the learner pick a point along the scale. It includes 5 points so learners realize they have a range of responses. The text area requires learners to defend their positions. Its size strongly encourages them to be brief.

Label to guide analysis

Vague prompts lead to vague answers. Text-input areas are especially difficult because they provide few constraints or hints as to the form of the answer. To help learners stay on track, label and size the field in a way that implies the form of the answer.

Label a text input area with either a simple question or an incomplete statement that the learner is to complete. Phrase the label so that it requires analysis to write a response.

> In the cases studied, buy-back marketing plans failed when ….
>
> Harassment complaints are most likely when ….
>
> The three main causes of brake-rotor failure are ….
>
> Editors should use Smart Blur rather than Gaussian Blur when ….

As a rule, make text-response areas about 25 to 50% larger than the size of the response you want. Most people will fill one-half to three-fourths of the available area.

Do not require learners to enter more than one answer in a field. If an activity has three questions, provide three text boxes, one for each question.

Prompt higher-level thinking

If learners must make judgments about objects, products, or ideas, they will need practice. Often activities that ask learners to critique an item draw vacuous responses like "Just great" or "It sucks." To provoke deeper responses, ask questions like these:

▶ What are the advantages of this item?

▶ What is wrong with this item?

▶ How can this item be improved?

▶ How can this error be corrected?

▶ What would be the results of performing this action?

▶ What are the categories of these items?

▶ What are the critical characteristics of this item?

▶ What conclusions can you draw?

▶ What evidence can you offer?

▶ What follows from a principle?

▶ What is the pattern in these incidents?

▶ How does your opinion differ from those of others?

▶ How could you apply this principle?

Teamwork activities

Teamwork activities are good to teach teamwork, or any skill that is practiced by a group rather than just an individual. The communications capabilities of networks let individuals at separate locations work as a team. Teamwork activities use these capabilities so that learners in a class can work as coordinated teams to solve a single, complex problem—no matter where they are. Team members communicate using online meetings and discussion forums in order to complete their assigned tasks.

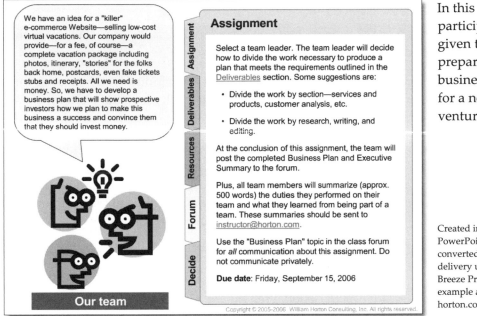

In this example, participants are given the task of preparing a business plan for a new venture.

Created in Microsoft PowerPoint and converted for Web delivery using Adobe Breeze Presenter. View example at horton.com/eld/.

In teamwork activities, the instructor assigns a design task and helps learners organize themselves into teams. Teams work independently, producing successively more refined versions of their work, which they submit to an integration team. The integration team merges the work of the other teams and submits the final project to the instructor for grading.

When to use teamwork activities

Teamwork activities are valuable to teach skills that learners apply as part of a team, rather than as individuals. Teamwork activities are also valuable in teaching teamwork skills in their own right. As more and more work requires coordinating with distant colleagues, teamwork activities will become a more common part of education.

Some common teamwork projects require learners to create:

▶ A financial plan for a new type of business.

▶ A report on the feasibility of a new product.

▶ Recommendations on the use of a new medical procedure.

▶ Proposed laws to cover new technology.

3

Do-type activities

Variations of teamwork activities

Teamwork activities is a broad category that you can adapt for classes of various sizes and for teaching various subjects. Here are a few suggestions:

For a small class. In a small class, each team can be a single individual. The instructor can take a more active role by integrating the parts and giving feedback on the work in progress.

For a large class. In a large class, have teams work in parallel. Divide the class into large teams and assign the same problem to each large team. Each large team must come up with its own solution and post it on the server for other teams to see. After seeing the solutions of other teams, a team may revise its own solution. At the end of the activity, each team must pick the best solution submitted by another team and justify its choice.

For language learning. For language learning, create teams of native and non-native speakers to solve a problem together. Teams must work in the language being learned.

Mosaic or jigsaw model. Take a large book, Web site, or other complex work made up of somewhat independent pieces. Divide the class into teams. Assign each team a part of the whole to review. Each team can further subdivide the work by assigning parts to individuals, or all the members of the team can work on the team's assignment. Then:

▶ Each team prepares a summary of its part and a critical review of it.

▶ An über-team assembles the pieces and writes a review of the whole.

▶ Individual members comment on the consolidated review, and the über-team revises it.

Best practices for teamwork

Make clear the grading criteria. Will grades be awarded to the class as a whole, to separate teams, or to individuals? Some learners may feel uncomfortable that largely unseen colleagues determine their grades.

Provide a suggested timeline for progress on the project. Lacking face-to-face contact, learners may not feel fully obligated to complete their share of work on time.

Challenge, but do not overwhelm. The goal of a teamwork activity must be appropriately challenging—not too difficult and not too easy. If learners have not worked in virtual teams before, they will require about twice as much time to complete an assignment as they would working together in a classroom.

Best practices for practice activities

Now for a few best practices for better practice activities, regardless of type.

Let learners decide how much to practice

In general, adults learn more effectively and efficiently when they decide how much to practice. Novices may need more practice to develop basic skills. Advanced learners may need only to refresh or refine their skills. Some with learning disabilities may benefit from extensive practice.

This means you may need to create many practice activities and to suggest a minimum number for learners to complete or a target score to achieve, such as "Practice till you achieve 85% correct" or "Try to earn 1,200 points."

Practice offline too

Let learners perform practice activities away from the computer. Rather than create an expensive simulation on the computer, give learners instructions they can follow while away from the computer—especially if they are learning a task that is normally performed away from the computer.

In this example, new bookstore clerks printed out this form and took it with them as they investigated where different kinds of books were shelved.

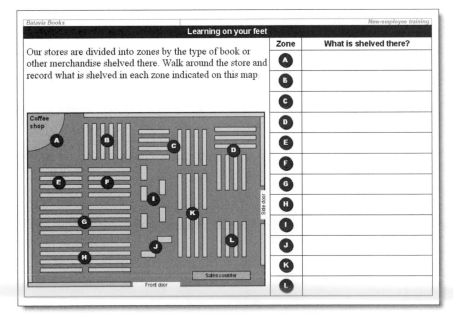

Built using Microsoft Word and PowerPoint.

Require the right skills

Ensure that learners apply the skills, knowledge, and attitudes that you are teaching. Minimize irrelevant requirements to complete the practice, such as:

▶ Purely mechanical tasks that are not part of the real task, such as typing things that could be clicked.

▶ Gathering materials and downloading many sample files. Gather all the materials into one Web page or one downloadable file.

▶ Unnecessary mathematical calculations. Provide a calculator (p. 189) or pick numbers that simplify the math.

Provide authentic challenge

Do not oversimplify practice. You may want to start with simple activities to introduce concepts and build confidence, but do not stop until learners confront realistically difficult tasks.

For example, in the *Using Gantt Charts* course, learners were required to interpret Gantt charts. Practice activities required them to deal with charts in a variety of formats and at a realistic level of detail, such as the ones shown here:

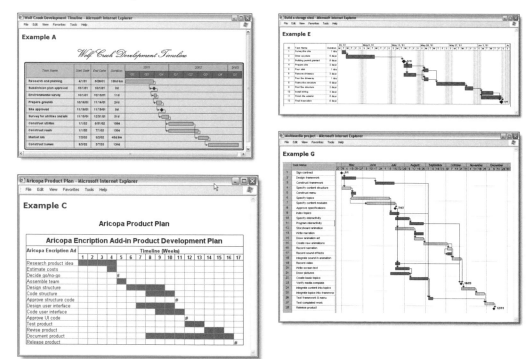

Combine practice with other activities

Practice activities can augment almost every other kind of activity, especially absorb activities. Here are some especially useful combinations.

▶ Follow presentations (p. 49) and readings (p. 78) with practice sessions to let learners refine their ability to apply what was presented.

▶ Precede games (p. 141) with practice sessions to help learners develop the simple skills that the game requires them to integrate and apply at a higher level.

▶ Combine research (p. 194) and reading (p. 78) with guided analysis (p. 113). Have learners conduct research to identify documents to read. Use guided analysis to help them make use of what they read.

DISCOVERY ACTIVITIES

Much of what we learn is by discovery. We conduct experiments or just try things out. We explore. We delve into things that arouse our curiosity. We systematically investigate subjects, and sometimes we just poke about. We prod and probe and provoke, just to see what will happen. We scrutinize and examine. We inspect and study situations to see what they can teach us. For many people, this is how most practical knowledge is acquired.

About discovery activities

Discovery activities do not present ideas, but lead learners to discover ideas on their own. They transform trial-and-error into trail-and-aha learning.

When to use discovery activities

Discovery learning is an alternative to presentation-based teaching. Use discovery learning:

▶ **For exploratory learning**. Some people learn by being told or shown, but many must discover skills and knowledge for themselves—especially those who are skeptical, concrete thinkers, or creative.

▶ **To reveal principles**. Experiments guide learners to discover principles, trends, and relationships for themselves. Many learners give more credibility to concepts they discover for themselves and tend to remember them longer.

▶ **To stimulate curiosity about a subject.** Discoveries can focus attention on a subject and motivate learners to seek explanations for what they discover.

Types of discovery activities

There are three main kinds of discovery activities useful in e-learning.

▶ **Virtual laboratories** (p. 127), where learners interact with a system to discover principles and refine thinking. Virtual laboratories are useful for hard knowledge.

▶ **Case studies** (p. 131), where learners analyze a complex, real event or situation to understand its underlying causes and concepts. They then draw conclusions, abstract principles, or make recommendations.

▶ **Role-playing scenarios** (p. 135), where learners interact with others in situations to infer the best practices, behaviors, and strategies. Role-playing scenarios are good for soft skills.

How discovery activities work

Discovery activities guide learners in conducting experiments and analyzing situations so that learners can observe and record their findings.

The instructor or the computer prepares learners by giving instructions on how to perform an analysis or experiment and by assigning specific questions to answer. Learners perform the assigned activity and record results or observations.

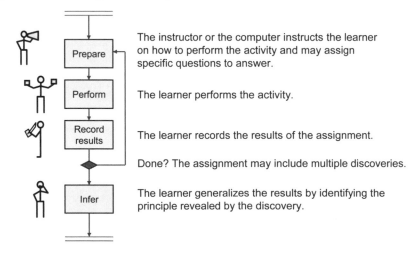

Prepare — The instructor or the computer instructs the learner on how to perform the activity and may assign specific questions to answer.

Perform — The learner performs the activity.

Record results — The learner records the results of the assignment.

Done? The assignment may include multiple discoveries.

Infer — The learner generalizes the results by identifying the principle revealed by the discovery.

This basic cycle of performing activities to answer questions may be repeated several times before the learner generalizes results to an overarching principle or summarizes them as a procedure or formula.

Virtual-laboratory activities

A virtual laboratory provides an on-screen simulator or calculator that learners can use to test ideas and observe results.

The learner gets the assignment, learns to operate the laboratory equipment, and then embarks on a series of experiments, carefully recording the results of each. After the last experiment, the learner generalizes what has been learned.

3

Do-type activities

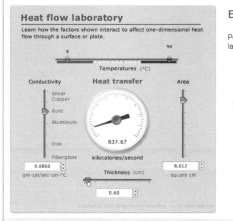

Here, mechanical designers conduct experiments to learn how heat flow depends on factors such as temperature, area, thickness, and thermal conductivity.

Lab built using Microsoft Excel and Crystal Xcelsius. Embedded in PowerPoint and converted for Web delivery using Adobe Breeze Presenter. View example at horton.com/eld/.

This virtual laboratory teaches HTML. Learners can use the arrow buttons to advance through a series of progress-sively more challenging goals shown at the right. Learners enter HTML in the text-entry area at the left and see their results in the middle column.

Built using Adobe Dreamweaver and custom JavaScript. View example at horton.com/eld/.

Clicking the button in the Result panel processes the learner's HTML and shows what it produces. The learner can compare the result to the goal and adjust accordingly. Learners who are stumped can click the check mark above the HTML area to see the solution for the currently displayed goal.

Over the decades, learners have consumed forests of grid paper drawing charts and graphs to detect trends and patterns in numerical data. Learners can now plot data right in their Web browsers by clicking and dragging.

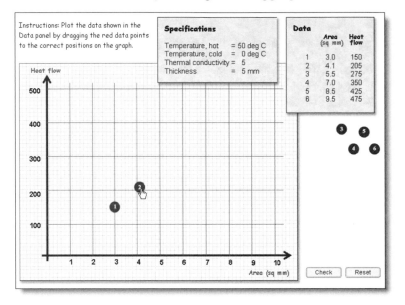

This example provides measurement data and allows the learner to plot it by dragging dots into place on the virtual graph paper. Doing so reveals a simple relationship between area and heat flow, which makes even the most dull-witted learner shout "Eureka!"

Built using Adobe Flash. View example at horton.com/eld/.

Plotting data points is tedious and teaches nothing by itself. So why not just show the graph with the points already plotted? The act of plotting the data forces learners to more actively process it, and more active processing leads to deeper learning. Just make sure that learners discover the relationship hidden in the data. Provide a hint or draw the trend line on the graph, if necessary.

When to use virtual laboratories

In a virtual laboratory, learners can try all kinds of experiments without risk of damaging equipment or injuring themselves, fellow learners, or lab technicians. They can also conduct experiments not possible in even the most generously funded real laboratory. Use virtual laboratories:

▶ **Instead of real laboratories**. You can use virtual laboratories to replace real laboratories. Once built, virtual laboratories have no additional costs for supplies, maintenance of equipment, or replacement of broken parts. Learners do not have to drive (or fly?) to the laboratory. Virtual laboratories are never crowded, never closed, and never broken. They never blow up.

▶ **To prepare learners to use real laboratories**. Virtual laboratories prepare learners for efficient work in real labs. Virtual labs can start as simple, limited representations of the real lab. As learners master simple experiments, the lab can reveal more controls and variables so that in the end the virtual lab has the same richness and range of experimentation as the real laboratory.

▶ **For abstract experiments**. Virtual laboratories are not limited to simulating real laboratories. With a virtual laboratory, learners can swap the orbits of planets, tinker with the global economy, or crossbreed a piranha and a panda. Use virtual laboratories to let learners experiment with concepts of any scale and any level of abstraction.

Best practices for virtual laboratories

Focus on what you are teaching

Focus your efforts on what you are teaching. If the purpose of the activity is to teach someone to use real laboratory equipment, then make the simulation richly detailed.

If the purpose of the laboratory experiment is to teach principles, design the activity to make discovering the principles efficient and reliable. Do not let operating laboratory equipment get in the way of learning. Make sure that every click and each pixel contribute to the goal, rather than just adding busy work. Just because the real-world lab equipment requires a lengthy calibration process does not mean that your virtual laboratory need include the same inconvenience.

Challenge learners' assumptions

Design experiments to challenge what learners believe to be true. Such a strategy can correct misconceptions and lead to exciting discoveries. Have learners state their perceptions or beliefs. Then have them conduct an experiment to learn how their ideas compare to reality.

Prescribe experiments

Do not just give learners a laboratory and assume they will make up their own experiments. Assign experiments to perform. The best format for such an assignment is a set of questions that laboratory experiments can answer. Before receiving the questions, the learners may not care about the subject, but the questions challenge them to prove that their initial guesses are right.

Allow independent experiments too

Let learners conduct their own experiments. In designing virtual labs, allow imitation, then innovation. Here is an example of what I mean.

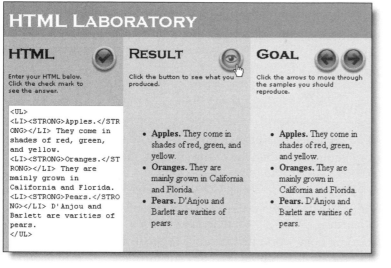

When I created the HTML Laboratory, I stocked it with goals for the learner to achieve. This was imitation.

What I didn't foresee was that many learners would try out variations of the goals I set.

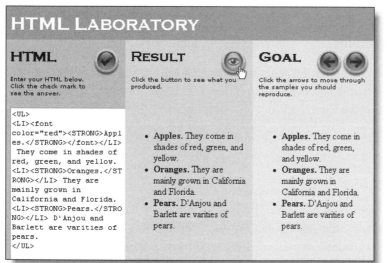

For instance, a learner might want to make the word *Apple* red. So the learner typed in the additional code and clicked the Result arrow. Voila, the word *Apple* is now red. That's innovation.

Built using Adobe Dreamweaver and custom JavaScript. View example at horton.com/eld/.

By letting learners conduct their own experiments, I added value to this laboratory and made it more active.

Reuse your virtual laboratories

Developing a simulated laboratory is a lot of work. Consider whether you can use the same laboratory in multiple activities or even in multiple courses.

Case studies

Schools have used case studies since—well, since there were schools. Case studies provide relevant, meaningful experiences in which learners can discover and abstract useful concepts and principles.

Case studies can be the basis for a reading activity, if we just wanted learners to absorb information from the study. However, case studies make fine discovery activities when learners must actively apply analytical and problem-solving skills to the events cited in the case study.

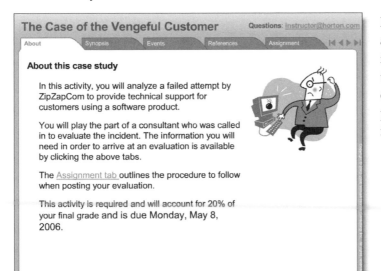

In this example, learners are asked to analyze a failed attempt to provide technical support for customers of a software product. Here you see the introduction.

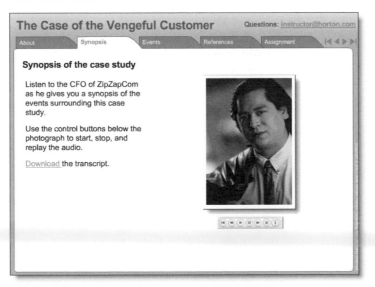

Here is the synopsis of the case study. It is narrated by the CFO. A transcript is available for learners to follow along. Notice the other tabs that contain a chronicle of events, reference documents, and the assignment.

Created in Microsoft PowerPoint and converted for Web delivery using Adobe Breeze Presenter. View example at horton.com/eld/.

In a case study, learners are given a comprehensive example to study. The case can be a real-world event, process, or system. Learners are also given materials that describe or perhaps even simulate the case. After working with these materials, learners attempt to answer questions about the case or to generalize the principles revealed by the case.

In e-learning, case studies differ from classroom case studies in the variety of material available through the Internet, in the use of interactive multimedia presentations, and in the multiple perspectives possible through collaboration. E-learning case studies can include a richer mix of materials for learners to examine and can more realistically mimic real-world cases.

When to use case studies

Case studies teach abstract, general principles from specific, concrete particulars. As such, they mimic the way most people learn most of what they know: by observing and analyzing their own experiences. Case studies are good for teaching complex knowledge that cannot be reduced to a simple formula. They are especially good for teaching the judgment skills necessary to deal with complex, contradictory situations common in real life.

Variations of case studies

Case studies can take many forms. Here are some of my favorites.

Instructor-led case studies

The instructor welcomes participants and introduces the case to study. The instructor then assigns a list of questions to answer and provides access to material describing the case. Learners individually study the case materials and post their answers to a discussion forum where they review and critique each other's answers. Learners continue to refine their answers until time runs out. Then learners post lists of the principles, trends, heuristics, and guidelines they inferred from the case. Finally, learners generalize their findings and specify how this knowledge can be applied to future cases in the real world. The instructor grades participants based on whether they identified the correct principles without oversimplifying the situation.

Virtual field trips

The case study can be presented as a virtual field trip (p. 89) that takes learners out into the real world to observe objects and events as they actually occurred. Learners can navigate a locale by clicking links that jump from page to page. They can traverse a series of events by moving along a timeline.

Observe-and-comment activities

Learners may observe a video or animation sequence (or just read a narrative) of people interacting. Such a scene may be organized as a drama presentation (p. 58). Learners can view the sequence as many times as they wish. Then they comment about what they have seen, answering such questions as:

▶ **What happened?** What did the people do? What did they think? How did they feel? What did the people gain or lose? What did they learn?

▶ **What does it mean?** What does the experience mean to you? How does it apply to your real-world experiences?

▶ **What will you do?** What have you learned? How will you think or act differently in the future? How will you apply what you have learned?

Mini-case studies

You can provide realistic, real-world experience by presenting a series of concise but complete examples. The formula is simple: Start with a statement of the situation. Introduce any characters, objects, or organizations of importance. Spell out crucial relationships among them. Then alternate questions and answers about the situation. Questions should require the learner to carefully examine the situation, infer facts not stated, apply principles, and deduce conclusions.

As a follow-up, pose additional questions to learners. Have them submit their answers to a discussion forum (p. 427). Or challenge learners to make up their own case studies and submit them to a discussion forum for use and critique by other learners.

Reaction papers

Have learners express their reactions after carefully examining a work in the field of study. The work can be a simple example, a report, or a physical artifact. To structure the activity, give learners a form to fill in. Include areas for them to enter:

▶ **Personal goals**. What do you hope to gain by examining the work?

▶ **Summary**. What does the work say? What does it mean to all those who come in contact with it?

▶ **Reaction**. What is significant about the work for you? What does your own background and experience tell you about it?

▶ **Utility**. How can you apply what you learned in this activity to your own work?

Best practices for case studies

Provide a rich mixture of case materials

Traditionally, case studies have used just paper memos, transcripts of interviews, and sometimes videotapes. Today case studies can include a much wider variety of materials. Some of the materials you can use include these:

▶ Conventional business documents, such as reports, contracts, instruction manuals, e-mail messages, memos, and letters.

▶ Blueprints, drawings, and specifications of products and systems.

▶ Patents, depositions, rulings, and other legal documents.

▶ Spreadsheets of numerical data.

▶ Charts, graphs, diagrams, and other technical and business graphics.

▶ Video or audio interviews.

▶ Simulations of an actual system.

Where possible, include live documents, such as word processing and spreadsheet files, that the learner can experiment with.

Guide study of the case

Prompt discovery of the important principles illustrated by the case study. Give specific guidance that will make good use of learners' time. Tell learners:

▶ **What the case study shows**. Do not be too specific. Just explain how the case relates to the subject under discussion.

▶ **What to notice**. What are the important features? Where should learners focus attention? Again, do not be too specific. Just give some clues as to where to start their examination of the case.

▶ **Questions to answer.** The answers form the deliverable for the activity. They direct learners' searches and control what discoveries they are likely to make on their own.

▶ **What to think about**. Ask questions that guide learners to think about how this case relates to others or to the subject of the lesson or course.

Role-playing scenarios

Children learn much adult behavior by playing at being an adult. Likewise, adults can learn much by playing the role of someone else.

In a role-playing scenario, the instructor states a goal and assigns learners roles in achieving that goal. Learners research their roles. They then collaborate via online meetings and discussion forums to play out their roles to achieve the goal.

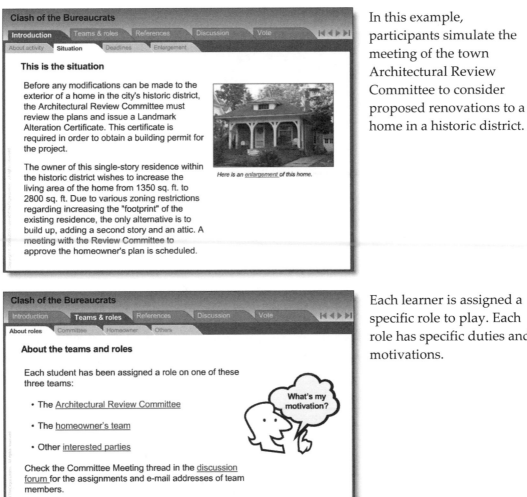

In this example, participants simulate the meeting of the town Architectural Review Committee to consider proposed renovations to a home in a historic district.

Each learner is assigned a specific role to play. Each role has specific duties and motivations.

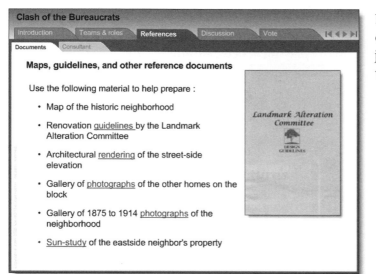

Learners have access to detailed reference materials, just as their real counterparts would.

Learners must complete a series of activities in their roles and submit materials for others to examine.

Created in Microsoft PowerPoint and converted for Web delivery using Articulate Presenter. View example at horton.com/eld/.

When to use role-playing scenarios

Role-playing is a valuable way to teach subtle, interpersonal skills and to reveal the hidden complexity of many human endeavors. Here are some common uses of role-playing activities:

▶ Force someone to view events from a different perspective. Give an environmental activist the role of a real-estate developer. And vice versa.

▶ Allow someone to experience events online that they would not experience in real life. For example, let a man experience sexual harassment as a woman.

▶ Demonstrate the many perspectives necessary for a complex undertaking. Have a management team guide a project from initial idea to successful product.

▶ Teach interpersonal skills. Hold a committee meeting to find an effective compromise among competing ideas, groups, and individuals.

Variations of role-playing scenarios

Role-playing scenarios can be used to mimic all the different situations that bring individuals into contact and possibly conflict. Here are some forms that make good learning activities:

Behavior critique. Teach learners the correct behavior for a particular situation, model and critique bad behavior. Assign someone the role of demonstrating inappropriate behavior. Assign the rest of the class the role of reacting to the bad behavior.

Court trial. Put a concept, historical figure, or organization on trial. Assign roles of judge, accused, prosecutor, defense attorney, witnesses, and jury.

Board meeting. Simulate a meeting of the board of directors of a corporation, university, hospital, or other organization. Assign each participant specific goals, attitudes, and personality. Spell out known and secret relationships among those at the meeting. Give the meeting an agenda and a time limit.

Murder mystery. Teach investigative skills by having learners play roles in a murder investigation. Each member receives a role. For each role there are publicly known facts that everyone has access to and privately known facts that only the role-player knows. Role-players can be asked or tricked into revealing these hidden facts. Each role-player also has secret motivations. Role-players are either suspects or investigators. Investigators must solve the mystery by interviewing the suspects, examining artifacts, and exchanging notes. If a murder mystery does not fit your situation, substitute one of these investigations:

▶ Finding hidden treasure.

▶ Learning the cause of an airplane crash.

▶ Discovering the cure for a disease.

▶ Locating a missing person.

Who am I? Each learner picks and researches a different well-known person from the field of study. Each learner then writes a speech from this person's viewpoint and in this person's style. Learners post their speeches to a discussion forum. Learners comment on each other's speeches. Comments are made from the perspective of the person being impersonated. Learners defend the positions taken by their characters. At the end, each learner must guess the identity of the other impersonated characters.

Best practices for role-playing scenarios

Role-playing scenarios can be entertaining, energizing, and hugely educational. Or time-consuming and frustrating. The difference is careful design of the situation and assignment of the roles.

Introduce the scenario fully

Spell out the details of the scenario. What is the general situation and what problem does it pose for learners? What roles must learners play? For each role, what are the motivations and behaviors? How is success defined and how will the activity be scored?

Provide all the documents and other sources of information that would be available in the real situation. These can be abbreviated, but should contain enough detail to fully enable learners to carry out their roles.

Assign roles related to the subject

In team assignments, give learners roles that relate to the subject or metaphor of the assignment. Pick roles rich with interrelationships and opportunities for conflict and cooperation. For example, the activity involving the Architectural Review Committee had the following roles:

The homeowners	Just want to build an addition to their home. Priority is getting more space for the least expense. Have a new baby on the way, so time is of the essence.
Architect	Wants to get the committee to approve plans already drawn. If plans are rejected, the architect will lose the commission. Really needs the job.
Building contractor	Wants to complete the job as quickly and inexpensively as possible. Does not worry much about architectural purity. Does worry about cash flow and completing the job before winter weather sets in.
City historian	Concerned with maintaining the architectural purity of the historic neighborhood. Classic bureaucrat with a fragile ego. Resents the power of the city attorney.
Head of committee	Also concerned with architectural purity. Has no formal architectural training. Just a busybody with lots of time on his hands.

City attorney	Insists that building codes be followed scrupulously and does not care that codes are somewhat vague and that they conflict with the guidelines of the Architectural Review Committee. Considers the city historian undisciplined and not too intelligent.
Neighbors	Concerned that the new addition will block their view of the mountains or shade their back yards. Generally get along with the homeowners but are jealous that the homeowners can expand and they cannot.

Otherwise use generic roles

If you cannot use roles associated with the subject of the activity, you can always use some of these generic roles. These are all roles that learners should find familiar.

Presenter	Initially offers content. May present material developed by a team.
Journalist	Writes periodic articles summarizing happenings in the scenario.
Researcher	Tracks down facts. Resolves factual disputes.
Judge	Rules on the relevance and appropriateness of material.
Editor	Edits, enhances, and polishes the work of others. Does not criticize.
Brainstormer	Suggests new ideas and new areas for research.
Devil's advocate	Argues unpopular and unfounded positions. A gadfly.
Mediator	Helps resolve disputes before appealed to Judge.
Lawyer	Identifies and comments on legal issues raised by activities.
Coordinator	Schedules and tracks activities. Makes assignments.

Match role to personality and skills

Assign roles carefully. Emphasize positive, creative roles rather than negative, critical roles. Be especially careful whom you assign to power positions, such as Manager, Judge, and Critic. Consider the personality of learners. Do they have the right mix of humility and assertiveness? Can they handle the power? Are their social skills adequate?

Also consider the basic skills of learners. If a role requires extensive writing, pick someone who can write clearly and quickly. If a role requires public speaking, pick someone with speaking experience and skills.

Have learners use their role names in messages

For class activities, have learners in chats and discussion forums post their messages using the names of their roles (Instructor, Tech Support, or Juror 4), rather than their personal name.

Best practices for discovery activities

Resist the urge to lecture

Not that you would, but many designers find it difficult to let go of control. In discovery activities, we have to trust that learners will discover the trends, principles, and concepts we are teaching. And we have to design the activity so that learners actually do make the intended discoveries. And we have to test and refine and test and refine even more. Designing discovery activities is like teaching by remote control.

Provoke experiments and interaction

In team activities, it is not unusual to wait for minutes or hours for action to begin because everyone is waiting for someone else to take the lead. In a new environment like a computer-mediated scenario, people may hesitate to take action. To overcome this reluctance, start with a specific trigger event that requires a response from all learners.

Include a synthesizing activity

Just performing experiments or reading case studies can leave learners with a lot of information but little knowledge. Include a synthesizing activity that requires learners to consolidate observations into a coherent theory. One simple way is to ask learners to summarize what they learned into a formula or a concise set of best practices.

Balance realism and complexity

Make the activity realistic enough that learners recognize it and can see similarities to their own situations. But do not become so obsessed with realism that you leave out the learning experiences or make the situation so specific that learners cannot map it to their situations.

Combine discovery activities with other activities

Discovery activities combine productively with other types of e-learning activities.

▶ Start with a brief presentation (p. 49) introducing an area of study. Have learners conduct experiments (p. 127) or play roles in a scenario (p. 135) to discover key principles and arouse curiosity. Then follow up with a discussion activity (p. 463) to extend the principles and satisfy curiosity.

▶ Include optional virtual-laboratory activities (p. 127) when teaching any subject where learners may doubt what you are teaching unless they discover it for themselves.

▶ Incorporate stories (p. 70) into case studies (p. 131) and role-playing activities (p. 135). The story-teller can be a key figure in the case under study or an imaginary character in the role-playing scenario. Story-telling activities can flesh out a role-playing activity when you do not have enough learners to fill all the roles.

GAMES AND SIMULATIONS

Games and simulations let people learn by playing. Sounds like fun. Games for learning can be fun, but they are always purposeful. They teach first and entertain second. Learning games can draw on the established conventions of quiz shows, board games, and video games to arouse curiosity and harness competitive urges. Simulations let us safely verify that learners can perform dangerous tasks. How do you think most learners would respond if you asked them whether they would rather take a test or play a game?

About games and simulations

Games and simulations allow learners to practice tasks, apply knowledge, and infer principles—all while having fun. Games and simulations may provide a complete model of a real-world system or just a rapid-fire series of questions to answer.

Example of a learning game

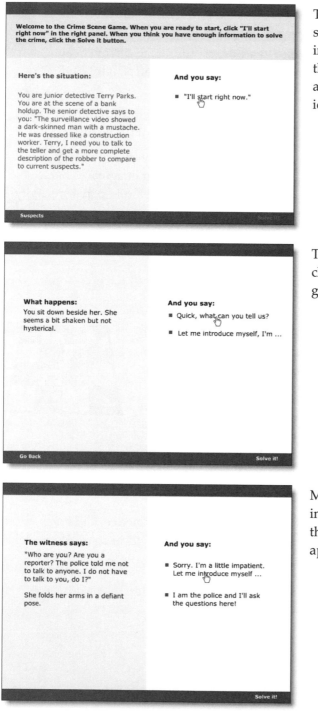

This game teaches interviewing skills in the context of a police investigation. Learners are assigned the task of interviewing a witness to a bank robbery to elicit clues to the identity of the robber.

The game provides the learner with choices that affect the course of the game.

Most feedback is provided by events in the game. Events reveal whether the learner's previous action was appropriate.

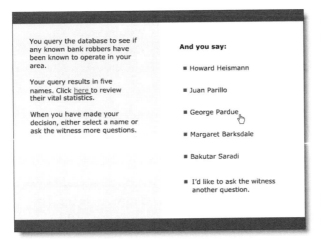

At any point, learners can try to solve the mystery.

Created in Microsoft PowerPoint and converted for Web delivery using Articulate Presenter. View example at horton.com/eld/.

What are games and simulations?

What exactly are learning games and simulations? The terms are used rather loosely, so we should define them before offering best practices.

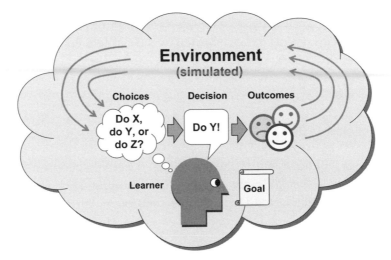

The most important ingredient is the learner. Perhaps this person is learning to use a piece of software or to interview job candidates. Or to apply calculus to solving problems in particle physics.

In the game or simulation, the learner has a goal. Usually this goal is presented to the learner by the computer. The goal is typically a task the learner is learning to perform. For software simulations, the goal typically requires the learner to perform a common task with a computer tool. For other tasks, the learner might have to interview a simulated job candidate or earn points by answering questions on the subject of study.

The learner operates inside an environment. That environment is simulated, of course. For a software simulation, the window looks like the display the learner would see when operating the computer program. For the job interview, the window might show the job candidate seated across a desk from the learner.

The environment presents the learner with choices. What do I do next? Which command do I use in this computer program? What question do I ask the job candidate? What approach will solve my problem? The learner must decide among choices and take action. The learner may indicate a choice by clicking a button, typing in text, or some other action.

The learner's actions have consequences or outcomes in the simulated environment. The learner may see the display change. Or the simulation may make a rude noise and an error message may appear. Such feedback is intrinsic to the game or simulation.

These outcomes may have additional effects in the environment, some of which may be invisible to the learner. These changes in the environment present the learner with new choices, and the cycle continues.

This cycle of making decisions and seeing results is the essence of the game or simulation. For software simulations, each cycle corresponds to one input from the learner. For the job-interview, each cycle consists of one question by the learner and an answer by the job candidate. In combat simulators used to train soldiers, the entire cycle may take only a second. In business simulations involving developing and marketing products, the cycle may represent months.

Is it a game or a simulation?

Experts and linguists will howl, but I believe the main difference between the terms *learning game* and *learning simulation* are just ones of positioning. True, simulations tend to look more realistic, while games tend to feature scorekeeping. However, pedantic reasons to distinguish the two are trumped by pragmatic concerns. Hence this recommendation:

> If *game* sounds frivolous, call it a *simulation*.

> If *simulation* sounds too stuffy or expensive, call it a *game*.

Just be sure to design it so it teaches. That said, henceforth I will use *game* to refer to both learning games and simulations. Feel free to pick whichever one appeals to your learners and satisfies your chain of command.

When to use games

Developing effective games is difficult, time-consuming, and expensive—typically 100 times the cost of a simple multiple-choice text question. Getting games to work well over the Web is even harder. When are games worth this effort?

Costs of failure are high. Failures that endanger life, public safety, and financial success justify expensive remedies. Brain surgeons, nuclear power plant operators, and stock market investors must perform at a high level of skill.

Learning with real systems is not practical. The real activity may take too long, for example, testing genetic modifications to plants. Training on real systems may be too expensive, for example, learning to fly the latest product from Boeing or Airbus. Failure may be too embarrassing, for example, triggering a false alarm in a security system that summons the police.

Learners need individual attention. Games are self-customizing. Learners experience a unique series of events in response to their own knowledge, skills, and instincts.

Many people must be educated. Since the major costs for a game are in developing and perfecting it, additional learners add little to the total costs. Spreading the costs over a few hundred or a few thousand learners recovers those costs.

Tasks are complex and time is short. Games can telescope weeks of education into days. Games let learners skip rapidly through subjects they have already mastered and spend more time on just the areas in which they need improvement. Games are highly efficient coaches.

Skills to be taught are subtle and complex. Simulations work well for subjects when the greatest challenge is not acquiring factual knowledge but applying skills, knowledge, and attitudes in complex, unique situations.

You have time and budget to see the project through. Games may be effective, but they are seldom easy or inexpensive to develop. Sophisticated, realistic games can require 500 to 1,000 hours of development for each hour of learning. Even though simpler games require much less development time, they do require substantial time to design, plan, and specify.

Types of learning games

The different types of learning games are limited only by the creativity of designers. Here are a few more examples to give you some ideas of the variety of learning games you can use in e-learning.

► Quiz-show games (p. 146).

► Word puzzles (p. 147).

► Jigsaw puzzles (p. 148).

► Adventure games (p. 149).

► Software simulations (p. 150).

► Device simulations (p. 151).

► Personal-response simulations (p. 152).

► Mathematical simulations (p. 152).

► Environmental simulations (p. 154).

Quiz-show games

To make tests less intimidating and more engaging, restyle them as game shows, similar to ones common on TV.

In this example, learners are challenged to score a number of points by correctly answering questions about Visual Basic. To reach their goals, learners answer a lot of low-point questions or fewer high-point questions. They can answer questions from a few categories or across several different categories. Each correct answer adds to the total score, and each incorrect answer subtracts from the total score.

Built using Adobe Dreamweaver and custom JavaScript. View example at horton.com/eld/.

Quiz-show games are good for testing factual knowledge, provided answers are clearly right or wrong. Such games can seduce voluntary learners into taking tests. In just a few minutes you can ask 25 fill-in-the-blank test questions. They provide incentive to study and learn. A game might be a good sensitizing activity or pre-test at the beginning of a module. The desire to win the game provides incentive to learn the needed facts.

Quiz-show games can easily implement an important element found in many games—graduated difficulty. The game is easy to start, but hard to master. Almost everybody will get some of the 100-point questions right, but few can get all the 500-point questions right.

Word puzzles

Word games, such as crossword puzzles, make learning terminology fun. Most are just fill-in-the-blanks tests dressed up as a game.

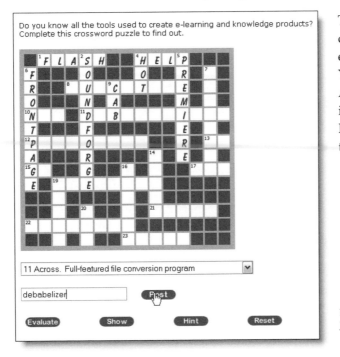

This crossword puzzle is from a course on technologies needed for e-learning. Here's how it works. You select a clue, in this case 11 Across. Then you type the answer into the answer field and click **Post**. The answer now appears in the puzzle.

Built using Adobe Dreamweaver and custom JavaScript. View example at horton.com/eld/.

Word games are good to test knowledge of terms. They are also good to motivate reading of text to identify names of people, products, concepts, animals, locations, and so forth. They combine well with scavenger-hunt activities (p. 196).

Jigsaw puzzles

Do you teach subjects that involve whole-to-parts relationships? Do you spend time telling learners how a product, organization, or other subject is organized? If so, jigsaw puzzles and scrambled-tiles games offer a way to let learners discover such relationships and to test learners on such relationships.

A scrambled-tile puzzle can help learners recall images, visualize relationships, or notice discriminating details.

This activity on listening skills asks learners to assemble an organization chart based on an overheard conversation among company executives.

Built using Adobe Dreamweaver and custom JavaScript. View example at horton.com/eld/.

Learners click on the tile they want to move and then click where they want to move it. They continue the process until the picture has been assembled. The game directs learners' attention to specific reporting relationships.

This same kind of puzzle has been used to teach remodeling contractors how the components of a particular architectural style are combined in specific houses and to teach JavaScript programmers the Internet Explorer document object model.

Conceptual and abstract subjects require practice too, yet we often forget to provide realistic practice activities for such subjects. One way to do so is to create a concrete game for learning abstract concepts.

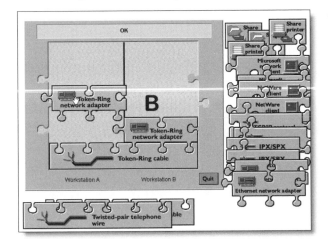

This jigsaw puzzle requires learners to drag and drop the puzzle pieces into place to configure a network. As they drop a component into place, they get feedback on how well the component works in the slot to which it is assigned and how it interacts with surrounding components.

Built using Adobe Director. View example at horton.com/eld/.

The task is not as simple as it looks. There are more pieces than slots and only compatible components can be used together. There is no fixed solution: any combination of components that would work in the real world work here.

With this activity, learners explore the abstract world of multi-layered standards regarding data-communication protocols—but in a fun, tangible way. Such games are difficult to create but are very effective in teaching subjects that have more than one right answer.

Adventure games

Adventure games let learners proceed toward a goal by making decisions that help or hinder their progress. These games resemble the early computer adventure games in which the player sets out on a quest and must pick up objects and choose paths carefully. Such games are often called social-interaction simulators when they are used to simulate the interaction between people.

This example lets learners practice their management skills by responding to an "employee's" request to take a sabbatical. The adventure of arriving at a correct response requires checking personnel files, reading company policy, and calling other managers.

Created in Microsoft PowerPoint and converted for Web delivery using Impatica for PowerPoint. View example at horton.com/eld/.

Software simulations

Software simulations are becoming a standard way to learn to operate computer software.

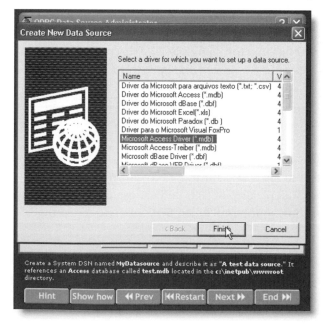

This simulator lets learners practice setting up connections between the operating system and various databases—without any risk of damaging data or the system. The simulator behaves like the real control panel—except the simulator restricts learners to the task being taught and provides instructions if needed.

In this step, the learner has selected the correct driver for the database and must now click **Finish** to continue.

Built with Adobe Captivate and TechSmith SnagIt. View example at horton.com/eld/.

Device simulations

Device simulations teach how to operate a piece of equipment. In device simulations, learners simulate pressing buttons by clicking on their images. They may simulate turning a knob by dragging its edge left or right.

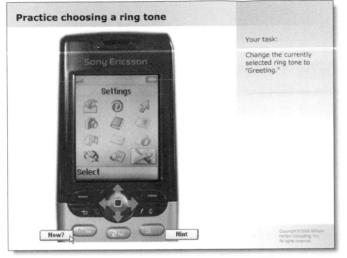

This example lets learners practice how to select a ring tone on a mobile phone.

Built using Adobe Captivate, PowerPoint, and Adobe Breeze Presenter. View example at horton.com/eld/.

And this one teaches how to operate an anesthesia delivery unit. Mistakes are a lot less costly in this simulation than in the real operating room. This is one case for which I would call this a *simulation*, not a *game*. If life is at stake, we do not play games.

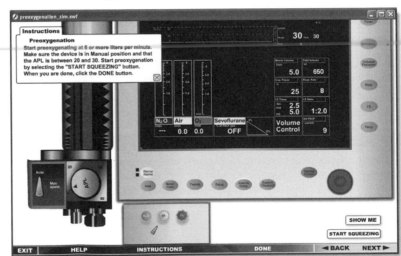

Designed by William Horton Consulting and built in Adobe Flash by Web Courseworks (webcourseworks.com).

Personal-response simulations

Personal-response simulations pose a series of complex decisions for learners to make. Learners can make changes to many separate factors and immediately see the results. Learners can tweak and tune their answers to try to improve results.

Meal 2 of 3

You want to lose a little weight. Your doctor advises you do so by keeping your evening meal to fewer than 600 calories.

Le Menu du Jour

Appetizer	Grapefruit, raw, pink
Soup	Beef broth, boulln, consm, cnnd
Pasta	Nothing.................
Entrée	Salmon, baked, red
Side	Broccoli, raw, cooked, drained
Beverage	Tea, brewed
Dessert	Nothing.................
Bread	Nothing.................

Select a dish from the pull-down list next to each category you wish to order from. Click **?** to look up the dish in our database and learn about its nutrients.

When you have selected your meal, click **Place my order** to see how well you did ordering your meal.

Place my order

In *The Diet Game*, learners practice ordering restaurant meals to meet complex dietary requirements. Meals consist of several different foods, each with different nutritional ingredients. After placing their order, learners see how well they did. They can then try other combinations of foods.

Built using Adobe Dreamweaver and Active Server Pages. View example at horton.com/eld/.

The Diet Game is a front end for a database of nutrition information published by the U.S. Department of Agriculture.

Mathematical simulations

Mathematical simulations let learners perform math in a fun, visual, intuitive fashion.

Would you rather learn to manage the finances of a training department by filling in numbers on a spreadsheet like this?

Self-directed e-learning

Decisions			
Enrollment fee		$100	USD
Relative quality		100%	% of competition
Service life of course		3	years
Consequences			
Enrollments		2250	
Development costs	$	300,000	
Financial results			
Revenue	$	225,000	per year
Amortized costs	$	100,000	per year
Profit	$	125,000	per year
ROI		125%	

Spreadsheet built using Microsoft Excel.

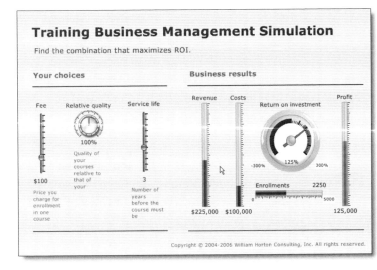

Or by dragging sliders in a game like this?

Built using Crystal Xcelsius and Microsoft Excel. View example at horton.com/eld/.

Another example lets learners develop better investment habits by repeatedly making risky investments until they discover the dangers of treating investment as gambling.

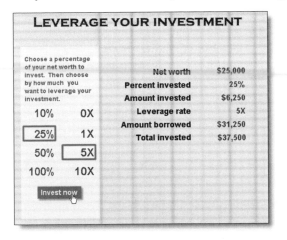

Learners decide what percentage of their net worth they want to invest and by how much they want to leverage it. Here a learner has decided to invest half his net worth and to leverage it by 10X, that is, to borrow $10 for every dollar of his own money invested.

The learner then clicks **Invest now**.

Built using Adobe Flash. View example at horton.com/eld/.

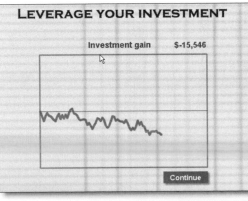

The game shows the fluctuations of the stock price. At any time the learner can click the **Sell** button to sell the stock and reap the gain or loss. The game then reverts to the earlier screen where the learner's net worth is revised to show the gain or loss. The learner can then try again and again.

Possible subjects for mathematical simulations include finance, science, engineering, and medicine.

Environmental simulations

Environmental simulations let learners experiment with a complexly interrelated system, such as a natural environment.

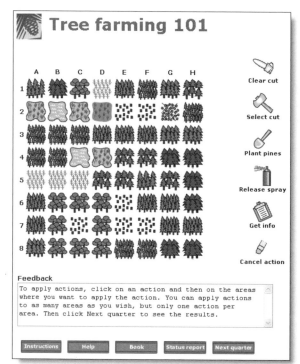

This game teaches private landowners in the southeastern United States to manage their forests more effectively, regardless of their particular goals. In it, learners manage a tree farm.

In the game, learners confront fluctuating prices, pine beetles, cash flow difficulties, and the fact that a tree takes 30 years to grow. This game lets learners discover both ecological and economic principles and learn to apply them to the simulated environment.

Built using Microsoft Notepad, Microsoft Paint, and a whole lot of custom HTML and JavaScript. View example at horton.com/eld/.

This simulation runs quarter by quarter for hundreds of years if necessary. Each quarter, the learner reviews the results from the last quarter and decides what actions to take. Actions include things like selectively cutting an area, clear-cutting it, replanting it, or having the area appraised. Actions can be individually applied to each of the 64 stands on the map.

The results for a quarter depend on actions taken by the learner, and also on variables such as rainfall, fluctuations in prices for saw timber and pulp wood, emergency needs for cash (daughter gets accepted at Harvard), forest fires, and disasters such as tornados and lightning.

Just as in the real situation, learners must look beyond the superficial appearances. To do so, they can call up a detailed status report.

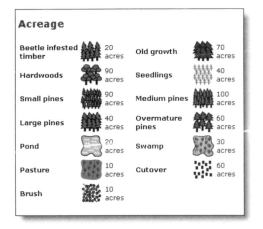

The status report shows the land use and conditions of trees.

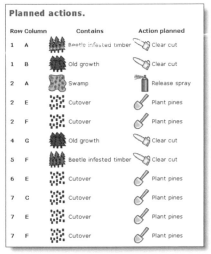

The status report also lists the actions ordered by the learner over the next quarter. This list gives learners a chance to reconsider actions, just as in the real world.

This game is a bit unusual in that learners can set the goals. They can mix economic, aesthetic, and environmental concerns to most closely match their goals for their real-life timberland. By making the goals flexible, we encourage learners to try out various approaches.

Design games for learning

Commercial computer and video games can cost millions of dollars and take years to develop. Few schools or training departments have budgets that large. On the other hand, I have seen effective learning games created by one person in a week. A good learning game requires good design more than it requires massive amounts of programming and intricate graphics.

Design to accomplish learning objectives

Designing effective games is as much art as science. For branching-style games, I have developed a procedure to create a game that teaches specific learning objectives.

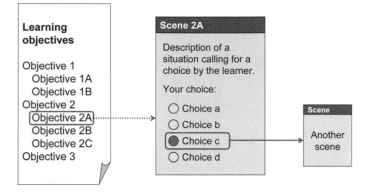

Each objective represents something the learner should or should not do, for example, desirable or undesirable behaviors. Each objective is taught by one or more scenes. A scene represents a situation in which the learner must make a choice. Choices test achievement of the objective. Making the right choice suggests that the learner has accomplished the objective. Each choice can then lead to another scene.

In such games, I include two types of scenes: scenes to test objectives and additional scenes to flesh out the story, called *context scenes*. Scenes to test objectives correspond directly with the learning objectives. The second kind of scene is used to prepare learners to make a decision.

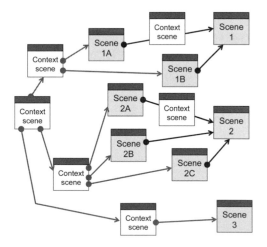

A context scene may describe the reasons for the decision. It may provide background information that the learner must consider. Most often it provides a natural transition between one decision and the next. As such it may display the consequences of the previous decision and lead naturally to the next decision.

Express the goal as a specific task

In the game, exactly what are learners to accomplish? Give learners a single, understandable goal against which their results can be measured.

☹ No	☺ Yes
Make money by investing in stocks, bonds, and real estate.	Re-balance a portfolio of stocks, bonds, and real estate to reduce federal taxes by 40%.
Order a balanced meal at the simulated restaurant.	Order a meal with under 1,000 calories that has twice the daily recommended amounts of iron and calcium.
Pick a diverse team.	Pick the smallest team with all the required skills for launching a new product simultaneously in Japan, China, and the United States.

Create the game's scenario

Include the necessary components

Create an imaginary world for learners to interact with. This may include:

▶ **Definite roles for the learner**. Define a character or characters for the learner to play. Give the character specific motivations and abilities.

▶ **Objects for the learner to interact with**. Provide tools the learner must use to accomplish difficult tasks. Tools include control panels of devices, sources of information, vehicles, and in some cases, play money.

▶ **Adversaries and allies**. A game may include other characters to help or hinder the learner. These characters may be other live participants in the simulation or may be simulated characters.

▶ **An environment**. The environment organizes and structures the game. It sets the scene and provides a context for the interaction. The environment includes everything the learner **does not** interact with directly—things like imaginary streets, buildings, rooms, and furniture.

Define clear, colorful characters

When simulating interpersonal relationships, provide learners with well-fleshed-out descriptions of the characters they will encounter in the game. If possible, include photographs or drawings of these characters. Encourage learners to print or display these descriptions in a separate window.

Add challenges

What challenges will learners face in accomplishing the goal of the game? These challenges should mimic the ones learners will face in real life and be crafted so that they provide opportunities for learning, not just frustration. Include obstacles that learners know about and can anticipate and plan for. Also include some unexpected events that require spontaneous action.

Teach in feedback

In games it is the feedback that teaches. We must systematically design that feedback.

Provide intrinsic feedback

The smooth flow of the game can be interrupted by delivery of feedback. Most good games deliver feedback intrinsically, that is, within the context of the game. Correct actions continue the action of the game in the direction the learner indicated. Indications of the correctness of the action may be subtle, such as a smile from a character or the accomplishment of a minor goal.

The witness says:	And you say:
"Who are you? Are you a reporter? The police told me not to talk to anyone. I do not have to talk to you, do I?" She folds her arms in a defiant pose.	■ Sorry. I'm a little impatient. Let me introduce myself … ■ I am the police and I'll ask the questions here!

Here the witness's words and body language provide clear feedback that the previous question was too abrupt.

Likewise, negative feedback can be delivered in the context of the game. The intended action fails. Another character responds through negative body language, gestures, or facial expressions. A door remains closed.

If you must inject explicit feedback, keep it short and clear. Just "Correct" or "Incorrect" is usually sufficient. Resist the temptation to explain why an action was wrong. Have the game play reveal the cause of the failure.

Or educational feedback

Another approach does interrupt play to provide explicit feedback aimed at delivering specific educational messages. For example:

> Correct. You can also use the keyboard shortcut Ctrl-S to save your file.

> No. Save As would save your file under another name. You want the plain Save command.

> Incorrect. Let me show you what you should have done.

Such feedback may be justified to correct a misconception that could cause problems if not immediately corrected.

Give extreme feedback for extreme failures

If the learner does something severely wrong, correct the learner immediately lest the learner continue unaware of the severity of the failure. For example:

▶ In *The Crimescene Game*, making a racist comment got you fired on the spot.

▶ In the simulation for an anesthesia delivery unit, actions that could endanger the patient drew immediate warnings.

Hold detailed feedback until the end

One way to provide detailed feedback without interrupting game play is to save up the feedback and deliver it in an after-action review.

The Crimescene Game

Ask the right questions and quickly solve the case

Situation	You chose ...	Feedback	Cost	Total
What happens: You sit down beside her. She seems a bit shaken but not hysterical.	Let me introduce myself, I'm ...	Good choice. You put the witness at ease.	0	35
The witness says: "Oh, I'm pleased to meet you Detective Parks. How can I help you." She smiles warmly.	I just need to ask you a few questions.	This was your only choice.	0	35
The witness waits while you decide which of the questions you want to ask.	What can you tell us about the robber's height and weight?	Good choice. This question may help the witness visualize the perpatrator and help her remember some distinguishing feature. However, estimating height and weight can be difficult and unreliable. Be prepared to ask a follow-up question.	0	35
The witness says: "He was about 5 feet 6 inches tall. And he weighed about 150 ~ pretty ~	Tell me about your sister.	Bad choice. This question may tend to get the witness off the subject.	-5	30

An alternative version of *The Crimescene Game* ended with a detailed critique that recapped learners' actions and commented on each of the actions.

Built using Microsoft Notepad and custom JavaScript. View example at horton.com/eld/.

Best practices for games

There are many exciting games, many colorful games, and many games with screens that flash and twirl. There are far fewer games that teach. Often the difference is in whether the game is truly designed to educate or just to amuse. Make sure your learning games actually cause someone to learn.

Emphasize learning, not just acting

Make sure your games require applying the knowledge and skills you are teaching.

▶ Simulate the thought-processes, not just the physical actions. Avoid games that measure only how quickly and accurately the learner can move the mouse, unless that is the skill you are teaching.

▶ Require the learner to make the same kinds of decisions as in the real activity. In most learning games it is more important that the learner make authentic decisions than that the learner execute those decisions in a realistic way.

▶ Avoid arbitrary limitations on how the learner accomplishes the goal. If there are three ways to do the task in the real world, allow three ways in the game.

Challenge learners

Make the game easy to start but difficult to master. You can design competition into the game so players compete against one another. Or challenge learners to top the best scores of others or their earlier best efforts. As learners gain more skill at the game, limit how long they can take for each turn. One good technique for challenging all learners is called scaffolding and fading.

These callouts illustrate three levels of scaffolding:

Scaffolding refers to the support we provide learners to ensure they succeed. As learners learn the task, reduce scaffolding or support so they work more on their own. One way to reduce scaffolding is to let intermediate or advanced learners figure out details from general instructions that you provide.

The low-scaffolding example provides a general prompt that requires learners to take several related steps at a time. Learners must decide what individual actions are required, locate the place to carry out each action, and perform them all. This is certainly more challenging and realistic than with detailed instructions for each action, as shown in the high-scaffolding example.

What do we let learners figure out on their own? In a computer simulation, we might start by requiring them to decide where to click. We let them find the needed button, icon, or other object on the screen. We might tell them to enter data, but let them decide in which field to enter it. We might also let learners decide how to format the data. We can also phrase our prompts so we tell learners what they must do, but not the order in which to perform actions.

It should come as no surprise that this best practice requires sensitivity. You must balance the need to wean the learner from explicit prompts and instructions against the danger of leaving the learner clueless. Might we suggest a couple of rounds of testing?

Explain the game clearly

Provide instructions for your game. Explain the goal clearly. Make clear any limitations, such as the amount of time available. Learners may reject any game that imposes arbitrary or unfair rules. And it is learners who decide which rules are unfair. Cover these points:

▶ **What is the goal?** What is the learner to accomplish in the game? How is success defined? Can learners set goals for themselves?

▶ **What roles do learners play?** Are learners expected to play the role of a particular character? What are the motivations, values, and goals of that character?

▶ **How do learners get started?** Learners often hesitate to take the first step. To get the game under way, suggest a starting strategy ("Why don't you begin with safe investments?") or a hint ("Psssst! Look in your in-basket"). Or require action within a short amount of time: "We need your decision in 2 minutes" or "An alarm just sounded on the master control panel. Better check it out." Smoothly and naturally propel learners into their roles within the game.

▶ **What are the rules?** If the game mimics a situation, spell out the rules that people in that situation would know. If the game behaves in unrealistic ways, make these exceptions clear. You do not need to tell learners how to beat the game, just how to play it well enough so that they are learning the things they would learn in the real world.

▶ **How do they operate the game?** Tell learners how to operate the learner interface of the game. How do they translate real-world actions, such as making a phone call or selling a stock, into clicking, typing, dragging, and dropping? In some designs, this information is in a separate Help facility.

Provide multiple ways to learn

Supplement trial-and-error learning with other methods, too. Learning by trial and error can be frustrating, and there is the danger that learners remember their first attempts, not the correct ones. To make learning more reliable, incorporate additional sources of learning from the world of the game, for example, business reports, memos, and e-mail messages, technical manuals and industry standards, company policies and procedures, meeting minutes, and other sources.

Where possible, just link to real documents available on the network. Such exhibits provide a low-bandwidth alternative to video and sound. Or, for greater realism, make these exhibits available to learners only after they have taken actions that would make them available in the real world—such as asking for them or joining a professional association.

Manage competitiveness

Excessive competitiveness can get in the way of effective learning. If learners are highly competitive anyway, the game may not produce the desired outcome. Sales representatives and trial attorneys may compete more aggressively than you anticipated. Other groups may feel uncomfortable competing directly against their friends or co-workers. Ask yourself whether your learners need to learn to compete or to cooperate? Design the game accordingly.

Make the game meaningfully realistic

Many novice designers equate realism with photo-realistically rendered 3D graphics or virtual-reality worlds. For learning purposes, though, realism has a somewhat different meaning. The game need not closely mimic the task for which it prepares the learner so long as it exercises the skills and knowledge needed in the real task. A game is realistic (hence effective) if it:

▶ Implements the causal relationships and principles of the real-world system that learners must master.

▶ Contains details necessary for the learner to map components of the game to their real-world counterparts.

▶ Lets learners control the aspects of the game they would control in the real world.

▶ Makes learners feel they directly control the subject of the game without awkward intermediate steps.

In other words, it is more important that the game work like the real-world system than that it look like the real-world system.

Program variety into the game

Design games so that the answer or response is different each time. That way, learners can repeatedly play the game. They cannot cheat by knowing the answers ahead of time. Either design the game to generate a new problem each time, or inject vagaries from the world being simulated: weather, equipment failures, outbreaks of the flu, or market fads.

Let learners play multiple roles

In games, let learners play multiple roles. Have them play once "by the book," again "on gut instinct," and finally "as bad as you can be." Games let learners experience the consequences of alternative behaviors. To teach the consequences of negative behavior, assign learners the persona of an evil or careless person, and let them experience life from that perspective. Instead of telling learners why they should follow rules, let learners break the rules and experience the consequences.

Combine games with other activities

Games work well alone and in combination with other learning activities. Here are some productive combinations:

▶ Combine presentations (p. 49) and readings (p. 78) with a game on the same subject. The game gives learners opportunities to apply what they learned in the presentation or reading. And a reading or presentation can provide more depth on the principles discovered in the game.

▶ Include software simulations in the online manual or Help file (p. 388) for computer software. The game will give learners reasons to look things up in the documentation, and the documentation can cover tasks beyond those of the simulation.

▶ In a complex game, have learners conduct research (p. 194) to learn how to proceed in the game. Give learners a virtual laboratory (p. 127) in which to conduct experiments to discover information needed in the game. A medical diagnosis game could require lab tests. An architectural simulation could require testing the strengths of different proposed materials.

Use games as e-learning courses

Games also form the basis for an entirely new kind of course—although many would call it a *learning environment* rather than a course.

Although seldom complete in itself, a learning game can serve as the heart of an entire e-learning. Here's how that might work: A typical learning game starts with a brief introduction that frames the game by telling what is simulated and what will be learned in the game. At this point, we might give the learner a choice of learning by the game or by a conventional tutorial. Most would pick the game. Surprised?

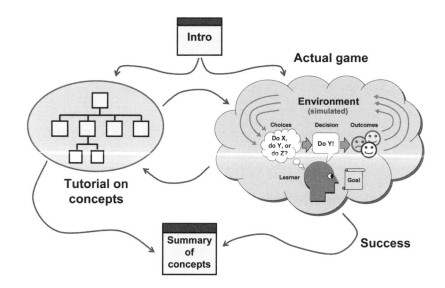

At some point, the learner realizes that, to win the game, it would help to know more about the subject of the game. Then the learner jumps to the conventional tutorial for a little study. After learning a bit more about the subject, the learner returns to the game. Learners may switch back and forth several times during the e-learning.

Once the learner achieves the goals in the game, there follows a quick review of the concepts. There is no test, because the game is the test. If learners can perform the task in the game, they can do it in the real world.

Of course, there are many variations possible in this flow. Some learners prefer to start with the tutorial and learn about the subject before trying their hand at the game. Others forgo the game altogether, and others never taste the tutorial.

IN CLOSING ...

Summary

Do-type activities are the path between information and knowledge, between explanations and skills. They put brains into action, exploring, discovering, practicing, refining, and perfecting knowledge and skills. Learners should spend at least half their time in meaningful do activities. Do activities include:

▶ **Practice activities** that exercise and refine a wide range of skills from simple mechanical skills to complex analytical or interpersonal skills.

▶ **Discovery activities** that use exploration and experimentation to lead learners to discover new concepts, principles, and facts for themselves.

▶ **Games and simulations** that let learners discover new knowledge, try out their growing skills, and monitor their progress—all while having fun.

For more ...

Do activities are often scored. That turns them into tests. Check out Chapter 5 for more ideas on tests. Some connect activities require doing things. Perhaps some of them could serve as do activities as well. Look at Chapter 4 for some ideas.

To find more on do activities, search the Web for combinations of these terms: *e-learning, interactivity, game, simulation, practice, case study, role playing*.

To create games, simulations, and other highly interactive forms of do activities, you may want to invest in tools such as these:

▶ Captivate (www.adobe.com).

▶ Quandary (www.halfbakedsoftware.com).

▶ Xcelsius (businessobjects.com).

▶ Articulate Presenter (www.articulate.com).

▶ Impatica for PowerPoint (www.impatica.com).

4 Connect-type activities

Linking learning to life, work, and future learning

Connect activities help learners close the gap between learning and the rest of their lives. They prepare learners to apply learning in situations they encounter at work, in later learning efforts, and in their personal lives. If *absorb* activities are the nouns and *do* activities the verbs, then *connect* activities are the conjunctions of learning.

ABOUT CONNECT ACTIVITIES

Connect activities integrate what we are learning with what we know. Often simple and subtle, connect activities are regularly neglected by designers who leave learners to make connections on their own.

Connect activities bridge gaps. They do not so much add new knowledge and skills as tie together previously learned skills and knowledge. In doing so, they add higher-level knowledge and skills. To know whether an activity is a connect activity; we have to ask the purpose of the activity. If the purpose is primarily to teach something new, it is a do or absorb activity. If the purpose is to link to something already known or prompt application of learning, it is a connect activity.

167

Common types of connect activities

Connect activities range from simple stop-and-think questions to complex real-world work assignments. Here are types of connect activities that have proven themselves in classroom and online learning:

- ▶ **Ponder activities** (p. 169) require learners to think deeply and broadly about a subject. They require learners to answer rhetorical questions, meditate about the subject, identify examples, evaluate examples, summarize learning, and brainstorm ideas.

- ▶ **Stories told by the learner** require learners to recall events from their own lives. (This activity is discussed, along with stories told by teachers, in Chapter 2.)

- ▶ **Job aids** (p. 183) are tools that help learners apply learning to real-world tasks. They include glossaries, calculators, and e-consultants.

- ▶ **Research activities** (p. 194) require learners to discover and use their own sources of information. These include scavenger hunts and guided research.

- ▶ **Original work** (p. 206) requires learners to perform genuine work and submit it for critique.

When to feature connect activities

Learners often fail to apply what they learn. For example, a manager passes a course on how to interview people of different cultures. Six months later she botches an employment interview of a shy Iranian woman wearing a traditional head scarf. A math student may get an A in introductory calculus but later a D in advanced calculus. Why? He did not apply the concepts from the introductory course to the advanced course, which assumes the introductory material as a prerequisite.

If you are familiar with Donald Kirkpatrick's four-level evaluation model, you know the importance of application. Application is right there on level 3, called *behavior*. It asks whether learners apply what they actually learned (level 2) to their subsequent behavior. Unless application occurs, intended organizational results (level 4) never occur.

By the way, if you are not familiar with Donald's model, you should be. Add *Evaluating Training Programs* by Donald and his son to your Amazon shopping cart. And be sure to read Chapter 11 (wink, wink).

Connect activities aim squarely at increasing application of learning. So use connect activities when:

- ▶ **Application is crucial**. The success of individuals, organizations, or societies depends on learners applying skills and knowledge. Every day people die because safety instructions are ignored. Economies sag because their workers are not competitive in a global economy.

▶ **Application is not adequate**. Perhaps learning is applied but not in enough depth or by enough people. For example, many companies hire expensive management consultants to teach their employees subjects like Six Sigma or TQM. Six months later the posters are peeling off the walls and the slogan-embossed pencils have been ground down to the nibs, and the only lasting result is a few additional coffee mugs in the break room. The teaching may have been great, but there was scant application.

▶ **You teach a general subject**. Broad principles and concepts can be applied in varied situations. You cannot include enough examples and custom activities to prepare learners to apply the learning in every possible situation they may encounter. For example, a course on business writing might be applied by an engineer to write a technical specification or by a marketing manager to write a sales proposal.

▶ **Learners doubt applicability of material**. College students apply binge learning to pass courses they are required to take but for which they see no practical value. Two weeks after the end of the term, they have forgotten most of what they learned. Much compliance training in industry fares no better. Learners get their tickets punched and go on just as if nothing happened. Why? They never saw how what they were learning applied to their lives.

▶ **Learners cannot make connections by themselves**. Sometimes it takes extraordinary efforts to see the connection between abstract subjects and daily life. This "in the clouds" stigma plagues mathematics, science, philosophy, and dozens of other subjects. Many learners lack the experience, motivation, or creativity to make connections on their own.

Connect activities can solve these problems without a lot of extra effort. As a rule, connect activities require only about 10% of learners' time. Sometimes a rhetorical question may be all you need.

PONDER ACTIVITIES

Ponder activities require learners to think deeply and broadly about what they are learning. They focus attention on the subject and invite learners to adopt a new perspective regarding the subject.

About ponder activities

Ponder activities are simple learning experiences that prompt the learner to examine ideas from a new perspective. They say:

> Stop and think about it!
>
> Zoom back and see the big picture.
>
> Look at it from a different angle.

Ponder activities are like classroom activities during which the teacher performs an out-of-the-ordinary activity to break the routine and to get learners to look at the subject afresh.

When to use ponder activities

Use ponder activities when you need learners to think about a subject in a new way. Use them to:

► Encourage broader and deeper thought about a subject.

► Make learners aware of how ideas and values apply in their lives.

► Reduce tunnel vision resulting from stress or anxiety.

► Trigger conceptual breakthroughs by getting learners to integrate separate ideas in new ways.

Types of ponder activities

Ponder activities come in several flavors. Here's a list of types and what they do.

► **Rhetorical questions** (p. 171) ask thought-provoking questions to direct attention to an aspect of the subject.

► **Meditations** (p. 172) promote a relaxed, open consideration of the subject.

► **Cite-example activities** (p. 176) require learners to identify real-world instances of a concept or category.

► **Evaluations** (p. 177) ask learners to judge the importance or value of an item under study.

▶ **Summary activities** (p. 179) require learners to identify and recap important principles, concepts, facts, tips, and other items of learning.

▶ **Brainstorming activities** (p. 181) collect suggestions for solutions to a problem from a group of learners.

How ponder activities work

Ponder activities are usually simple one-shot experiences without any sequence. If they involve more than a couple of steps, they are probably part of another type of activity. The utter simplicity of ponder activities makes it easy to integrate them into other more complex activities. We often interleave ponder activities with do and absorb activities without the learner noticing the connect activity as a separate event—especially if it is a simple form such as a rhetorical question.

Rhetorical questions

Rhetorical questions provoke thought. They may not require a visible response from learners, but they do require learners to think deeply in order to answer the question for themselves. We sometimes call them *stop-and-think* questions.

In the *Using Gantt Charts* course, I included these questions in one topic:

```
Find a Gantt chart at your work. Can you see how it was constructed? Could you
have constructed it?
```

There were no checkboxes for learners to click and no text boxes for learners to type in their answers. Thinking about the answers was enough.

When to use rhetorical questions

Use a rhetorical question as a simple way to get learners to think about a subject. For example, when:

▶ Real-world examples abound and you only need to direct learners' attention to them.

▶ All you need to do is to get the learners to think about an aspect of the subject.

▶ You lack time, space, or energy to do more.

4

Connect-type activities

Best practices for rhetorical questions

You can ask rhetorical questions about any topic you teach, such as a policy, procedure, principle, concept, attitude, or value. So how do you ask good rhetorical questions?

Ask stop-and-think questions. Teachers since Socrates have peppered students with rhetorical questions designed to direct their thoughts to aspects of a subject. Here are some proven thought-starters:

▶ Why do you think this is so? Why did this happen?

▶ What other results could you expect?

▶ Where will this idea apply? Where will it not apply?

▶ How can you apply this idea?

▶ How important is this idea to you?

▶ How consistent is this idea with other things you know?

Make questions personal. Feature the second person singular: "How will **you** …?" "Why do **you** …?" Get learners to think about their own experiences, knowledge, attitudes, and values.

Require thought about the subject and the learner's world. Just asking questions about the subject makes the question seem like a test. So put the question in the learner's context. "In the work that you do, what is the best way to …?"

Require some action if necessary. "Find an example of this idea and then answer these questions about it ….."

Trigger thought about when, where, how, and why to apply learning. Ask questions learners would have to answer before applying learning for real. "How often will you apply this idea?"

Meditation activities

The word meditation may conjure the image of someone sitting cross-legged, repeatedly chanting "om." Although such forms of meditation might provoke a relaxed state appropriate for learning or lead to mystical insights—that is not what I have in mind by a meditation activity. Meditation involves a relaxed consideration of a subject with a mind open to insights that may occur.

Meditation activities are not tightly focused. The big picture and content are more important than interior details. Meditation activities may involve more than cognitive aspects of a subject. They may delve into emotional meanings and implications for the learner's values and attitudes. Meditations may use non-verbal and non-explicit media such as music and abstract graphics.

Example of a meditation activity

On one project, I needed to broaden the concept of vision from just a "vision statement" to something involving the feelings of the group and how those feeling guide the group's actions.

A secondary purpose was to help the learners—the vision committee for a Christian church congregation, who have other jobs, demanding families, and busy lives—to let go of their daily concerns long enough to work together in this course.

To accomplish these objectives, I began each lesson with meditation activities. The lesson started with a page featuring a stained-glass window. On each window was a different flower from the Christian Bible. The purpose was to draw learners out of their noisy world by letting them look at a beautiful image. The choice of a window was not accidental. The window reinforced the message that vision looks outward and colors how the organization sees the larger community of which it is a part.

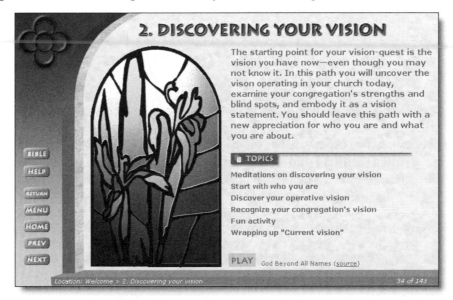

Built using Adobe Dreamweaver and Flash. View example at horton.com/eld/.

To further help learners disengage from daily concerns, the page included a button to play music associated with spiritual values.

The second page of the lesson included meditative activities designed to further the contemplative mood necessary to work as a team to discover a common vision. The main activity on this page presented different styles of music and challenged participants to pick one that reflected their vision. This activity provoked lively discussion as learners asked each other, "Why do you feel that way?"

Built using Adobe Dreamweaver and Flash. View example at horton.com/eld/.

Rounding out the meditation were quotations from sources sacred and common—again reinforcing the point that an organization's vision connects it to the surrounding world rather than isolating it.

When to use meditation activities

Meditation activities are especially valuable for subjects that may trigger emotional resistance, for example, leadership style, negotiation, ethical behavior, politics, and dealing with angry people. They are also good when discussing basic human values or teaching aspects of spirituality.

Use meditation activities to:

► **Relax tense learners**. Help them disengage from outside concerns that could interfere with their learning.

► **Broaden the focus and emphasize context**. Get learners to step back and see how a subject fits into a broader scheme.

► **Involve other sensory modalities and "intelligences"**—for variety, sure, but in a purposeful way that learners will find natural and sponsors will pay for.

► **Prepare for work requiring openness and creativity**. Meditative activities can disengage critical and analytical modes of thinking when they might interfere.

▶ **Encourage holistic thinking**. Help learners resolve conflicts and inconsistencies between what they are learning and what they believe.

I have also used meditation activities to reduce tension in "hard" subjects such as law and computer programming by reminding learners how these subjects fit into the larger universe of human endeavors.

More kinds of meditation activities

Here are some more simple meditation activities:

▶ **Coloring book**. Learners must pick colors for a symbol and justify the implications of their choices.

▶ **Symbolize**. Search a clip-art library for all the different ways to represent a group, concept, value, or principle. Justify the choice.

▶ **Chant**. Repeatedly say the name of a concept or organization to sense its hidden associations.

▶ **Deep watching**. Experience a video segment normally, then with the sound turned off, then with only the sound, then in slow motion, and finally speeded up.

▶ **Meaning quest**. Search the Web to collect or compare quotations on a subject or definitions of a term.

▶ **Deja viewing**. Identify ancient analogies to modern technologies and recent historical events.

Best practices for meditation activities

Meditation activities are subtle and benefit from sensitive design.

▶ **Have a good reason for the activity**. Many designers throw in colorful artwork or music for no good reason. Your reason for a meditation activity may be intellectual, emotional, or spiritual—but not just decorative.

▶ **Clarify your purpose**. What do you want the activity to achieve? Excitement or a calm, receptive mind? Are you trying to make a subtle point? Or is your goal to get learners to put aside a bias or prejudice?

▶ **Explain the reason** for the activity lest learners think you are being "weird for weird's sake."

▶ **Vary the type** of meditation activity. Different learners will respond to different types of activities. Use different media. Consider music, symbolic graphics, animation, and video.

4

Connect-type activities

Cite-example activities

Challenge learners to identify instances of a concept or category you have described and illustrated. Such an activity connects the concept or category with things the learner is already familiar with or can easily find in the world.

This activity requires learners to identify existing examples, not to create original examples. Creating original examples is part of the Original work activity (p. 206).

A course on information architecture challenged learners to find examples of Web sites organized according to different principles.

Built using Adobe Dreamweaver and Active Server Pages.

In the *Using Gantt Charts* course, I introduced dependency markers and then challenged learners to cite examples.

Can you think of some examples of this kind of dependency relationship on projects you have worked on?

That's right. Sometimes a rhetorical question is all you need.

When to have learners identify examples

Requiring learners to identify examples achieves several educational goals, such as:

▶ Rounding out the definition of a term or category.

▶ Making a concept more concrete and specific.

▶ Verifying that students can correctly apply terms and categories.

▶ Proving the applicability of learning.

The response of one student to such an activity shows its value: "Wow. This stuff really exists. I never knew."

Best practices for cite-example activities

▶ **Require searching to find examples**. Require learners to do more than pick from lists you provide. To simplify the search, give learners a starting point. If extensive searching is required, combine the cite-example activity with a research activity (p. 194).

▶ **Simplify submitting examples**. Let learners submit by entering Web addresses of the examples; by uploading or e-mailing a photograph, sound recording, or video clip; or by giving directions on how to find the example, such as providing its GPS coordinates. In an online meeting, have learners identify examples by entering them in chat (p. 429) or describing them orally by audio-conferencing (p. 442).

▶ **Specify the type of examples sought**. Clearly define the category or concept for which examples are sought. Show a few examples as a model of the type examples learners should identify. Also specify any quality standards ("legibly formatted"), required characteristics ("at least three levels deep"), or technical limitations ("1 MB max").

▶ **Encourage personal examples**. Ask learners to look for examples in their own experiences, work, personal life, and prior education.

Evaluation activities

Require learners to rate the importance of items of learning. Learners must judge from their personal perspective, such as in the context of a project in which the items of learning might be applied.

Pick access methods

For a real or imaginary online document you are creating, choose which access methods you would recommend. To the right is a list of the access methods we discussed in this lesson.

First, write the goal of your document. Then type 5 to 7 of the most important access methods you will employ.

Goal of the course:

Access methods (from most to least important):

[Enter] [Compare] [See all]

Click **Enter** to add this decision to your journal. Click **Compare** to see what other learners have chosen for their courses. Click **See all** to review the decision you have made so far.

Available methods
Autoscanning
Bookmarks
Context sensitivity
Full-text search
Grazing
Guided tour
History list
Home topic
Index
Keyword search
Map
Menu structure
Natural language search
Picture gallery
Table of contents

This example required learners to rate the utility of various access methods for an online document or Web site they were creating.

Built using Adobe Dreamweaver and Active Server Pages.

An evaluation activity can be used as a whole-class activity as well. In an online meeting you can have the class vote on the value for each item. Let them re-vote after considering the opinions of others.

When to use evaluation activities

Asking learners to rate the importance of ideas they have been taught challenges them to critically examine those ideas from a personal perspective. Such re-examination is valuable to:

▶ Get learners to start winnowing the ideas they will actually apply.

▶ Force reconsideration of individual items and their practical advantages and disadvantages.

▶ Replace rote rule-following with sensitive judgments.

Best practices for evaluation activities

▶ **Personalize ratings**. Remind learners to evaluate items from their unique individual perspective. Ask them "How important or valuable is this idea *to you*?"

▶ **Set a context for evaluation**. State the area for which importance is rated. Use phrases like "in the work you do" and "in your math courses."

▶ **Require criteria.** Have learners state the criteria they used to judge the idea. "Rate the importance from 1 to 10 and explain how you arrived at that number."

▶ **Require precision**. Avoid vague ratings like "good and bad." Require a numeric rating along a scale or require learners to rate the relative importance of a group of ideas.

Summary activities

Summary activities ask learners to recap what they have learned. Learners must review a subject area, select what is important, organize the selection logically, and express it clearly in their own words.

Summarize your findings

Read the Fire Management Plan document. Summarize the main points of the fire management plan as it relates to prescribed burns. Then explain what parts of the plan may be useful in formulating a wildland fire management plan for the Indian Peaks Wilderness Area.

Summarize how this plan addresses prescribed burns:

Explain how this policy might aid our own planning efforts:

Enter   Compare   See all

Click **Enter** to add this decision to your journal. Click **Compare** to see what other learners have chosen for their courses. Click **See all** to review the decision you have made so far.

This example challenges learners to summarize a document and how the ideas of the document apply to their work.

Built using Adobe Dreamweaver and Active Server Pages.

When to use summary activities

Summarizing prior learning has several effects on learning. It:

▶ Prepares learners to apply learning by having them rehearse recalling needed information.

▶ Prepares learners to teach or inform others, such as members of their team or study group.

▶ Triggers a systematic, personal review of an area of learning.

These activities let you monitor learners' level of understanding. Do learners recall the main points? Are the points logically integrated and prioritized? Have learners translated learning into their own vocabulary?

Best practices for summary activities

Simplify creating the summary. A blank text area is not always the best way for learners to express a summary. For some subjects, you may want to have learners draw a picture and submit it by e-mail or post it to a discussion forum. For other subjects, you may want to structure the form of the summary. You could, for example, let learners construct a summary by selecting and sequencing statements from a list.

Clarify what to summarize. Have learners summarize a specific lesson, topic, or activity. Have learners summarize specific learning experiences—books, articles, presentations, regulations, or other documents.

Assign summary activities to a group. Have learners compare separate summaries and then consolidate them. First, each learner individually creates a summary and posts it to a discussion forum (p. 463). Then, as a group, the class discusses the summaries either in an online meeting or on the forum. Together they identify points to include in the master summary and how these points should be organized.

Set a context for the summary. Rather than have learners write a conventional academic summary, consider requiring a format that they might need to produce in the real world or in an ongoing scenario, such as one of these:

▶ Press release.

▶ Advertisement.

▶ Poster.

▶ Block diagram or organization chart.

▶ Book jacket and blurb.

▶ Headline and first few paragraphs of a newspaper story.

▶ Storyboard for a 60-second TV news spot.

▶ 20-second sound bite.

▶ Review or synopsis.

Brainstorming activities

Brainstorming is a common part of most creative activities. Brainstorming is the process of generating lots of new ideas. In a brainstorming session, the leader poses a problem for which participants suggest solutions. The goal is to produce as many ideas as possible. In brainstorming, no ideas are rejected or criticized.

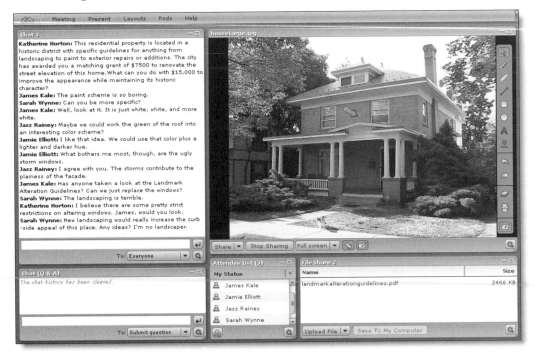

Meeting conducted with Adobe Breeze Meeting.

This example of brainstorming is from a class for architects and building contractors on how to remodel homes. The purpose of the session is to show learners how creative thinking can help them work within a tight budget. The session starts as an online meeting using a whiteboard (p. 431) and a chat window (p. 429) where learners rapidly suggest ideas.

The brainstorming session shifts to a discussion forum (p. 427). Here we see the Brainstorming activity thread and the responses posted to it.

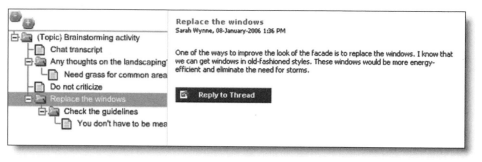

Discussion forum provided by The Learning Manager.

When to use brainstorming

Brainstorming can be taught as a valuable skill in its own right. It is an important aspect of teamwork, problem solving, and creative thinking. Brainstorming can also be useful anywhere learners need to solve problems in an original way.

How brainstorming works

Brainstorming sessions can take several forms. One common form involves both synchronous and asynchronous events. In an online meeting, the instructor poses the question to answer or problem to solve. Individual learners, using chat, contribute answers as fast as they can think of them until either the flow of ideas slows or the time allocated to the live phase of the activity expires.

The instructor then transfers the brainstorming from chat to a discussion forum in which learners continue adding ideas at their own pace. At the end of the allotted time, the instructor grades participants based on the quantity, not the quality, of the ideas they contributed.

Best practices for brainstorming

Brainstorming is a simple activity with great potential to motivate learners and develop creativity. To achieve this potential, consider some of these ideas:

Use more media. If you have the capability, use other media. Audio-conferencing (p. 442) speeds the process, as many people find typing slows their production of ideas. If you use audio, remember to record the session and post a typed transcript or summary to the discussion forum. A shared whiteboard (p. 431) lets learners contribute ideas by sketching or pasting in their drawings or clip art. For visual subjects, a whiteboard is especially valuable.

Skip the online meeting. If learners are familiar with brainstorming, you may want to conduct the whole brainstorming session in a discussion forum. This is a good alternative if it is difficult to get all learners together at the same time. Some brainstorming participants find it hard to be creative when it is four hours past their bedtime.

Set a context. You can give the brainstorming a more realistic flavor by situating it in a life-like scenario. Tell a story of a real problem. Ask learners to pretend they are characters in the story. Have them offer solutions from the perspective of their characters.

Enforce the prime rule of brainstorming. Make sure all participants understand the one and only rule of brainstorming: **There are no bad ideas**. Emphasize that participants cannot criticize ideas, but can add better ideas. Remind participants that they score points for the number (not quality!) of ideas.

Ask thought-provoking questions. Ask open-ended questions that can have many answers. For example: What if X? How do we make X better? Why should we do Y?

Keep ideas flowing. Prime the pump with a few ideas of your own. Periodically restate the question in a new way. Reverse the question. For example, after asking how to make something better, ask how to make it worse.

Combine ponder activities with other activities

Ponder activities are simple connect activities that bond well with other activities.

▶ Combine ponder activities with research activities (p. 194) so learners can explore the significance of what their research revealed.

▶ After a presentation (p. 49), have learners summarize the presentation, evaluate its importance, and cite examples to illustrate its principles.

▶ Sprinkle rhetorical questions like pixie dust throughout your e-learning.

JOB AIDS

Job aids help learners apply knowledge and skills to real-world tasks they encounter on the job—or anywhere else in life. Job aids are not formal education, but they can shape the need for learning and in some cases can substitute for learning. We lump them with connect activities because they prepare and encourage learners to apply learning on the job.

About job aids

Job aids are as much a category of tool as a specific learning activity. The term *job aid* covers a lot of ground, from a recipe on an index card to an elaborate electronic performance support system. The idea of a job aid is to provide help to someone performing a task right when and where they need it.

When to use job aids

Use job aids as part of your e-learning efforts when:

▶ The subject is too complex for learners to recall all important details.

▶ Tasks are critical or have negative side effects if not performed exactly as specified.

▶ Rote memorization would distract from learning more important principles and concepts.

▶ A job aid can replace unnecessary training and education.

For a lot of performance problems, a job aid is the perfect solution. Yet many training departments have developed whole courses when a job aid would have solved the problem for 1% of the cost. Why? They are training departments, not job-aid departments. Before you develop a course, consider whether a job aid is a better idea.

Types of job aids

Job aids are as varied as the jobs they aid. Here are some job aids that have made the transition to e-learning. Because the last 3 make special use of electronic media, they are described in more detail later.

▶ **Checklists** record the essential steps in a procedure or components of a system. Format the checklist for printing. For online checklists, use checkboxes so learners can keep track of items completed.

▶ **Reference summaries** recap crucial information in a field. They are sometimes called a *crib sheet* or *cheat sheet*. One common form is the pocket-sized card listing commands in a computer program or their keyboard shortcuts.

▶ **Glossaries** (p. 185) define the key terms, abbreviations, and symbols of a field.

▶ **Calculators** (p. 189) perform mathematical calculations for learners, thus eliminating the need to memorize formulas or consult complex tables.

▶ **E-consultants** (p. 192) dispense advice on complex situations. They can range from simple if-then tables to full expert systems.

How job aids work

There is no real flow, as job aids are used by themselves or as a part of a do activity. When the need arises, the learner obtains the job aid and follows its advice. Obtaining the job aid may involve downloading it from a Web site or just reaching in a pocket for a creased and stained page printed out six months ago.

Glossaries

Learning a new subject often requires acquiring a new vocabulary. A glossary lets us look up the meaning of terms as we encounter them. A good glossary can define terms, spell out abbreviations, and save us the embarrassment of mispronouncing the shibboleths of our chosen professions.

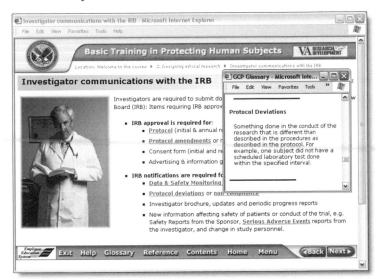

In this example, a term within the content is linked to a pop-up window that displays the term and its definition.

Designed by William Horton Consulting. Built by William Horton Consulting and VA Research and Development using Adobe Dreamweaver.

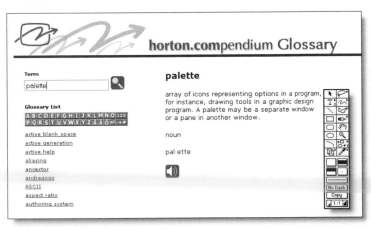

In this Web-based glossary, learners can look up terms by two methods: by typing the term into the text box at the upper left, or by looking up the term using the letter buttons.

Built using Adobe Dreamweaver and Active Server Pages.

In addition to the definitions, a glossary can include:

► Illustrations or links to pop-up illustrations.

► Synonyms and other related words, each linked to its definition.

► Pronunciation, both spelled out in text and linked to a voice pronunciation.

► Part of speech of this word, for example, noun or adjective.

► Usage notes to help learners use the term appropriately.

When to create a glossary

Glossaries are almost mandatory in e-learning that contains terminology unfamiliar to learners or that aims to teach correct use of terminology. A glossary makes strange words familiar and guides learners in their use. Consider creating a glossary for subjects when:

► Practitioners use many specialized terms and abbreviations. Every complex endeavor is subject to the Tower-of-Babel effect.

► Correct use of terminology is crucial to success. Misusing terms can cause legal penalties or just severe embarrassment.

► People of different specialties (and hence different vocabularies) must collaborate. An architect may use a technical term for something that a general contractor refers to by its common name and the construction worker calls by yet another term.

► Specialists and non-specialists must work together. Often reports written by a specialist must be typed and edited by those not versed in the esoteric terminology of the specialist's field.

Before you create e-learning on the concepts and principles of a field, consider whether a glossary would meet your requirements.

Best practices for glossaries

Glossaries are relatively easy to create. Effective glossaries, though, require close attention to linguistic and technical issues.

Use the classic formula for definitions

The classic form for a definition has two parts. The first part (called the *genus*) tells the general category to which the term belongs, and the second part (called the *differentia*) tells how it differs from other items in the category. For example, in this definition:

chromostereopsis – illusion of depth caused by the fact that objects of different colors come into focus at different distances.

The genus is "illusion of depth," and the differentia is the rest of the definition. OK, it's an old-fashioned way of writing definitions and the terms are from a dead language, but the formula is easy to follow and leads to definitions that are easy for learners to understand.

Clarify when the term applies

Provide general definitions before specific ones. For each specific definition, begin with the area in which this definition applies.

> **filter** – a device or process to limit what is included. In camera-work, a sheet of material in front of the lens that restricts which colors of light reach the film or sensor. In photo-editing, any process that systematically alters the recorded image, such as blurring, sharpening, or tinting.

Notice how this glossary entry includes a general definition and two specialized definitions differentiated by the context in which they apply.

Phrase definitions for clarity

If the definition refers to something besides the term, make the definition a complete sentence. For example:

> **linked list** – a data structure in which each member stores an item of data and a pointer to the next member in the list. In double-linked lists, each member contains pointers to both the previous and next member in the list.

Do not use a term within its own definition.

 No | ☺ Yes

display control panel – a control panel where you can control the display of your computer's monitor.

display control panel – a utility for changing the size, number of colors, and other characteristics of the image shown on your computer's monitor.

Separate the term and its definition

Format the term and definition so they are clearly separate. This is crucial for multi-word terms.

 No | Yes

peep-hole effect misinterpretations caused by receiving information without being aware of the context in which it applies.

peep-hole effect
misinterpretations caused by receiving information without being aware of the context in which it applies.

Cover a particular field

Design your glossary so it covers an entire field of study, not just the terms needed for a single course. That way you can offer your glossary as a separate product and your glossary can support multiple courses. Do focus on a specific area of knowledge. A glossary is not a replacement for a general-purpose dictionary. There are already plenty of general-purpose dictionaries on the Web. And don't forget to clearly label the field your glossary covers.

Evolve your glossary

Start simple and make your glossary more sophisticated as you increase its size and functions.

1. Start with a simple, single-page list of terms and definitions. Or just link terms in your text to their definitions in a separate window.

2. If the list of terms gets longer than 5 or 6 scrolling zones, add letter buttons at the top of the page to jump directly to the first term beginning with each letter.

3. As the list grows beyond a size that will load quickly, break it into separate pages, one for each letter or group of letters.

4. If your glossary grows beyond a couple of hundred terms, or if it needs frequent revision, consider storing the terms, definitions, and other data in a database and generating each definition in response to a request from the learner.

5. Add advanced search features. For example, let learners search for terms whose definitions contain specific words. Or let learners look up terms by how they are pronounced.

Borrow a glossary

Before you start your glossary project, check to see whether someone else already publishes a glossary for your field. Glossaries exist for most technical and business subjects, and most are free. If a glossary is on the Web, link to it.

Link related definitions

If the definition of one term includes words defined elsewhere in the glossary, consider linking each of these terms to its definition. This is especially important in a field in which novices would have trouble understanding definitions otherwise.

Calculators

One popular job aid is a job-specific numerical calculator. Such a job aid lets workers compute numbers directly, rather than having to recall formulas, perform calculations, or look up answers in complex tables. On-screen calculators may also eliminate the need to teach complex formulas.

Case study of an online calculator

Let's consider a case study of just such a calculator. Photographers frequently need to calculate camera settings for a particular shot. Such calculations involve relationships among aperture or f stop, shutter speed, film speed, and exposure value.

Photographers could calculate the desired values from formulas they have memorized.

Built using Adobe Dreamweaver.

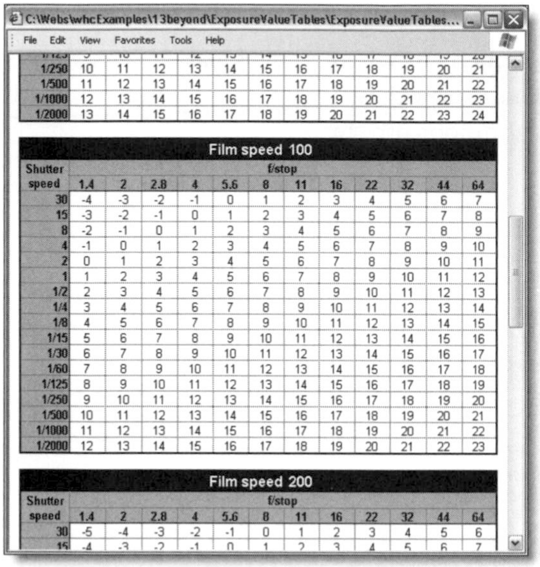

1/250	10	11	12	13	14	15	16	17	18	19	20	21
1/500	11	12	13	14	15	16	17	18	19	20	21	22
1/1000	12	13	14	15	16	17	18	19	20	21	22	23
1/2000	13	14	15	16	17	18	19	20	21	22	23	24

Film speed 100												
Shutter speed	f/stop											
	1.4	2	2.8	4	5.6	8	11	16	22	32	44	64
30	-4	-3	-2	-1	0	1	2	3	4	5	6	7
15	-3	-2	-1	0	1	2	3	4	5	6	7	8
8	-2	-1	0	1	2	3	4	5	6	7	8	9
4	-1	0	1	2	3	4	5	6	7	8	9	10
2	0	1	2	3	4	5	6	7	8	9	10	11
1	1	2	3	4	5	6	7	8	9	10	11	12
1/2	2	3	4	5	6	7	8	9	10	11	12	13
1/4	3	4	5	6	7	8	9	10	11	12	13	14
1/8	4	5	6	7	8	9	10	11	12	13	14	15
1/15	5	6	7	8	9	10	11	12	13	14	15	16
1/30	6	7	8	9	10	11	12	13	14	15	16	17
1/60	7	8	9	10	11	12	13	14	15	16	17	18
1/125	8	9	10	11	12	13	14	15	16	17	18	19
1/250	9	10	11	12	13	14	15	16	17	18	19	20
1/500	10	11	12	13	14	15	16	17	18	19	20	21
1/1000	11	12	13	14	15	16	17	18	19	20	21	22
1/2000	12	13	14	15	16	17	18	19	20	21	22	23

Film speed 200												
Shutter speed	f/stop											
	1.4	2	2.8	4	5.6	8	11	16	22	32	44	64
30	-5	-4	-3	-2	-1	0	1	2	3	4	5	6
15	-4	-3	-2	-1	0	1	2	3	4	5	6	7

Or they might look up the answer in complex tables such as those shown here. Notice that the document is five times as long as shown, and it requires five scrolling zones to cover just the four items in the formula.

Exported Microsoft Excel spreadsheet to create Web page.

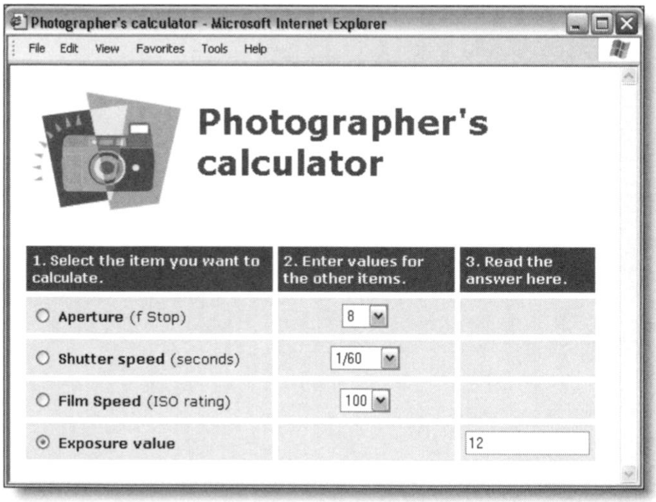

Or photographers could use a job-aid like this calculator, which lets them select the item to calculate, pick values for the other items, and then read the answer.

Built using Adobe Dreamweaver and custom JavaScript. View example at horton.com/eld/.

A better approach might be to make the calculator run on a mobile device so photographers could slip it into a pocket or camera bag.

Built using Adobe Flash. View example at horton.com/eld/.

On-screen calculators remove unnecessary barriers to successfully applying what the learners know about a subject.

Best practices for calculators

Incorporate such calculators into your e-learning to relieve learners of the tedium of manual calculations.

▶ **Link to publicly available calculators**. Do not waste time replicating existing calculators, such as the Windows calculator. If calculations in your subject are simple, just tell learners how to use a standard calculator.

▶ **Make entering numbers easy**. Let learners input numbers by mouse or keyboard.

▶ **Use calculators to promote your e-learning**. Put the course emblem or department logo on the calculator. Include a link to launch an e-learning course on the concepts and principles supported by the calculator. Give away calculators freely. Demonstrate them in classroom courses.

▶ **Test and refine your calculators**. Make sure they cover the real-world situations your learners encounter. Survey practitioners to learn the range of values the calculator should handle.

E-consultants

E-consultants give advice. An e-consultant is a form that the learner fills in to describe a problem—a virtual interview. When the learner clicks the **OK** or **Submit** button, the form analyzes the learner's answers and recommends actions to take.

Disciplining the Employee Who Violated Security Regulations

Deciding how to discipline an employee who violated security regulations or policies is a complex and crucial decision. Use this eConsultant to assess the factors and reach a preliminary decision—which you must then review with your manager and the legal department.

Did the violation break any laws or government regulations? (Legal Department can tell)	⦿ No ○ Yes
Was the violation accidental?	○ No ⦿ Yes ○ I do not know
Did unqualified persons obtain the information?	○ No ⦿ Yes ○ I do not know
What categories of information were compromised?	☐ Government Top Secret ☑ Government Secret ☑ Company Proprietary ☐ Company Confidential
Has this employee violated security before? (Check with Human Resources)	○ No ⦿ Yes
If Yes, is the employee currently on probation?	⦿ No ○ Yes

(Advise me) (Reset)   (Email security) (Email HR) (Email Legal)

Advice:

This is a serious breech and should be dealt with forcefully. Notify Human Resources to put the employee on probation for a security violation.

All violations involving government-classified materials must

This e-consultant helps managers decide how to deal with security violations by employees. Choices include a written warning, quarantine away from secure information, dismissal, or prosecution. This Web page replaces a complex, three-staged if-then diagram in the employee handbook. Notice there are links to the Security, Human Resources, and Legal Departments should the supervisor face a more complex problem than the form can describe.

Built using Adobe Dreamweaver and custom JavaScript. View example at horton.com/eld/.

The e-consultant is used at the time a problem arises. It asks a series of questions, as if conducting an interview. Then it dispenses advice based on an organization's policies and procedures.

E-consultants are sometimes called soft-skills calculators because they deal with situations too complex to be reduced to a single, simple mathematical formula. Use them when a situation has a lot of conditions mixed with irregularities and exceptions.

When to use e-consultants

E-consultants work well for any complex decision that can be divided into separate decisions and governed by a moderately complex set of rules. These include management decisions, such as go/no-go decisions on a project or selecting among alternative suppliers; technical decisions, such as selecting among design strategies; or any kind of problem-solving activity, such as diagnosing problems or recommending further tests.

Best practices for e-consultants

▶ **Do not try to handle every situation**. Cover the most common and most critical ones. It is better to create a job aid that lets 90% of people solve 90% of the problems than to create one that solves 95% of problems but only 50% can use.

▶ **Refer learners to human advisors** and other sources of information. Link to e-mail addresses and give phone numbers of people who can help analyze the problem and recommend solutions.

▶ **Phrase questions so they can be understood** by someone under the stress of making a critical decision. The people most in need of advice may be the ones least able to understand complex questions.

Best practices for job aids

Designing job aids is not difficult so long as you keep in mind that they are first and foremost tools for use in the work environment.

Design for how the job aid will be used. If a job aid will be used to guide a learner in performing a procedure on the computer screen, keep it compact so it does not cover up too much of the learner's work area. If the job aid guides a procedure done away from the computer, design it for printing out.

Keep job aids compact and concise. As a rule, design the job aid so it fits in a single scrolling zone of the browser at its default size, or on a single piece of paper, if it will be printed out.

If printing out, format for paper. If a job aid will be printed out, make sure it prints on a single sheet of paper. Consider formatting the printable version in Adobe Acrobat PDF format so that you can control the layout more precisely than with HTML. And remember to allow for differences between A4 and U.S. paper sizes.

Make job aids stand alone. A job aid should work outside the context of your e-learning and should not require extensive training to use.

Do not make job aids into tutorials. A job aid is not a training tool. Making it into one destroys the unique value it has as a job aid. Use job aids to supplement and complement training, but not as training.

Use job aids to simplify e-learning. Just as job aids simplify work, so too can they simplify taking e-learning. Use calculators to relieve learners of having to make tedious calculations. Use reference summaries and task-specific instructions to guide them in using tools within your e-learning.

Replace courses with job aids. Do not develop a course if all people need is a job aid. Do not teach formulas if a calculator eliminates the need to learn the formulas. Do not teach concepts and terms if a glossary is what people really need. Instead, teach how to use the job aid and you may not need to teach the theory, concepts, procedures, principles, and other details encapsulated by the job aid.

Do not short-circuit learning. If you really need to teach a concept or procedure, do not give learners a job aid that obviates learning the concept or procedure. At least teach the concept or procedure first, and then let learners have the job aid.

Use job aids as mementos. Give learners job aids that they can continue using after your e-learning. These mementos will remind them of what they learned and where they learned it. Put your logo onto the job aid. Link it to your Web site.

Combine job aids with other activities. Include job aids where they will simplify other activities. Design activities to encourage learners to begin using job aids. Use reference summaries to summarize key points from a presentation (p. 49) or reading activity (p. 78). Include calculators in practice (p. 106) and guided-analysis activities (p. 113) that require performing calculations as part of the activity. Combine practice activities with reference summaries and checklists.

RESEARCH ACTIVITIES

Research connects learners to the whole world of knowledge by teaching them to learn on their own. In our complex world, research is a basic skill. Rote memorization of facts will not do. There is too much to learn, and what is accurate and applicable today is erroneous and inappropriate tomorrow.

About research activities

Research activities teach learners to gather, analyze, and report on information. Because they involve information, research could qualify as an absorb activity. Because they require performing actions to gather information, they could be considered do activities. I have classified them as connect activities because the most valuable effect of research is to connect learners with the universe of knowledge on which they must draw to lead successful lives.

Technologies that let us instantly access large bodies of information have called into question the very definition of what it means to know something.

> The verb to know used to mean, having information stored in one's memory. It now means the process of having access to information and knowing how to use it. – Herbert Simon, Nobel Laureate

This view shifts the mission of education from putting facts in people's heads to giving people the tools they need to learn what they need when they need it, that is, conduct research. The editor of the *Harvard Business Review* put it even more bluntly:

> It's not what you know, it's how fast you can access all the things you don't know. And if you get that time down to a few seconds, then you effectively know everything. – Thomas Stewart, *The Wealth of Knowledge*

The ability to find information when needed is now basic education.

Types of research activities

Research is often a natural part of other types of activities, such as readings or discovery activities. Two main types of research are learning activities in their own right.

▶ **Scavenger hunts** (p. 196) challenge learners to identify reliable sources of information to answer questions and enable tasks.

▶ In **guided research** (p. 199), learners consult various sources of information and opinions on a topic and then summarize their findings.

Although similar, these two forms differ in their purposes. Scavenger hunts teach learners to find reliable sources of information, whereas guided research teaches learners to draw conclusions from information.

How research activities work

In research activities, the learner considers a question or assignment, gathers data, and then uses the data to answer questions or solve a problem.

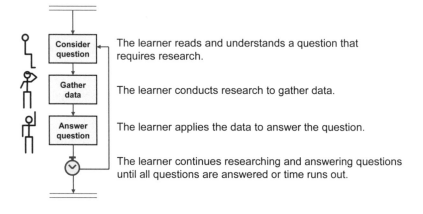

The learner reads and understands a question that requires research.

The learner conducts research to gather data.

The learner applies the data to answer the question.

The learner continues researching and answering questions until all questions are answered or time runs out.

Scavenger hunts

Scavenger hunts send learners out on a quest for answers and sources of reliable information on the Web or corporate and campus intranets.

The scavenger-hunt activity specifies the questions to be answered. It may specify additional information the learner must submit, such as the location where the answer was found, the method used to find it, the reason why it is the correct answer, conclusions drawn from the answer, and the category into which it fits.

The activity may recommend sources of information, or learners may be on their own to locate sources. Using these sources, learners answer the specific questions posed by the activity. Relying on the answer to the specific questions and on sources identified earlier, learners may answer a more general or abstract question. Submissions may be automatically scored or graded by an instructor.

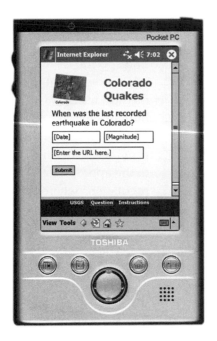

This example, designed to run on a mobile device, asks learners when the last recorded earthquake occurred in Colorado and its magnitude. Learners are also prompted to enter the URL of the page where the answer can be found. To simplify search, the activity includes a link to the U.S. Geological Survey Web site, the official source for such information.

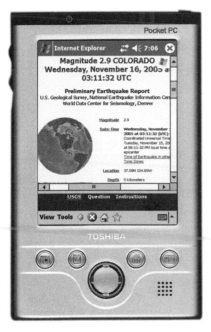

After locating the answer, learners click the **Question** button to return to the question and enter the answer and where it was found.

Built using Adobe Dreamweaver.

Learning a rapidly advancing body of knowledge requires learning how to keep current with changes in the field. For instance, programmers must have access to the latest information on a programming language, database technologies, and the various code libraries they use daily in their projects. Such information is quite volatile because producers are frequently releasing new versions of their tools as well as the inevitable patches, bug fixes, and work-arounds. With such volatility, printed documentation and classroom training cannot keep up. The programmer who relies on the tools and documentation that came in the box is left behind.

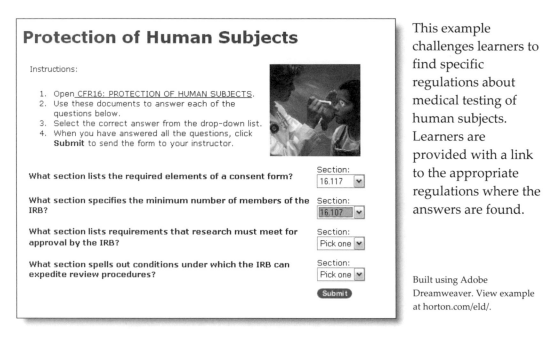

This example challenges learners to find specific regulations about medical testing of human subjects. Learners are provided with a link to the appropriate regulations where the answers are found.

Built using Adobe Dreamweaver. View example at horton.com/eld/.

When to use scavenger hunts

Use scavenger hunts to teach learners to find their own sources of reliable information. This is especially valuable in fields in which the best, most up-to-date, most accurate information is found only online. In such fields, knowing where to find information is an essential skill in its own right. Use scavenger hunts to teach learners to:

▶ Find information on the Internet or intranet.

▶ Navigate a large reference document, such as a specification or technical manual.

▶ Retrieve information from a database.

Best practices for scavenger hunts

Keep the activity simple. Scavenger hunts do not have to be complex. They can be as simple as a list of 5 to 10 short questions that learners can answer by consulting Web resources.

Show the value of information. To emphasize the importance of data gathered in the scavenger hunt, have learners use that data in calculations or in making decisions.

Focus on the goal of the activity. Emphasize that merely answering the question is not enough. The goal of the scavenger hunt is to identify reliable sources of information for use in the future. Require learners to identify the sources of their answers and to judge the accuracy of information provided by those sources.

Simplify scoring. To automate scoring, let learners pick from lists of pre-identified locations. If learners must type in locations, match them to a list of acceptable locations. Submissions with unmatched locations are routed to a human evaluator. If the location is OK, it is added to the list.

Challenge learners. To give the scavenger hunt more of a game flavor, add a countdown timer that imposes a visible time limit on searches.

Guided research

As its name suggests, guided research activities coach learners in performing research in the subject of learning. Learners are assigned a research topic. The topic may be a complex question or a series of simple questions. The learners individually or in teams gather the information necessary to answer the questions. Learners evaluate the information they have gathered, select relevant facts, and organize them. An instructor or facilitator may then grade the reports prepared by learners based on the extensiveness of the research, accuracy of the facts, and logic of the organization.

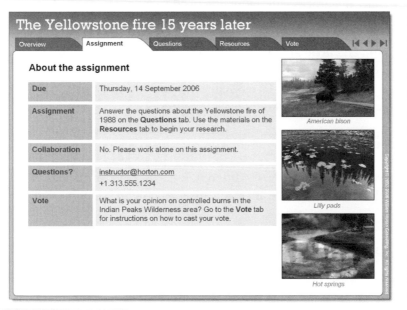

In this course for professional foresters, learners are asked to consider the conclusions that were drawn after fires swept through Yellowstone National Park in 1988.

Created in Microsoft PowerPoint and converted for Web delivery using Adobe Breeze Presenter. View example at horton.com/eld/.

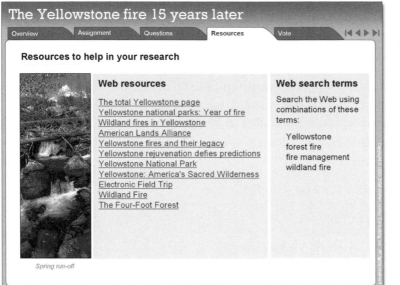

The **Resources** tab provides resources to begin the research. It includes links to useful documents as well as search terms to use to find more documents.

When to use guided research

Because guided research works well with individuals, teams, and entire classes, make it a staple of instructor-led e-learning. Use it to teach learners how to conduct informal research on a subject, especially if learners will frequently need to prepare reports summarizing their research efforts.

Although locating information and analyzing it are a part of guided research, these activities are not the primary focus. Use guided research when you want to teach learners to evaluate, select, and organize information. To teach just information-gathering, use a scavenger hunt. To teach analysis, use a guided-analysis activity.

Variations of guided research

You can adapt guided-research activities for many different kinds of e-learning and for different class sizes—even classes of one. Here are some ideas on how to adapt guided research to your needs:

Personal perspectives

Rather than have each learner perform the same research task, pick a complex subject and assign each learner a different perspective to research. For example, a course on project management could research the case of the Swedish ship, *Vasa*, which sank on its way out of Stockholm Harbor on its maiden voyage in 1628. Perspectives to research would be:

▶ **Engineering**. What design flaws caused the ship to capsize and sink? Was naval engineering advanced enough at the time to have prevented the failure?

▶ **Managerial**. How did the management process of designing and building the ship contribute to its failure?

▶ **Social**. What social pressures contributed to the bad design?

▶ **Legal**. What were the civil and criminal proceedings that followed?

▶ **Historical**. How did Swedish history influence the design of the ship? How did the failure affect events afterward?

▶ **Aesthetic**. What features of the ship were symbolic or decorative? What was the role of aesthetics in design at that time? Did aesthetics contribute to the failure?

▶ **Scientific**. Why were the remains found virtually intact? How was the ship recovered and preserved? What did scientists learn by restoring it?

Learners can consider the research of all the different perspectives to augment their own.

Scrapbook

One popular form of guided research is the scrapbook. Here learners gather and organize knowledge on a subject. They create a scrapbook by cutting and pasting (not linking) resources. Learners can later post their scrapbooks to a forum for others to comment on.

Give learners instructions such as these:

> Visit the resources listed below. Collect text, pictures, statistics, bits of multimedia, and quotations important to your role and assignment. Assemble the pieces into a scrapbook, annotated with brief explanations of what they mean and why you selected them.
> Prepare a table of contents showing the logical organization of the materials you have collected.

Day in the life

Have learners research a real, historical, or fictional character and then write about what this person experiences on a typical day. Pick a person who has contributed to the subject matter of the course or who is an exemplary practitioner in the field. Or pick an ordinary person typical of a social class or profession.

Self-derived best practices

One form of research for practical subjects is to have learners spot, analyze, and express best practices in examples of excellent work in the field of study.

Start by presenting sources of dozens or hundreds of examples of excellent work for learners to peruse. You can pick them yourself or select museum exhibits, award winners, or items frequently cited by experts. Next, direct learners to specific aspects of the examples. You may list characteristics to notice or ask specific questions about the examples. Or you might give learners specific categories in which to compare the examples. Then, ask learners to pick the best example in the category and state why it is the best. Instruct learners to repeat the process in another category. Finally, ask learners to generalize what the best examples have in common.

Criteria for comparison should ask questions an expert would ask but not be weighted to suggest an answer. You may want to include a worksheet to guide analysis and structure the activity.

Ongoing research

For a research project, require learners to keep and periodically submit logs of their research activities. The instructor can identify additional sources, suggest more efficient techniques, and challenge questionable resources. Once a week, require learners working as a team to submit a brief summary of their findings.

Best practices for guided research

Assist learners in locating reliable sources of information. Provide links or search terms that will reveal answers to some questions but not all. Require learners to find analogous resources. Guide the research.

Emphasize the importance of evaluating, selecting, and organizing facts. Make guided research more than simply recording information found at the end of a Web search. Require learners to judge the accuracy of what they find, select the best evidence, and combine it into a coherent argument or explanation.

Use probing questions to guide research. Ask questions that require combining information from multiple sources. Require learners to sort out contradictory information or to separate fact from opinion. Ask why and how, not just when and what.

Best practices for research activities

Design to connect

Ensure that research activities connect learners to life and prior learning.

► Emphasize locating sources of information and the process of analyzing data, not just the results that answer individual questions.

► Offer learners multiple sources of information to choose from and require them to consult multiple sources.

▶ Require analysis and synthesis to teach learners to apply what they gathered through research.

Use the Web as a source of material

Both kinds of research activities benefit from the vast library of resources available on the Web. Amidst the sex shops, bigot-blogs, and watch-me Webcams are a treasure of case studies, reports, books, manuals, historical documents, databases, dictionaries, news, music, images, and cataloged data on every subject imaginable. Much of it is free. Before you start shoving material online for use in research activities, consider whether your time might be better spent designing an activity that relies on available Web resources.

Starting points for research. There are thousands of Web sites that can direct you to useful sources of information. Some are maintained by search engines, some by government agencies, some by universities, and some by communities of passionate amateurs. Here are some of these sources to consider as a starting point. Don't recognize the URLs? Well, check them out.

▶ **wikipedia.com** for articles on a vast variety of subjects.

▶ **dictionary.com** for definitions of words.

▶ **urbandictionary.com** for the meaning of the latest slang and jargon.

▶ **etymonline.com** for the history of words and phrases we use.

▶ **earth.google.com** for 3D views of everywhere in the world (no kidding).

▶ **scholar.google.com** for scholarly papers and books.

▶ **images.google.com** for pictures of just about anything you can imagine.

▶ **print.google.com** for access to the text of millions of books.

▶ **uspto.gov** for thousands of patents describing a myriad of devices and methods.

▶ **www.sec.gov** for information on companies publicly traded in the USA.

Product literature and documentation. Today the Web sites for most companies provide detailed operating instructions, marketing literature, repair procedures, reference manuals, technical specifications, and documentation for their products and services. Use these materials in e-learning that involves selecting, operating, designing, evaluating, manufacturing, or recycling such products. Go to the company's Web site and click on **Products** or **Support** to start finding such resources.

Magazines and journals. Even paper-based magazines, trade journals, and scholarly journals now make articles, abstracts, and back issues available over the Web. Some charge for access to complete articles or back issues, but most provide free access to summaries of current articles.

Professional associations. If more than a few people perform a job activity, there is probably a professional organization with a Web site from which learners can get useful information regarding the principles, ethics, standards, job categories, skill requirements, and other aspects of the job. Of special interest to us designers of learning will be Web sites of user-groups for products used by professionals. One sterling example of the valuable resources available on such sites is the National Association of Photoshop Professionals (www.photoshopuser.com).

Most professional association sites reveal their full riches only to members of the association. You may want to encourage learners to join or may need to restrict yourself to the freely available resources.

Government agencies. Increasingly, government agencies are making their collections of regulations, artwork, and scientific data available over the Internet. For example, NASA makes available 3D Landsat and Shuttle Radar imagery for the whole planet (worldwind.arc.nasa.gov). The U.S. Library of Congress (www.loc.gov) offers free access to maps, photographs, video clips, and librarians. The European Union On-Line (europa.eu.int) provides information on governance of the European Union. The United Nations provides similar information (www.un.org).

News networks and newspapers. Almost all major news-reporting organizations have Web sites that provide up-to-the-moment and archived articles and video clips on politics, technology, business, science, nature, entertainment, education, sports, medicine, travel, and law. Here are just a few to get you started:

- news.bbc.co.uk

- www.cnn.com

- www.wsj.com

- www.msnbc.com

- www.nytimes.com

- news.ft.com

Keep in mind that each of these organizations has its own perspective. Several have multiple divisions. For example, the *Financial Times* has separate Web sites for the UK, the U.S., Europe, and Asia.

Discussion forums and newsgroups. If more than a thousand people worldwide are interested in a subject, you can bet there is a discussion forum or newsgroup on the subject. Such online discussions provide a great resource to introduce learners to subjects as they are practiced in the real world. They can also be a way to introduce learners to the petty bickering, narcissistic self-promotion, bombastic pontificating, and personal invective common out in the real world.

Have learners access a forum or newsgroup, lurk for a while, then join in the conversation, and finally report on what they have learned. Suggest that learners report on what the real function of the group appears to be. For what kinds of questions is it a good source? For which kinds is it not an effective source? Is its function primarily scholarly, job-related, or social?

Direct observation sites. Live Webinars have shown babies being born, hearts being bypassed, and sex being had. But not all Web sights are so spectacular. Some have solid educational value. David Iadevaia, an astronomer and professor at Prima College in Tucson, Arizona, lets learners look through the telescopes at what he or other researchers are seeing (www.api-az.com. Webcams let us view live images of hungry piranha (piranhapictures.com), prisoners being booked into a jail (www.tnasco.net/cont/jailcam.php), or a volcano smoldering (www.fs.fed.us/gpnf/volcanocams/msh/). If you want learners to see it, just type the subject and the word Webcam into a search engine and see what's out there.

Combine research with other activities

Join research and other types of activities for a richer, more reliable learning experience.

▶ Combine guided analysis (p. 113) and guided research to teach learners to identify sources of information, to extract facts from them, and to analyze the facts in detail.

▶ Follow presentations (p. 49) or readings (p. 78) with research activities to teach learners how to learn more on their own.

▶ Have learners conduct research to locate materials for reading activities (p. 78).

ORIGINAL-WORK ACTIVITIES

Original-work activities are the ultimate final exam—they require learners to apply learning to their own work. Learners must solve a real-world problem and submit their solutions for critique by an instructor or by fellow learners.

About original-work activities

Original-work activities encourage learners to begin applying learning to current projects.

When to use original-work activities

Original-work activities let you and your learners verify that they can apply learning to real work or future studies. Use original-work activities to:

▶ Verify that learners can apply what you are teaching.

▶ Require integration and synthesis of separate areas of learning.

▶ To serve as a final exam or practicum.

Types of original-work activities

There are several ways learners can perform original-work activities. The ones listed here represent different ways of conducting an original-work activity but not distinct activities. You can combine some of these types quite productively.

▶ **Decision activities** (p. 207) require learners to submit decisions made at critical junctures in a real project.

▶ **Work-document activities** (p. 208) require learners to create a document that would be a part of actual work, such as filling in a form, creating a slide presentation, or writing a specification.

▶ **Journal activities** (p. 209) provide a way for learners to collect decisions into an ongoing document that they can review and take away at the end of the e-learning.

▶ **Comparison activities** (p. 210) allow learners to compare their work to that of other learners.

▶ **Group critique activities** (p. 210) require learners or small teams to submit their work for review by fellow learners.

How original-work activities work

Original-work activities are a two-step process: First the learner creates original work and then the instructor or fellow learners critique it.

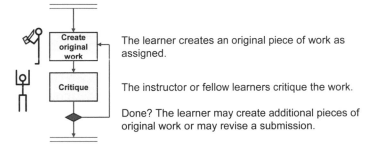

The learner creates an original piece of work as assigned.

The instructor or fellow learners critique the work.

Done? The learner may create additional pieces of original work or may revise a submission.

Decision activities

Invite learners to make decisions for real projects and to submit their decisions for critique. The decision may take the form of a small component of work.

Layer a cluster in your document

Imagine that you are creating an electronic course for an area with which you are familiar. What kinds of information would you put on each of three layers?

Type the requested information into the text boxes, then press **Enter** to post the information to your personal journal.

First layer   Deeper layers

ACTIVITY

Subject area:

First layer:

Second layer:

Third layer:

This example asks learners to make decisions on layering information for a project. Learners get to pick a subject from their work or studies. And that's what makes it original work.

Built using Adobe Dreamweaver.

Such a decision activity is simple and easier to evaluate for an instructor who may not know all the particulars of the learner's field of work.

4

Work-document activities

Much work and study requires producing official documents or giving presentations. One form of original-work activity requires learners to submit a real document from their work.

This example requires the learners to specify colors for a Web site they are designing. They do so on a form downloaded as part of the activity.

Built using Adobe Dreamweaver and Microsoft Word.

Think about the work activities the learner engages in. What are the products of those activities? Any of these work products could be the basis of an original-work activity. For example, consider the work of a social worker and resulting documents.

Interviewing people	Recording, transcript, or report of the interview.
Recording data	Form filled in to record the data.
Recommending actions	Report with supporting documents.

Consider the wide variety of work products you can have learners submit:

▶ Writings.

▶ Plans.

▶ Procedures.

▶ Policies.

▶ Spreadsheets.

▶ Reports.

▶ Designs.

▶ Sketches.

▶ Slide presentations.

▶ 3D models.

▶ Advertisements.

▶ Musical compositions.

▶ Video clips.

▶ Animation sequences.

▶ Audition tapes.

Journal activities

Original work is ongoing. A journal activity can collect the pieces of work in a workbook, database, or discussion forum, where it can be reviewed and updated.

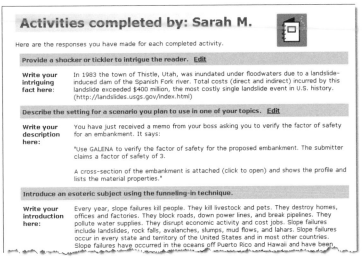

This example shows a journal activity. Each individual activity like this is written to a database. Once entered, the learner can revise it by making changes and clicking the **Update** button. Clicking the **See all** button reveals the entire journal.

Built using Adobe Dreamweaver and Active Server Pages.

The journal displays all the learner's entries so far. Each entry has an **Edit** button the learner can click to make changes to the entry.

Journal activities are good after a learner has completed a significant piece of work. The Journal then contains the completed work, along with a clear trail of its creation and refinement. The journal activity is like the decision activity repeated over and over again for all the key decisions of an entire project.

Comparison activities

The comparison activity is a variant on the decision activity. It lets learners compare their decisions to those of other learners. Learners see how others decided or did an analogous piece of work.

Often the comparison is a great source of inspiration. It lets learners reinterpret the activity in a more useful manner. It is also an important source of feedback in learner-led e-learning, where there is no instructor to critique the work, and in asynchronous e-learning where there are not enough learners at the same point in the course for a group critique.

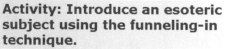

Activity: Introduce an esoteric subject using the funneling-in technique.

Here is how others responded to these questions.

Team: Terri D.

Write your introduction here:	Let me set the context for our course, Using Gantt Charts. What do project sponsors care about? They want their projects good, fast, and cheap!
	Think of your project parameters as represented by this triangle: the base reprsents SCOPE, one side represents TIME, and the other side represents RESOURCES (both human and financial).
	These three elements, scope, time, and resources are interrelated. So, you can have a project be relatively good, relatively fast, and relatively inexpensive. But, they are RELATIVE.
	We can't cover all the aspects of project management in this short course, but we'll focus on the results of this planning as depicted in a Gantt chart.

Team: Jerry S.

| Write your introduction here: | Vibration radiate outwards in all directions and if the blast is large enough... can be felt world wide. Part of the nuclear test ban treaty is to verify compliance. Monitoring stations are set globally. The State Department, Arms Control and Disarmament Agency is the responsible group in the US. Separating small nuclear detonations with large coal mine blasts is challenging. The video shows the global network of monitoring stations and then pans to a coal mine in Wyoming. The point is.... Vibrations can be felt anywhere from a coal mine blast. |

Team: Sarah M.

| Write your introduction here: | Every year, slope failures kill people. They kill livestock and pets. They destroy homes, offices and factories. They block roads, down power lines, and break pipelines. They pollute water supplies. They disrupt economic activity and cost jobs. Slope failures include landslides, rock falls, avalanches, slumps, mud flows, and lahers. Slope failures |

Here is the journal activity we saw earlier. Now, by clicking the **Compare** button, the learner can see how other learners performed the same activity.

Built using Adobe Dreamweaver and Active Server Pages.

Group-critique activities

The group-critique is the most complex form of original-work activity. Group critiques have learners help other learners to refine their work. Group-critique activities take advantage of discussion forums to help learners learn from other learners. In the simplest form of group critique, a learner prepares an individual answer to a question, posts it for others to critique, and then revises it before submitting the final version.

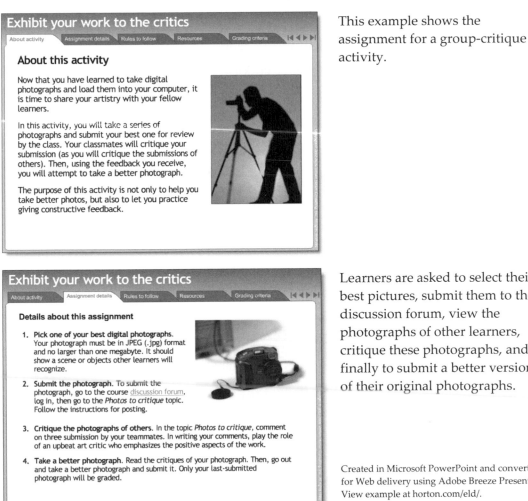

This example shows the assignment for a group-critique activity.

Learners are asked to select their best pictures, submit them to the discussion forum, view the photographs of other learners, critique these photographs, and finally to submit a better version of their original photographs.

Created in Microsoft PowerPoint and converted for Web delivery using Adobe Breeze Presenter. View example at horton.com/eld/.

A typical group-critique activity works like this: First, the instructor assigns an original-work activity for learners to perform. Individual learners then post their preliminary work to a discussion forum, where learners ask questions, critique, and suggest changes. Learners can then revise their answers and resubmit them for another round of critique. In the end, the instructor evaluates learners based on the final quality of their answers and on the helpfulness of their comments to others.

You can vary the basic group critique by changing how the critique is performed, what is critiqued, and what kinds of comments are solicited.

Group critiques teach learners to give and accept criticism. Use them to:

▶ Teach learners to refine their work by incorporating the ideas of others.

▶ Condition learners to accept and filter the criticism of their peers.

▶ Teach learners to offer helpful criticism.

▶ Offload from the instructor much of the work of evaluating and critiquing learners.

The value of group critiques depends on the quality of the comments offered by the group. For best results, guide participants in offering practical, encouraging comments. Monitor and moderate critiques. And be prepared to jump in if the comments degenerate into personal attacks. Remind reviewers that part of their grade depends on the helpfulness of their comments.

Best practices for original-work activities

Specify criteria for critiques

Provide objective criteria for critics to use. Focus the critique on the work, not the person who created it. Make clear that personal criticisms are not helpful. Have learners suggest criteria for evaluation of their work. You may want to go so far as to provide a form to structure the critique.

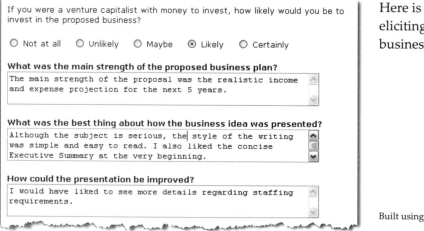

Here is the form eliciting a critique of a business plan.

Built using Adobe Dreamweaver.

Offer helpful comments

The instructor can promote helpful comments by offering some as an example. If learners seem reluctant to criticize the work of others, the instructor can start the process and establish a pattern of helpful comments. Two kinds of helpful comments include questions that require the learners to rethink their work and suggestions for improvement. Neither directly criticizes the work or the learner who submitted it.

Use revision features of word processors

If the whole class uses the same word processing program, you can have learners prepare a detailed, precisely formatted document in the word processor. Learners can use the revision features of the word processor to insert their comments into the body of the document.

Clarify what learners must submit

▶ Give learners a form to fill in or a template. For example, if learners must prepare presentations, give them a slide file with necessary slides containing placeholders for the kind of information you require.

▶ Remind learners to remove personal, proprietary, or secret information before submitting their work.

▶ Require learners to provide the context against which their work is to be evaluated, for example, the goals it is to accomplish.

Combine original work with other activities

▶ Have learners conduct research (p. 194) so they can perform original work up to professional standards, so they can compare their work to that of experts, and so they know criteria to use in critiquing the work of others.

▶ Assign original-work activities that require learners to assemble their own libraries of reference materials and create their own job aids.

▶ If training teachers, have them redesign the course for you. Use their materials the next time you offer the course.

IN CLOSING ...

Summary

Connect-type activities ensure that people can apply what they learned. They do not usually teach knowledge and skills, but make existing knowledge and skills more useful. Connect activities range from a simple stop-and-think question to a full-scale work project. To design effective connect activities; start with a clear idea of what you want to connect.

To connect this	To this	Use this type connect activity
Individual principles, concepts, and other bits of learning.	The learner's work or studies.	Ponder activities, such as identifying examples.
Major themes in your e-learning.	The learner's life.	Stories told by the learner.
Procedures and policies.	The learner's professional work.	Job aids and original-work activities.
Limited information in your course.	The larger body of knowledge in a field.	Research activities.
Current information.	New information that the learner will encounter.	Research activities.

For more ...

Because the primary purpose of connect activities is to ensure that learners apply what they learn, search the Web for combinations of these words: *education, training, learning, transfer, performance,* and *application.*

Connect activities seldom work alone. Be sure to consider do activities (Chapter 3) and absorb activities (Chapter 2) as partners.

5 Tests

Assessing learning

Educational experts underrate them. Instructional designers disregard them. Course authors overlook them. Learners fear them. We may cloak them as games or puzzles. We may put off writing them until there is not time enough to do them well. Whether we call them *tests*, *assessments*, *quizzes*, *drills*, *examinations*, *competence monitors*, or *demonstrations of mastery*, they, nonetheless, remain essential for gauging a learner's progress. And they represent an opportunity for clever designers to engage learners and provide objective feedback.

DECIDE WHY YOU ARE TESTING

Before you begin writing test questions, make sure a test is warranted. Unless your reasons for testing are clear, your tests will fail.

When are formal tests needed?

Tests are difficult to create and administer. Often informal practice activities may be sufficient to teach a subject. In *Tests That Work*, Odin Westgaard lists 3 conditions for using formal tests with recorded scores:

▶ Learners require specific skills, knowledge, and attitudes.

▶ You do not know whether learners possesses those skills, knowledge, or attitudes.

▶ A test is the best way to provide that assessment.

Otherwise, use some other kind of activity, such as an unscored practice activity or a survey.

Why are you testing?

Before deciding to test, list your goals. Here are some reasons for testing. Some are good, and some are not.

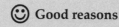 Good reasons	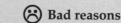 Bad reasons
▶ Let learners gauge progress toward their goals.	▶ Fulfill the stereotype that all e-learning courses have tests and all tests are unpleasant.
▶ Emphasize what is important and thereby motivate learners to focus on it.	▶ Reinforce the instructor's power over learners. Pay attention or else.
▶ Let learners apply what they have been learning—and thereby learn it more deeply.	▶ Torture learners. Training is supposed to be painful. Tests can ensure that it is.
▶ Monitor success of parts of the e-learning so that the instructor and designers can improve it.	▶ Artificially bolster learners' self-esteem by giving them easy tests with gushingly positive feedback.
▶ Certify that learners have mastered certain knowledge or skills as part of a legal or licensing requirement.	▶ Use a testing tool you paid a lot of money for.
▶ Diagnose learners' skills and knowledge so they can skip unnecessary learning.	▶ You can't think of any other way to add interactivity.

Consider testing carefully. Contradictions lurk within these lists. What learners want to learn may not square with what instructors want to teach. Knowledge required for certification may not be sufficient to actually do a job.

If sorting through this long list is too complex, let me simplify it. The reasons for testing usually boil down to a choice between teaching and measuring performance. Ask yourself, Am I more interested in using tests to enhance learning or to accurately measure learners' abilities? Although these 2 goals are not opposites, achieving each requires compromises in the other.

What do you hope to accomplish?

Consider your purpose for testing when you decide how to test, whether to record scores, and what feedback to give learners.

Purpose for testing	How to test	Record scores?	Feedback
Measure the progress of learners.	End-of-module-tests.	Yes.	Numeric, at end of test.
Help learners measure their own progress.	Frequent short tests.	No.	Descriptive and numeric.
Certify learners' knowledge.	Proctored, legally defensible tests.	Yes.	Pass-fail or overall score. May also provide scores for sub-components so learners can study and try again.
Certify learner's skills.	Observed accomplishment of prescribed tasks.	Yes.	Pass-fail or overall score. May also provide scores for sub-components so learners can study and try again.
Motivate learning.	Informal pre-tests.	No.	Recommended areas of study.
Teach new knowledge and skills.	Informal, frequent, before presentation of content.	No.	Presentation of just the content that testing indicates the learner needs.
Diagnose learners' skills and knowledge.	Comprehensive test.	?	Complete profile of what the learner already knows and needs to learn.

Purpose for testing	How to test	Record scores?	Feedback
Measure the effectiveness of learning modules.	Comparison of test scores between different modules and between modules before and after revisions of pre- and post-tests.	Yes.	--

What do you want to measure?

To design a test, you must know exactly what you want to measure. This is not a problem if you followed the procedure in Chapter 1, because you already know the specific learning objectives for your e-learning, lessons, and topics. Review the learning objective for the unit of content covered by the test. Chapter 6 on topics contains some advice on tests appropriate for specific types of learning objectives (p. 299).

Watch out for the "as-shown-above syndrome." Learners do not always start at the beginning of the e-learning and proceed straight through to the end. Learners may jump into the middle of a topic in the middle of a lesson in the middle of the e-learning. Many consider this their right. They will consider you unfair if you test them on material not found in the section supposedly covered by the test—or in a clearly identified prerequisite section.

Once you have decided why you are testing and what you hope to measure, you can make tactical decisions on what kind of test to use. Let's look closer at the decisions you must make.

SELECT THE RIGHT TYPE OF QUESTION

Any activity that can be scored by a computer or human can be a test question. For that reason, there are an unlimited number of test questions possible. In this section, we restrict ourselves to the types that are especially common in e-learning.

Throughout this chapter, I use the term *test question* rather than *test item*, even though some test items are not literally questions. Good test items at least imply a question. Anyway, it helps to think of test items as questions put to the learner.

Consider the type question you need

Before you decide to use a multiple-choice or matching-list question, take a moment to consider what kind of information you are trying to gather and what you are willing to do in order to get this information.

Subjective or objective?

Questions can be subjective or objective. *Subjective* test questions require human judgment to evaluate. They are sometimes called *open-response* questions because the exact form of the response is up to the learner. A composition question is an example of a subjective test question. Subjective questions are good for subjects without clear categories and ones that require finesse and judgment. Subjective questions usually require a human being to evaluate the answer and provide feedback. Subjective questions are limited to instructor-led e-learning.

Objective questions are ones with clear standards for correctness. They are sometimes called *closed-response* questions because the learner must select an answer from choices provided by the designer. Multiple-choice questions are objective. Objective questions are easily scored by computer. Objective questions are good for mature subjects with established categories and well-accepted practices and principles. Objective questions can require subtle and sophisticated judgment, but they work best for questions with right-wrong answers.

Scored by computer or human?

Some types of test questions are easily scored by the computer. For example, multiple-choice, sequence, and matching item questions can be completely scored by the computer—as can simple fill-in-the-blank questions. Computer-scored questions make up in immediacy of feedback what they may lack in subtlety of evaluation.

More complex questions, such as text-entry questions that take more than a word or 2, may require human evaluation. Human evaluation can better handle questions asking for subtle judgments, complex reasoning, and expressions of attitude. They do, however, require a human evaluator with the time, skills, and sensitivity to evaluate answers. Feedback comes only after a delay for scoring.

Common types of test questions

You can use a variety of test questions. This section introduces the most popular types. It is weighted heavily toward simple ones that can be created by a variety of simple tools and that can be scored by the computer.

Type question	Example	Use to measure the learner's ability to:
True/False (p. 221)		Make categorical, either-or judgments.
Pick-one (p. 224)		Recognize the one correct answer in a list. To identify a member of a category or assign an item to a category.
Pick-multiple (p. 228)		Recognize multiple correct answers in a list. To recognize characteristics that apply to an object or concept.
Fill-in-the-blanks (p. 231)		Recall names, numbers, and other specific facts.
Matching-list (p. 234)		Identifying associations between items in 2 lists, as between events and their causes or terms and their definitions.
Sequence (p. 236)		Identify the order of items in a sequence, such as chronological order or a ranking scheme.
Composition (p. 238)		Create an original explanation, story, sketch, or other piece of work.
Performance (p. 242)		Perform a step of a procedure, typically in a simulation.

True/False questions

True/false questions require learners to decide between 2 alternatives, typically saying whether a statement is true or false.

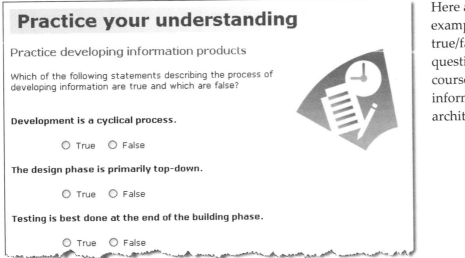

Here are examples of true/false questions from a course on information architecture.

When to use true/false questions

Use true/false questions to test learners' abilities to make definite judgments. True/false questions require learners to make a binary decision:

- ▶ Is a statement right or wrong?
- ▶ Will a procedure work or not?
- ▶ Is a procedure safe or unsafe?
- ▶ Does an example comply with standards?
- ▶ Should you approve or reject a proposal?
- ▶ Which of 2 alternatives should I pick?

Before using a true/false question, consider other types of questions as well. True/false questions are restricted to simple cases and may encourage guessing:

However, a well-designed true/false question that requires the same thought processes as the real-world activity is more accurate and valuable than a three-dimensional, immersive simulation that invokes only the decision-making skills of a twitch-and-splat videogame. And true/false questions are simple enough that learners can answer them quickly.

Questions need not have yes/no or true/false answers. Any mutually exclusive alternatives will do. Phrase the answer as a binary choice if that is more natural.

Watch out for cases in which the choices are not mutually exclusive or there really are more than 2 choices possible. Here is such a case:

The atmosphere of earth contains more gases than the 2 listed here. Although the percentage of nitrogen is more than that of other gases, the atmosphere does contain trace amounts of carbon dioxide.

Note: If your testing tool does not provide an explicit true/false test or if it does not let you change the labels for answers, use a pick-one question with just 2 answers. Or use a pick-multiple question that requires a series of related true/false judgments by asking, "Which of the following statements are true?" and then making each statement a choice.

Require thought

To make true/false tests effective, design them so they require thought rather than guessing.

▶ Ask more than one true/false question on a subject. The odds of getting them all right by guessing diminish with each additional question.

▶ For each subject, phrase true/false questions in different ways so that sometimes the right answer is false and other times it is true.

▶ Analyze your true/false questions to ensure about the same number are true as false.

▶ Phrase the question in neutral terms so you do not imply an answer.

Phrase the question to fit the answers

Make the question simple and straightforward. Do not ask what the learner thinks or feels or believes unless that is what you are testing.

No

Do you think that the following statement is true or false?

Yes

Is the following statement true or false?

Often a statement followed by true/false radio buttons provides sufficient instructions.

Portugal is a member of the European Union.

○ True ○ False

In true/false questions, phrase the question and answers so that the answers match the form of the question. Do not ask a yes/no question and then label the answers true/false.

No

Does granite contain biotite?

○ True ○ False

Granite contains biotite.

○ Yes ○ No

Yes

Does granite contain biotite?

○ Yes ○ No

Granite contains biotite.

○ True ○ False

Discourage guessing

Many learners guess on a true/false question, figuring they have a 50-50 chance of being right. Unless you are teaching a course in probability or gambling, you should discourage such behavior. You can discourage guessing in several ways:

▶ **Penalize guessing**. In scoring true/false questions, give 1 point for right answers, 0 points for unanswered questions, and –1 point for wrong answers. Thus guessing is no better or worse than not answering.

▶ **Require higher scores**. Statistics to the rescue! The odds of getting 5 of 10 true/false questions right by guessing are 50%. But the odds of getting 80% correct are only about 5%.

▶ **Ask more questions**. Increase the number of true/false questions to 20 and the odds of getting 80% right by guessing drop to less than 1%.

Consider alternative forms for true/false questions

Most true/false questions are formatted as a pair of radio buttons, but any form that clearly implies a choice between opposites or between just 2 alternatives will do.

Graphical alternatives

Here are some graphical alternatives that have been used, with appropriate labels, in true/false questions:

Pick-multiple test

A series of related true/false questions can be converted to a single pick-multiple question, for example:

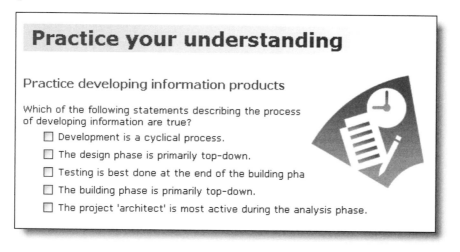

Pick-one questions

Multiple-choice questions display a list of answers for learners to choose from. There are 2 main types of multiple-choice questions: *pick-one* and *pick-multiple*. Pick-one questions ask the learner to pick just one answer from the list. Only one answer is correct.

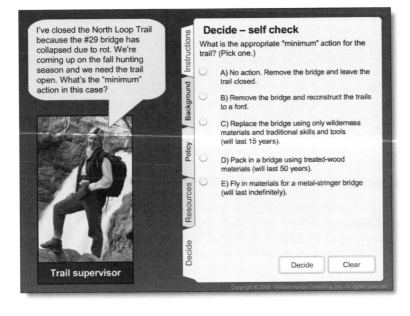

In this example from a course on wilderness management, learners are presented a scenario and asked the correct action to take in order to remedy the problem while complying with specific regulations.

Created in Microsoft PowerPoint. Test added using Adobe Breeze Presenter. Topic converted for Web delivery using Breeze Presenter. View example at horton.com/eld/.

When to use pick-one questions

Use the pick-one format for questions that have one right answer. They work well for activities that require people to assign items to well-defined categories, for instance:

▶ **Rating along a scale**. Ranking loan applications by degree of risk.

▶ **Recognizing a member of a specific category**. Picking the plant that is a member of a particular species.

▶ **Recognizing the main cause of a problem**. Diagnosing the most common cause of a flat tire.

▶ **Picking superlatives:** Picking the best, worst, greatest, least, highest, or lowest member of a group.

▶ **Selecting the best course of action.** Learners must weigh tradeoffs to choose among plausible actions.

Consider alternative forms for pick-one questions

Traditionally, pick-one questions present their answers as radio buttons and pick-multiple questions as checkboxes. Even if you need variety, do not reverse these forms. That would confuse learners. Instead, consider an alternative form.

Selection lists for multiple pick-one questions

If you want to ask several pick-one questions about a subject or if space is tight on the page, consider using a series of selection lists.

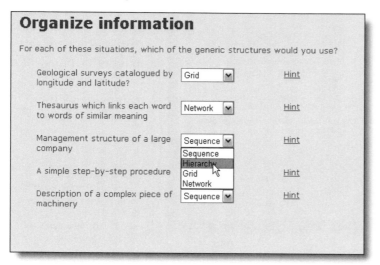

In this example, the selection-list format works especially well since all the questions have the same set of possible answers.

Built using HTML and custom JavaScript. View example at horton.com/eld/.

It does, however, mean that learners must know how to make a choice in a selection list. Most people figure out checkboxes and radio buttons on their own. Operating a selection list should be a problem only for the novices at filling in Web forms.

Click-in-picture questions for visual choices

If you want to let learners select among visual alternatives, you can present the choices as pictures and have learners indicate their choices by pointing and clicking. Because such questions are used primarily for visual subjects, they are treated as a separate type of question called a "click-in-picture" question.

Click-in-picture questions ask the learner to select an object or area in a picture by pointing to it with the mouse and clicking the mouse button. They are a visual equivalent of the pick-one question.

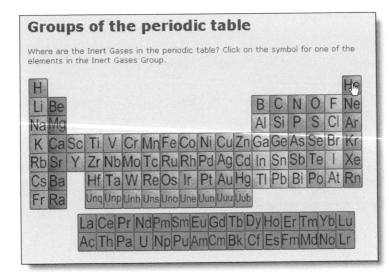

Groups of the periodic table

Where are the Inert Gases in the periodic table? Click on the symbol for one of the elements in the Inert Gases Group.

Here, learners are asked to identify a class of chemical elements by pointing to an area in the periodic table.

Built using HTML and custom JavaScript. View example at horton.com/eld/.

Use click-in-picture tests to measure visual recognition of objects or areas. Use them to ask questions such as these:

> What button would you press to trigger an emergency shutdown?
>
> Who in this picture is not wearing required safety gear?
>
> What country is home to our company's largest factory?
>
> Click on the flag of the province where Mandarin Chinese is the official language.

Use click-in-picture questions instead of text pick-one questions when it is more important that learners know where something is or what it looks like than what it is called.

For pick-in-picture questions, use clear images and write clear instructions.

▶ Explain exactly what learners are to select. An area? An object? A point on a scale?

▶ **Make targets visually distinct**. Make them visually separate objects or areas with distinct borders.

▶ **Make targets large enough** so that learners with only average eye-hand coordination can quickly select them. Make targets at least 20 by 20 pixels as a minimum size.

▶ **Show the scene the way it would appear in the real world**, if simulating real-world activities, such as pushing buttons on a control panel.

Select along a scale for value judgments

To ask learners to express a relative value, you can request that learners select along a well-understood scale. For example, in a chemistry lesson you might ask:

Where along this scale of pH values would you rate hydrochloric acid? (Click on a value.)

← Increasing acidity ——————— Neutral ——————— Increasing alkalinity →

0 1 2 3 4 5 6 7 8 9 10 11 12 13 14

The learner can select a position along the scale by:

▶ Clicking on the scale (as in this example).

▶ Moving a sliding icon to a position along the scale.

▶ Entering a number corresponding to a position along the scale.

▶ Selecting from defined positions along the scale.

For scales where the learner must pick a position, include an odd-number of choices. This provides a neutral position so learners are not forced into a position. The neutral position removes the implication that the learner must make an either-or choice. And the neutral choice makes the question appear more objective.

Keep scale intervals equal and meaningful. It is usually OK to round numbers if that is how learners are accustomed to seeing the scale.

Pick-multiple questions

Pick-multiple questions let the learner pick one or more answers from a list of possible answers.

In the <u>storage shed plan</u>, what tasks depend directly on Task 7: Pour the driveway? (Pick all the apply.)

☐ Task 4: Prepare site
☐ Task 5: Pour slab
☐ Task 6 Remove driveway
☐ Task 8: Frame the structure
☐ Task 9: Roof the structure.

In this example, the learner can pick all answers that are correct.

When to use pick-multiple questions

Use pick-multiple questions for asking questions with more than one right answer. Pick-multiple questions can be more sophisticated than pick-one or true/false questions. Pick-multiple questions require making a series of related judgments. For instance:

▸ Picking items that meet a criterion.

▸ Deciding when a rule applies.

▸ Making a quick series of yes-no decisions.

▸ Picking examples or non-examples of a principle.

Use a pick-multiple question to discourage guessing. The odds of guessing correctly are much less when the learner must select a specific combination of items.

Type question	Odds of guessing correctly
True/False	1:2
Pick 1 of 4	1:4
Pick 1 of 5	1:5
Pick multiple of 4	1:16
Pick multiple of 5	1:32

Each additional answer in the pick-multiple list reduces the odds of guessing the correct combination by half.

Pick-multiple questions are a compact way to ask several related true/false questions.

What are the characteristics of fluorite?
(Select all true statements.)

☐ Fluorite is colorless in its pure state.

☐ Fluroite has a hardness of 5 to 5.5 on the Mohs scale.

☐ The United States is the world's largest commercial producer of fluorite.

☐ Fluorite has a monoclinic crystal structure.

☐ The formula for pure fluorite is CaF_2.

This example asks 5 true/false questions. The point value of this question would of course be higher than 5 individual true/false questions to reflect the difficulty of getting all of them right.

Consider alternative forms for pick-multiple question

Here are some alternatives that you may want to try.

Graphical pick-multiple questions

Let learners select items by clicking on them in a picture.

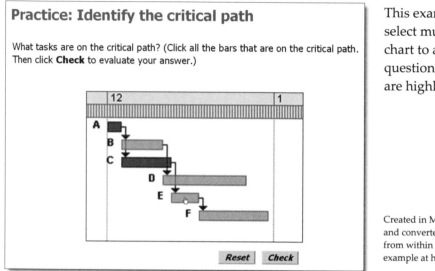

Practice: Identify the critical path

What tasks are on the critical path? (Click all the bars that are on the critical path. Then click **Check** to evaluate your answer.)

Reset   Check

This example has learners select multiple bars on a chart to answer the question. Selected bars are highlighted.

Created in Microsoft PowerPoint and converted for Web delivery from within PowerPoint. View example at horton.com/eld/.

Use click-in-picture tests to measure visual recognition of objects or areas. Use them to ask questions such as these:

> In what countries on this map does our company have sales offices?
>
> What items are allowed in carry-on luggage?
>
> What elements in the periodic table were discovered by Marie Curie?

Use graphical pick-multiple questions when it is more important that learners know where objects and areas are or what they look like.

Use clear images and write clear instructions.

▶ **Explain exactly what learners are to select**. Areas, objects, a range along a scale? Refer to the graphic ("on the map").

▶ **Make targets visually distinct**. Make them visually separate objects or areas with distinct borders.

▶ **Make targets large enough** so that learners with only average eye-hand coordination can quickly select them. Make targets at least 20 by 20 pixels as a minimum size.

If your tool does not offer a pick-multiple question

If your testing tool does not include a pick-multiple test question, you may be able to ask the same type question as a series of true/false questions. Each choice of the pick-multiple question becomes a true/false question.

Fill-in-the-blanks questions

Fill-in-the-blanks questions require learners to type in the answer to a question. Typically, these are short answers to very specific questions.

> **Question 1:**
>
> In the <u>storage shed plan</u>, how many calendar days does it take to frame the structure (Task 8)?
>
> 7

In this example, learners type in the number of days.

Fill-in-the-blanks questions require learners to supply missing words or numbers. The blank can occur within a sentence or at the end of a question. Multiple blanks can be sprinkled through a paragraph of text or across a table.

When to use fill-in-the-blanks questions

Use fill-in-the-blanks questions to verify that learners have truly learned the names of things. Use them to test recall of:

▶ Technical or business terms.

▶ Part numbers.

▶ Abbreviations.

▶ Commands and statements in a programming language.

▶ Vocabulary in a foreign language.

How to design a fill-in-the-blanks question

The most difficult aspect of designing fill-in-the-blanks questions is phrasing the question so that the computer can evaluate the answer.

▶ Make sure the context provides enough clues so that the learner can fill in the blank. Ensure that the introduction and context make clear exactly what is requested. One way to do this is to put the blank after a clearly phrased question rather than within a vague statement. Test your questions.

▶ Phrase the question to limit the number of correct answers. If possible, write the question so only one answer is correct.

▶ Phrase the question so that the answer can be evaluated based on the presence or absence of specific words or phrases, but not on the exact order or syntax of the answer.

▶ Accept synonyms (other words with the same meaning), grammatical variants, and common misspellings. Watch out for differences between British and American and Canadian and Australian English.

▶ Tell learners how to phrase their answers. Give an example of a properly phrased answer. Make clear whether the answer is to be text or numbers or mixed.

▶ If the question is complex, break it into separate questions, each with a simple answer. Do not ask 2 questions to be answered in one input box.

▶ Tell the learner the length, format, required parts, and other constraints on a free-form input. If you do not state a length, most learners will assume they can fill the input box.

Although automatic scoring of free-form text is not practical in most cases, you can write your question so that the completeness can be evaluated. For example, if you ask learners to compare various gemstones, the system could scan the learner's answer for the names of gemstones ("ruby," "diamond," "opal," and so forth) and for characteristics ("color," "hardness," and so forth).

Where possible, validate the form of the input right on the page before evaluating whether it is the correct answer or not. By "validate" I mean check for small mistakes that do not indicate subject-matter knowledge. For example, suppose you ask for a number. An engineer would probably not enter "One hundred ten," but you cannot be sure. A validation check examines the input to determine whether it is a number or text. If the input is not a number, the validation check throws up a caution and invites the learner to correct the form of the input.

Cloze questions

Questions with multiple blanks are sometimes called *cloze* questions. Such questions have been used for hundreds of years and are a staple of education.

Here is a classic example used to test knowledge of French grammar, syntax, and spelling.

> **Enter the correct feminine and masculine articles.**
>
> La salle a manger est- elle plus grande que la cuisine? Non, elle plus petite que la cuisine.

Cloze questions work just like the paper workbooks in which students have to write their answers. With the e-learning version, learners fill in their answers by typing or by picking from selection lists.

5

Tests

This example uses selection lists from which learners pick words in a programming language to complete a function.

This function returns the screen coordinates for an object on a Web page, taking into account the location of the Web page, the scrolling zone, and the HTML container the object is inside of. Complete this function by selecting the appropriate Internet Explorer 5 properties from the select lists.

```
function agtGetCoordinates(theObject, XorY) {
    var parentElement = theObject
    var offsetsX = 0
    var offsetsY = 0
    while (parentElement. [tagName ▼] != "BODY") {
        parentElement = parentElement.offsetParent
        offsetsX += parentElement. [offsetLeft ▼] + parentElement.clientLeft
        offsetsY += parentElement. [offsetTop ▼] + parentElement.clientTop
    }
    elementX = window. [screenLeft ▼] + theObject. [Pick one ▼]
        + document.body. [Pick one ▼] + offsets
        elementY = window. [Pick one ▼] + theObject.
        + document.body. [Pick one ▼] + offsets
    XorY = XorY.toLowerCase()
    if (XorY == "x") {
        return elementX
    } else {
        return elementY
    }
}
```

Pick one
tagName
offsetLeft
clientLeft
offsetTop
clientTop
screenLeft
screenTop
scrollLeft
scrollTop

Built in HTML and custom JavaScript. View example at horton.com/eld/.

As you can see, a cloze question is really just a tightly integrated series of fill-in-the-blanks or multiple-choice questions.

When to use cloze questions

Use cloze questions to measure learners' ability to apply knowledge within the context of a specific problem. Learners use a partial answer to figure out the complete answer. Use cloze questions:

▶ **To test incremental knowledge**. Learners know part of a subject and apply what they know to infer answers.

▶ **Where context matters**. Learners infer the correct answer from surrounding text or code.

▶ **To measure ability to apply verbal knowledge in context**. Learners guess the right words from the words that come before it and the words that follow it.

▶ **To ask complex questions.** Learners answer questions with multiple interrelated parts.

▶ **To provide scaffolding.** The context provides the support learners need early in learning a subject. Learners need not have mastered the knowledge supplied by the context.

How to design cloze questions

Make filling in the blanks simple and predictable so learners focus on answering the question.

▶ **Introduce the context.** Explain where the incomplete sample comes from and what it attempts to accomplish. For example, "Here is a paragraph from a Russian tour guide suggesting sights to see on your first day in St. Petersburg."

▶ **Explain the goal.** Tell learners what criteria they should use to fill in the blanks. For example, "Pick words that turn the paragraph into a concise summary of ...."

▶ **Use a selection list** to let learners pick among several plausible alternatives if there are too many possible right answers.

Matching-list questions

Matching-list questions require learners to specify which items in one list correspond to items in another.

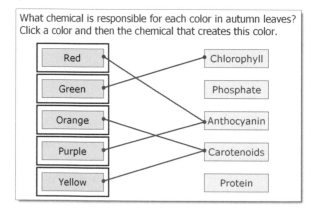

In this example, the learner chooses chemicals responsible for the respective colors of autumn leaves.

Created in Microsoft PowerPoint and converted for Web delivery from within PowerPoint. View example at horton.com/eld/.

The lists need not be formatted as stacked lists of words. You can require learners to move icons or images to corresponding locations on the screen.

In this example, learners must drag elements of a Gantt chart into place to represent relationships among tasks of a project. Such drag-and-drop questions test the ability to assign items to the correct category or to arrange the parts of a system into a whole.

Built using Adobe Dreamweaver. View example at horton.com/eld/.

When to use matching-item questions

Use matching-item questions to measure knowledge of the relationships among concepts, objects, and components.

Use them to match:	With:
Questions	Answers
Terms	Definitions
Pictures	Captions
People	Titles or accomplishments
Tools	Their uses
Diseases	Symptoms or cures
Parts of one whole	Locations within the whole
Items	Their categories, their rankings along a scale, or their opposites

How to design matching-item questions

Make matching easy so that learners can focus their attention on the relationships between items in the 2 lists.

▶ **Write list items clearly.** Use familiar terms or provide a glossary for the learner to look up terms.

▶ **Keep the lists short so that they both fit in the same display.** If they do not fit, give the learner a button to jump back and forth. Generally 7 items are plenty.

▶ **Do not mix categories within a list.** Include only comparable items in each list.

▶ **Let learners indicate matches simply.** Rather than having them type the letter or number of the matching item, let them select it from a list of choices, drag it from one list to another, or draw lines between items.

▶ **Eliminate the "process-of-elimination" effect** by including more items in one list than the other, by letting one item match more than one item in the other list, or by letting learners choose "None" if an item has no match in the opposite list. In instructions, tell learners of these possibilities.

Sequence-type questions

Sequence questions ask learners to put items into a sequence from beginning to end by some rule or according to some principle. Learners are presented with a list of items in an incorrect order. They must move the items to put the items into the right relative positions within the list.

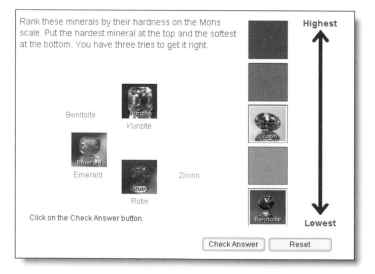

This example asks learners about the relative hardness for 5 minerals. Learners drag pictures of the minerals into the appropriate slot before clicking the **Check Answer** button to see which items are in their correct positions.

Built using Adobe Flash Learning Interactions. View example at horton.com/eld/.

When to use sequence questions

Use sequence questions to measure learners' ability to put items into a meaningful order. They ask learners to make judgments about the relationships among items in the list. Use sequence questions to test a learners' ability to sequence:

▶ Historical events by date.

▶ Steps of a procedure by order performed.

▶ Phases of a process by the order in which they occur.

▶ Logical arguments in inductive or deductive order.

▶ Innovations by a chain of dependencies.

▶ Rankings of value.

▶ Properties of objects, such as size, weight, or importance.

▶ Remedies by probability of success.

▶ Diagnoses of symptoms by probability.

Sequence questions are also valuable in polling, especially for subjective questions, such as value.

Communicate the desired sequence clearly

Make the sequence activity clear, simple, and fair.

▶ **Do not use sequence questions if there is more than one right sequence**. Even if your scoring procedure would accept all correct answers, learners may still feel the question is unfair. In general, avoid sequence questions when the sequence is subjective.

▶ **Use only distinct items familiar to learners**. Do not require learners to guess what items mean or conduct research during the test.

▶ **Specify the criterion for the sequence**. For instance, specify ("in chronological order"). Also specify the direction of the sequence ("from earliest to latest dates").

▶ **Specify only one criterion for the sequence**. Avoid complex criteria, such as "by primary and secondary constituents" or "by technology and then by year developed."

Score fairly

Ensure fair scoring of sequence questions. Simple scoring can be a problem. The nature of the sequencing task means that one item out of place can render the answer incorrect, even though the learner knew the relative positions of all other items.

Such strict scoring may be appropriate if the question is about steps in an emergency procedure. In other cases, it may unfairly penalize the almost-right answer. Some solutions:

▶ Give partial scores for items near their correct location.

▶ Score each item individually so the ones in correct final position win some points.

▶ Use sequence test questions for practice when scores are not recorded.

Consider alternative forms for sequence questions

If your testing tool does not provide a sequence question (and many don't), consider asking the question in some other form:

▶ Use a matching-item question to match items with their positions in the sequence.

▶ Number the items in a list and have learners enter the numbers of the items into a fill-in-the-blanks question.

Composition questions

Composition questions ask learners to write an essay, draw a picture, or write a song. They ask for an original analysis, opinion, or other piece of work. Composition questions are just scored original-work activities (p. 206). By far, the most common form is the essay question, but other media can be submitted as well.

Tang Dynasty ceramics

Write a 300- to 500-word essay describing Tang Dynasty ceramics.

[Type your essay here.]

Submit

This example asks for short, free-form answers.

Built using HTML.

Composition questions are most commonly used in instructor-led e-learning. They ask subjective or open-response questions. They require human evaluation.

When to use composition questions

Use composition questions to evaluate complex knowledge, higher-order skills, and creativity. Typical uses include questions that require learners to:

▶ Synthesize an original solution to a problem.

▶ Recognize and express complex or subtle relationships.

▶ Analyze a complex object or situation.

▶ Form and justify an opinion by weighing evidence.

▶ Resolve conflicting opinions and contrary evidence.

Do not use composition questions when answering them would place too much of a physical burden on learners. For example, entering long amounts of text on a mobile device without a keyboard would prompt learners to be unnaturally brief, to use extreme abbreviations, or just to skip the question altogether. Better to substitute another type of question that can be answered more easily.

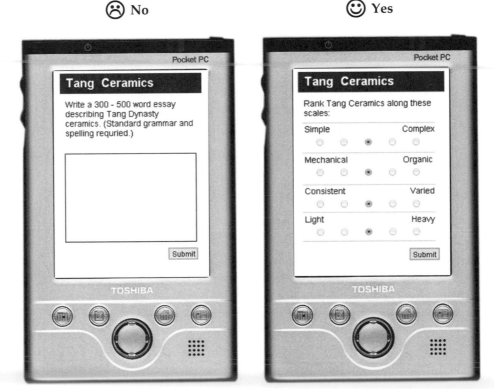

Built using Adobe Flash.

Designing composition questions

▶ **Require breadth and depth in answers.** Ask questions that require considering more than one aspect of the subject and going beyond surface details.

▶ **Require original thinking.** Do not reward "parroting" material from the course, instructor, textbook, or other sources.

▶ **Disallow copy-and-paste responses.** Do not let learners include the words or other works of others as answers, except as clearly identified quotations or examples. And require an original explanation of why the item was included and how it supports the learner's original answer.

▶ **Let learners respond in the medium of their choice.** If the subject is writing, it makes sense to require a written response. However, if the subject is business, let learners submit their answers as a voice recording, a PowerPoint slide, or a video clip.

▶ **Be specific.** Do not say "List a solution" when you mean "Explain the least-expensive solution." Precise questions filter out trivial or obscure answers. Mention any constraints on the answer. Tell learners the requirements for a good answer.

▶ **Guide responses.** Give learners a model or template for structuring their response. The problem with many open-response questions is that they are too open.

▶ **Limit the number of composition questions.** They are tiring. After about a half-dozen such questions, all you are measuring is stamina.

Scoring composition questions

Write specific scoring guidelines (commonly called *rubrics*) to guide instructors in scoring answers and providing feedback. In such scoring guidelines, specify objective requirements for an acceptable answer:

▶ Characteristics of the answer. Length. Format.

▶ Items it must include. Facts it must mention. Media it must use.

▶ Relationships among items.

▶ Conclusions the learner should draw.

▶ Recommendations it should make.

List examples of ways the learner may answer the question. Include both right and wrong answers, along with the feedback each should trigger. List signs of common mistakes, such as incorrect statements or items often omitted.

Here is part of a rubric for an assignment in a management course. It helps the facilitator evaluate learners' responses.

Assignment 2.2	Grading criteria

• If learners list the skills and talents needed to build, promote, and *deploy*, make sure they include:
  b. technical support
  c. subject-matter experts
  d. facilitators
  e. administrators
 	
These positions are clearly listed in Table 10-1 of *Leading E-learning*. Failure to do so indicates that they are not looking beyond the development phase and have lost sight of the fact that this plan includes deployment.
 	
• If learners recommend staffing levels, they need to justify their numbers. AND make sure that this section is consistent with the previous section on skills needed.
 	
• For outsourcing, make sure they justify why or why not. Why should e-learning be or not be a core competence?
	If learners identify and address all three points—the missing skills, justifying their staffing recommendations, and making a persuasive argument about whether to outsource or not— they get an A. If the writing is clear and well-structured, give them an A+.
	
	If they identify and address two out of the three issues, give them somewhere between an A- and a B-.
	
	If they identify and address only one of the three issues, give them a C.
	
	If they take a whole different approach, make sure they explain it. You will have to make a judgment call whether the new approach will work or not. You need to be careful not to stifle their creativity.
	
	Add or subtract points either way to reflect the quality of their answers.
	
	If you feel that some learners just got off to a bad start, you can be a bit more lenient in the grading. Quite frankly, it is a judgment call.

Writing such rubrics is basic instructional design—and it is hard work. It is essential if the composition will scored by someone other than the author of the course. That is true whether the course is offered in a classroom, online, or by some other method. Such objective guidelines are especially important in e-learning because anxious learners may be hyper-sensitive to test scores and they may expect computer-like objectivity in every aspect of the course.

Alternative forms for composition questions

Essay questions are not the only possible form of a composition question. Consider including a button to let learners record a voice answer or upload a recorded audio file. Or a similar button to record an answer from a video camera. Or require learners to create their compositions using a template you supply. You might have them download, fill in, and submit PowerPoint or Word template placeholders for required elements of the composition.

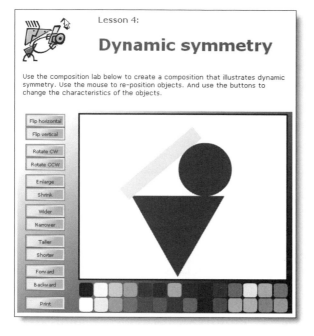

In this example, the learner must drag and drop and flip and flop shapes to create an abstract visual composition that meets a design goal.

To see another example, visit www.wildlifeart.org/Rungius/home.html.

Built using Adobe Flash and Dreamweaver. View example at horton.com/eld/.

Performance questions

Performance tests require the learner to perform actual work. Each step of the work that can be scored individually serves as a separate test question.

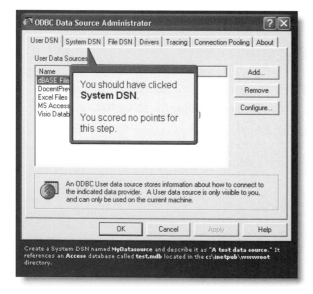

In this test, the learner performs the steps to create a system data source name in a simulation. Each step of the simulation is scored. Because the learner did not perform this step correctly, a message is displayed telling the learner that no points were scored for that step and telling the learner how to proceed to the next step.

Built using Adobe Captivate. View example at horton.com/eld/.

Performance questions measure learners' abilities to perform complex activities. If learners accomplish the assigned task in the performance test, they pass and can presumably perform the real activity.

When to use performance questions

Performance questions help us test whether someone can perform a task. When should you use them?

▶ You are testing the ability to perform a procedure rather than abstract knowledge about a subject.

▶ The procedure is complex; requiring learners to make decisions, not merely follow a sequence of steps.

▶ The speed of performing the task is important to its success.

▶ You are qualifying people to perform a task in the real world.

Performance questions are not limited to tasks that are performed on the computer. You can use "gatekeeper tasks" (p. 113) as performance questions to verify that learners have successfully performed a step in a non-computer task.

Performance test questions that require simulation can be expensive and time-consuming to develop—typically 100 times the cost of a simple multiple-choice test question. Often they are worth the expense, but not always. Use simulations for performance questions when:

▶ Other types of test questions cannot adequately measure performance.

▶ Having learners perform the task on a real system could be dangerous.

▶ Using a simulation simplifies scoring the activity and integrating it with other types of test questions.

How to design performance questions

Simplify the test. A performance test should measure ability to perform a task, but not teach that task. Do not expose the learners to more choices and options than necessary to test for the target objective.

State the goal clearly. Tell learners exactly what they must accomplish to pass the test. Spell out any restrictions. Must they accomplish the goal using a particular method or feature? How long can they take?

Explain the question. Make sure learners know how to answer performance questions. If they must operate a simulation, tell them what buttons they can press, what knobs they can turn, and what switches they can flip.

Reveal the limits. No performance question or test is a perfect copy of the real-world task. How does the test differ from the real world? What are the limits on actions learners can take? If using a simulator, tell learners what dangerous aspects of the real system are harmless in the simulator and what features and capabilities are turned off.

Spell out scoring rules. If the test is not graded pass/fail, spell out the criteria for awarding points. Are learners rewarded for the quantity of work accomplished? Are they penalized for the amount of time they took, the number of actions used, or minor mistakes made along the way?

WRITE EFFECTIVE QUESTIONS

To test learning, you must translate your learning objectives into test questions. Nowhere is precise, clear language more necessary. Questions are effective only if all learners understand them and can answer them the way you intended.

Follow the standard question format

Although many different types of test questions are possible, they share a common anatomy. Here is a typical test question with its parts labeled.

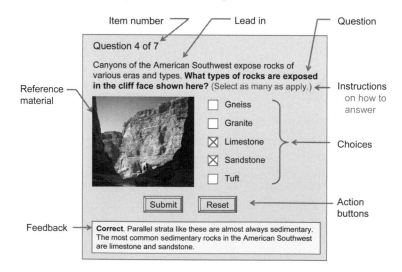

Let's look at the parts of a typical question and how to design them.

Part	Description
Item number	Indicates the place of this question in sequence. For long tests and timed tests, the number helps learners budget their time. It gives them a sense of progress as they move through the test.
Lead-in	Provides background information or context for the actual question. Use a lead-in to keep the actual question simple. A lead-in can be necessary if questions appear in random order or are chosen from a pool. The lead-in makes the question more independent of other questions.
Question	The question is the specific sentence the learner must respond to. Usually it is phrased simply as a question. For more on questions, look through the rest of this chapter, especially the segment starting at page 244.
Instructions	Instructions tell the learner the procedure for answering the question and any limits on how the question may be answered, for example, how many items should be selected or how many words can be entered. Learn more about instructions starting on page 247.
Choices	True/false, pick-one, and pick-multiple questions have learners select their answer from a list of choices. See the segment starting on page 254 for advice on designing choices for test questions.
Action buttons	Learners must signal that they are ready for their answers to be evaluated. Most often this is done by clicking a button such as **Submit**, **Evaluate**, or **Next question**. The learner may have other buttons to erase the current answer, return to the previous question, or exit the test. The exact labels are not as important as picking words that communicate clearly to the learners what will happen when they click the button.
Feedback	Feedback may be presented after each question or at the end of the test. If feedback is presented with each question, it may appear in an area below the question or in a pop-up window. The feedback can range from "Correct" or "Incorrect" to complete explanations of the answer and links back to related content. For aiding learning, meaningful feedback is crucial. See the section starting on page 262 for advice on giving feedback.

Ask questions simply and directly

Simple questions are easier to understand, to answer, and to score. Direct questions seem more objective and fair to learners.

Phrase questions precisely and clearly

Unless learners can understand the question, they cannot answer it. The difference between a clear and an unclear question may be just a single word or punctuation mark. Take a little extra time to make sure your questions ask what you want them to.

Use the simplest language possible. Tests put learners under stress. Those learners may have varying language skills. Some may be taking the test in a second language or may suffer from reading difficulties such as dyslexia. Use of language not understood by all can even pose a legal problem if it penalizes certain groups relative to others.

Phrase questions as questions

If possible, phrase the test question as a simple, standard question. Use the canonical question format:

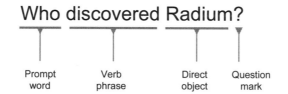

This is the form familiar to young children and new speakers of English. (If you are writing questions in another language, just use the standard format for questions in that language.)

The prompt word alerts the learner immediately that this is a question, and the question mark confirms it. No question about it: this is a question.

The prompt word announces that this is a question and specifies the type of answer requested. We are all familiar with Rudyard Kipling's 6 honest serving men: what, who, when, where, why, and how. Use them like this:

Use	To ask for
What	An object, process, or event.
Who	A person or a group.
When	A time, date, or place in sequence.

Use	To ask for
Where	A location.
Why	A reason, cause, or justification.
How	A procedure or process.

These are sufficient for 90% of the questions we ask. And no, I didn't forget *which* ....
Which is usually inferior to *what* in asking test questions. Do not ask "Which of the following is ...?" when you could ask "What is ...?"

Put background information before the question

Do not supply new information in a question. For complex questions, supply background information in a lead-in to the question. Phrase the lead-in as simple declarative sentences.

 No   Yes

How is the tropical disease known as dengue (breakbone fever or dandy fever) and characterized by acute fever, chill, headaches, muscular and joint pain, and skin eruption, transmitted?

Dengue is a tropical disease. It is also known as breakbone fever and dandy fever. Its symptoms include acute fever, chill, headaches, muscular and joint pain, and skin eruption. **How is dengue transmitted?**

Sometimes after moving the background information to the lead-in, you discover it is not necessary. Then delete it. Many times, however, background information is necessary to clarify the context of the question or fully identify a term in the question.

Include instructions on how to answer

If learners might not know how to indicate their answers, put instructions immediately after the question proper. For example:

> What chemicals are responsible for leaf colors? (Drag each chemical over the color it produces.)

Where might such instructions be necessary?

▶ In pick-multiple questions to tell learners they can pick more than one answer.

▶ If not picking any answer is an option.

▶ In a drag-and-drop activity wherein learners might not know that objects are movable.

▶ In fill-in-the-blanks or essay questions when spelling, punctuation, and capitalization matter.

Ask yourself whether 95% of your learners will figure out how to answer the question without any instructions. If not, add instructions.

Phrase questions and answers simply

To ask questions that all learners will interpret exactly as you intended, just use language as simply and directly as possible.

KISS—Keep It Simple for Students

The challenge in a test should be answering the questions, not interpreting them. Tricky wording is a special problem for anxious and impatient readers—especially ones reading in a second language.

▶ Stick to simple sentences. Avoid complex sentences with embedded clauses.

▶ Use standard spelling and punctuation. Begin each choice with a capital letter and end it with a period.

▶ Use common terms familiar to the learner. Provide a glossary for any technical terms you must use.

▶ Use blank space to distinguish questions, instructions, choices, and action buttons.

▶ Keep questions short; say no more than 10 or 12 words. Include only necessary words.

▶ Phrase choices so they match answers the learner may recall when reading the question.

▶ Keep choices short—a single line if possible.

▶ In negative test questions, emphasize the word **NOT** or its equivalent.

Remove ambiguity

Take special care to avoid ambiguous language in questions and answers. Some common problems include these:

▶ **Ambiguous terms**, such as "can not," which could mean "possibly not" or "not possible."

▶ **Fancy words** that not all learners will recognize. If a simpler word works, use it. Do not try to show off your vocabulary.

▶ **Double negatives**, such as "When should you not reject …?" If possible, ask the question in the positive sense, such as "When should you accept …?" At least untangle the logic. If you can ask a question in a positive form, do so. If you cannot, keep the form simple and emphasize the negative word.

▶ **Indefinite questions**, such as "Do you think that 3 + 5 is 7?" Is the question about mathematics or opinion? Take special care with phrases like "Does it seem that …?" or "Does it appear that …?"

▶ **Unrecognized humor.** Learners may take a humorous comment literally or be annoyed by your casual attitude to what to them is a nerve-wracking experience.

▶ **Metaphors, irony, or other figures of speech** that are unfamiliar to learners. Many such expressions are specific to a particular culture or language. Consider this question: "What military commander pulled a hail Mary on the day after Christmas 1776?" Answering depends on knowledge of a sports metaphor based on the name of a prayer.

Ask just one question at a time

Phrase questions so that only one answer is required. Do not ask or imply a second question, as does this shameful example:

This example asks 2 questions. The first asks how to cut heating costs and the second asks what component wastes energy.

Rephrase the question to something like this:

Your best customer wants to cut heating costs. What feature of the ThermoKAV would you disable?

○ Instant-on
○ Heat boost
○ Precision thermostat
○ Humidifier option
○ Particulate filter

Now the example asks a single question.

One form of compound question is useful, but it must be designed with care. This is the what-and-why question. It asks learners to pick an answer and the reason why it is the best answer.

You are photographing an automobile race. What exposure mode should you select?

- ○ Shutter-priority mode so you can avoid motion blur.
- ○ Aperture-priority mode so you can control the depth of field.
- ○ Aperture-priority mode so you can capture more saturated colors.
- ○ Programmed mode because it is the most flexible.
- ○ Shutter-priority mode so glints do not fool the light meter.

This example asks not only for the correct choice but for the correct reason as well.

Use this form for subjects where the real-world answer to questions often is "It depends." Phrase the question clearly, and make sure every choice has both the what and why parts. Set up a pattern among choices and stick to the pattern.

Emphasize important words

In phrasing questions, emphasize small crucial words on which the meaning of the question depends—words that could cause the learner to misinterpret the question if not read correctly. Here is an example:

> What items is *not* an example of romdibulation?

Usually the most critical words are reversing or constraining words: *not, only, just, one, first, last,* and so forth. Emphasize the word, but not by underlining it, as learners are likely to interpret underlined words as hypertext links.

Ask application-related questions

Phrase your questions so that they resemble the kinds of decisions learners will have to make when applying the knowledge and skills you are teaching. Phrase questions so they re-create what would actually occur on a job. Here are some suggestions:

Set the scene

Set the scene using questions that might come from a customer, the boss, a subordinate, an angry co-worker, or a friend.

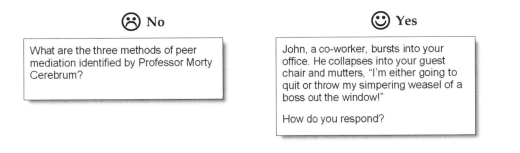

If you cannot imagine the question being asked in the real world, then why are you asking it in a test?

To ensure you are asking more application-related questions:

▶ Base your questions on performance objectives rather than enabling objectives (p. 14).

▶ Put the learner into the question. Present a situation and ask, "What would you do?"

▶ Ask questions that are more life-like in what they require the learner to decide or do, even if this means asking fewer questions.

▶ Establish a realistic scenario, introduce a problem, and then ask several questions about that problem.

Ask in the mode of application

Test-writers tend to ask questions verbally. This may be OK for learners who are verbal, but it is not fair for those with limited language skills. Nor is it accurate for tasks performed visually or physically.

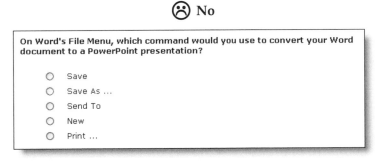

☺ **Yes**

Select the command to convert your Word document to a PowerPoint presentation:

The pick-one question above uses words to ask for knowledge about a task performed visually and kinetically. The simulation mimics the real situation and requires exactly the same abilities as does the real task.

Match the type of test question to the way knowledge and skills will be applied after learning:

How applied	Type test question
Verbally	Text questions, such as pick-multiple, pick-one, or fill-in-the-blank.
By locating something	Click-in-picture question (p. 226).
Software task	Simulation of performing the task.
Physical task.	Performing the task and then answering a *gatekeeper* question about the results (p. 113).
Making yes-no decisions	True/false question based on information used to make the decision.

Avoid common mistakes

Inexperienced test-writers often write questions they later regret. Let's review some common mistakes and see how to avoid them.

Prevent obsolescence

Avoid questions whose answers may change over time. In rapidly changing fields, new developments or a new version of software can change the answer to such questions.

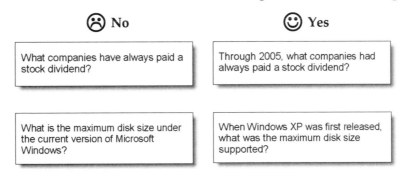

Be careful when asking absolute questions

Absolute questions assume rigid categories with razor-sharp boundaries. Beware questions like these:

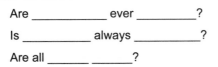

A single exception changes the answer. Learners can be quite clever in tracking down that one obscure, minor, nearly unknown exception you forgot about.

Avoid absolute words in questions and answers. Absolute words include *all, every, entirely, everybody, completely, altogether, always, exactly, no, none, never,* and *nobody.* Also take care with extreme words such as *most, almost, nearly, barely,* and *hardly.*

Avoid "all of the above" and "none of the above"

Take special care with answers of the form "all of the above" or "none of the above."

> **PDQ Corporation offers hourly employees which of these benefits?**
>
> ☐ Medical
> ☐ Prescription
> ☐ Dental
> ☐ Optical
> ☐ None of the above
> ☐ All of the above

Do you see the Escheresque logic in this question? Right. For "All of the above" to be true, "None of the above" must also be true. But if "None of the above" is true, then "All of the above" cannot be true. No combination of answers is logically possible.

In pick-one questions, an "all of the above" choice violates the form of the question, suddenly shifting from pick-one to pick-multiple. "All of the above" is also grammatically inconsistent with the form of the question. Instead of including an "all of the above" choice, simply change the question style to a pick-multiple.

In general, forego "none of the above" and "all of the above" as choices. But if you do use "none of the above" and "all of the above" answers:

▶ Always make "None of the above" the last choice.

▶ Do not use these choices just to fill out a list of choices. Try to think of more plausible answers.

▶ Remember to turn off the randomize-answers feature of your test tool as it could put these choices anywhere in the list.

Make answering straightforward

Multiple-choice tests are simple to construct but may encourage learners to guess rather than think about the answer. Also, by listing incorrect answers, multiple-choice tests may cause learners to remember the wrong answers rather than the right ones. To avoid these problems, encourage learners to think carefully about their answers. Make sure learners understand all their choices in pick-multiple, pick-one, and true/false questions.

Make all choices plausible

Make all answers equally plausible to someone who has not yet learned the subject. Make each choice a natural response to the question. To test the plausibility of each choice, read aloud the question, immediately followed by the answer. To be plausible, all choices should be equivalent in length, grammar and syntax, complexity, specificity, and scope.

Keep all answers about the same length

Make all answers approximately the same length. Or at least make sure that the longest answer is not always the right one. Guess which of these answers is right:

> **A customer asks to speak to a supervisor. What do you say?**
>
> ○ Are you sure?
> ○ No, I think I can help you.
> ○ Certainly. I'll page one if you'd like. It'll take
>   a couple of minutes. But first, why don't you
>   let me see if I can solve your problem.
> ○ Good luck finding one.

Make all choices grammatically equivalent

Make all choices grammatically similar. Double-check that each answer is compatible with the question, especially if the answers are offered as potential completions of a lead-in phrase.

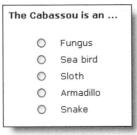

> **The Cabassou is an ...**
>
> ○ Fungus
> ○ Sea bird
> ○ Sloth
> ○ Armadillo
> ○ Snake

Can you spot the not-too-subtle hint in this example?

Yes, Armadillo is the only grammatically correct answer. To correct this problem, simply rephrase the question something like this: What is a Cabassou?

Make choices parallel

Phrase all answers at the same level of abstraction, generality, and degree of common usage.

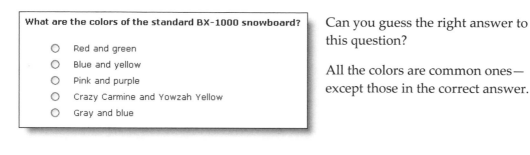

Can you guess the right answer to this question?

All the colors are common ones—except those in the correct answer.

Simplify selecting answers

Reduce the effort required to indicate the correct answer. Minimize the amount of typing and the degree of eye-hand coordination required.

▶ Let learners choose the answers in multiple-choice tests by clicking on the items. Clicking on the text should have the same effect as clicking on the associated radio button or checkbox.

▶ If multiple-choice answers are presented visually, let learners answer by clicking on the pictures.

▶ Do not number choices that learners select by clicking on them. Numbers or letters before a choice imply that the learner selects by typing the number or letter.

○ A. True

○ B. False

Unfortunately, most test-creation tools insist on numbering all answers.

Keep choices concise

Do not repeat words in each answer that could be put in the question.

What are the differences between hornblende and biotite?

☐ Although both biotite and hornblende can be black in color and both occur in granite, only hornblende contains sodium.

☐ Although both biotite and hornblende can be black in color and both occur in granite, hornblende crystals are triclinic and those of biotite are monoclinic.

☐ Although both biotite and hornblende can be black in color and both occur in granite, hornblende is harder than biotite.

☐ Although both biotite and hornblende can be black in color and both occur in granite, biotite cleaves in one dimension while hornblende cleaves in two dimensions.

In this example, notice how much text is repeated in each question.

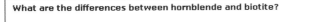

> **What are the differences between hornblende and biotite?**
>
> ☐ Only hornblende contains sodium.
> ☐ Hornblende crystals are triclinic and those of biotite are monoclinic.
> ☐ Hornblende is harder than biotite.
> ☐ Biotite cleaves in one dimension while hornblende cleaves in two dimensions.

Now notice how much easier it is to compare the answers when the repeated information is removed.

Put choices in a meaningful order

List choices in an order that helps learners find the correct answer. For example:

If choices:	List choices in this order:
Are numbers	From least to greatest.
Are events	Chronological order.
Vary by a common characteristic	Increases or decrease in that characteristic.
Have no inherent order	Alphabetical or random order.

Express choices simply

Keep the noise out of your questions by expressing choices simply and directly. Do not require mental efforts just to untangle the question or choices.

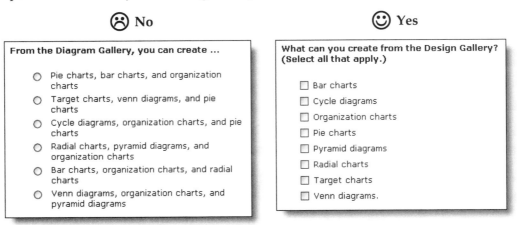

☹ No

> **From the Diagram Gallery, you can create ...**
>
> ○ Pie charts, bar charts, and organization charts
> ○ Target charts, venn diagrams, and pie charts
> ○ Cycle diagrams, organization charts, and pie charts
> ○ Radial charts, pyramid diagrams, and organization charts
> ○ Bar charts, organization charts, and radial charts
> ○ Venn diagrams, organization charts, and pyramid diagrams

☺ Yes

> **What can you create from the Design Gallery? (Select all that apply.)**
>
> ☐ Bar charts
> ☐ Cycle diagrams
> ☐ Organization charts
> ☐ Pie charts
> ☐ Pyramid diagrams
> ☐ Radial charts
> ☐ Target charts
> ☐ Venn diagrams.

Beware of compound choices, of irrelevant details in questions and answers, and of words or symbols unfamiliar to learners.

Vary your pattern

Vary the position of the correct answer in a list of choices. Amateur test designers are less likely to make the first or last answer the correct one. Skillful test-takers who need to guess will pick the third of 4 choices. For 5 choices, they opt for the third or fourth. Not a sure thing, but it does put the odds in their favor. So analyze your answers to make sure the correct answer occurs throughout the range of answers. Or use a tool that can shuffle answers so each time the question appears the answers are in a different order.

COMBINE QUESTIONS EFFECTIVELY

To create an effective test, you may combine test questions written separately at different times, perhaps by different test-writers. Your test may need to include questions to test multiple learning objectives or a high-level objective. What must you, as a designer, think about as you compose a multi-question test?

Ask enough questions

Include enough test questions to accurately gauge the learners' understanding in the subject. Consider the number of learning objectives the test must cover. For a single, simple objective, 3 well-designed pick-one questions may be adequate. More complex objectives will require more test questions and more sophisticated test questions.

Also consider the purpose of your testing. To give learners a general indication of how well they are doing, you need fewer questions than you would to legally certify that learners can perform a dangerous task.

Don't forget to consider how what you are teaching will be applied. If your subject will be applied in widely varying situations, you may need a wider variety of test questions to accurately predict learners' ability to apply learning. You cannot cover every situation, but you can ask questions that span the range of application.

Make sure one question does not answer another

In a series of test questions, one question may ask about a subject mentioned in another. Often one of the questions provides unintended information that indicates the answer to the other.

What does the Fraud-D-Techt feature do?

○ Informs customers of bank holidays
○ Spots fraudulent transactions
○ Verifies checks are completely filled in
○ Maintains anti-virus software on the bank's servers

What feature spots fraudulent transactions?

○ Check-o-matique
○ Detectafraud
○ Fraud-D-Techt
○ SecureTrans

Can you guess the answers to these 2 questions?

Notice how the first question provides a clue for the second question, which provides a clue for the first question.

Make questions independent. Answering one question should not affect a learner's ability to answer subsequent questions. Make sure that the wording of one question and its answers do not imply the answers to subsequent questions.

Sequence test questions effectively

Most tests consist of a sequence of questions. Consider how separate questions are best combined for a comprehensive test.

Ask multiple questions about one scenario. For complex subjects, create a series of test questions based on the same situation, scenario, or description. Make it easy for the learner to refer to the original explanation. Either display the scenario in a separate frame or window from the questions or link back to the original explanation from each question. Repeat salient facts in each question.

Ramp up the difficulty. Let learners warm up on simple questions. Learners who cannot answer any of the first 3 questions are likely to despair and not sincerely try later ones. Or they may spend so much of their time on the initial difficult questions that they do not get to the easy ones within the time limit of the test. Vary the difficulty of test questions so that no one completely fails and yet few get a perfect score. Start with the simpler questions. In that way, learners taste success and are motivated to continue trying.

Keep the sequence short. Few people like long tests. Four or 5 questions make a nice pop quiz. A dozen are enough for almost any sequence. A test containing more than 15 questions is a police interrogation. If you feel these limits are too restrictive, break your test into multiple short tests and sprinkle them among the presentation of material.

Enable navigation. If practical, let learners skip back and forth among the questions, answering the ones they can and skipping over the ones they cannot. Either put all the questions onto the same Web page or include navigation buttons to skip among the pages of a test. Make sure that skipping over a question does not lock in an answer until the time limit expires.

Vary the form of questions and answers

To keep a series of questions from becoming monotonous, vary the way questions and answers are phrased.

▶ **Mix different forms of questions**: pick-multiple, fill-in-the-blanks, matching list, performance. Mix different media. Ask questions visually and verbally.

▶ **Design each question to test for a different common misconception**. Ask different kinds of questions, such as what, when, why, where, and how.

▶ **Vary the form of questions**. Ask learners to pick the right answer. Then the one wrong answer. Then the best answer. Ask which of a list of statements do apply, then which do not apply.

▶ **Vary the position of the correct answer** in multiple-choice lists. However, if several questions have the same list of answers, do not vary the order of the answers.

▶ **Arrange test questions in a predictable pattern.** For example: pick-one, pick-one, pick-one, pick multiple, pick-one, pick-one, pick-one, pick multiple, and so on. Learners should concentrate on the questions, not their format.

Such purposeful variety makes testing more robust. The results do not depend on learners' verbal skills or ability to answer one kind of question.

GIVE MEANINGFUL FEEDBACK

After learners answer a question, they crave feedback. Did I get the right answer? No? Why not? What's wrong with my answer? What did I misunderstand? How can I correct my misunderstanding? Provide such feedback.

Report test scores simply

As soon as possible, tell learners how well they did on the test. For example:

Congratulations. You passed.	or	Sorry. You failed.
Your score: 85. Passing score: 75.		Your score: 66. Passing score: 75.
Continue with the next lesson.		Review the summary and retake the test.

Relieve the anxiety and let the celebration or remediation begin. Report scores simply and directly. Tell learners 3 things: their scores, the passing score, and the effect of their scores. Learners immediately know how well they did and what they should do next.

Provide complete information

Tests can teach too. Feedback on test questions can correct misunderstandings and augment knowledge. For each answer, consider including:

▶ **The question**. Repeat or re-display the question. If questions are numbered, include the question number.

▶ **Right/wrong flag**. Avoid vagueness. Do not say "Almost" or "Not quite" but simply "Wrong" or "Incorrect."

▶ **The correct answer**. Do not make learners repeatedly answer a question hoping they guess the right answer. A 5-choice pick-multiple question can be answered 32 ways. That's a lot of guessing.

▶ **The learner's answer**. Learners may not have entered what they thought they did.

▶ **Why the correct answer is right** (and, if necessary, why the learner's answer is wrong).

▶ **Link to the original presentation** or a remedial one on this subject. Also include instructions on how to resume after reviewing the material.

> **Score Card**
>
> **Score: 110 of 230**
>
> Question 1:
>
> **Correct**. You use InStrRev to return the first place within a string that another string occurs, from the end of the string. 50 of 50 points.
>
> Question 2:
>
> **Incorrect**. The Mid function returns a specific portion of its input text string. 0 of 25 points.
>
> Question 3:
>
> **Correct**. The filter property limits the file types shown in the Open File dialog box. 25 of 25 points.
>
> Question 4:
>
> **Incorrect**. You should review these text manipulation functions again. You got 2 of 6 right. 10 of 30 points.

Here is a simple example of helpful feedback. It annotates the learner's answer to provide the necessary feedback.

Briefly acknowledge right answers. Tell learners they were right. Be enthusiastic, but do not be effusive. For positive feedback, all you need to say is "Correct," "Right," or "Yes." Anything more would interrupt the learner's momentum.

If your primary goal is teaching rather than measurement, you may want to ignore this advice and supplement the feedback for right answers. You may want to tell the learner why the right answer was right (the learner may have guessed).

For right answers, you can challenge learners to think about how they got the right answer and to consider other methods.

> Right. How did you get your answer? Did you calculate it in your head? The math was pretty simple. What would you do for a more complex case?

The feedback for a correct answer can teach additional information. You already have the attention of a happy, receptive learner. Use it.

Question 4: **Correct**. Summarizing the customer's complaint shows that you were listening to her. It is also a good way to get her to agree to your interpretation of the problem before you continue.

Notice how this example adds related information?

Keep the feedback brief, or the learner will not read it. Most of the time learners are satisfied to know they got the question right.

Gently correct wrong answers

For an incorrect answer, gently but clearly point out the problem. Help learners overcome their misconceptions.

Use a neutral term

For negative feedback, use a neutral term, such as "incorrect" without any exclamation points, please. You can also use "sorry" or "not quite," although these may seem a bit patronizing. Do not say, "Wrong!!!" or "Gotcha" or "I don't think so."

Tell why answers are wrong

Tell learners why their answers were wrong. For pick-multiple questions, make clear why each choice was right or wrong.

> The correct answers are Doyle and Scribner.
>
> Doyle and Scribner are both common methods of measuring the lumber volume of trees. Cordage is a measure of the volume of cut wood and is used for pulpwood. IDN and Wocon are just made-up terms and have nothing to do with forestry.

Do not embarrass or insult the learner

Do not shout at people if they get something wrong—no flashing headlines or embarrassing noises.

You ...

Failed

... the test.

You got 6 of 10 questions correct. This is **NOT** an acceptable score. To pass you must get at least 7 of 10 questions correct.

Perhaps you did not pay attention while taking the lesson or did not have the prerequisite knowledge to take this lesson or this course.

In any case, you must repeat the lesson and achieve an acceptable score on the lesson post-test before you will be allowed to take subsequent lessons.

How would you like to receive this feedback? The word *Failed* appears in a blood red color and jiggles on the screen, accompanied by a chorus of boos. Also notice the condescending tone.

Built using Adobe Dreamweaver. View example at horton.com/eld/.

Acknowledge partial success

Give learners credit for the questions they got right. Encourage learners to try again. Give them choices so they feel in control. Notice how this feedback acknowledges an almost-passing score and suggests alternatives for how the learner should proceed.

Your score: 72

Passing Score: 75

Because your score was close to a passing score, we recommend you review the summary topic and then retake this test.

Or, you could just retake this test. (You will see new questions.)

If you feel you understand the subject well enough, you can proceed to the next lesson. Or, if you prefer a more in-depth review, you can restart this lesson.

Avoid wimpy feedback

Compared to the computer games that players love, much e-learning gives timid feedback. In a game, you always know exactly how well you are doing. If you fail to perform, the game mocks you or your character dies. I am not suggesting we abuse or decimate our learners; just consider a bit more direct approach. Avoid weak and vague feedback messages like these:

> Good try, but you could have done better.
>
> We're sorry, but that is not the best answer.
>
> Almost. Would you like to try another guess?
>
> Close, oh so very, very close.
>
> Oh, too bad.
>
> Bummer!

Simply say "Right" or "Wrong" and explain why the answer was right or wrong.

Give feedback at the right time

When will you tell learners how they scored on the test? Sooner is better, but sometimes delays are necessary even with automatic scoring. You can deliver feedback automatically after each question or after the whole test. Or you can deliver feedback after evaluation by a human being. This section discusses the merits of each approach.

After each question

Scoring each question as the learner answers it provides immediate feedback but can interrupt the flow of the test. In general, I prefer this approach. It makes tests more fun and prevents misconceptions. It makes tests seem a bit more like games.

Immediate feedback corrects misconceptions before they take up residence in the learner's brain. If feedback comes only after answering a whole series of questions, learners will have transferred their answers to long-term memory before they realize which were wrong. Immediate feedback also keeps the learner from missing several related questions because of a single, simple misunderstanding.

Getting feedback piecemeal, however, can make the test take longer and prove frustrating to impatient learners, especially ones with a high level of knowledge who get few questions wrong. Immediate feedback can also make it harder for learners to answer a series of closely related questions. Interruptions for feedback break the continuity of the test. If you do choose to provide feedback after each answer:

▶ Make each question complete in itself. After reading the feedback, learners are unlikely to remember details of the preceding question.

▶ Let learners skip over lengthy feedback for correct answers. Make the feedback brief and let learners click a button to advance to the next question.

▶ Do not reveal too much. In the feedback to one question, do not give away the answer to another question.

▶ Do not require immediate remediation. Otherwise learners would bail out of the test after their first wrong answer. At the end of the test, provide a recap with links to let learners review material for questions they got wrong.

▶ If the test is timed, stop the timer while the learner is getting feedback and restart it only when the learner advances to the next question. Make sure learners understand that they can take all the time they want to read feedback.

After test is complete

Postponing evaluation until learners have answered all questions is more efficient and more economical, but less fun. By evaluating answers only at the end of the test, you reduce the number of screens the learner must view and the time required to take the test. Learners can quickly navigate back and forth among the questions, answering them at will.

Feedback at the end can comment on understanding of the whole subject of the test. By evaluating at the end, your feedback can be more targeted. If several questions test the same concept, learners see the feedback just once, not over and over again.

However, postponing evaluation can prove frustrating to some learners. Misunderstanding one question can cause them to miss other questions. Guess whom they blame!

If you do design tests with evaluation only at the end of the test, follow these common-sense guidelines:

▶ Make questions independent and self-contained. Misunderstanding one question should not lessen chances of getting other questions right.

▶ Keep tests short. Learners should be able to complete the whole test in 10 to 15 minutes.

▶ At the end, provide clear feedback on questions the learner got wrong with links to the original material or to new material on the subject.

After a delay for human evaluation

If a test question is complex and its answer must be carefully considered by the instructor or fellow learners, immediate feedback is not possible. The answer must be transmitted to an evaluator who scores it and sends back a reply. Throw in time zones, weekends, holidays, and work priorities, and the delay can be several days.

For tests with delayed evaluation, use the strengths of human evaluation to offset the problems caused by the delay.

► Give priority to scoring tests. Guarantee 48-hour turnaround if you can do so without compromising the quality of evaluations. Find stand-ins if instructors are unavailable. Consider having learners perform non-critical evaluations. Base part of the final grade on the promptness and quality of such evaluations.

► Let learners proceed with the e-learning, even if a passing grade is normally required before beginning the next lesson.

► Schedule tests on days when the evaluator will be able to respond immediately. Some instructors like to schedule tests on Friday so that they can grade them during the quiet time over the weekend.

► Warn learners about potential delays. If learners decide when to take tests, publish a calendar indicating when the instructor will be available to grade tests. One course had this policy: "You will receive your grade within 2 business days at the office of the instructor."

PERFECT YOUR TESTING

Few tests are perfect the first time out. With careful monitoring and revision, however, you can eliminate the most common problems.

Hint first

Instead of giving the correct answer as feedback to an incorrect guess, consider displaying a hint and challenging the learner to try again. Or include a **Hint** button to let learners request a little help answering the question.

> Answer the following questions about the <u>multimedia project plan</u>.
>
> | Question | Answer |
> |---|---|
> | Which task has a lagging-start dependency with a previous task? | Pick one ▾ |
> | How long does this lag delay start of the dependent task? | Pick one ▾ |
> | How much is the dependent task delayed if the previous task ends 3 weeks late? | Pick one ▾ |
> | If the preceding task is delayed 6 weeks, how many other tasks, including the dependent task, are delayed? | Pick one ▾ |
>
> (Evaluate)   (Show)   (Hint)   (Reset)
>
> ```
> Lagging-start dependencies look a lot like float
> lines. What distinguishes the two?
> ```

Notice how clicking on the **Hint** button reveals a fact that makes answering the question easier.

Built using Adobe Dreamweaver and custom JavaScript. View example at horton.com/eld/.

Use advanced testing capabilities

We can use computer capabilities to make testing fairer and more sophisticated. We can pick questions from a pool of available questions and can randomize the order of questions and choices within questions. These capabilities require a testing tool that provides these features or one that includes a scripting or programming language you can use to implement this feature yourself.

Pool test questions

In question-pooling, test questions are pulled from a pool of available test questions. That is, the test designer creates more test questions than necessary for a single test. The test delivery system then selects questions from the pool at the time the test is delivered. For example, suppose we have created Questions A through H on a subject. Tests on this subject could pull questions from that pool as follows:

Test 1	Test 2	Test 3	Test 4
Question A	Question C	Question E	Question G
Question B	Question F	Question A	Question F
Question C	Question H	Question C	Question A
Question D	Question A	Question G	Question H

When should you use question-pooling? Question pooling is great when tests are taken more than once. By drawing questions from a pool, we make sure that the learner does not see exactly the same questions time and time again. This is especially important when we are using pre- and post-learning tests to measure learning. If the post-test merely repeated the questions from the pre-test, we would not know whether results indicated learning or just familiarity with the test questions. Question pooling is also useful when learners may need to retake a test, for instance, after failing a first attempt.

Another use for question pooling is to make cheating harder. One student cannot tell another student what questions are on the test.

Question pooling can pose some problems for test designers. It thwarts designers who want questions to appear in a specific order. Many designers want to start with simpler questions before more difficult questions or to put questions in a logical or chronological order. With question pooling, one question cannot build on or refer to a previous question. If test scores are to be comparable between students and offerings of the test, all questions in the pool must be of the same difficulty. With question pooling there is a statistical possibility that the questions on an individual test will not cover the subject evenly.

Don't forget that question pooling requires test designers to create more questions. This requires more research, analysis, and testing. Budget and schedule accordingly.

A critical question to ask is how questions are selected from the pool. One way is randomly. Other ways apply a scheme, such as picking questions from separate pools, ensuring that questions are not repeated on subsequent tests taken by the same learner, and as groups of related questions.

Just remember that question pooling requires sophisticated technology and more work on your part.

Randomize questions

When you randomize questions, they appear in a different order each time a test is administered. For example, for a simple test:

Test 1	Test 2	Test 3	Test 4
Question A	Question C	Question D	Question B
Question B	Question B	Question A	Question A
Question C	Question D	Question C	Question D
Question D	Question A	Question B	Question C

Should you randomize the order of questions? Randomizing the order of questions can make the test seem fresh the second time taken, and it will make cheating harder. However, it does require you to design your questions independently. That means questions cannot refer to other questions. You cannot sequence questions in chronological or logical order. You cannot progress from simple to hard questions.

The randomizing feature is most often combined with the question-pooling feature so that questions are selected at random from a large pool of questions.

Shuffle answers

With randomized or shuffled answers, the choices for a pick-one or pick-multiple question appear in a different order each time the test is taken. For example, the answers to a pick-one question in chemistry might appear different on subsequent tests:

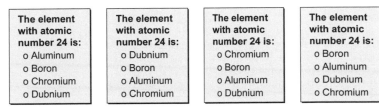

Should you shuffle the order of answers in your test questions? Shuffling the order of choices will make the test seem fresh the second time taken and will make cheating a little harder. However, it does require you to write questions so the order of choices does not matter. That means answers cannot refer to earlier answers (Be careful with pronouns like *it*, *these*, and *they* that refer to words in earlier answers.) It also means answers will not appear in alphabetical, numeric, chronological, or logical order. This can make scanning the choices harder, especially for test-stressed learners.

Automatically generate questions

Some advanced testing tools have the ability to automatically create fresh test questions from a formula or pattern. For example, with the learning management system called The Learning Manager (www.thelearningmanager.com), I can define a question in geometry with placeholders rather than fixed numbers.

> What is the area of a rectangle {number1} units high and {number2} units wide?

And I can then define a procedure to generate specific numbers to replace those placeholders in actual questions.

```
number1 = rndnum(1,10,1);
number2 = rndnum(1,10,1);
correct = number1 * number2;
format(number1, "%.0f");
format(number2, "%.0f");
format(correct, "%.0f");
```

The first line picks 2 whole numbers between 1 and 10 at random. The third line defines the correct answer is the product of these 2 numbers. The final tree lines format the numbers as whole numbers.

The first time the question appears, a set of numbers is generated and a correct answer calculated.

What is the area of a rectangle 6 units high and 2 units wide? `12`

The next time the question appears, different numbers fill the placeholders and the correct answer is different.

What is the area of a rectangle 7 units high and 5 units wide? `35`

Each time the question appears, different numbers fill the slots.

What is the area of a rectangle 3 units high and 9 units wide? `27`

Good uses for automatically generated questions include:

▶ Simple mathematics, such as arithmetic and unit conversions.

▶ Subjects requiring calculations, such as accounting and engineering.

▶ Drill and practice on estimating quantities.

Monitor results

One of the best ways to improve tests is to examine the log files after a reasonable number of learners have taken the tests. Look for the symptoms of easily corrected problems, such as these:

Questions with lower than normal success rates.	These questions are too hard or are unclearly phrased.
Questions with higher than normal success rates.	These questions may be too easy or something is giving learners a clue to the correct answer.

| Questions that many learners skip. | These questions may be hard to understand, take too long to read, or be too difficult to answer. |
| Large number of questions left unanswered on timed tests. | You may need to increase the time or decrease the number of questions. |

Ask yourself this question: Do people who have the required skills and knowledge pass the test, while those without the skills and knowledge fail?

Make tests fair to all learners

Sometimes learners may feel tests are unfair. They believe that tests ask improper questions or do not give all learners an equal chance to answer questions correctly.

Prevent common complaints

Common complaints about unfair tests and test questions include:

▶ Questions outside the scope of stated objectives or unit of learning.

▶ Questions that depend on irrelevant skills or on knowledge not mentioned in prerequisites.

▶ Culturally biased questions that rely on knowledge that one culture might possess but another might not. Or complex, tricky language that is especially difficult for second-language readers.

▶ Unfamiliar terminology: Unnecessary jargon, metaphors, and slang.

▶ Unreasonable time limits that unfairly penalize second-language learners and those with vision or reading problems.

Test your tests

As a check on e-learning design, make each test question pass a test itself. This test has 3 questions:

▶ Which objective does this question test?

▶ Where was the learner taught this objective?

▶ Can someone with subject-matter knowledge but minimal reading skills answer the question?

Unless you can easily answer each item, rewrite your test question.

Solicit feedback from learners

Invite learners to comment on tests. However, request the feedback only after the test has been graded. This delay gives learners time to calm down so that their responses are more reasoned and less emotional. And learners can respond based on the actual grade rather than the anticipated one.

Let learners report questions they consider unfair. Require them to state why they feel the question was unfair. And ask them what change would make the question fair.

Avoid trick questions

Trick questions are ones designed to trick learners into making an incorrect answer. Writers of such questions often claim that they are just trying to teach learners to pay close attention. Trick questions teach learners to fear tests and distrust the test-writer. Trick questions penalize even successful learners. Writing trick questions is unethical and probably immoral. If you do it, you should be sentenced to take an endless test made up entirely of trick questions where each incorrect answer triggers a sting by a big nasty wasp.

There is no limit to the number of tricks evil designers can play on learners. Here are a few of the most common abuses:

- ▶ **Red herrings** that embed cues to prompt incorrect responses. For example, asking "Which consumes more oxygen, an 80 kg human jogging uphill or a 3 kg rabbit calmly browsing lettuce?"

- ▶ **Trivia questions** that ask for skills and knowledge that the learner will never need to apply. "What color eyes did Napoleon have?"

- ▶ **Late requirement,** which asks for something that was not taught in the course or in a required prerequisite.

- ▶ **Context-less queries,** which do not provide a specific enough context to enable an answer. For example, "How frequent are tornadoes?" Many such questions require a comparison but give no standard for the comparison.

- ▶ **Required confessions,** which require a response that admits to wrongdoing. For example, "How do you feel when you drive faster than the speed limit?"

- ▶ **Overlapping categories,** where the scope or range of choices overlap so that more than one pick-one answer could be correct. "What is the hardness of malachite on the Mohs hardness scale? (Pick one) (a) 1 to 2, (b) 2 to 3, (c)3 to 4, (d) 4 to 5." The hardness of malachite can range from 3.5 to 4, so both the third and fourth answers could be correct.

5

▶ **Demoralization,** where the designer puts the hardest questions first to dishearten and fluster learners.

▶ **Duplicated distracters,** where the same wrong answer is restated in different words in subsequent choices. "Why was Brian fired? (a) He was rude. (b) He was discourteous. (c) He violated policy. (d) He was offensive. (e) He broke the law."

▶ **Linguistic lofting,** where the designer deliberately uses words that only some of the learners will recognize, even though understanding the terms is not a prerequisite or objective of the course.

▶ **Breakstep sequencing,** where numeric choices are not in numeric order. For example, "What is the altitude of the ozone layer? (a) 10 km (b) 20 km (c) 40 km (d) 80 km (e) 30 km."

▶ **Apples-and-oranges comparisons,** where completely different categories must be compared. For example, "Which is better, the climbing capacity of the V10 engine in the VW Touareg or the hill-descent electronics of the Land Rover Discovery?"

How do you know whether a question is unfair? Ask learners. Include only questions your learners will agree are appropriate.

Test early and often

As soon as you teach something, test on it. Help learners lock in learning and give them an opportunity to confirm their progress. Asking questions about knowledge learners have just acquired helps them consolidate and integrate the knowledge. Having learners perform procedures immediately after learning them makes performance fluid and sure.

Include more short tests, rather than just a few long ones. In a large course, include several tests evenly spaced throughout the course—not just one big exam at the end.

Many courses present a series of ideas and then test on them all. By the time learners reach the test, they have forgotten what they learned about the earlier concepts and are intimidated by the big test.

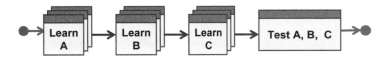

Instead of one big test at the end, sprinkle small tests throughout learning. Thus learners do not proceed without learning. Because these tests are small, they are less intimidating. After teaching and testing the final idea, present a brief review and a short test on all the ideas.

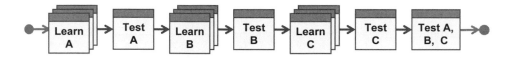

Design the smaller tests so that they accurately predict performance on the larger tests. Give learners lots of practice activities and just a few recorded tests. Tracking the learner's every attempt and recording every score discourages quick, spontaneous action. The rapid cycle of assessing a situation, forming a hypothesis, testing it, getting feedback, and revising the hypothesis is a valuable learning event in its own right. Give learners lots of opportunities to practice without the fear that their every mistake is being recorded in ink.

Set the right passing score

If your test is used to make decisions about learners—and not just to provide general feedback to them—you will need to set a passing score. This passing score (or cut score) is the number of points the learner must earn in order to adequately master the unit of learning covered by the test.

Before you set a passing score, consider exactly how you will use this score. Will you use it just as a goal for learners to shoot for? Will you require learners to repeat the module until they have achieved the passing score? Will the score be recorded as part of their job records? Will the score qualify the learner for a job-relevant certification? Obviously, the more effect the test score has on the learner's future, the more objective and systematic you must be in setting the test score—and in other aspects of testing.

One way to think of the passing score is as a target level of competence between minimal competence and complete mastery.

But what should that target threshold be? There are several ways to set the score. Here we list 3 in order of increasing rigor.

Professional judgment

If you are experienced teaching the subject of the test and know where and how learners will apply the knowledge or skills being taught, you can just use your professional judgment to set the passing score. You know the subject and how well learners must learn. Translate your professional judgment into a test score.

In setting a passing score, consider:

▶ How crucial is the skill or knowledge to future learning. A foundation skill must be mastered to a high level.

▶ What is the danger if the subject is not mastered? Will someone's life be put at risk? Will work quality suffer?

▶ How difficult is the subject to novices? Is a high score unrealistic?

Consensus of experts

Ask the help of subject-matter experts. Base the passing score on the judgment of a half-dozen experts in the subject of your test. An expert would be expected to score well above the passing score, a standard deviation or more.

One way to make more precise use of your experts is to have them examine each question and then specify the odds that a minimally proficient learner (someone who should just barely pass the test) would get this individual question correct. You can then add up the probabilities to get the number of questions necessary to pass.

For example, say a test has 5 questions and your experts estimate the probabilities of getting the questions right are 0.8, 0.7, 0.8, 0.4, and 0.6, respectively. Adding up these numbers tells us the number of correct answers needed for a passing score:

$0.8 + 0.7 + 0.8 + 0.4 + 0.6 = 3.3$ questions required to pass.

If questions have different point values, you would need to multiply each probability of passing by the number of points awarded for each question. Suppose the questions in the preceding example have point values of 10, 10, 20, 20, and 10, respectively. Now our required score becomes:

$0.8 \times 10 + 0.7 \times 10 + 0.8 \times 20 + 0.4 \times 20 + 0.6 \times 10.$

$8 + 7 + 16 + 8 + 6 = 35$ points required to pass

And while you are at it, have your experts take the test. Better still; have them take the test before making their estimates.

Contrasting groups

The contrasting-group method statistically compares the scores of experts and novices and sets the passing score between these two.

1. Recruit 2 groups of test-takers. The "expert" group consists of people who have mastered the subject of the test and should pass handily. The "novice" group consists of people who know little or nothing about the subject and who should fail the test. About two dozen test-takers should be sufficient.

2. Administer the test to the 2 groups under identical conditions. If possible, have them all take the test at the same time.

3. Compile test scores and identify the mean and standard deviation of the scores for each group.

4. Set the passing score between one standard deviation below the mean for the experts and one standard deviation above the mean for novices.

5. Nudge the passing score up or down within this range to make testing more or less stringent.

Define a scale of grades

Rather than a pass-fail threshold, give learners ranges of scores along with recommendations of how to proceed. For example:

90-100 points. Excellent! Please skip ahead to the <u>next lesson</u>. You may want to <u>attempt the test</u> for that lesson to see whether you can also skip that lesson.

80-89 points. Good. You understand the basics and can continue with the <u>next lesson</u>.

65-79 points. You should improve your score before beginning the next lesson. Please <u>review the summary</u> and attempt this test again.

0-64 points. You need to work on this subject before proceeding. You should *repeat the lesson* or explore <u>alternative learning resources</u> before re-attempting this test.

Pre-test to propel learners

A pre-test is a test taken before beginning a lesson or course. It covers the same ground as the associated unit of learning, just like the post-test or final exam that comes at the end of the unit. Pre-tests may test for prerequisites of the following unit, for the content of the unit itself, or for both.

Why pre-test?

Pre-testing offers several benefits to learners and to designers. Pre-tests:

▶ Motivate learners by challenging them to fill in the gaps revealed by the pre-test.

▶ Make clear what the unit of learning will cover.

▶ Ensure that learners take prerequisites before beginning the unit of learning.

▶ Streamline learning by letting learners skip material they already know.

▶ Help designers identify modules they can omit (because everybody passes the pre-test) or additional modules to develop (because everybody fails the pre-test.

Use pre-test results

Depending on your purposes for pre-testing and the sophistication of your learning management system, you can use the results of pre-testing to route learners to different locations.

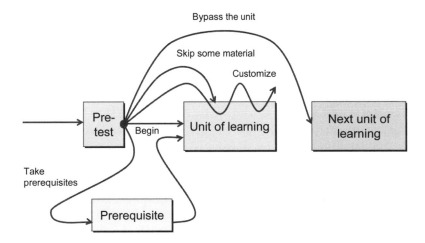

If learners ...	Route them to ...
Completely pass the pre-test.	The next unit in sequence.
Partially pass the pre-test.	A starting point within the current unit.
Show that they lack prerequisite knowledge.	A prerequisite course or lesson.
Pass the prerequisites portion of the pre-test.	The beginning of the current unit of learning.
Pass portions of the pre-test for the current unit.	A custom path through just the components the learner did not pass in the pre-test.

EXPLAIN THE TEST

One of the most common complaints about tests is that the rules are unclear or that the procedures are not explained fully. If learners do not understand the "rules" of a test, they may not score well and will blame the creator of the test. Take the time to tell learners how to take the test.

Prepare learners to take the test

Learners are curious beings, especially when it comes to tests. They want to know all the rules and regulations and restrictions—before they begin the test. But no one wants to read a bunch of boring rules. So keep the rules as simple as possible, express them concisely, and encourage learners to know the rules before they begin the test. Here is a comprehensive list of the kinds of questions learners ask.

▶ **Why am I being tested?** Learners who see the value of a test to them try harder and score higher. Tell learners that the test will give them confidence, help them quickly correct misunderstanding, and progress more quickly.

▶ **Is the test graded?** What effect will this test have on the overall grade? What is a passing grade? What grade should the learner achieve before going on to the next lesson?

▶ **What does the test cover?** Just the current lesson? All lessons up to this point?

▶ **Is the test timed?** How much time is available? What is the penalty for taking too much time?

▶ **When must the test be taken?** Before a deadline? During a specific period? At a certain hour and day? Before advancing to the next lesson?

▶ **How long is the test?** How many questions are on the test? (Especially important if the questions scroll off the bottom of the screen or are on subsequent pages).

▶ **How are answers scored?** How many points are awarded for each question? What are the penalties for incorrect answers, incomplete answers, and unanswered questions?

▶ **How accurate must my answers be?** Do spelling, capitalization, and grammar count? How precise must calculations be? Does the order of entries matter?

▶ **What form does the test take?** What kinds of questions are used: multiple-choice, true/false, fill-in-the-blanks, or others? Does everyone get the same questions or are questions picked at random?

▶ **Can I take the test later?** If so, how do I skip the test? How do I take the test later?

▶ **Should I guess?** Tell learners how unanswered questions are scored so they can decide whether to guess at answers. National testing services typically deduct 1 point for missing answers and 3 points for incorrect answers {Westgaard, 1999 #1951}.

▶ **Can I retake the test for a better grade later?** How many times? Which score is recorded: the first one, the last one, the best one, or an average of all attempts?

▶ **What resources may I use to take the test?** Specify what calculators, computer programs, books, Web sites, search engines, or other sources of information learners can use. Include links to these items so all learners have equal access.

▶ **Are questions weighted equally?** Do some questions score more points than others? If weightings vary, state the point value of each question as it appears.

▶ **How realistic are the questions?** Are drawings to scale? Are numbers realistic?

▶ **Must questions be answered in sequence?** Does advancing to the next question automatically trigger scoring the current question?

▶ **What if I experience a computer failure?** What if the computer, network, or the testing program crashes during the test? What effect will this have on my score? How do I restart or resume the test?

Keep learners in control

We want learners to feel in control as they take tests. That way they focus on the content of the test. The key to control is information and having appropriate choices.

▶ **Explain before starting the timer.** Explain the test before it begins. Give all the instructions for a test before starting the timer. After presenting the instructions, require learners to select a "**Start test**" button to actually begin the test, especially if the test is timed.

► **Let learners skip optional tests.** If tests are optional, let learners skip them. Make this easy with explicit buttons.

Evaluate	Next Lesson

► **Make status clear.** Let learners know how much they have done and how much they have left to do. Some systems display a console showing the time and number of questions:

Test 14: Using ADO 2	
Questions answered	**Time remaining**
4 of 10	5:36 of 10:00

CONSIDER ALTERNATIVES TO FORMAL TESTS

Testing in e-learning obviously has limitations and is not always the best way to evaluate the progress of learners. Before you start designing tests, take a few minutes to consider alternatives to tests.

Use more than formal, graded tests

Not all assessments need to be formal, graded tests. Use a mixture of different forms of assessment:

► Formal graded tests.

► Open-book tests during which learners can consult reference materials.

► Performance tests requiring completion of actual work.

► Self-graded tests by which learners evaluate their own performance.

► Self-evaluations of practice activities or original work.

► Evaluations by boss, peers, subordinates, or customers.

► Learning games and puzzles that require learning to win or solve.

► Research projects that require gaining original knowledge.

► Tests taken by teams instead of individuals.

Help learners build portfolios

Instead of testing on knowledge, have learners create tangible evidence of their learning. Base grading on a work-ready portfolio the learner assembles during the course. The portfolio can consist of samples of a variety of work products or the completion of a single, complex plan or report.

For those already working in the field of the course, the portfolio can consist of materials immediately useful on the job. For those preparing for a new field, the portfolio can consist of samples that demonstrate competence to practice in the field.

Have learners collect tokens

Rather than requiring learners to pass a series of tests, challenge them to collect tokens that represent completion of activities. Each test or activity is worth a certain number of tokens in proportion to the scope and value of the knowledge it requires.

Gauge performance in live online meetings

In online meetings, include activities that reveal the level of learning by students. Here are some activities you can use:

▶ **Polling**. Ask questions to see who "got it."

▶ **Application sharing**. Have learners demonstrate tasks with software.

▶ **Oral exams**. Ask specific learners.

▶ **Student teachers**. Have learners teach short segments.

▶ **Open-ended questions** that must be answered through chat.

And in discussion-forum activities

▶ **Take home tests** that learners submit the next day.

▶ **Homework** that learners prepare and submit for grading.

▶ **Portfolios** of original work by learners.

IN CLOSING ...

Summary

▶ Develop and perfect tests by the same cyclical process used for other parts of e-learning.

▶ Use tests to let learners gauge their progress and administrators measure the effectiveness of your e-learning.

▶ Write test questions so they measure skills and knowledge, not the ability to decipher tricky phrases or to make lucky guesses.

▶ For simple questions, provide feedback immediately so that misconceptions are identified and corrected before they take root.

▶ Test early and often. Use unrecorded tests for frequent practice. Make tests more like challenging games and less like school examinations.

▶ Test your tests. At a minimum, make sure that experts pass the test and novices do not.

▶ As always, design first and then pick your tool. If you have already selected a tool to create and administer tests, do not moan, groan, or whine. Just do the best you can.

For more ...

For more sophisticated tests, consider using learning activities (Chapters 2, 3, and 4). Most activities will, however, require grading by the instructor.

Before buying a tool for authoring tests, try out the types of tests it provides and investigate how you can add tests of your own design. Consider these tools:

▶ CourseBuilder for Dreamweaver (www.adobe.com).

▶ Hot Potatoes (www.halfbakedsoftware.com).

▶ Perception Questionmark (www.questionmark.com).

▶ Quiz Rocket (www.learningware.com).

▶ QuizMaker (www.articulate.com).

▶ Captivate (www.adobe.com).

Simulations integrate teaching and testing. Consider a learning game (p. 142) or whole simulation course (p. 164).

Topics

Accomplishing specific learning objectives

Topics accomplish individual learning objectives. They may consist of a single page or many. They may center on a single activity or may span multiple complex activities. They may mix text, graphics, voice, music, animation, and video. They may take minutes or hours to complete. But each topic accomplishes one learning objective and accomplishes it fully. That's what makes them topics. This chapter will show you how to design e-learning topics to accomplish your learning objectives.

WHAT ARE TOPICS?

A topic is the lowest-level learning object in a course or other knowledge product. It is the building block of instruction that accomplishes a single learning objective. Typically, a topic requires a combination of absorb, do, and connect activities and includes an assessment to gauge accomplishment of the objective.

Examples of topics

The term *topic* may still seem abstract and remote. Let's fix that by looking at some concrete examples of topics. One is very simple, another a bit more ambitious, and one complex indeed. As we look at each, we will point out its instructional design and its visible components.

A simple topic

Here is an example of a simple topic. (You might remember it from Chapter 1, where I used it to illustrate a low-level learning object, containing the three essential learning activities.) It consists of a single Web page and is about as simple as a topic can be.

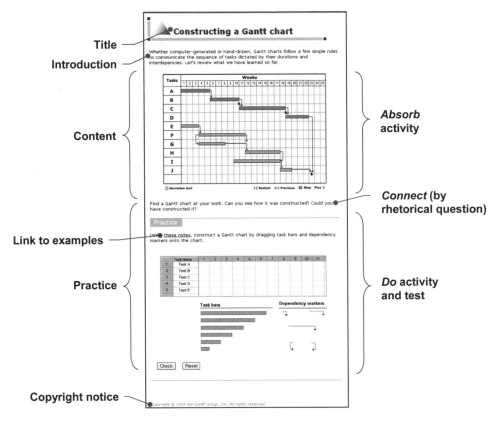

This simple topic accomplishes a simple objective, namely teaching how to interpret dependency markers in a Gantt chart. Though only a single page, this topic has the main components of a learning object.

It has a title that announces and labels the topic. A short paragraph introduces the topic and summarizes its content. Next follows a narrated animation that explains what dependency markers are and how to recognize them. After the animation is a short paragraph that emphasizes the key point and then links to another topic for more information on dependency markers. Next the learner is invited to display a real Gantt chart and interpret the meaning of dependency markers found there.

Although simple, this topic contains the necessary learning experiences. Learners **absorb** the concept by reading a definition and experiencing the animation. The practice provides both a **do** activity and a test. Learners **connect** with future learning through the link to another topic.

A typical topic

Our next example is a bit more complex. It teaches the learner to make a difficult decision requiring research, analysis, and judgment.

This topic is from a prototype course for managers of wilderness areas. It is called a *micro-scenario* because it presents a situation based on real events that requires the learners to make a decision just as they would in the real world.

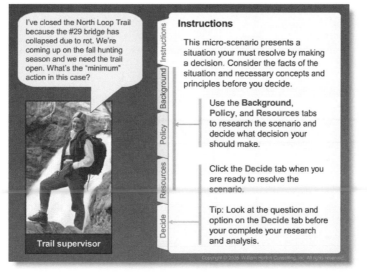

The **Instructions** tab welcomes learners to the main activity of the object and provides directions on how to complete the assignment.

Created in Microsoft PowerPoint and converted for Web delivery using Adobe Breeze Presenter. View example at horton.com/eld/.

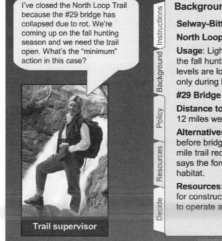

The **Background** tab supplies details about the situation learners must investigate and find a solution for. Learners must **absorb** these details before searching for a solution.

The **Policy** tab reveals the most important constraints on a solution, namely regulations that govern the situation described in the Background. Learners must **absorb** this information before attempting to apply it.

The **Resources** tab presents a list of links to documents. Learners must research both the situation of the specific wilderness area as well as the generic information on regulations. This research **connects** learners to resources they will use in the future.

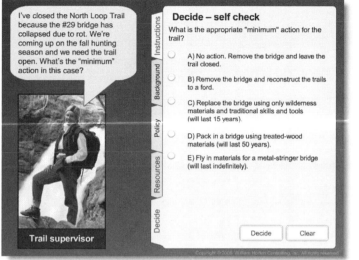

The final tab, **Decide**, lets learners choose a solution. These choices are all plausible, so learners must conduct research and carefully analyze the situation to pick the right answer. Learners' decisions provide an assessment on how well the objective was met. This is a **do** activity.

Test was built using Adobe Breeze Presenter.

A complex topic

As an example of a complex topic, we look at the learning object that teaches how to set the material properties in a computer program called *GALENA*. The material properties are necessary for *GALENA* to analyze the safety of a dam or other slope. To enter material properties, the user of *GALENA* must make several separate entries on a dialog box in the program.

The topic has several tabs, each of which reveals a different part of the topic.

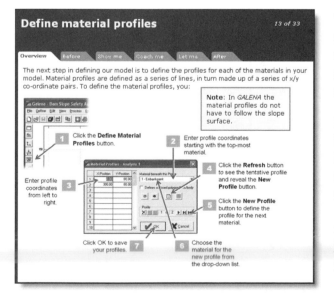

The **Overview** tab presents a concise preview of what learners will learn about how to define material properties. This overview serves as a summary as well.

Learners may **absorb** the instructions provided here. Or learners may print the page and use it as a job aid, which helps them **connect** to real work.

Tabbed interface built using Adobe Dreamweaver and custom JavaScript. Screens captured with TechSmith SnagIt. Illustrations created in Microsoft PowerPoint.

6

Topics

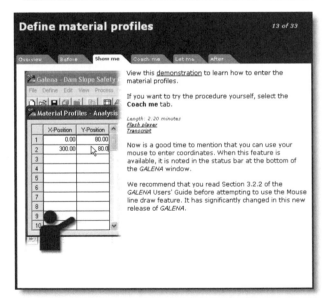

The **Before** tab supplies background information learners need before beginning the other activities. It explains the parts of the model that will be built in this topic.

Learner **absorbs** this information.

The **Show me** tab lets learners watch a demonstration of how to perform this step. This tab contains links to launch the demonstration and to display a transcript of its voice narration.

The demonstration appears in a separate window because the actual program requires a window larger than that of the course.

Experiencing this demonstration is an **absorb** activity.

Demonstration built with Adobe Captivate.

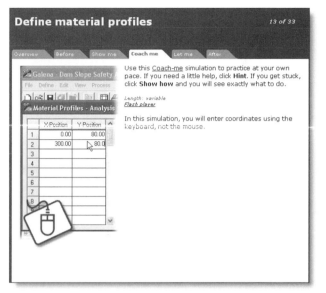

The **Coach me** tab lets learners practice performing the procedure. From this page, they launch a simulation in which they try to perform the procedure just demonstrated. Learners get feedback and can request hints or instructions.

Performing this simulation is a **do** activity.

Simulation built with Adobe Captivate.

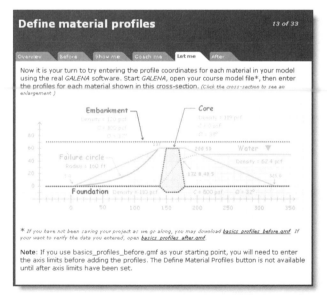

The **Let me** tab gives learners instructions for an activity performed with the real software. It provides a starting model and instructions of what learners are to do with the model. Learners must apply knowledge gained from the previous two tabs.

Performing an activity without assistance with the real software is a **connect** activity.

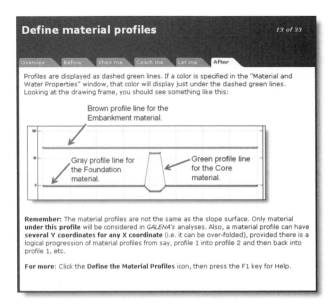

The **After** tab helps learners verify that the let-me activity was performed correctly. It also provides hints for how learners can verify their own success when using the software for their own models. And it suggests additional topics to pursue.

As a wrap-up, this tab helps learners **connect** to future learning.

Anatomy of a topic

Let's look at the components you might find in a simple, topic-level learning object. This list is comprehensive, so don't try to include all these items in every topic you create.

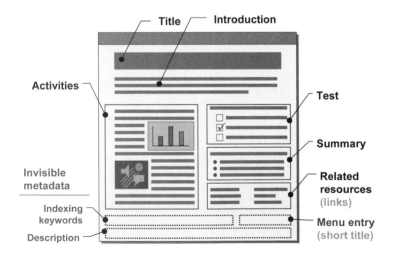

The first thing the learner might notice would be the title of the topic displayed as a banner or headline at the top of the page.

Following the title might be a brief introduction to help put the content in context or motivate the learner to consider it carefully. Further contextual information might be provided by some kind of you-are-here indicator.

The primary focus of the page will be the activities. This part of the topic may include text, graphics, and other media. These components will provoke the necessary learning experiences. A test will provide practice and feedback to let learners monitor how well they accomplished the objective of the topic. And a summary may be included to help learners retain key ideas from the topic and to make sure that those merely skimming are exposed to all critical ideas.

To be completely self-contained, the topic would need to include a lot of material of interest to only a few learners. As a compromise, the topic may link to related resources for those who want to follow up on personal interests or to dig deeper into the main subject.

In addition to these visible components, the topic may have invisible items, typically to make it easier for learners to find the topic. The topic may contain indexing keywords that can be compiled to present an alphabetical index or that may be searched for by search engines. The topic may also have a description that can, for example, be scooped up and displayed as a catalog of available topics. Invisible items like keywords and description are part of what are called metadata, that is, information about the topic. Another part of the topic is the menu entry that the learner clicked on to jump to this topic. Although the entry is displayed separately, it is properly thought of as part of a self-contained topic.

DESIGN THE COMPONENTS OF THE TOPIC

Although topics may differ widely, most contain some standard components, such as a title, introduction, learning activities, assessments, and metadata. The objective gives rise to all the components of the topic, and it is the objective against which the results of these components are judged. Let's see how to translate the learning objectives of a topic into these components.

Title the topic

A small but essential part of the topic is its title. The title announces the topic to the world and makes promises on its behalf.

Titles are crucial

Titles are crucial for success of the topic. The title is often the first part of the topic the learner sees, for instance, in a menu showing available topics or at the start of a lesson that lists the topics of the lesson. The title is displayed in search results. The title is almost universally cataloged by search engines and is the highest priority text for a search match.

The topic title is also important because it is a promise to the learner. The title strikes a bargain with the learner: Take this topic and you will gain what the title implies.

Base the title on the objective

Make the title appropriate for each type of objective.

Type objective	Format for title	Examples
Do procedure X to accomplish Y.	_____ ing _____	Interpreting dependency links. Replacing a trail bridge. Defining material profiles.
Decide X.	Selecting _____ Choosing _____	Picking your prescription plan. Selecting your team members. Saying no to fraud.
Create an X that does Y.	Building a _____	Building trust among team members. Writing your first VB program.
Know X about Y.	[Name of X] [Statement summarizing X]	Dependency links. VAT differs by province.
Believe X.	Why _____? [or just a statement of X]	Why slope stability matters. Leveraged investments are risky.
Feel X about Y.	[Statement that implies X about Y]	Everyone brings something to the team. Slope failures kill people.

Compose a meaningful title

The title is the first part of a topic that learners read. A good title efficiently tells the learner what question the topic answers. A good title is:

▶ **Distinct**. Easily distinguished from names of other topics, lessons, activities, and other components.

▶ **Context-free**. Do not depend on the context or other surrounding information to make sense of the name. For this reason, avoid pronouns in titles. "Why this is so" is meaningless out of context.

▶ **Understandable**. Use standard grammar and terms meaningful to the reader. Be careful about using official terminology that learners will understand only after completing the topic.

▶ **Scannable**. Make the meaning obvious in a glance without further reading. Put the most important words at the beginning of the title so they are noticed and not cut off if the list of titles is narrow. Change "How you can make friends" to "Making friends."

▶ **Thematic**. The learner can predict the contents of the topic from the title. See whether learners can match titles to the objectives of the topics.

▶ **Motivational**. The learner recognizes "what's in it for me." Compare "Filling in the 3407/J form" to "Reducing bank fraud."

Every topic should have a unique title that learners will understand, even when they see the title apart from the topic. Often learners must pick a topic from a list of topic titles. A knowledgeable learner should be able to guess the content of the topic from its title.

And a short title, too

When you title your object, take a few seconds to coin a shorter form of the title. This shorter form may better fit onto narrow menus. This may be more effective than having the display chop off all but the first few words of the title or else wrap the title to several lines.

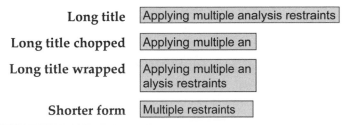

Long title	Applying multiple analysis restraints
Long title chopped	Applying multiple an
Long title wrapped	Applying multiple an alysis restraints
Shorter form	Multiple restraints

To shorten a title, pick out the most important verbs and nouns from the long title. Abbreviate if necessary, but make sure learners will recognize the abbreviation. If possible, provide a tool tip or hover text that displays the full title when the learner moves the cursor over the short title.

Here are some examples of long and short titles:

Original title	Short form of the title
Interpreting dependency links	Dependency links
Replacing a trail bridge	Replace bridge
Defining material profiles	Profiles

Introduce the topic

Do you just dive into the heart of the topic, or do you provide an introduction to gently ease the learner into the subject? And how should you introduce the subject of a topic?

Do you need an introduction?

When learners may jump from topic to topic, introductions are especially important. How much of an introduction should you include? That depends on how the learner gets to the topic.

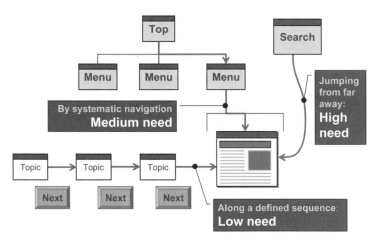

Learners may get to the topic along a trail of topics by repeatedly pressing the **Next** key. Because each topic introduces the next, very little introduction is needed. Sometimes the learner may get to the topic by systematically navigating a hierarchy of menus. Because the path is systematic, the need for an introduction is moderate. Other times the learner may jump to the topic from a distant topic or find the topic using a search process. In this case, the need for an introduction is high.

Examples of introductions

Here are some examples of introductions based on the objective of the topic and how the topic will be accessed.

Example: Interpreting dependency links

Objective   Teach how to recognize and correctly interpret dependency links to a mid-level manager or supervisor who can interpret task bars on a Gantt chart.

Introduction   Restatement of prerequisite knowledge to set the context: "Dependency links show the relationship between the start and finish of two tasks. For example, the requirement that Task A must be completed before Task B can start."

Example: Replacing a trail bridge

Objective   Teach how to decide the "minimum action" necessary to maintain a trail in a wilderness area to a wilderness manager who understands the principles of "minimum action" and has access to underlying regulations and Web-based resources.

Introduction   Immediate presentation of the scenario problem the learner is to solve. The problem is stated in a speech balloon over the image of a trail manager standing beside a stream.

Example: Defining material profiles

Objective   Teach how to use the Material Profile dialog box in *GALENA* to define the cross section for a layer of material in a slope-stability model to an engineer responsible for safety of slopes in open-pit mines who can use *GALENA* to create a model of a slope up to the point of defining cross sections.

Introduction   Context of the topic in the overall process and a restatement of prerequisite knowledge: "The next step in defining our model is to define the profiles for each of the materials in your model. Material profiles are defined as a series of lines, in turn made up of a series of x-y co-ordinate pairs."

Base the introduction on the type of objective

As with all other components of the topic, we look to the objective for guidance. Make the introduction appropriate for each type of objective.

Type objective	Type introduction
Do procedure X to accomplish Y.	Why perform the procedure. What it accomplishes. When to perform the procedure. One-sentence overview of the procedure.
Decide X.	Statement of the question or issue to be decided. When the decision is necessary. Statement that the decision is often made incorrectly.
Create an X that does Y.	Why create X. Mention Y and its value to the learner.
Know X about Y.	Context of Y into which X fits. Restatement of prerequisite knowledge. Question that X answers.
Believe X.	Current belief (that does not include X). Startling reason to believe X.
Feel X about Y.	Context of Y. What is Y? Statement of how the learner probably feels about Y now.

For more examples of introductions, see *Secrets of User-Seductive Documents* (horton.com/html/whcsed.asp).

Design a good introduction

A good introduction welcomes and orients the learner. It helps the learner see how the topic relates to other topics and to the course as a whole. A good introduction should:

▶ Confirm that learners are in the right location. It lets learners verify that they jumped to the right topic. It provides enough information to let them decide whether to continue with the topic or resume searching elsewhere.

▶ Orient learners who jumped directly to this topic from far away. It provides enough of a preview that learners understand what the topic will do for them.

▶ Set the context for the rest of the content of the topic. Prepares learners to interpret what they read, see, and hear.

▶ Motivate deeper study. The introduction gives learners reasons to study hard.

For most topics, only a short introduction is necessary. A couple of sentences and a single graphic usually suffice.

Test learning for the topic

The topic should verify that it accomplished its objective. A simple test will do this. It will verify learning to reassure the learner and to assist the developer in improving the topic. Chapter 5 shows several types of formal tests you can build into your topics. In addition, many of the activities suggested in Chapters 2, 3, and 4 can help learners and designers gauge how much learning occurred.

Examples of tests based on objectives

The test used to measure success of the topic must verify that its objective was accomplished. Here are some examples:

Example: Interpreting dependency links

Objective   Teach how to recognize and correctly interpret dependency links to a mid-level manager or supervisor who can interpret task bars on a Gantt chart.

Test   Referring to a Gantt chart, answer 5 questions such as which task depends on a particular task or which tasks must be completed before another task can begin.

Example: Replacing a trail bridge

Objective   Teach how to decide the "minimum action" necessary to maintain a trail in a wilderness area to a wilderness manager who understands the principles of "minimum action" and has access to underlying regulations and Web-based resources.

Test   Require learners to decide among 5 courses of action. Selection will require judgment and compromise. Choices represent tradeoffs among invasiveness, economy, and longevity. For example, one choice is more disruptive of the environment but will not have to be repeated every few years.

Example: Defining material profiles

Objective	Teach how to use the **Material Profile** dialog box in *GALENA* to define the cross section for a layer of material in a slope-stability model to an engineer responsible for safety of slopes in open-pit mines who can use *GALENA* to create a model of a slope up to the point of defining cross sections.
Test	Assessment is provided in two ways:
	The steps of the coach-me activity can be individually scored and an overall score reported (a la SCORM) to a LMS.
	The final let-me activity tests learners' ability to perform the procedure unaided.

Pick test for type of objective

The type of test you use depends on the type of learning objective. Here are some suggestions to get you thinking along these lines:

Type objective	How assessed
Do procedure X to accomplish Y.	Require the learner to recognize situations in which the procedure should be applied and to perform the procedure.
Decide Y.	Give the learner situations that call for the decision and the necessary information and other resources and observe whether the learner makes the correct decision.
Create an X that does Y.	Give the learner the assignment to create X and the resources necessary to do so. Observe whether the learner does so successfully.
Know X about Y.	Test whether the learner can recall and interpret facts, principles, and concepts.
Believe X.	Verify that the learner's statements and actions are guided by the belief.
Feel X about Y.	Verify that the learner's statements and choices reveal the desired emotion.

Specify learning activities for the topic

Learning activities are the heart of the topic. They power the learning. Chapters 2, 3, and 4 can suggest specific activities for you to consider.

Examples of learning activities in topics

Once again, here are our titles and objectives. For each objective a selection of absorb, do, and connect activities is listed.

Example: Interpreting dependency links

Objective   Teach how to recognize and correctly interpret dependency links to a mid-level manager or supervisor who can interpret task bars on a Gantt chart.

Activities   **Read introduction**. Definition of dependency links. Statement of why they are important.

View animation, pointing out dependency markers and how they connect tasks.

Read and think. Summary of what dependency markers do and an invitation to find them in your own Gantt charts.

Example: Replacing a trail bridge

Objective   Teach how to decide the "minimum action" necessary to maintain a trail in a wilderness area to a wilderness manager who understands the principles of "minimum action" and has access to underlying regulations and Web-based resources.

Activities   **Read**. Description of the situation and summary of the regulations. Situation is that a trail bridge has collapsed due to rot. Regulations permit actions to reopen the trail, provided they are the "minimum action" as defined in legislation.

Research the situation. Read about the wilderness area and the trail to learn how it is used. Examine maps to scout out alternative routes and to identify resources that could be used to rebuild the bridge.

Research regulations. Examine laws, regulation, articles, and case studies to identify issues that must be considered in making a decision.

Decide. Choose among 5 plausible alternative courses of action.

Example: Defining material profiles

Objective	Teach how to use the **Material Profile** dialog box in *GALENA* to define the cross section for a layer of material in a slope-stability model to an engineer responsible for safety of slopes in open-pit mines who can use *GALENA* to create a model of a slope up to the point of defining cross sections.
Activities	**Read**. Overview of the steps of the procedure.
	Read and view. Aspects of the ongoing example that will be filled in during this phase.
	Watch and listen. Demonstration of setting material profiles in *GALENA*.
	Perform simulated process. Learners repeat the process demonstrated. Receive feedback and hints as necessary.
	Perform procedure for real. Learners define a specified material profile using *GALENA*. Learners then compare results to targeted results.

Pick activities for the type objective

Let's look at the kinds of learning experiences that you might need for each of the different types of learning objectives. This is only a starter set. Volumes have been written about how to pick activities to teach various objectives. Still, this should get you started.

Type objective	Learning activities to consider		
	Absorb	**Do**	**Connect**
Do procedure X to accomplish Y.	Watch a demonstration of the steps. See examples of conditions that trigger the procedure.	Practice performing the steps.	Identify personal situations in which the procedure will apply. Identify how it must be modified to apply.

Type objective	Learning activities to consider		
	Absorb	**Do**	**Connect**
Decide Y.	Read or watch presentations on: ▶ Rules for deciding. ▶ How to gather information. ▶ Reasons for each option.	Practice deciding for various assumptions.	See consequences of decisions. Decide for situations in the learner's life.
Create an X that does Y.	Presentation of the requirements of Y. Demonstration of how to use tools.	Practice creating an X that does Y.	Create an X for the learner's Y.
Know X about Y.	Read, listen, watch a presentation on X.	Practice identifying X in various situations.	Identify situations in which this knowledge applies. Apply knowledge to a personal situation.
Believe X.	Presentation or readings on: ▶ Reasons for X. ▶ Facts suggesting X.	Infer X from facts and reasons.	Acknowledge change of beliefs. Apply new beliefs to personal situation.
Feel X about Y.	Presentation and readings on reasons to feel X. Image associating X and Y.	Respond to situations in which Y triggers X.	State the personal effect of feeling X.

6

Topics

Summarize the topic

If a topic consists of more than a single scrolling zone of information, you may want to include a summary.

When to include a summary

The summary gives the learner another chance to learn. It also helps learners verify that they acquired the necessary knowledge. A good summary may be all that is needed by learners returning for a refresher or for learners who already know much about the subject and only need to extend their knowledge a little bit.

Include a real summary

Many topics have a page or section titled "Summary," but lack any true summary. A real summary states the key points the learner should know before ending the topic. Many so-called summaries merely restate the objectives. I think lazy designers are to blame.

No	☺ Yes
This module taught how to:	To **set a starting time**, select the time and then type in minutes and seconds.
▶ Set a starting time using the keyboard.	To **adjust the time,** use the **up** and **down** buttons.
▶ Use buttons to adjust the time.	To **specify what to pick**, select the **Team** or **Person** checkbox.
▶ Pick a person at zero time.	To **specify people** to pick from, click the **Specify people** button. For teams, click the **Specify teams** button.
▶ Pick a team at zero time.
▶ Specify the people to pick from.
▶ Specify the teams to pick from.

Combine overview and summary

One way to simplify your topic is to design the summary as an overview and put it early in the topic.

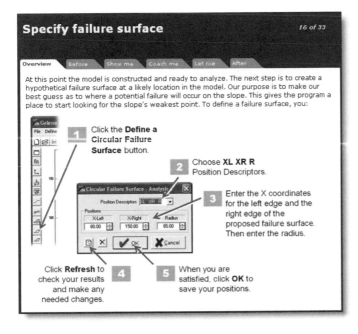

The *GALENA Slope Stability Analysis* course does just this. The topics for each procedure begin with an **Overview** tab that serves as both a preview of the steps to be learned and a summary of those steps.

Tabbed interface built using Adobe Dreamweaver and custom JavaScript. Screens captured with TechSmith SnagIt. Illustrations created in Microsoft PowerPoint.

6

Topics

Link to related material

Real life is seldom simple. Problems defy simple solutions, and work demands a wide mix of skills and knowledge. Topics must provide a variety of learning experiences and reference materials.

Make it easy for learners to read related topics and materials. Put hyperlinks to other topics learners may need. In each topic, present just one main idea. Link to other topics, rather than include their information.

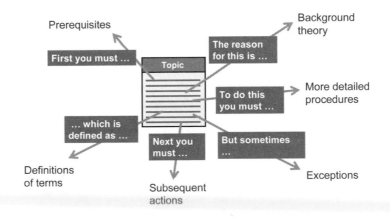

Link to reference materials or to other topics for background theory, more details for a procedure, exceptions to a rule, subsequent actions for a procedure, definitions of terms, and prerequisites or requirements before beginning an activity.

Connect related knowledge

Continually ask yourself, "What other information would help the learner?" Use hyperlinks to let learners quickly find all the different kinds of information they need to answer their questions. Consider linking these kinds of information (Notice some hyperlinks are two-way and others are just one-way):

Steps in a procedure	↔	Concept involved
A step in a procedure	↔	The next step in the procedure
One way of doing a task	↔	Another way
Overview	↔	Specific details
Term	→	Definition
Principle or concept	↔	Concrete examples that illustrate it
General rule	↔	Exceptions to the rule
Parent topic	↔	Child topic
Knowledge or skill	→	Prerequisite knowledge or skill

Let's look at how some topics and lessons expand the potential learning experiences by linking to related materials.

The *Designing Knowledge Products* course begins each lesson with references to prerequisites and related information. These links take the learner to topics in other lessons or to documents found elsewhere on the Web.

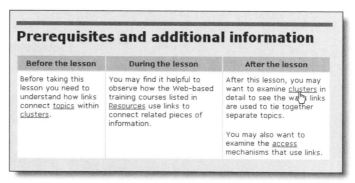

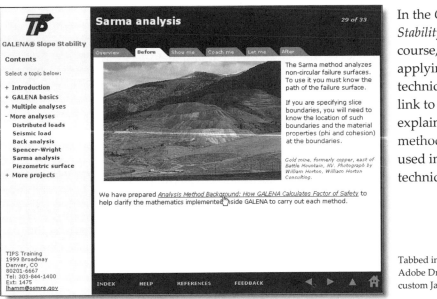

In the *GALENA Slope Stability Analysis* course, the topic on applying an analysis technique contains a link to a document explaining the method of calculation used in the technique.

Tabbed interface built using Adobe Dreamweaver and custom JavaScript.

6

Topics

Learners who were interested in learning more about the mathematics involved in the technique could download and read this document.

Document created in Microsoft Word and converted to PDF using Adobe Acrobat Professional.

GALENA® Slope Stability

Analysis Methods Background

How GALENA calculates factor of safety

By Lou Hamm

Presented by TIPS Training ... at the speed of technology

Limit free-form hyperlinks

Limit free-form hyperlinks. These are links that jump diagonally across the organizational hierarchy. Such links lead to the *tangled vine dilemma*. If you include a topic in your e-learning, you must include all the topics it links to. And all the topics they link to. And all they link to. And so on and on.

One mildly painful solution may be to enable free-form navigation only through the menu, the index, a search facility, or automatically generated next and previous links. The solution is painful because finding related topics now requires consciously searching for them. But the result is that the topics and lessons you create can be reused freely.

One technique to use is to suggest search terms to the learner who needs to find related topics, for example, "For more detailed instructions, search for "editing sentences and words."

Write metadata

Metadata is just descriptive labeling. The term metadata means "information about information." It is just a fancy way to refer to the descriptive labeling that can be used by learners to find topics they want to take and by developers to find topics they want to include in their courses.

Industry standards define specific metadata items (p. 402), and many authoring tools leave slots on their dialog boxes where you can enter metadata for your topics and other components.

Include keywords and a description

Two metadata items are especially important for designers of topics: the description and keywords. Although these items may not be visible to learners as they take the topic, they can help learners and developers find the topic when they need it.

The keywords may be used like index terms in a book. The learner may enter them in a search field to find a topic that matches these terms. The description may appear in a catalog of course topics. Here are some examples:

Example: Interpreting dependency links

Description	Shows what dependency link markers look like and explains what they mean.
Keywords	dependency links
	dependency markers
	links, dependency
	markers, dependency

Example: Replacing a trail bridge

Description	Teaches managers to conduct research necessary to decide the minimum action for maintaining a wilderness trail.
Keywords	minimum action
	trail bridge
	ford
	bridge outage
	maintaining a trail
	trail maintenance

Example: Defining material profiles

Description	Teaches how to add a profile to indicate the cross section for a material in the slope.
Keywords	material profile
	profile, material
	cross section

Assign indexing keywords

If your e-learning is large, you will need to include an index and possibly a keyword search facility. That means you must assign indexing terms to topics. The terms you assign depend on the content of the topic and on the objective it accomplishes.

Anticipate questions of learners

When do you use the index of a paper book? When do you do a Web search? When you are seeking the answer to a question—that's when. This suggests that we choose keywords to match questions learners may have and that our topics may answer.

1. Compile a list of questions that learners may have. Consider all the ways a learner might ask the question. Remember, the learner may not know the official terminology yet.

2. Identify which topics answer these questions.

3. Assign keywords to each topic by picking words prominent in the questions that the topic answers.

Add more terms

Consider additional terms. Here are some candidates:

▶ Unique nouns and verbs from the title, body text, and figure captions.

▶ Names of things. Include prominent proper nouns, official nomenclature, and parts lists.

▶ Objects and concepts shown in graphics, especially ones not explicitly named in the text.

Include more than standard words

Further enrich your keyword by including familiar:

▶ **Abbreviations**. How many people know what NASA or UNESCO stands for? How many would type out the full form of a more common abbreviation, like IBM or CIA?

▶ **Part numbers**. Many mechanics know the numbers of frequently replaced parts better than the names of these components.

▶ **Slang and jargon**. Learners may have a workplace vocabulary that does not square with the official terminology used in your topic.

Speak the learner's language

Remember, not everybody uses the same words or spells them the same way. Learners may not yet know the official names of things. So, in your keywords, include synonyms, that is, words with the same meaning. For example:

copy → duplicate, replicate, reproduce

build → create, make, generate

Vary the grammatical form of the words. Some search engines can do this automatically. If yours cannot, consider including multiple forms of each important word. For example:

> copy → copying, copies, copied

> build → building, built

Account for spelling variations. British and American spellings may differ. And some words may have competing spellings or different forms for the plural or collective. For example:

> color → colour

> appendixes → appendices

Do not over-index

These techniques are good for keyword searches, but can cause a problem in displayed indexes. If you plan to include an index, use a subset of your keyword list so that the displayed alphabetical index will not end up with too many nearly identical entries in a row.

Describe your topic

Another important piece of metadata is the description of your topic. This description may be displayed to the learner as a preview of the topic or an inducement to take it. There are no hard-and-fast rules for writing the description, but here are some commonsense suggestions:

▶ **Write the description for the potential learner**. It is easier for an instructional developer to understand a description written for learners than vice versa.

▶ **Tell learners what the topic offers them**. I do not recommend the usual boring recitation of the instructional objectives—in a bullet list nonetheless—but a simple statement of what the learner will be able to do as a result of the topic.

▶ **Keep the description short**. A few sentences are usually enough. If learners are curious, they can examine the topic itself.

▶ **Choose terms that the learner will understand**. Do not use terms that the learner would understand only after completing the topic.

DESIGN REUSABLE TOPICS

Just dumping content into templates does not make for effective learning. Just structuring topics as learning objects does not in itself make the content usable or reusable. To be useful and reusable, topics must be designed with reuse in mind. And reuse can only come if the topic is useful in the first place.

Craft recombinant building blocks

Reusable components are discrete chunks, not flowing passages. They are like building blocks that can be stacked to build a wall, a house, or a cathedral.

Design discrete chunks of reusable content

Effective topics are coherent, self-contained, complete, and consistent.

Reusable content is coherent. It aims to accomplish one purpose or answer one question. It confines itself to one subject and does not meander into non-essential material.

Reusable topics are self-contained. They may be consumed in any order. Sure, consuming topics in a specific order, such as the steps of a procedure, may make them more valuable and understandable, but no one should become hopelessly confused when encountering a topic out of sequence.

Reusable topics are complete. They contain everything necessary to accomplish their goal. They may contain the necessary presentations, practice activities, and other content directly. Or they may contain other more-specific topics.

Reusable topics are consistent. We can mix and match them with little concern that learners will become confused as they navigate the course (p. 313).

Use recipe cards as a guiding metaphor

If you need a role model of reusable objects, think of recipe cards. Each is self-contained and complete. It contains all the knowledge necessary for a cook to prepare one dish. It is concise and focused. It does not mix too many different types of information or stray from the subject. Recipe cards follow a consistent format.

Imagine taking a stack of recipe cards and throwing them in the air. After they flutter to the floor, pick one at random. It still works. Sorting the cards out by type of dish or nutritional characteristics may add value, but no one will be poisoned by a recipe card taken out of context. That is a goal we should work for in designing reusable topics.

Design consistent topics

Prevent the whiplash experience that occurs when learners, moving through a sequence of topics, are buffeted by an unpredictable sequence of pedagogical designs, colors, navigation schemes, icons, writing styles, backgrounds, layouts, sound levels, media, and test questions. In developing your topics, standardize:

▶ Visual appearance.

▶ Navigation schemes.

▶ Instructional strategies.

▶ Testing approaches.

This advice goes double if topics are created by multiple departments and triple if multiple companies are involved.

Avoid the "as-shown-above" syndrome

What happens if our topics are not self-contained? Imagine the introduction of a topic where you find the phrase "In a previous topic you learned how to …." But what if the learner chose to skip that topic? Or jumped directly to this topic from a search engine? The presumption that learners all follow a single path through the course indicates that the topics are not truly self-contained.

The *as-shown-above syndrome* is the tendency of designers to assume that everybody takes the course in exactly the sequence the designer intended. You see it in phrases and assumptions like these:

▶ "As shown above" and "As shown below" (where the items mentioned are not on the current screen or even in the current topic).

▶ "Earlier you read that… ."

▶ "By now you have learned how to… ."

▶ "Repeat the preceding steps" (when the preceding steps are in another topic or have scrolled off the screen).

▶ "… will be explained later" (But will the learner be reading later?).

▶ Abbreviations spelled out only the first time they are used and terms defined only the first time they are used.

▶ Warnings, cautions, notes, and conventions in the beginning of the course.

▶ "The next step in the process is …." (when the learner arrived at this topic directly from a search).

▶ Links labeled <u>Return to X</u> (when we did not come from X).

The solution is to make no hard assumptions about which path learners will follow. If understanding one idea requires understanding another idea, state the other idea, or link to it, or at least signal the requirement. Make it easy for learners to find needed information out of sequence. Here's where an index pays for itself. As do a good menu and a search facility.

INTEGRATE FOREIGN MODULES

Sometimes the best way to build your e-learning is to include topics, activities, and lessons developed by others. Technically, you can do so just by linking to these "foreign" modules. However, content developed by someone else following different standards may look different, teach differently, and further different objectives than your topic or lesson. Such modules may prove confusing to learners accustomed to your e-learning's "native" topics and activities.

Well, you must design a "docking module" to fit between the foreign content and your topic.

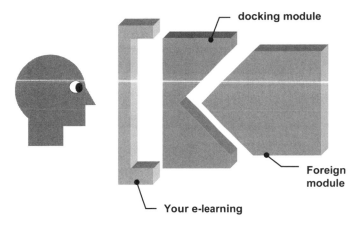

The docking module helps the foreign module fit into your course so that learners can make the transition from your course to the foreign module and back again.

Example of a docking module

Here is an example of a module designed for one course but appearing within another.

The brief introduction to the foreign module tells learners where the module comes from and guides them in navigating the module.

It also tells learners what file formats are used and what portions of the module should be ignored.

COMBINE LEARNING ACTIVITIES

The individual learning activities of Chapters 2, 3, and 4 and the topics of Chapter 6 can be combined to accomplish more ambitious goals and to create richer, more sophisticated learning environments.

Simple, single learning activities hardly make for revolutionary learning—until you start combining them in creative ways to build much richer learning experiences. How could you combine simple activities to teach a complex subject?

First, what do you want to teach? Think of an especially difficult concept or procedure. Now, what coordinated combination of learning experiences can accomplish your goal? You will need to list them and sketch a diagram showing relationships among the separate experiences.

Suppose we want to teach remodeling contractors how to obtain approval from the architectural review committee for a historic neighborhood.

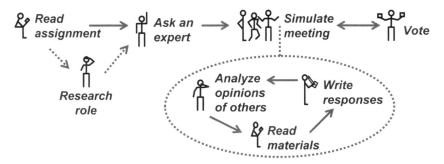

The first activity might ask learners to read the assignment for the lesson. This is usually the first step for a complex activity. Because we want to use a role-playing activity, we encourage learners to research the roles they will play.

Our first collaborative activity might be a chat session during which learners can ask questions of an expert on the procedure of obtaining the necessary permits. Learners would participate in this activity in their assigned roles.

Next learners might simulate the meeting of the review committee. During and after the meeting, participants might vote on whether to grant the requested permit. The meeting should be designed to foster a cycle of activities, the first of which is analyzing the opinions of others.

Learners might then read materials to try to develop arguments to sway the opinions of others, sparking the need to write responses to those opinions. This would provoke more discussion, which would require more analysis, thus starting another cycle of analysis, research, and communication.

The next step is to create learning activities to provoke these planned learning experiences.

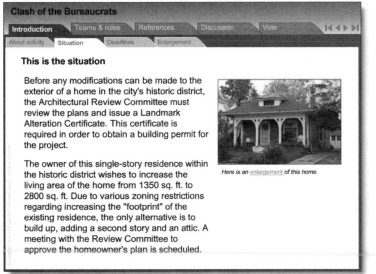

Here is the resulting lesson. It is a compound activity designed to provoke the required learning experiences. Notice the different tabs for different aspects of the activity.

Created in Microsoft PowerPoint and converted for Web delivery using Adobe Breeze Presenter. View example at horton.com/eld/.

This is the way to design lessons. Start with objectives and decide what learning experiences will accomplish those objectives. Then create materials to provoke and sequence those learning experiences. The key to effective lessons is to think first of the balance and flow of learning experiences and only later about content.

WAYS OF ORGANIZING LESSONS

Lessons can be organized into several generic structures, such as a linear sequence, a branching hierarchy, or a two-dimensional grid. Although these generic structures have their place, most e-learning is structured in ways that reflect the needs of learners and the nature of the subject matter. We call these organizations "purpose-specific" and design them around the subject matter and the learners' need for knowledge.

Common kinds of lessons

Let's briefly recap the lesson types and where to use them.

Structure	Description	When to use it
Classic tutorials (p. 323)	After an introduction, learners proceed through a series of topics, each teaching a more difficult concept or skill. At the end of the sequence are a summary and a test. Within the topics, teaching skills and concepts are examples and practice activities.	To teach basic knowledge and skills in a safe, reliable, and unexciting way.
Book-like structure (p. 329)	The lesson is organized as a hierarchy of general and specific areas. Learners can navigate the lesson sequentially as if turning pages, drill down to a specific topic, or consult an index or table of contents (main menu).	For subjects with a clear, accepted structure, especially if the lessons will be used for refresher learning or just-in-time learning.
Scenario-centered lessons (p. 333)	The lesson centers on a major scenario about a problem or project. After an introduction and preparation, the learner engages in a variety of activities all relating to accomplishing the goals of the central scenario.	To teach complex concepts, emotional subjects, or subtle knowledge that requires rich interaction with the computer or other learners.
Essential-learning tutorials (p. 340)	After an introduction, learners proceed through a series of tests until they reach the limits of their current knowledge. Then they are transferred into the main flow of a conventional tutorial, which ends with a summary and test.	To let impatient learners skip over topics on which they are already knowledgeable.

Structure	Description	When to use it
Exploratory tutorials (p. 345)	Learners find knowledge on their own. Learners navigate an electronic document, database, or Web site in which they accomplish specific learning goals. To aid in this task, they may use a special index and navigation mechanisms. Once learners have accomplished their goals, they view a summary and take a test.	To teach learners to learn on their own by developing their skills of navigating complex electronic information sources.
Subject-specific structure (p. 351)	A free-form structure where each topic, activity, or page can potentially lead to any other. In practice the structure is organized by the logical organization of the subject or the flow of a scenario.	For subjects that have a distinct organization you want to teach. And for simulations when other structures would interfere with learning.

E-learning courses have evolved several ways of structuring lessons. These have the advantage of much experimentation and refinement. Before you start to design your own lesson structures, take a few minutes to consider some of the models presented here. These models are not meant to be solutions to your problems. Use them as a starting point for your own solutions.

Classic tutorials

Most e-learning lessons today are organized as the classic tutorial. This structure enables the same flow of learning experiences teachers have used for 50,000 years.

Architecture of classic tutorials

In the classic tutorial, learners start with an introduction to the lesson and then proceed through a series of topics teaching progressively more advanced skills or concepts. At the end of the sequence, learners encounter a summary or review of the concepts and a test or other activity to measure whether they accomplished the objectives of the lesson.

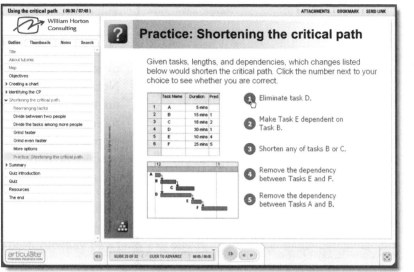

Associated with the topic is a practice activity. This activity asks learners to identify changes to a project that would shorten the critical path. Clicking a change reveals feedback for the item.

Practice activity created with Adobe Captivate.

Following the last lesson is a summary that recaps the important concepts in the tutorial.

The final element of the tutorial is a short, 4-question quiz.

Quiz created with Articulate Quizmaker.

When to use the classic tutorial structure

The classic tutorial structure is the safe, reliable choice. It is familiar to learners, especially to those who have taken conventional e-learning lessons. Learners seldom get lost in such a simple structure. It is flexible enough to adapt to many purposes, yet simple enough to create largely from templates. The tutorial structure also works well for simple training tasks, especially for cognitive subjects. Simple subjects typically require a clear explanation and a bit of practice. It is readily implemented as learning objects.

One drawback to the classic tutorial is its linear structure. Impatient or advanced learners resist plodding all the way through the sequence. We may need to give learners some alternative navigation paths.

The classic tutorial may not be the most efficient or effective, but it is simple and safe. With this structure, novice instructional designers cannot make mistakes so big that a little testing will not detect them.

Variations of the classic tutorial structure

There are hundreds of variations on the theme of the unstructured tutorial. Here are a few of the ways I have bent and twisted the classic tutorial structure to fit specific objectives.

▶ I find that many American and Canadian learners, upon first entering the lesson, experience an immediate itch to jump to the test to see whether they already know what the lesson teaches. For them, I put a button on each page to let them jump directly to the test at any time.

▶ Some learners, who are returning to the course as a refresher, will want to jump directly to the Summary—hence another button.

▶ I have also observed what I call "page flipping" behavior in this structure. Learners skip through the main sequence, without paying close attention, just scanning to see what topic the sequence contains. Only after they get well down that road do learners decide to actually take the lesson. For them, I include a menu so they can decide where to begin and what to repeat.

▶ In the classic tutorial, examples and practices are separate items off the main path. If examples and practices are short and simple, you may want to incorporate them onto the page of the skill or concept they demonstrate.

Best practices for the classic tutorial structure

The classic tutorial structure works well most of the time. As long as you keep it simple—and test to detect and correct problems—you should be able to use it for much of what you teach. When you use the classic tutorial, keep these suggestions in mind:

▶ **Do not try to teach too much**. Limit each sequence to no more than 7 to 10 simple skills or concepts; 3 to 5 would be better.

▶ **Do not omit practice activities**. Let people apply what they learn as soon as they learn it. Otherwise the main sequence turns into a boring page-turner.

▶ **Do not follow the structure mechanically**. Be practical, not dogmatic. Omit the parts of the structure you do not need. If you do not need an example, leave it out. If one topic does not require practice, fine. Consolidate short topics. I frequently put examples right on the main topic page.

▶ **Do not skimp on examples**. While you are being practical and omitting parts you do not need, take care to keep enough examples to ensure that learning really occurs.

▶ **Share control with learners**. Do not force-march learners from the beginning to the end of the tutorial. Let them skip topics they have already mastered. Let them repeat topics as many times as necessary.

7

Lessons

Book-like structures

The book structure fits e-learning to an organization and metaphor that has been proven over the past 500 years.

Architecture of the book structure

The book structure resembles the organization and features of a reference book. It usually starts with an introduction or overview. From the introduction, learners may jump to the starting topic of specific sections. From each of these high-level topics, learners may jump to subtopics. For example, learners could jump from the intro to section 1 and from there to topics 1A or 1B. Each of these mid- and low-level topics could be a learning object.

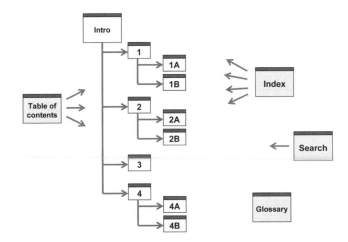

E-learning organized in the book structure usually contains a table of contents that serves as a main menu from which learners can jump directly to any main topic or subtopic. The e-learning may also contain an alphabetical index like the one typically found at the end of a book. The index enables learners to find a topic by the type of knowledge it conveys. Because learners can jump around the structure, they may encounter terms that they do not recognize. To prevent confusion, the book structure may offer an online glossary whereby learners can look up the meaning of abbreviations and technical terms. One addition to the book metaphor may be a search facility that lets learners type in a word or phrase to search for in the text of the e-learning.

As you can see, the book structure makes it easy to access individual topics, even out of sequence.

Books are not tutorials

The book structure is similar to the classical tutorial but differs in some subtle ways:

▶ Both contain hierarchical and sequential access, but the book structure emphasizes and encourages hierarchical (top-down) access.

▶ Topics are designed to be accessed in a sequence determined by the learner rather than the designer. Topics must be carefully designed so they can be consumed in any order.

▶ The book structure provides access mechanisms familiar in books, such as a table of contents (menu) and an alphabetical index. It may also include a glossary. And it may include a search facility.

Example: *Designing Knowledge Products*

The course *Designing Knowledge Products* uses a book structure.

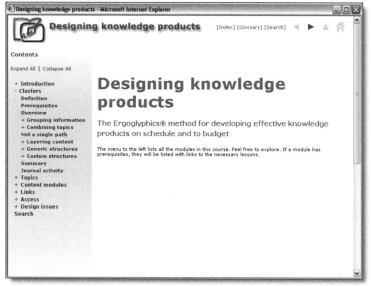

Originally created in 1996, it organized instructions on producing electronic courses and documents as an electronic document. The book structure was appropriate because it was familiar to designers who would be designing online documents and because it illustrated a strategy they might want to emulate for their Web sites and online documents.

Built using Adobe Dreamweaver and Active Server Pages.

Contents

Expand All | Collapse All

+ **Introduction**
- **Clusters**
   Definition
   Prerequisites
   Overview
      + **Grouping information**
      + **Combining topics**
   Not a single path
      + **Layering content**
      + **Generic structures**
      + **Custom structures**
   Summary
   Journal activity
+ **Topics**
+ **Content modules**
+ **Links**
+ **Access**
+ **Design issues**
Search

Looking at the first page, you can see the table of contents to the left

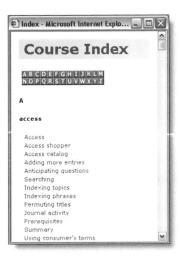

Clicking the **Index** link displays the alphabetical index. Clicking on a letter at the top of the panel scrolls the index to entries beginning with that letter.

Clicking the **Glossary** link displays a glossary window. There the learner can type in a term to look up the definition of that term or can click a letter button to scroll to glossary entries beginning with that letter.

Built using Adobe Dreamweaver and Active Server Pages.

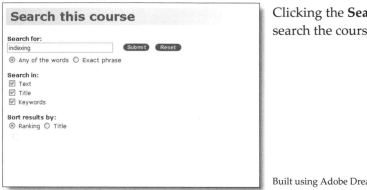

Clicking the **Search** link lets the learner search the course for specific topics.

Built using Adobe Dreamweaver and Active Server Pages.

When to use the book structure

When should we use the book structure? This structure works well for large, complex subjects with a well-understood organization. The hierarchical structure accommodates a large number of topics, making them accessible and revealing interrelationships among them. If content can fit into a hierarchical organization, the book structure is a good choice.

Use the book structure for just-in-time learning when finding pieces of knowledge is critical. Because content is logically and clearly organized, learners can reliably find individual topics when needed. The table of contents, index, and search facility simplify finding topics quickly.

Best practices for book structures

A book is not a course. The book structure is a good metaphor, but it takes careful design to make it seem natural for e-learning.

Organize content logically. The more logical the organization, the better learners can find individual topics. The most logical organization is the one expected by learners. If learners find the organization familiar, they can anticipate the location of specific topics. If learners do not have a consistent expectation of how the content is organized, then organize the lesson as suggested by experts in the field. That way the structure teaches learners to think as experts.

Do not overdo the book metaphor. Forward navigation does not require a hand to pull the page across the screen. You do not have to use a parchment background for displays. Displays need not be shaped as pages of a book. Adapt the structure of the book; do not mimic its minor details.

Index, index, index. Although indexing is hard work, it does make the content accessible to learners not yet familiar with the official terminology of the subject.

Enable drill-down navigation. Title topics clearly and list subtopics so that learners can select ever-more-specific topics until they get to a single topic that teaches what they want to learn.

Create self-contained topics. Learners do not always read from the start of the book. They may jump to a topic from the table of contents, index, or search facility. This means each topic must be self-contained. Chapter 6 on topics can help you do that.

Scenario-centered lessons

Some multifaceted learning activities are almost lessons in themselves. Almost. To turn them into lessons you must wrap them in a context and integrate them into your overall course structure. One way to do this is to design multiple activities that explore different aspects of a single, rich scenario to reveal different perspectives and to accomplish multiple objectives.

Architecture of scenario-centered lessons

The scenario-centered structure organizes learning around a main scenario. The scenario consists of an important and difficult task or problem. The scenario usually contains an ongoing example upon which individual topics or activities focus. For example:

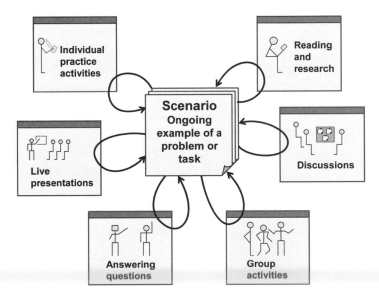

In the center is a complex problem or an **ongoing example**. After a brief introduction, the learner prepares for the activity. The scenario may occasion **reading and research** activities. All of the research and reading relates to issues raised in the scenario. For example, learners may have to research a solution to an obstacle in the scenario. They may have **discussions** about issues raised in the scenario. These discussions may involve ideas uncovered by research. The discussions may occasion more research. **Group activities**, such as brainstorming and role playing, may elaborate aspects of the scenario. **Questions** may be posed to learners about situations revealed in the scenario. **Live presentations** may be conducted to provide conceptual knowledge needed for the scenario or to discuss aspects of the scenario. **Individual practice activities** may require learners to make judgments and decisions relating to the scenario.

Because all the activities depend on the scenario and their goals are interdependent, it may be hard to make the individual activities into objects. It may make more sense to make the entire lesson into an object.

Example: Economics of learning

I taught an online seminar on economics of learning. It featured some pretty boring spreadsheets and formulas for calculating return on investment. Participation zoomed when I introduced a cast of imaginary characters and a crisis involving the characters.

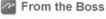

The hero of our story

Position: Chief Learning Officer

Company: Technology and Research Associates, aka TaRA

In job: 5 years

With company: 10 years

Problem: Rightsizing, downsizing, cutbacks, and outsourcing have plundered her once seven-figure budget and her corner office with floor-to-ceiling windows.

Charlotte O'Hara

I started with a hero to care about. I put the hero in difficult circumstances to win sympathy and arouse a desire to help the hero on her quest for redemption.

Presentation created in Microsoft PowerPoint.

From the Boss

Memo

Sales drive this company. Our sales force has to sell, sell, sell! And you have to support then any way you can—even if that means cutbacks in your own departments.

William Sherman
CEO
aka
"Scorched-Earth Bill"

The hero had a nemesis—not exactly a villain but certainly a challenge. The nemesis presented the learner with a predicament to overcome. The predicament called for immediate action.

To add interest, I gave the hero allies who provided advice and information that might otherwise appear in dry commentary. The idea of the scenario was to tell the story through the experiences and actions of people.

The hero had her moment of crisis and discovery.

I ensured that all actions took place in the context of helping the hero deal with the crisis. Abstract principles and formulas were presented as they applied to the situation faced by the hero.

In the end, the hero—with the learner's help—triumphed. The learner shared emotionally in that triumph.

By centering all the activities of the seminar on one woman's quest, the seminar gave personal meaning to some pretty dry subject matter.

Example: Graduate management course

Here is an example of a scenario-centered course. The course is titled *Managing the Design, Development, Delivery, and Evaluation of e-Learning.*

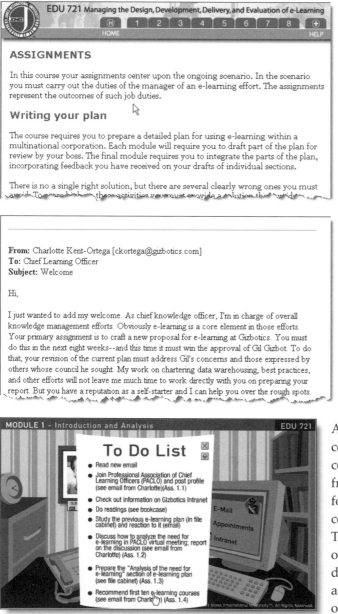

It is a graduate course in the master's of education degree program by Jones International University. In this course, the learner plays the role of the newly hired chief learning officer of a fictitious company. The centerpiece of this course is a single activity.

Learners are introduced to this activity in a welcome e-mail at the beginning of the course. The central activity requires the learner to craft a proposal for implementing e-learning at a fictitious company.

All other activities are in the context of this simulated company. Assignments stem from a to-do list rather than a formal syllabus. All items contribute to the overall goal. Tasks include drafting sections of the proposal as well as dealing with weekly crises, such as calming a nervous employee or revising an annual budget.

Likewise, weekly reading assignments relate to issues raised on the to-do list. Reference materials include a simulated corporate Web site, a previous version of the proposal, and various books and papers.

Online discussions with fellow learners take place in the format of online meetings of a professional association to which learners all belong. Each week's topic of discussion concerns an important issue or problem in the ongoing scenario.

Interview of ... Mia Majors	
Mia says:	**And then you respond:**
I'm a little worried whether we have the technology and our people have the technology skills to take e-learning. What I mean is, we are the last to get updated computer workstations. And we do not have the technical staff to help learners get started.	▸ What do you like about e-learning? ▸ Let me ask you a question on a different subject. ▸ Thank you. Those are all the questions I have.

Other activities include simulated interviews with executives who either support or oppose the proposed use of e-learning. A successful interview wins support for the proposal.

Designed by William Horton Consulting. Built by William Horton Consulting and Jones International University staff using Adobe Dreamweaver and Flash.

Questions asked of the instructor must be phrased as requests to the learner's boss in the simulation. Everything the learner experiences in this 8-week course relates directly or indirectly to the task of drafting the proposal.

When to use scenario-centered lessons

Use a scenario-centered lesson for complex concepts, emotional subjects, or subtle knowledge best taught by engaging learners in rich interaction. Use this structure for objectives that cannot be accomplished with a single large activity or a series of simple independent activities.

The scenario-centered structure works well for teaching subjects when the correct answer is based on conflicting needs and contradictory information, that is, when judgment is required. Because this structure exposes the learner to multiple perspectives and includes different formats of interaction, it builds a complete understanding of a complex situation.

This structure is also good to add continuity to the learning experience. And because it centers on a real situation, it provides context for abstract concepts and principles.

Variations on the scenario-centered lesson

The scenario-centered lesson structure is as varied as the activities on which it is centered. Here are some variations you might try:

Link to alternative materials. One common variation is to link to other learning and reference materials on the subject of the lesson. Include these links in the Introduction, Preparation, or Summary.

Add a practice session. If the activity is not truly interactive, you may want to graft on a practice activity so that learners get a chance to practice what they have learned.

Test by other means. Resist the urge to include a formal test of knowledge. Instead use a relevant activity, such as some kind of work product, to confirm that learners have mastered material taught in the lesson.

Include secondary scenarios. If your course teaches a complex activity, you may want to include some secondary scenarios that deal with special issues or problems. You can design your main scenario so that the secondary scenarios appear a natural part of the overall scenario.

Best practices for scenario-centered lessons

Pay attention to the quality of the core scenario. It is the heart of the lesson. Test its effectiveness with actual learners before you add the other components of the lesson. Do learners readily understand the task or problem—and do they care about its resolution?

Prepare learners. Provide everything necessary for learners to engage the scenario, for example:

- ▶ **Goals of the scenario**. What do the people in the scenario hope to accomplish? And what are the learning goals?

- ▶ **Context**. How does the scenario fit into the course as a whole?

- ▶ **Prerequisites**. What learners must know before beginning the lesson.

- ▶ **Rules of behavior**. What can learners do and not do in the lesson? How do learners interact with the instructor and fellow learners?

- ▶ **Instructions**. What tasks must be performed and what documents created? What are the deadlines?

- ▶ **Additional resources**. Include links to needed information, software, or other resources.

Explain the scenario. Unless learners understand the scenario, they may miss the points it is designed to make and may misconstrue the principles it is meant to illustrate. Explain what information is available about the scenario so that learners know how to fully understand the scenario. Tell learners what assumptions they must make. If the scenario is not completely realistic, explain its limits and ask learners to work within these limits or to use their imagination as to what lies beyond the limits of what is provided.

Monitor discussions and other activities to keep learners on track. It is easy for learners to misinterpret some aspect of the scenario or become fixated on some minor detail. Do not censor or interrupt discussions, but do gently nudge conversations back to the heart of the matter.

Tell learners how to ask questions and get help. Can they get help within the framework of the scenario, for example, by e-mailing one of the characters in the scenario? Or must they address questions to an external Help desk or facilitator? Be clear on the type of support provided and the mechanism for requesting assistance.

Essential-learning tutorials

There is nothing harder or more wasteful than trying to teach people something they already know. In the essential-learning tutorial, learners skip topics they do not need to learn. The essential-learning tutorial targets missing knowledge and skills. In the essential-learning tutorial, learners dive into the lesson at their thresholds of ignorance and proceed to the end, or until they satisfy their needs.

Architecture of essential-learning tutorials

The essential-learning tutorial is organized to enable learners to skip topics they have already mastered. The exact organization may vary, but the idea is to use testing to identify what learners already know and therefore do not need to learn.

Here's how an essential-learning tutorial might be organized. After an introduction, learners begin a gauntlet of tests. The tests are progressively more difficult. That is, each one assesses more advanced levels of knowledge or skills than those before. Learners continue down the test series until they fail to pass a test. At that point, they are directed into a parallel sequence of content topics. Thus learners enter the sequence at the upper limit of their abilities.

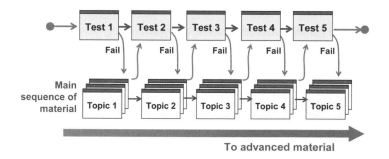

For example, a learner would not begin with Topic 1 but with a test on the objective of Topic 1. If the learner fails the test, the learner is enrolled in Topic 1. If the learner passes the test, the learner progresses to a test on the objective of Topic 2. Failing this test enrolls the learner in Topic 2. And so it goes, with the learner progressing through a series of tests, each covering the objective of a topic in the sequence. Failing a test shunts the learner into a sequence of topics. After completing the sequence and demonstrating mastery of the material, the learner can continue with the next sequence of topics or return to the series of tests. This way, the learner bypasses material already understood.

The topics in an essential-learning tutorial can be learning objects. And the tests can come from those already defined as part of the corresponding learning object.

Example: Visual Basic tutorial

Here is an example of an essential-learning tutorial. It teaches Visual Basic programming skills.

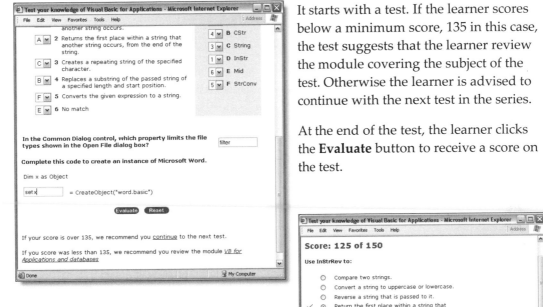

It starts with a test. If the learner scores below a minimum score, 135 in this case, the test suggests that the learner review the module covering the subject of the test. Otherwise the learner is advised to continue with the next test in the series.

At the end of the test, the learner clicks the **Evaluate** button to receive a score on the test.

The score card reveals the test results. Here the learner scored 125 out of a possible 150. The numeric value of the score indicates how well the learner understands the material.

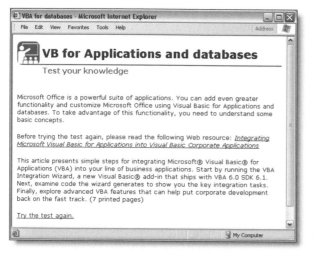

Because the learner scored less than the score required to skip the module, the learner is directed to the topic on the subject of the test.

Built using Adobe Dreamweaver and custom JavaScript.

In this example, the learner can choose to ignore the advice and continue with the testing sequence, take the module, or quit altogether. Some other variants of the essential-learning tutorial do not give the learner this choice.

Example: Coach-me simulations

Coach-me simulations have learners attempt the simulated task on their own. Learners receive hints or explicit directions only if needed.

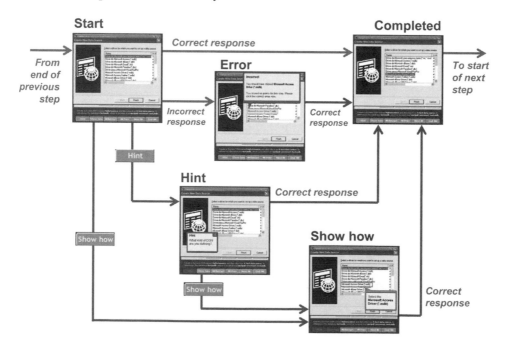

This diagram shows the common structure for each step in a simulated task. At the start of the step, the learner sees a simulated screen, without any prompting. If the learner makes the correct response, the simulation shows the results and a brief note confirming the correct response. The learner can then continue with the next step.

A learner who needs a little assistance can click a **Hint** button to reveal a suggestion for what to do. The suggestion does not tell the learner exactly what to do, but does guide the learner to think of the solution. A correct response then puts the learner back on track.

If the hint is not sufficient, the learner can click the **Show how** button to receive precise instructions on where to click and what to type. Once the learner follows the directions, the simulation continues.

In this architecture, the learner does not have to request a hint before receiving explicit instructions. The learner can always click the **Show how** button to receive explicit directions. The learner can also advance to the next step by pressing the **Next** button.

Thus learners proceed through the simulated procedure until they reach a step they cannot perform. Then they can get help by asking for a hint, asking for explicit instructions, or by attempting the step and getting feedback.

When to use the essential-learning tutorial

Use essential-learning tutorials to reduce the time spent learning a complex, varied subject. For such subjects, it is difficult to predict what aspects of the subject an individual learner knows already. By using this structure, you can match learning precisely to the needs of the individual.

Likewise, use the essential-learning tutorial to efficiently educate people from widely varying backgrounds. With a wide variety of learners, it is not practical to make everyone start at the level of the least knowledgeable learner and proceed to the goals of the most ambitious learner. Often, learners are too impatient to endure training on subjects they have already mastered. This structure lets advanced learners skip the parts that are too basic for their needs.

Variations on the essential-learning tutorial

The essential-learning tutorial is a simple structure that you can easily adapt to your needs. Here are a few variations you may want to consider:

Let learners quit as soon as they meet their goals. This structure lets learners dive in at the level of knowledge they possess. You can also let them jump out when they reach the level they desire. Let learners know that they can quit the lesson when they feel they have learned all they need.

Return to the test stream. If it is not so easy to tell what knowledge is basic and what is advanced, you can simply return learners to the test stream once they complete a content topic. It is probably best to return them to another version of the test they failed so they can confirm that they have indeed learned the material.

Generate lessons. Generated lessons tailor a lesson to each learner based on answers to a test or questionnaire presented at the start of the lesson.

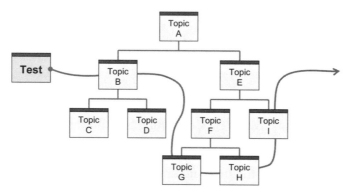

After a brief introduction, the learner takes a test or fills in a questionnaire. The test analyzes the learner's answers and threads a sequence of topics that exactly meets the needs of the individual learner. The lesson concludes with a summary and test.

Best practices for essential-learning tutorials

Validate your tests. Unless your tests accurately measure the learner's current knowledge, they will be ineffective in directing the learner to needed topics.

Make the test gauntlet more sophisticated. Use a more flexible and sensitive testing scheme. Give learners a graduated series of problems to solve. Each time learners get a question right, they skip ahead five questions. If they get one wrong, they go ahead to the next question. If they get three questions in a row wrong, they go directly to a topic at that level of difficulty.

Vary the kinds of tests. The test sequence can contain more than traditional true/false, multiple-choice, and short-answer questions. You can use any self- or computer-scored activity to decide where learners should jump into the content path. No one likes taking a long series of tests, so add variety with different types of questions, and throw in some games, too.

Focus each topic on a single learning objective. That way testing can precisely pinpoint the learner's needs and provide just the modules to meet those needs. Make each topic a distinct learning object.

Monitor usage and feedback to refine the tutorial. Look for modules that everybody bypasses. Are they really needed? Or are the tests for those topics too easy? Look for complaints from learners that they are taking topics that they already know. Perhaps the tests for these topics are too hard. Keep refining tests and topics until learning is highly efficient.

Exploratory tutorials

In an exploratory tutorial, learners discover knowledge on their own. They are given goals and an electronic collection of knowledge, which they must explore in order to achieve these goals. Learners may be given navigating tools to help in the task.

The exploratory tutorial is an extended version of the scavenger-hunt (p. 196) and guided-research (p. 199) activities.

Architecture of exploratory tutorials

The exploratory tutorial consists of two parts. One part is an external source of information. Typically this is an online knowledge product that existed before you created the tutorial. The external information source may be any type of information source that can be accessed online. It may be an electronic document, such as a manual, report, or specification. It could also be a database, a Help file for a computer program, a Web site, or even an online museum. The tutorial leverages the external information source to produce education or training.

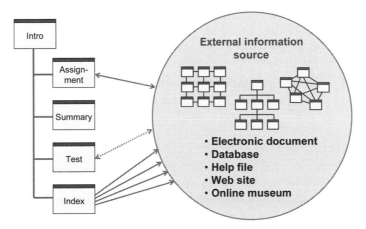

The exploratory tutorial itself might begin with an **introduction** that provides an overview of the tutorial and previews its contents. From the introduction, learners can access several kinds of activities and resources.

One essential activity is an **assignment** that causes learners to interact with the external information source. Typically it will require the learner to look up information in the external information source. To accomplish multiple objectives, the exploratory tutorial poses questions that together cover the objective. Questions are sequenced to reveal prerequisites first and to proceed from simpler questions to more difficult ones.

Because the external information source is vast and may cover more subjects than the ones relevant to the tutorial, the exploratory tutorial may include a **summary** of the subject. This summary would cover just enough of the subject to meet the tutorial's objectives. Think of it as backup or learning insurance.

To verify accomplishment of objectives, the tutorial may include a simple **test**. Completion of the assignment should provide adequate preparation for the test. The test may be "open book," meaning that the external information source may be searched for answers to help complete the test.

One final topic is a special **index** that helps learners locate relevant topics in the external information source. Entries in the index link to specific pages or topics in the external information source. A simple form of an index is just a page containing links to different relevant Web pages.

You may create several exploratory tutorials for a single external information source, each emphasizing a different aspect of the subject or covering how to perform a different task.

Exploratory tutorials are not made up of lower-level objects because each objective is taught not by the tutorial but by interaction with an external information source.

Example: Text-components catalog

The *Designing Knowledge Products* course includes an exploratory tutorial teaching how to design paragraphs, bullet lists, checklists, and other pieces of text in Web pages and other online documents.

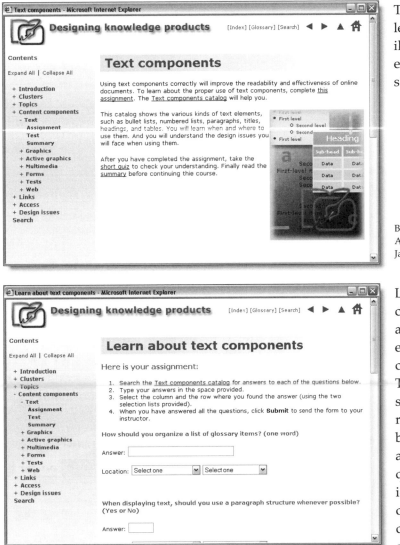

The Text-components lesson shown here illustrates the exploratory-tutorial structure.

Built using Adobe Dreamweaver, Active Server Pages, and custom JavaScript.

Learners are told to complete an assignment using an external text component catalog. The assignment is a scavenger hunt that requires the learner both to find the answers to specific questions and to identify the row and column (within the catalog) where the answer is found.

7

Lessons

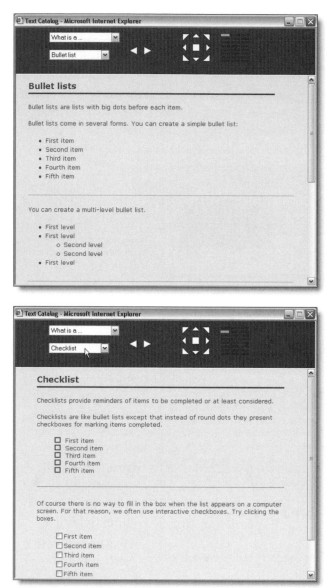

In the catalog, information is organized in a two-dimensional grid of three columns by eight rows. The three columns link to topics about each type of text component, namely what the component is, when to use it, and design issues when creating one of these components. The components themselves are organized into rows. They include bullet items, checklists, glossary items, indented lists, numbered lists, paragraphs, tables, and titles and headlines.

For example, selecting "What is a ..." and "Checklist" from the dropdown lists displays the topic explaining what checklists are, the first topic of the second row. Its location in the information source is indicated by the green rectangle in the dark-blue grid at the upper right.

Built using Adobe Dreamweaver and custom JavaScript. View example at horton.com/eld/.

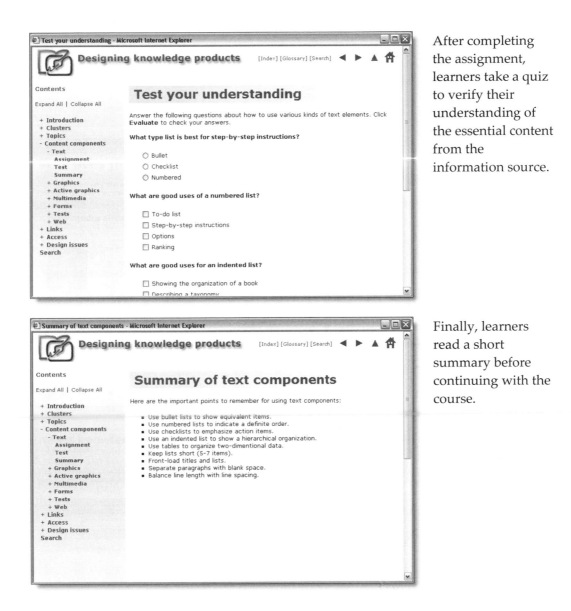

After completing the assignment, learners take a quiz to verify their understanding of the essential content from the information source.

Finally, learners read a short summary before continuing with the course.

When to use exploratory tutorials

Use exploratory tutorials for:

Saving time and money. Exploratory tutorials are inexpensive and quick to develop, as they leverage existing materials. They also fit well with learners adept at searching the Web to find answers to everyday questions.

Teaching how to learn. Exploratory tutorials accomplish learning objectives that involve learning to learn rather than learning specific facts, procedures, or concepts. Although specific questions may be used to guide the exploration, the learning goal is the ability to find and acquire new information rather than the answers to specific questions.

Teaching how to navigate online information. Exploratory tutorials teach how to use a large, complex source of online information. The exploratory tutorial both motivates and guides productive searching and reading activities. It prepares learners to search on their own.

Teaching searching skills. The exploratory tutorial teaches searching strategies that learners can employ to learn on their own. It shows them how to use an external information source for just-in-time learning. Such search skills will transfer to Web searches as well.

But not for novices. Exploratory learning is best for experienced learners who are comfortable navigating Web documents and who already understand the basics of the field of study.

And not for teaching a large subject. The exploratory tutorial is not effective to teach extensive content from the external information source. The information source is vast and the exploratory tutorial requires considerable work by learners to find information. Although the exploratory tutorial can teach focused aspects of the subject, it is not a good way to cover a large subject.

Variations on the exploratory tutorial

Many variations are possible based on the documents being explored and on the style of interaction.

Vary the kind of document the learner must explore. Some candidates for exploration include Web sites, blogs, podcasts, reports, white papers, specifications, brochures, manuals, e-books, databases, newsgroups, forums, chat archives, and Help files.

Vary the organization of the document the learner must explore. If you have control over the organization of the external reference documents you use, vary their structure based on the type of information they convey. A sequential structure is good for online versions of paper books. Many online documents can be organized as a hierarchy of topics and subtopics. Tabular information will fit well into a grid. Loose collections of data can be linked in a free-form structure.

Vary the tone of the activity. Several years ago, a popular computer game, *Where in the World Is Carmen Sandiego?*, required players to look up information in an included paper reference book in order to track down the elusive international criminal. That is exactly the same task as in this lesson structure. All of which suggests making this structure into a game or puzzle.

Best practices for exploratory tutorials

Exploratory tutorials must ensure that learners search and learn successfully.

Make finding information fun, like a game. Challenge learners to find the information needed to solve a problem or complete a scenario. Start with some easy questions and, as search skills develop, pose more challenging questions.

Explain the structure of the information source so learners can quickly understand how to navigate it. Such knowledge will make their searches more predictable and hence more reliable.

Suggest search strategies as appropriate. If learners are new to information searching or are unfamiliar with the information source, you may want to suggest ways to make initial searches more productive and less frustrating. For example, you may want to point out that an online document has an alphabetical index or recommend drilling down through menus.

Balance challenge and difficulty. Ask enough questions to accomplish your objectives but not so many that the lesson becomes tedious and repetitive. Three questions hardly justify a lesson; 20 questions become an inquisition. Make questions hard enough that learners must search to find the answers and easy enough that most learners can do so within a few minutes.

Subject-specific structures

The subject-specific structure is the most flexible. Use it when the subject or activity provides its own distinct structure to organize learning. It is sometimes called a *network* or *free-form* structure because it imposes no restrictions on the organization beyond those implied by the subject matter.

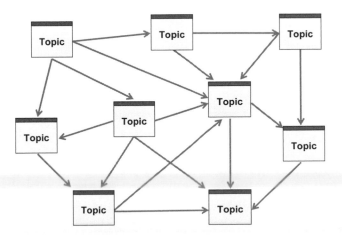

When to use a subject-specific structure

Use the subject-specific structure when more defined structures do not represent the structure of the subject or the navigational pathways needed through the subject. Use it to organize learning to match the underlying structure of knowledge, a work activity, or a complex process. Use it for:

▶ Scenes in a branching simulation.

▶ Multi-faceted subjects that learners can explore to satisfy their interests.

▶ Learners with different interests and goals. Creating many custom courses is not practical.

▶ Highly customized learning experiences.

And use it when no other structure works.

Example: *The Crimescene Game*

The Crimescene Game (p. 142 and p. 159) is a branching simulation. As such, it provides the learner with great freedom of navigation among the topics or scenes of the simulation. Here is a map of all the scenes. Learners encounter scenes in response to decisions they make. The oval with an A inside signifies the main menu of questions, or lines of inquiry. Learners return to this menu when they exhaust a particular sequence of scenes or pathway.

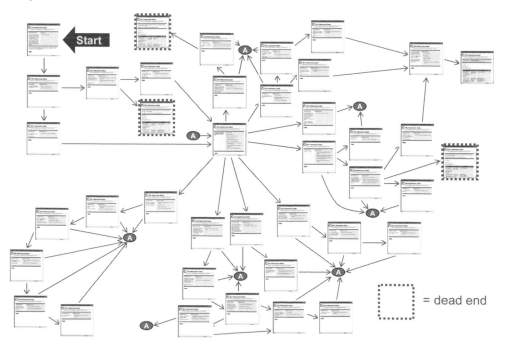

Best practices for the subject-specific structure

The subject-specific structure imposes no constraints on the designer, so it is up to the designer to use this structure with restraint and purpose.

Beware combinatorial explosion. Branching expands the number of topics exponentially. Suppose each topic branches to 4 others. One topic branches to 4, which branch to 16, which branch to 64, which branch to 256, which branch to 1,024, which branch to 4,096. And so on. Two practical strategies can control branching while providing needed flexibility.

▶ **Branch and rejoin**. After a few branches, pathways converge back to a central pathway or junction.

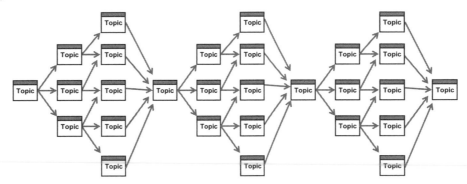

▶ **Loop back to central menu**. Learners depart on excursions from a menu of choices. After a few branches, learners are returned to the menu. This is the strategy used in *The Crimescene Game*.

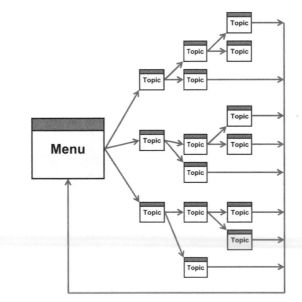

standards chosen. Alas, we must compromise design for pragmatic concerns like government regulations, learners' schedules, and limitations of authoring tools. Still, it is best for the designer to determine those compromises early in the design process rather than to have a finished design hacked away by unconcerned bureaucrats and lazy tool operators.

Design constraints apply at every level of design: curriculum through individual media components. These constraints both define and constrain the type of learning experiences you will deliver. In some cases the constraints are imposed by geography or the preferences of learners. In other cases they are design decisions you make. In either case, you must fully understand the implications of each constraint.

Some of the items in this chapter are things you observe and others are things you decide. All will constrain and guide your e-learning. Some of these decisions serve as policies governing the development of an entire curriculum or library of materials. Others may pertain throughout a course. Others may vary by lesson, topic, learning object, or learning activity. Some decisions may serve as a default that you follow throughout your work—except in special cases that warrant an exception.

WHAT IS A COURSE?

E-learning design asks us to define our course in new terms. No longer can we think of a course as what happens in a particular room during certain hours of the week. A course is now defined in terms of media and technologies—and the learning experiences they occasion.

Framework and content

Let's look at the architecture of an e-learning course. At the top level, a course consists of a framework and content.

The framework of a course provides a home and a stage for the content. The framework might contain a slot for the actual content as well as mechanisms to display its menu, an index, and a glossary.

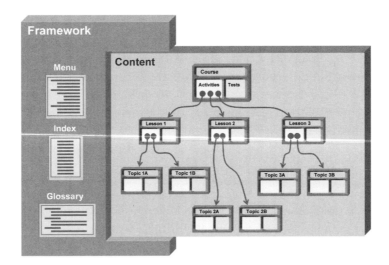

Much of the framework may be provided by a learning content management system that launches and administers the course or by the authoring tool used to create the course. Or the framework may be hand-crafted as part of constructing the content of the course.

What does a course actually look like? That is, what is its outward structure? Let's take a look at one.

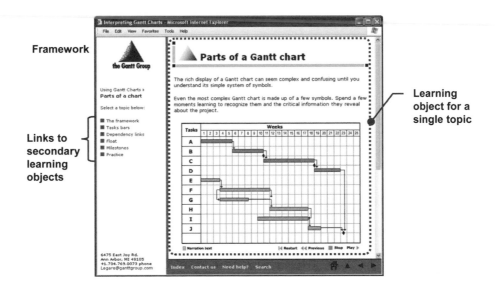

The framework consists of the basic window. Along the left edge are a title and a slot for displaying the table of contents. At the bottom are some generic links for getting information about the course and some buttons for displaying the index, sending e-mail, getting help, and searching. Because these actions are not associated with particular parts of the content, we think of them as part of the framework. In the larger area at the right is displayed the currently selected learning object. In the table of contents we find links to second-level learning objects.

A hierarchy of learning objects

The content is made up of learning objects. The content as a whole may be represented by a hierarchy of learning objects starting with the primary learning object.

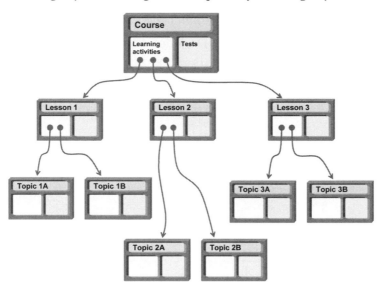

This primary learning object may refer to other, smaller and more specific learning objects. In this example, the primary learning object for the course refers to learning objects for Lessons 1, 2, and 3, which in turn refer to even more specific learning objects.

Each topic contributes items to be displayed as part of the framework. The titles of topics may appear in the main menu indented in a way that reflects the hierarchy of relationships among the topics. Each topic may contribute terms to the index and to the glossary.

CHOOSE THE KIND OF E-LEARNING

With computer and Internet technologies, we can create many different kinds of e-learning, each providing learners with a distinctive type of learning experience and each suited to different purposes and situations. Some kinds of e-learning are led by an instructor who charts the path and sets the pace for a group of learners. In other kinds, learners find their own way, set their own pace, and interact only with the computer. Let's consider the design decisions that will determine the nature of your e-learning.

Instructor-led or learner-led?

One of the first and most important decisions facing designers is the role (or lack of a role) for an instructor. For each component of e-learning, we must ask, "Who leads?" Is the e-learning paced and directed by an instructor or does the learner decide the sequence of activities and set the pace? As with many design decisions, this is not an either-or decision. Options range along a spectrum from pure instructor-led to pure learner-led.

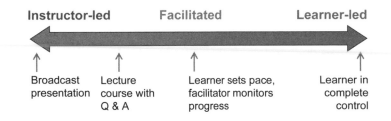

Only broadcast presentations are truly instructor-led, with the instructor totally controlling the content and pace while the participant is completely passive. Standalone e-learning courses, at least traditional ones, are taught with no instructor. The learner decides when to take the course, which activities to perform, and when to quit.

Between these two extremes are several alternatives. A degree of learner-leadership enters when lecture courses include question-and-answer activities. Some courses or activities may have a designated instructor or facilitator who monitors the progress of individual learners as they proceed at their own pace.

Both instructor-led and learner-led training offer advantages:

Advantages of instructor-led learning	Advantages of learner-led learning
▶ The instructor can answer questions and solve problems as they arise.	▶ Learners are not required to conform to the instructor's schedule.
▶ Instructors provide authority that some learners need for motivation.	▶ Learners are empowered by the ability to learn when, where, and as much as they wish.
▶ An instructor can adjust the course to suit the needs of specific learners.	▶ Learners develop self-reliance.
▶ Instructors can grade activities and tests too subtle for automated scoring.	▶ All learners get the same quality of learning experience.
▶ Instructors can sympathize, empathize, urge, cajole, and inspire learners.	▶ Learners are not intimidated by an instructor. They do not feel they are being judged.
▶ Instructor-led courses are quicker and less expensive to develop.	▶ Learner-led courses are less expensive to deploy and conduct.

Many e-learning courses deliberately shift from instructor-led to learner-led during the progress of the course. The course starts with the instructor firmly in charge, setting the pace, making assignments, presenting information, and grading results. As the course progresses, the instructor's responsibilities are taken up by teams and eventually individuals. By the end of the course learners are prepared to apply their learning alone.

For the course *Using Gantt Charts,* I decided to put the learner in control, but to include some degree of facilitation. My reasons were more pragmatic than pedagogical. First, I considered the economics. This course was free and earned no revenue to pay a facilitator or instructor. Second, the schedules of the sponsors made learner-leadership a necessity. The principals of the 2-person company were too busy and traveled too frequently to serve as instructors or even active facilitators. A third reason was the motivation of learners. Students in this course were managers who were learning for self-improvement. Highly self-motivated, these learners preferred to learn at their own pace, a desire reinforced by their hectic schedules.

Synchronous or asynchronous?

One of the most important design decisions is whether to make e-learning synchronous or asynchronous. Can learners control when they learn? What do these terms mean?

Synchronous	Asynchronous
In a strict sense, the term *synchronous* means that everyone involved in an activity must perform their parts at the same time. Such events are sometimes called *real-time* or *live* events. Such events include online meetings and phone conferences.	*Asynchronous* activities are ones that participants can experience whenever they want. Permanently posted Web pages and automatically scored tests are clearly asynchronous—learners can complete them at any time.

Unfortunately these terms are used inconsistently even within a single university or company. One designer will call a course synchronous, while another will call the same course asynchronous. The problem is the meaning of "at the same time." Some take it to mean within minutes or seconds, while others take it to cover a span of hours or days. Are forum messages answered in 2 days asynchronous or synchronous?

Courses are not purely synchronous or asynchronous. Courses are made up of a mix of activities and events that can be synchronous or asynchronous. Still other events and activities take place over a different period of time for each learner. Rather than considering synchronous and asynchronous as mutually exclusive terms, perhaps we should use a scale indicating how much latitude learners have in completing activities.

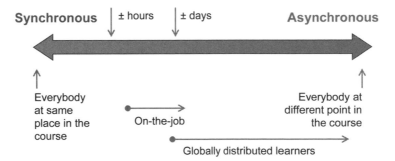

Some e-learning considered synchronous may include some activities and events that learners can partake of at their own pace. And an asynchronous course can still have deadlines, timed tests, and "respond immediately" messages.

If busy people must fit e-learning around meetings and other scheduled events, such e-learning can only be synchronous within a few hours. If learners are distributed around the globe, in many different time zones, in countries with different business, government, and religious holidays, it will be difficult for participants to stay in synch with one another closer than a day or two.

Your course can be asynchronous or have a mixture of synchronous and asynchronous activities. In designing your course, consider the advantages of each approach.

Choose synchronous activities when ...	Choose asynchronous activities when ...
▶ Learners need to discuss issues with other learners at length.	▶ Learners are from a wide span of time zones and countries.
▶ Learners need the motivation of scheduled events reinforced by peer pressure.	▶ Learners have inflexible or unpredictable work schedules.
▶ Most learners share the same needs and have the same questions.	▶ Learners cannot wait for a class to form.
	▶ Learners have unique individual needs.

Let's consider the example of the course *Using Gantt Charts*. I decided to make this course purely asynchronous. Why? Learners were distributed around the globe. Getting learners from 24 time zones to all log in at the same time seemed improbable. In addition, the learners were managers with unpredictable schedules. They found it hard to commit to a particular time slot more than a few hours in advance. These same learners were ambitious and did not want to be held back by slower learners or pushed ahead by faster learners. They wanted to go at their own speed.

What size class?

In e-learning a class is a group of individuals learning the same material on the same schedule. Unlike classroom training, the size of an e-learning class is not constrained by physical architecture but by decisions of the course designer and capabilities of collaboration technology. Classes of 10,000 are technically feasible, although seldom wise.

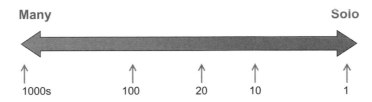

While larger classes are more economical, they provide learners with less individual attention. The class size also affects the possibilities for collaboration. With very small classes, smaller than 10, say, work can be done by the class as a whole. Larger classes may need to divide into separate teams. Over about 20 learners, the amount of interaction with the teacher begins to drop off and teams get less attention. Classes over 100 provide little individual attention to learners and few teams get much attention.

The size of the class is an important issue, as it affects both the economics and instructional effectiveness of the course. The size determines the number of times the course must be offered, how often a class starts, the learner-teacher ratio, and the potential for team activities. Let's look at the advantages of each class size:

Large class size	Small class size	Class of one
▶ More economical as fewer sessions are required.	▶ More individual attention from the instructor.	▶ Learner gets a private tutor or mentor.
▶ More people taught in less time.	▶ Whole-class activities are practical.	▶ No waiting for a class to form.
▶ More classmates to interact with.	▶ Classes start more frequently.	▶ Learning is private.
▶ Enough learners for all types of activities.	▶ Meets expectations of learners accustomed to small classes.	
	▶ Moderate instructor load.	

To decide on a class size, you need to consider both your organizational and learning objectives.

Let's take the example of the *Using Gantt Charts* course. I decided to design it for solo learners, without the requirement for group work. My reasons centered on the work schedule and learning styles of learners. Learners were managers with busy, unpredictable schedules that made teamwork impractical. Some wanted to take the course in very short segments, while others preferred to take it straight through. They were impatient learners.

What devices will learners use to take e-learning?

Today learners can take e-learning on a wide range of devices: desktop computers, laptop computers, tablet computers, personal digital assistants, mobile phones, and media players.

Desktop computers

The typical desktop computer consists of the main chassis with a separate monitor and keyboard. It may also include additional attachments such as printers, microphones, and video cameras. Desktop computers are the largest, most capable, and least mobile of the devices for taking e-learning.

They usually feature fast processors and can be loaded with adequate memory and large disk drives. They can have full-sized, ergonomically designed keyboards. Because they are used indoors under consistent lighting, their displays tend to be quite legible. In addition to a keyboard and mouse, they may have a range of additional input devices, such as a scanner, video camera, digitizing tablet, or trackball. And because they are large and heavy, they are less likely to be stolen than their more mobile cousins. Competition among manufacturers ensures that the cost for an almost-state-of-the-art desktop computer is moderate. And most desktop computers are deployed in environments with high-speed network connections.

The main disadvantage of the desktop computer is that it is not mobile at all. The learner has to come to it. If you are running a computer lab, the desktop computer is just fine. But if your learners want to study in stolen moments throughout the day, the desktop computer may not be the right target for your e-learning.

To design for desktop computers:

▶ Design the best e-learning you can. Use media wisely but freely.

▶ If learners must perform activities outside the vicinity of the computer, let them print them out.

Laptop computers

Laptop computers combine computer, keyboard, pointing device, and monitor in one box that closes for protection while traveling. Laptop computers are almost as capable as desktop computers today and they are mobile—or at least transportable. They are, however, more expensive.

Laptop computers today are 80% as capable as their desktop companions. And they can be easily moved from location to location. Learners can learn while riding on a bus or plane or while sitting on the beach. Today's models are rugged enough for all but the clumsiest users (I am living proof) and the most difficult environments.

Monitors, disk drives, and memory may be a bit smaller than on desktop models. The touchpad or other pointing device may not be as convenient as a mouse. The keyboard may not be as ergonomically arranged as the best one you can buy for your desktop. However, today's laptop computer is capable of playing just about any e-learning you develop.

Problems with the laptop have to do with its portability. Like other mobile devices, it can be stolen. And its battery life is not infinite—though one extra battery pack kept me running all the way from Tokyo to San Francisco. For that portability and the miniaturization necessary to make it possible, vendors charge a premium—typically two times the price of an equivalent desktop computer.

Laptop computers are good for people who cannot do all their learning or work at a fixed location but who do not want to compromise the learning experience. To design e-learning for laptop computers:

▶ Design your e-learning to work with a moderate amount of memory and disk space and to display on a moderate-sized monitor.

▶ Design for the noisy environments and frequent interruptions laptop users face.

▶ Do not depend on continuous high-speed network connections.

Media players

Media players display photographs, and play audio and video. They are commonly used to watch movies and play music while traveling. Media players are popular for their use for entertainment. Convincing learners to acquire one is thus easier. Most have small screens and are limited in the media formats they can play.

Use media players to present information. Forget about interaction, or combine the media player with another device.

To design e-learning for media players:

► Rely on graphics, audio, and video presentations. Do not require any interactivity.

► Use high-quality audio, but design video and photographs to work on the device's small screen.

Where will learners take e-learning?

Imagine your learners taking your course. Where are they? Are they in their offices, at home, in a dorm room, in a coffee shop, on the road, or in a corporate training center? Where should they be?

The success of a course can depend on where people take it. I know designers who decided that learners would take e-learning on specially equipped high-performance workstations in a quiet, calm, corporate training center. After they deployed their e-learning, they found the expensive training center vacant, as most learners took the e-learning from outdated laptop computers in hotel rooms and from their children's home computers, both using slow-speed dial-up connections. As a designer, you must design for where learners will actually take the courses.

Where people take e-learning controls what computers they use and what kind of network connection they have. It also affects how much noise and how many distractions they must contend with. The choice of computer in turn affects the ability of the course to display information and to play media. The speed, reliability, and availability of the network connection also limit the use of media, participation in live events, and use of confidential or secret information. The environment of the learner affects how much attention learners can give the course, how long they can participate in an activity, and how often they must put a hand over the screen to hide confidential information. Almost every aspect of design is affected by where the learner takes e-learning.

People take e-learning courses in several main environments. Let's look at each in turn, weighing its advantages and disadvantages while noting the design requirements it imposes for the course.

In the learner's office or cubicle

Many of the cited advantages of e-learning assume learners take courses at their desks connected to a corporate network.

Potential factor	Best practices when this factor applies
Learners must sandwich learning among other tasks, as time is available. Phone calls, visitors, and other interruptions are frequent.	Create the course with short, self-contained topics so the learner can fit learning between interruptions. Let learners bookmark topics so they can easily resume where they left off.
The environment is relatively quiet.	Use sound where appropriate. Provide or recommend a headphone if e-learning is taken in cubicles.
Computers are attached to a relatively fast network.	Use graphics, voice, and other media, where justified, to communicate clearly.
A computer tuned for accounting or software development may not welcome the plug-ins and other software needed for e-learning.	Design for computers learners actually have and the plug-ins they can download and install. Use file formats that can be displayed by commonly available players such as the Flash Player and the Acrobat Reader.
In-house technical support is available.	Provide instructions for technical support staff to help learners prepare their computers for e-learning.
Learners have access to corporate documents, databases, and information systems.	Design activities that encourage learners to practice applying learning to their own work.

In a non-office workplace

Not everyone works at a desk. E-learning is insinuating itself onto kiosks in bookstores, onto laptops at construction sites, into corners of fast-food restaurants, and onto the factory floor. These work environments pose some challenges for computers and e-learning in particular.

Potential factor	Best practices when this factor applies
Space is limited. The computer must fit into available space with no additional desk space.	Include everything necessary online. Do not require learners to refer to separate printed materials.
The computer is shared for other purposes, which may take priority over its use for learning.	Design learning in short episodes. Enable bookmarking so learners can easily resume. Allow learners to print out lengthy activities and work on them away from the computer.
A network may be unavailable. The local network may be isolated from the Internet for security reasons. Or, it may be dedicated to specific business purposes.	Offer courses from CD-ROM or DVD.
Noise may make computer sounds hard to hear. Earphones may pose a safety hazard.	Display visual equivalents to all voice and other important sounds.
Learners may be on call for other tasks, such as answering customer questions.	Design learning in short, self-contained episodes. Make displays especially legible at a greater than normal distance.
Learners may need to wear special safety equipment, such as clean-room suits, hard hats, and protective gloves.	Do not require extensive typing or precise pointing.

Potential factor	Best practices when this factor applies
Smoke, soot, grease, dust, and other contaminants may make computers impractical in some environments.	Consider alternative devices such as media players. Or allow learners to perform activities from printed assignments.
E-learning may refer to machinery and devices in the work environment.	Design activities that do not require looking at the computer. Use voice for instructions to learners.

In a learning center

Many companies and universities are setting up special rooms where employees can take e-learning. These rooms are called *learning centers* or *learning labs*. Most learning centers contain desks or cubicles with computers that are specially equipped to run e-learning. Some learning centers feature a facilitator or technician to greet learners, get them started, and provide help when requested.

Potential factor	Best practices when this factor applies
Learning centers provide a quiet place where people can learn without the noise or interruptions of their workplace.	Include complex activities that realistically prepare learners to apply difficult subjects in challenging environments. Use longer, more life-like activities than you might otherwise use.
Computers have all the necessary software installed and set up. They also have high-speed network connections.	Use multimedia, advanced browser capabilities, and large graphics as appropriate. For example, display detailed diagrams to explain complex processes and use voice-over narration or video to demonstrate difficult procedures.
Learning centers have on-site facilitators.	Train center staff to support your courses. Document the technical requirements and show facilitators how to get learners started.
Learning centers require people to be away from their desks for significant periods of time.	Design self-contained activities. Do not require learners to refer to documents or other items found only in their offices or dorm rooms.

Potential factor	Best practices when this factor applies
Learning centers are expensive to set up and administer. Unless all employees work on a single campus, multiple learning centers will be required.	Budget for centers. If centers must host your learners, the centers may require compensation.
Not all learners have access to the learning center.	Publish specifications and instructions so learners can set up their computers to match learning-center computers. Design activities learners can perform on their own. Tell learners how to phone the learning center to receive help.

At home

Many employees take e-learning at home during evenings and on weekends. Most of these employees say they cannot find enough quiet time at the office to complete lessons. Some companies encourage their employees to take e-learning on their own time and may subsidize the purchase of the home computer.

Potential factor	Best practices when this factor applies
Some learners have better computers at home than at work, especially those whose work computers are old or configured for purposes other than learning. Multimedia home computers sold today are quite capable of running e-learning courses.	Research the kinds of computers learners have at home and design accordingly. Design so your e-learning will work on a variety of computers. For example, all your office computes may run Windows, but many home computers may run the Macintosh operating system.

Potential factor	Best practices when this factor applies
Many learners find they have traded office distractions for family distractions. A child needs help with homework, the dog wants to be walked, or the spouse does not like being ignored.	Design to accommodate frequent interruptions. Design short, self-contained topics. Enable bookmarking so learners can resume where they left off. Increase efforts to motivate learners. Ensure that e-learning is interesting. Provide headphones for listening to audio. This will shut out noise and signal that the learner does not welcome interruptions.
Homes lack a technical support staff other than computer-proficient children.	Minimize the technical requirements, especially the number of plug-ins the learner must download and set up.
Learners at home must typically access courses by logging into the corporate intranet, oozing through the firewall, and logging into the course.	Streamline the process of accessing the course from outside the firewall. Anticipate and resolve security problems early. Test access after each security update. Do not depend on access to secret or confidential material.

While traveling

More and more professionals are mobile, spending increasing portions of their time away from the office. They check into their hotel room, plug in their laptop computer, and fire up their e-learning.

At first glance, this might seem like the worst possible scenario for taking e-learning, namely suffering from jet lag, sleep deprivation, and indigestion. However, learning while traveling has some advantages. Many find that e-learning courses ease the loneliness of travel, especially if the course includes collaborative activities. One traveling salesman put it this way: "It's better than hanging out at the hotel bar." For many traveling professionals, e-learning provides the only practical way to get the education they need.

Potential factor	Best practices when this factor applies
Learners are free of the distractions of office and home.	Design for the learner's full attention. Allow richer activities and tolerate more complex displays. But keep activities short, lest fatigue prove a problem.
The learner's laptop computer is old or damaged from years of travel.	Minimize the technical requirements. Design for a three-year-old laptop.
The process of establishing an Internet connection, logging into a corporate network, navigating through the firewall, and finding the course server can be complex and unreliable.	Package the entire course on CD-ROM or DVD, or let learners download entire lessons. Let learners download e-learning when connected and burn a CD-ROM for use while traveling.
A laptop can be stolen—and its cached or downloaded materials read by malicious eyes.	Limit use of confidential or secret information. Ensure that case studies, reading assignments, and research activities do not compromise security or reveal embarrassing information. For example, make sure that computer simulations or exercises do not involve confidential customer data.
Learners feel lonely and a bit homesick.	Design opportunities for spontaneous collaboration and discussion. Set up a student lounge where learners can meet and chat at any hour of the day.
The learner's schedule is erratic and subject to frequent changes.	Make live events optional. Let learners download a summary or transcript of the event. Better still, record the live event so learners can play it back at their convenience.
Learners are tired, stressed, and jet lagged.	Design short, focused activities. Let learners postpone recorded tests till they are rested and relaxed. Minimize long reading assignments or any monotonous activities.

Potential factor	Best practices when this factor applies
Learners lack access to a printer.	Minimize reading assignments or anything that requires printing out instructions.
Luggage space is limited.	Include all necessary material online. Do not require learners to lug along a fat textbook or other reference materials.

In a dorm room

Yes, on-campus students do take e-learning to supplement their classroom studies. The dorm-room environment combines features of the home and the office.

Potential factor	Best practices when this factor applies
High-speed network connections, at least on most major campuses, are the norm.	Use graphics, voice, and other media as needed. Remember that younger learners may expect a richer media experience and resist reading large amounts of text.
Learners may have some privacy, but be afflicted with noisy and nosey roommates.	Limit display of personal information. Consider supplying headphones or reminding learners to use their own headphones.
The computer may be one prescribed by the university. It may be years out of date. It may be optimized for playing games and much of its disk space used for downloaded music.	Design for the type computers learners have. Do not require storing large amounts of material locally.
Students may prefer to study while listening to music and carrying on a couple of instant-messaging sessions with friends.	Design e-learning in short segments. Make it easy to bookmark a location and return to it later.

Outdoors

With light-weight computers, PDAs, wireless networks, and better batteries, learners are choosing to move outdoors. They take e-learning in a park, on safari, and at a sidewalk café. The outdoors presents some special advantages and challenges for e-learning.

Potential factor	Best practices when this factor applies
Network connections are slow, intermittent, or nonexistent.	Design e-learning so it can be downloaded and taken when not on the network. Let learners download e-learning when connected and burn a CD-ROM for use when in the field.
Bright sunlight makes reading difficult.	Design displays with high contrast. Make text and graphics highly legible.
Sounds of traffic, nature, and passersby are loud. Noise makes hearing hard.	Either forego sound or recommend headphones.
Learners can carry limited weight.	Ensure e-learning works on lightweight laptops or other mobile devices. Include all necessary material online. Do not require learners to carry textbooks or other materials.
Learners may have to contend with heat, cold, wind, dust, rain, or snow.	Recommend a ruggedized computer. Make sure learners can operate your e-learning while wearing gloves or mittens.
Battery life is finite.	Keep learning sessions short. Enable learners to print out assignments they can carry instead of the computer.

In a moving vehicle

Learners may choose to learn in an automobile, bus, train, or airplane. For many of us, it is the only time available for professional education. More and more mobile devices are allowing learning to occur while traveling. Ford has announced a new model of its popular F150 truck equipped with a computer and wireless networking.

Potential factor	Best practices when this factor applies
The only space available may be the learner's lap, leaving no space for reference papers or peripheral devices.	Make the course self-contained. Ensure all necessary material can be displayed on the screen at the same time as the e-learning.
The learner must attend to announcements ("Fasten your seatbelts" or "Next stop Lyon") and guard against theft or other threats.	Keep learning activities simple. Do not require the learner's full attention. Let learners bookmark topics so that they can resume where they left off.
The ride may be bumpy, subjecting the learner and the computer to vibration.	Make text especially legible. Recommend a ruggedized computer if the road is really rough.
Lighting varies from bright sunlight streaming in a window to the darkness of a tunnel.	Keep all displays legible. Ensure adequate foreground/background contrast.
If driving, the learner may be limited to audio inputs and cannot brook distractions.	Do nothing that would unduly distract the learner from driving safely. No complex activities. Nothing visual. Better still, forego e-learning while driving. Have drivers learn after they safely arrive at their destination.
Network connection is slow, intermittent, or nonexistent.	Make e-learning available on CD-ROM or DVD. Let learners download entire lessons ahead of time.
Power may not be available.	Design to minimize disk access and network access, which consume more power.

Other places people can take e-learning

There is almost no limit to where people are taking e-learning. I have taken e-learning in a non-reclining, middle seat on an airliner halfway across the Pacific; on a computer lashed to a tree at 3,500 meters altitude; and in numerous restaurants and, yes, bars. Others have learned in a rowboat in the middle of a lake, in a tent during a rainstorm, and while standing in line at the grocery store. How do you design for such varied environments? Although I cannot give you specific advice, I can suggest some best practices.

Environmental characteristic	Best practices
Lighting is bright, dim, or variable.	Make displays especially legible. Ensure high foreground/background contrast and use adequate font sizes.
The environment is noisy.	Provide earphones or do not rely solely on voice or sound for any critical messages.
The learner is subject to vibration.	Reading will be slow and difficult. Pace activities accordingly. Make displays extra legible. Make click targets extra large.
The network is unavailable or intermittent.	Make e-learning available from CD-ROM or DVD. Let learners download entire lessons or courses beforehand.
The environment is dirty. The computer is subject to smoke, dust, soot, or grease.	Protect the computer. Use an alternate device, such as a media player, or print out activities to be performed from paper.
Learner must wear gloves or mittens, say outdoors in winter.	Do not require typing or precise pointing.
Space is cramped with little room for the computer and other materials.	Make all materials available on the computer. Do not require consulting external reference materials. Make sure your e-learning works on a small display monitor.
Distractions and interruptions are frequent.	Design e-learning in short, self-contained segments. Let students bookmark their locations so they can easily resume where they left off.

CONSIDER ALTERNATIVES TO PURE E-LEARNING

For many e-learning needs, the best solution may not be a single type of pure e-learning but an intelligent hybrid of different types of e-learning combined with a mix of other types of learning.

Organizations with large investments in classroom training and disk-based e-learning may prefer to reuse their well-tested training materials during a transitional period while they redesign their courses as pure e-learning. They may want to blend multiple types of learning or embed e-learning into other knowledge products.

Blended learning

To accomplish any difficult educational goal, we often must blend different media, instructional strategies, and design approaches. This process of crafting custom mixes of learning goes under the name *blending*.

Blending can be defined simply as the mixture of different forms of education or training for a single purpose. The only thing remarkable about this definition is that it does not limit itself to mixtures of e-learning and classroom learning. A blend can be any mixture of any form of learning possible: classroom, virtual-classroom, or standalone e-learning. It may mix informational, behavioral, cognitive, and constructive strategies. It may mix CD-ROMs, Web sites, books, online help files, video broadcasts, e-mail exchanges, and dozens of other media. It may be delivered on desktop computers, laptop computers, tablet computers, personal digital assistants, and even mobile phones. The proper blend may be custom tailored to an individual learning objective or even the individual learner.

Is blending really a breakthrough?

Blending has been touted as a breakthrough in education. But is it really? Imagine that you are attending an international medical conference. One of the speakers announces a major medical breakthrough. The speaker proudly points out that in clinical trials the new technique lowered mortality by 100%. That is, patients who applied the breakthrough technique all survived, but those who failed to practice the technique all died. You would probably be impressed and want to know the name of this miracle cure. So what do you think is the name of the breakthrough?

It is called breathing. And blending is just the same kind of breakthrough. All effective learning is a blend. And always has been. The only question is what that blend consists of.

To prove my point, how did you learn to drive? What blend of learning experiences taught you to pilot an automobile safely? Did you take classroom instruction? Did you read about driving on your own? Were you assigned reading by an instructor? Did you demonstrate your driving skill to your parents, instructor, or licensing official? Did you practice driving under the supervision of a licensed driver? Did you practice driving on your own? Were there other learning experiences that helped you learn to drive? For most people, learning to drive was a blend of activities, like most everything we learn in life.

Levels of blending

Blending is a complex issue. It involves so many possible ways of mixing learning activities and requires so many design decisions that we may be tempted to just try combinations at random or else stick with what worked in the past.

One way to simplify the task of selecting the correct blend is to consider different levels of blending, that is, different degrees of sophistication and potential success. For each level, let's describe what goes on at that level.

Level		Description
4	Personal	Custom tailoring detailed learning experiences to the needs of individual learners.
3	Tactical	Mixing methodologies, design approaches, and media for each individual topic.
2	Strategic	Mixing classroom and e-learning events based on subject matter and goals.
1	Mechanical	Sandwiching slabs of existing e-learning and classroom content.
0	Paralytic	Endlessly debating the proper blend while doing nothing.

I define level 0 as **paralytic** blending. This level is characterized by endlessly debating the proper blend while doing nothing. It is not really blending (hence it's number 0) but is quite common in nervous organizations.

Level 1 is **mechanical** blending. This level creates blends by mechanically sandwiching slabs of existing e-learning and classroom content. Neither classroom nor e-learning experiences are in any way tailored to the task at hand or the needs of learners.

Level 2 is called **strategic** blending. At this level we mix classroom and e-learning events based on the subject matter and our goals for learning.

Level 3 is **tactical** blending. This level takes a jump in sophistication. At this level we mix methodologies, design approaches, and media for each individual topic in the overall course. Level 3 requires thorough analysis of the subject and a hand-crafted instructional design.

Level 4 is called **personal** blending. As its name suggests, this level custom tailors detailed learning experiences to the needs of individual learners. This level is the most ambitious ideal. It requires extensive instructional design because each topic may require multiple versions. It also requires a sophisticated learning content management system (LCMS) to identify which module to dispense to which learners.

For now, we will look at strategic blending as it is both practical and worthwhile.

Level 2: Strategic blending

Level 2 or strategic blending mixes classroom and e-learning events based on subject matter and goals. Let's look at how we might perform strategic blending.

Decompose the skill

The first step in strategic blending is to decompose the skill into its components. Ask yourself these questions: What skill are you teaching? To whom are you teaching the skill? In order to acquire the skill, what must learners know? What attitudes must they have? What must they believe? And what must they be able to do?

Let's say we are designing a course on how to resolve disputes among subordinates. The course will be offered to new supervisors.

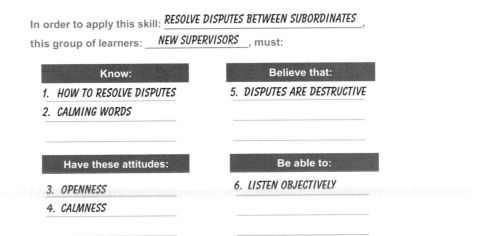

8
Strategic decisions

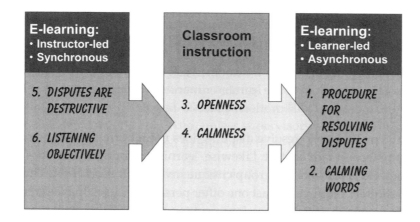

In the first e-learning segment, learners need to acquire motivation and basic skills necessary to complete the other activities. We will make it instructor-led to better support learners new to e-learning. And we will offer it in a synchronous meeting, to save money by reducing the effort required of the instructor and to motivate learners through peer support.

What do we teach in this first segment? As mentioned earlier, we start with topics that are basic and motivational, namely the knowledge that disputes are destructive and a technique for listening objectively. Don't let the numbers 5 and 6 fool you. Those are just the order in which we identified the objectives to teach. And, yes, some designers do absentmindedly teach objectives in the order in which they were identified.

The middle segment will be taught in the classroom. There we teach the segments that require face-to-face contact, specifically openness and calmness. In the classroom, learners can also apply their abilities to listen objectively as they demonstrate and hone their attitudes of openness and calmness.

Finally, after returning to the workplace, learners continue studying. For continued study, learners engage in more e-learning. The e-learning is learner-led and asynchronous so learners can continue at their own pace. In this third segment, they learn the well-defined procedure for resolving disputes and add to their vocabulary of calming words.

Embedded e-learning

E-learning can stand alone or it can be embedded within some other knowledge product.

Forms of embedding

E-learning can be embedded in a computer program, within the online help for a program, in a diagnostic procedure, or among other sources of electronic information.

Embedded in an application

You might choose to embed your e-learning in the user-interface of a computer program. For instance, here is a classroom timer application. On the Help menu are links to tutorials that explain the interface and some of the most common tasks users perform.

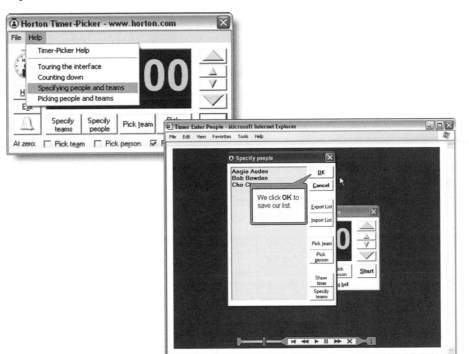

Demonstration built using Adobe Captivate.

Embedded in online Help

E-learning can also be embedded into online Help for a product or process.

This example looks like a conventional Help topic, which it is. However, if we select the **How to** item from the menu, the Help window displays a demonstration showing how to perform the procedure. Clicking the **Try a simulation** link brings up a simulation in which we can practice performing the procedure (as shown here).

Simulation built with Adobe Captivate.
View example at horton.com/eld/.

Embedded in diagnostics

E-learning can also be embedded in a business procedure, such as a diagnosis of a problem. The procedure might start with a general symptom that the troubleshooter has noticed. The procedure might then ask questions or suggest tests that help identify a more specific symptom. This procedure of refinement would continue until the cause of the problem is confirmed. The next step would be to remedy the problem.

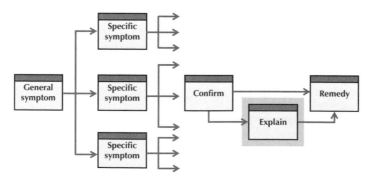

At this point, between confirming and fixing the problem, we might want to embed an optional explanation of the problem. Chances are troubleshooters would not choose the explanation the first couple of times they encounter this problem. But if the problem proves common or expensive to fix, they would become eager to learn why the problem occurs and what could be done to prevent it in the first place. That point at which the troubleshooter becomes eager to learn is a "teachable moment," and the explanation becomes embedded e-learning.

Here is an example of such e-learning that is embedded near the end of a diagnostic procedure. At the start of this diagnostic procedure for a media server, we see a list of symptoms and select one. Then, through a series of screens, we are asked questions to zero in on the cause of the problem. At the end of the diagnosis we find a repair procedure. At the bottom of this procedure is a link that displays this explanation of the cause of the problem.

Built using Adobe Dreamweaver, Microsoft PowerPoint, and TechSmith Camtasia.

Linked knowledge products

We can use hyperlinks to connect separate knowledge products, including e-learning. Such links provide pathways to related knowledge. One common use of such links is to connect a computer application, its Help file, online documentation, and e-learning.

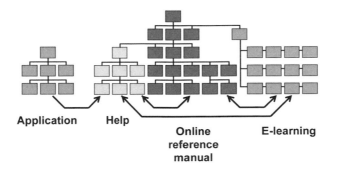

The user of the application presses a button and jumps directly to a relevant topic in the Help file. Increasingly, designers are linking these context-sensitive Help topics to other information in the online reference manual. A user who jumps into Help can jump further

PLAN FOR REUSE

Executives, managers, and instructional designers alike recognize that they can save money, deploy quicker, and increase quality by reusing perfected units of e-learning rather than constantly recreating them. Increasingly, designers are trying to design reusable learning objects.

Build from reusable parts

Reusable learning objects let us build from existing parts. That means we will not need to develop all the content we need for a particular project. Parts, once perfected, can be reused on several projects.

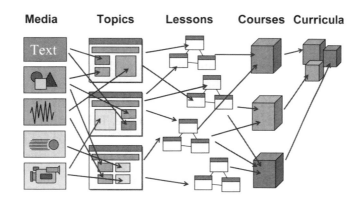

At the top level we can assemble a collection of courses from reusable courses. We can select from existing courses to construct a curriculum or library. To create courses, we can shop for existing lessons. Proven lessons may find their way into multiple courses. To create the lessons, we may combine existing topics. Relevant, well-crafted topics may appear in multiple lessons. Topics, likewise, may be composed by including existing lower-level media components. These media components may consist of reusable boilerplate text, standard graphics, narration segments, animations, and video clips.

Even though we may have to develop some original content, the costs will be less because that original content can be reused in subsequent projects. Or such is the dream.

Combine objects freely

Reusable components of content make it easy to publish various subsets of the content. This is useful when the material is used for many different purposes or is needed by different groups of people—in other words: whenever it is hard to anticipate your needs ahead of time.

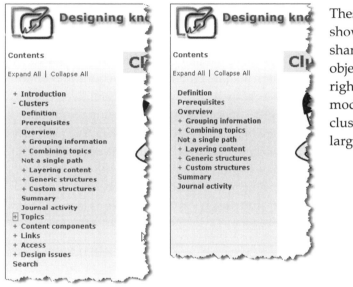

These two course menus show how two courses share certain learning objects. The course on the right only contains modules about designing clusters—a subset of the larger course on the left.

At what level will you reuse content?

As a designer, you must decide at what levels you will reuse content. This decision will affect the economics of your project. Here is an example of the decisions made for one project about what would be reused at each level of content.

	What will you reuse?	Why?
Curriculum	*Popular courses in certificate programs.*	*To cover broad subject areas.*
Course	*Generic courses on popular subjects.*	*Courses are available and inexpensive.*
Lesson	*(Nothing at this level.)*	*Lessons not modular enough at this level.*
Topic	*"Boilerplate" pages.*	*To save time and ensure consistency.*
Media	*Clip art.*	*To save money and ensure consistency.*

In making such decisions it is important to weigh the tradeoffs between money and time saved by reuse versus the extra effort required to make units of content reusable.

Reuse in different ways

The more ways you can reuse an object, the more value it offers. Our plan for reuse must consider different opportunities to reuse units of content.

Suppose we have an individual object. It may be a course, a lesson, a topic, or just a media component. We want to publish it on the Web. Immediately we run into a problem. We need two versions: one designed for learners with fast Internet connections and another for those with slower connections. Not everybody has a Web connection. Even those with connections in their offices and homes may be off the Net while traveling. For these learners we may want to offer our learning objects on CD-ROM or DVD. Well-developed materials may be quite useful in the classroom—the physical classroom as well as the virtual classroom. Each of these venues may require a slightly different form of the object. And let's not forget those who prefer to curl up with a good book. The need to publish material on paper is not going away. Even students in virtual classrooms clamor for paper handouts.

Here is a practical example of reuse. If shows how a PowerPoint presentation evolved to serve as the single source for most of the forms we just discussed.

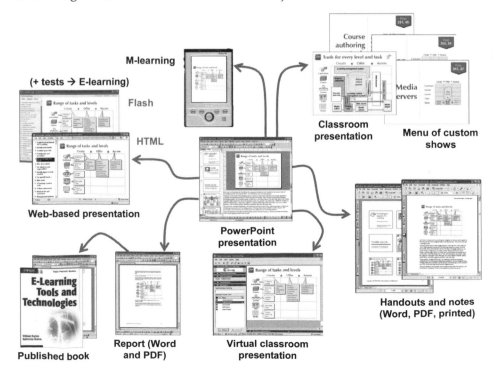

Being able to publish content in multiple forms is valuable if you need to distribute to the widest possible audience; incorporate new distribution channels as soon as they become available (e.g., mobile phones); or respond to new platforms, file formats, browsers, and so forth.

Follow standards for reuse

Standards for reuse simplify the process of reusing content created by various teams in different tools and running them in different management systems. Ideally, a school should be able to build a course by combining modules created in ToolBook by Jane's Multimedia with modules created in Flash by Peters Petagogee and be sure they can be launched and tracked by the SymunLegree LMS.

Types of reuse standards

Technical standards for e-learning help us mix and match units of content, authoring tools, and management systems. They help both producers and consumers combine components freely.

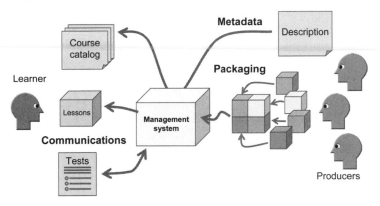

Producers design, develop, and distribute e-learning content. They may produce whole, monolithic courses, or they may produce individual learning objects such as lessons and topics that could be combined to build courses. These producers may use different authoring tools.

By following standards, these producers can integrate objects created by different teams using different authoring tools into a single course and import that course into a management system, such as an LMS or LCMS. The standards that say how separate objects must be produced so they can be integrated are called *packaging* standards.

Once the course is safely lodged on the management system, learners need to take the course. That means the management system must dispense individual objects and keep track of which learners have completed which courses, lessons, and objects. It may also need to conduct tests and record who passed and who failed—or even how each learner answered a particular question in a specific test. For tests and learning objects to communicate back completion and test scores, they must follow *communications* standards that define a language that both the module and management system understand.

Learners need to know what e-learning is available for them to take. Producers need to know what learning objects are available for them to reuse. For this to happen, the management system needs to publish a searchable catalog of all the available components and courses. That in turn requires a way for producers to describe their individual contributions. *Metadata* standards make this possible.

Standards bodies

Standards are often known by the name of the organization that specifies them. For e-learning technology standards, there are several main groups whose names you will encounter.

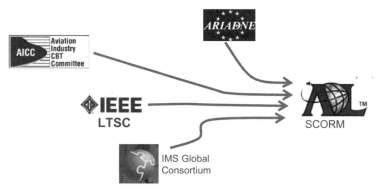

The oldest organization active in e-learning standards is the Aviation Industry CBT Committee or AICC for short. AICC was originally formed to help airframe manufacturers integrate training from various subcontractors into systems that could remain accessible over the decades an airplane was in service. Over the years, other industries realized they had similar needs and joined AICC so that today its membership is quite diverse.

Other standards organizations sprang up to serve different industries, to solve specific problems, and to give us more abbreviations to learn. The most important of these were the Institute of Electrical and Electronics Engineers (IEEE, pronounced "eye-triple-E") Learning Technology Standards Committee (LTSC), the IMS Global Consortium. And the European ARIADNE project and foundation.

For years these groups merrily issued specifications, which most people called standards. Unfortunately the "standards" were not always consistent and seldom easy to understand or implement. The joke in the e-learning field was, "The only good thing about standards is that there are so many to pick from."

The world's largest education institution, the United States Department of Defense (DoD, in case you have not had enough abbreviations) was not amused. So it chartered the Advanced Distance Learning (ADL) initiative, whose first combat mission was to "harmonize" the differing standards so they could be used. The name of that project was the Sharable Content Object Reference Model (SCORM) project.

SCORM fostered a lot of communication and real cooperation among the rival standards groups to the point that SCORM began gaining acceptance globally.

When I refer to SCORM as a standard, I am talking about a *de facto* standard. It is only a standard because vendors of tools and creators of content have begun following it. ADL has no legal enforcement powers. If you fail to follow SCORM standards, Military Police will not erase your hard disk. Of course, your customer may refuse to buy your course.

Packaging standards

Packaging standards refer to how you bundle up all the separate components of a course, lesson, or topic so that a management system can dispense the pieces properly. A complex course may consist of hundreds of separate files, each of which must be in a specific subdirectory for the course to work.

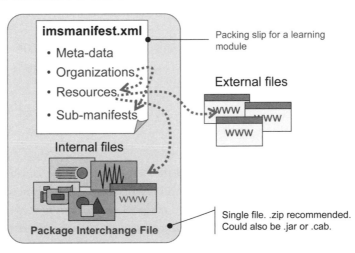

The core of the packaging specification within SCORM is a manifest. The manifest is a packing slip for the package, which could be anything from a whole course down to an individual sound clip. SCORM refers to these units as SCOs (rhymes with snows). This manifest must be named imsmanifest.xml, which might seem to be a bit weird. The "ims" on the beginning refers back to IMS Global Consortium, which wrote the original specifications for a manifest. The ".xml" at the end means that the file must follow the rules of XML (eXtensible Markup Language, a do-it-yourself version of HTML).

Within the manifest are four main sections:

▶ The **Meta-data section** describes the module. Entries within this section must follow metadata standards.

▶ The **Organizations section** tells what the module contains and how it is structured. The Organizations section lists two types of content: resource descriptions and sub-manifests, each of which is further detailed in subsequent sections. Think of the Organizations section as a table of contents for the module. The Organizations section may also specify how lessons and topics are sequenced, that is, what prerequisites learners must complete before starting a lesson or topic.

▶ The **Resources section** contains resource descriptions that identify specific files that make up the package. There are two types of files: local files that are actually scooped up and uploaded with the module to the management system and external files that are just URLs to resources available elsewhere on the Web.

▶ **Sub-manifests** contain the same Meta-data, Organizations, and Resources sections as the main module, but for included units of content. A sub-manifest may include other sub-manifests. For example, the manifest for a course may include sub-manifests for included lessons. The sub-manifests for lessons may include sub-manifests for topics.

The SCORM packaging standard also says how the dozens or hundreds of separate files can be bundled up with the manifest into a single file. The most common file format for such packages is the common .zip format, specifically PKZIP Version 2.04.g. Other formats acceptable are a Java archive (.jar) or Windows cabinet (.cab) file.

Design issues for packaging

Packaging standards present you with decisions you must make and limitations you must design around. For instance:

▶ What level do you package: curriculum, course, lesson, topic, test, or media component? The most reusable units seem to be whole courses and media components (individual graphics, animations, and sound sequences.) However, creating many packages adds to the work and recordkeeping necessary.

▶ How do you restrict the sequence in which learners can take lessons and topics? Do you enforce a strict linear path from beginning to end? Or do you let learners navigate freely within the course? Or do you selectively enforce prerequisites between topics and lessons?

▶ In what additional contexts will your package be reused? Can you design it to avoid the as-shown-above syndrome (p. 313)?

▶ Do you need to define packages within packages, i.e., sub-manifests? Will your LMS support that capability? Can you make packages truly independent enough that they can be included within other packages?

▶ What prerequisite relationships exist among your packages? This will affect the version of the SCORM standard you follow. Standards can restrict the complexity of relationships you can build into your course.

And you must ensure that your LMS and LCMS can handle the level of detail you desire.

Communications standards

Communications standards define a language whereby the learning management system can start up modules and communicate with them. In this segment, we will consider what the learning management system and modules need to communicate, what communications standards have been proposed, how they work, and what we must do to comply with them.

What objects communicate

Communications standards prescribe how (but not what) objects and management systems can communicate. All communication is initiated by the object. It can:

▶ Signal that it has started or is about to end.

▶ Send data to the management system.

▶ Request data from the management system.

What do the learning management system and learning module need to communicate? What could they possibly have to say to one another?

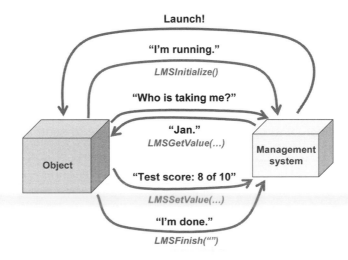

The LMS might want to start the module and have the module acknowledge that it is running. The module might ask the name of the learner so it can personalize responses, or the module might report back how much of the module the learner has completed. For tests, the LMS needs to record the scores. And the LMS needs to know when the learner has completed and closed a module.

Keep in mind that none of these communications needs is new. We never noticed them in traditional CBT modules because the communication was within a single integrated piece of software running on a single machine, rather than among distributed components running across the World Wide Web.

Design issues for communications

▶ What level do you track: course, lesson, or topic? Management systems may limit the levels you can track. Pure LMSs track only courses.

▶ What will you do with the data you record? One good use is to analyze navigation and pacing to improve the organization and user interface of your course.

▶ What events do you track at each level: just start and finish, one test result per object, multiple test results, or answers to individual test questions?

▶ What data items will you want to exchange about the course, about the module, and about the learner?

▶ Privacy laws and policies may restrict what data you collect and record.

▶ More data is not more information. You must filter, analyze, and organize the data to turn it into useful information. Do you really have time to do that?

▶ Knowing their every action is recorded can intimidate learners.

▶ Implementing the tracking adds time to the schedule for building the course.

Metadata standards

Metadata is a fancy name for descriptive labeling. It is like the spines of books or posters for movies. Metadata is literally data about data. For e-learning, metadata standards provide a consistent way to describe courses, lessons, topics, and media components. These descriptions can be compiled into a catalog and electronically searched. Learners can consult the catalog to find modules to take. Producers can consult the catalog to find units to reuse.

Example of metadata items

Metadata standards specify dozens of items, some optional and some required, some essential and others pedantically obscure. Here are some commonly specified items of metadata:

Name	Example	What it records
Title	Introduction to Gantt Charts	Official name of the course, lesson, topic, or media component.
Language	en-US	Code for the language used in the unit, American English, in this case.
Description	Overview of using Gantt Charts in business.	What the unit teaches.
Keyword	Gantt chart, project management	Terms under which this module might appear in an index or be searched for.
Structure	hierarchical	How the unit is organized internally.
Aggregation level	3	The size of the unit, a course, in this example.
Version	1.1	Number indicating sequence among revisions.
Format	text/html, image/gif, application/x-shockwave	File formats used in the unit.
Size	1200000	Size of the files comprising the unit (in bytes).
Duration	PT3H30M	Time required to complete the unit, 3.5 hours, in this case.
Cost	no	Does the unit charge a fee?

Other metadata items may record specific items of interest to you.

Specific metadata schemes

Metadata standards are very open-ended. There are individual metadata schemes that specify what items are mandatory and how to consistently describe items. That level of detail is best left to entire organizations and professions. If you are developing a scheme for your department, say, you may want to base your scheme on one of these:

▶ ARIADNE (www.ariadne-eu.org).

▶ CanCore (www.cancore.org).

▶ HEAL (www.healcentral.org).

▶ MERLOT (merlot.org).

▶ Dublin Core (www.dublincore.org).

Design issues for metadata

▶ Which metadata items do you record for your own use? And for reuse by others?

▶ For what levels do you include metadata: course, lesson, topic, and media component?

▶ How do you ensure consistency? Do you adopt a taxonomy, which is a specific vocabulary and classification scheme? Do you define keyword dictionaries? What quality checking procedures will you put in place?

▶ Who writes subjective metadata, such as descriptions and keywords? How do you ensure that such entries are accurate and objective?

▶ How will you handle items for which the standard does not define metadata items, such as the instructor's contribution to a course, collaborative events, and blended learning?

▶ How will you represent quality and effectiveness?

Related standards

There are many other standards that affect e-learning. Most of them pertain only to tools used to create and manage e-learning and do not directly affect design. However, there are a couple more you should know about.

AICC

Think of AICC as SCORM for dinosaurs. AICC standards for reuse date back to the 1980s. They inspired many of the features of SCORM standards. AICC standards are still found in some authoring tools and management systems—as well as content produced with and for those systems.

If you have content that meets AICC standards, you may want to continue to support those standards. If you are starting fresh, do not adopt these obsolete standards. Follow the more up-to-date standards, such as SCORM.

IMS Question and Test Interoperability

The IMS Question and Test Interoperability (QTI) specification spells out how test questions authored in one tool can be combined with questions authored in another tool and how they all can be delivered by a third tool. Since much of the work of authoring a course goes to writing test questions, developers are understandably reluctant to have to re-create their questions for each management system they might encounter. As more and more management systems and test-authoring tools follow this standard, test questions will become more portable.

Avoid a naïve view of reuse

Reuse is a beautiful goal and has great benefits in practice, but designers must honestly admit the challenges it poses.

▶ **Real-world knowledge is highly interrelated, and skills are interdependent**. Concepts that make good blocks in a schematic diagram sprawl and slither all over the place when you try to corral them into learning objects.

▶ **Technical incompatibilities have not been eliminated**. A module created with WebWonker cannot be integrated into a course managed with PathGrinder and displayed in the NoChoice browser on the Zebra operating system. Not everything is as standardized as some of the plugfests suggest.

▶ **Learners experience whiplash learning**. On one page, buttons are at the top, on the next they squat on the bottom. Tranquil earth tones abruptly shift to pulsing neon. Text-only pages alternate with multimedia extravaganzas. The experience is bumpy at best. Unless developers follow common standards for the user interface, visual appearance, and media usage, learners suffer.

FOLLOW QUALITY STANDARDS

Following SCORM or other technical standards does not guarantee that anyone will find your course usable (p. 36). Design standards can help ensure that human beings can use and learn from your e-learning. Two main types of quality standards are emerging.

▶ **Design quality.** A checklist to ensure that your e-learning follows generally recognized principles of instructional design and user-interface design.

The Guidelines specify three levels of actions at different priorities, Priority 1 being most urgent. These Guidelines have found their way, almost verbatim, into various government regulations, for example:

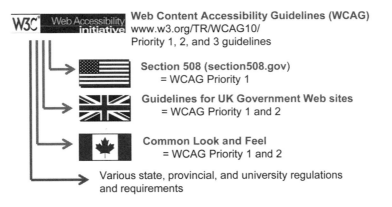

U.S. Section 508

The term *Section 508* refers to the 1998 Revision of Section 508 of the Rehabilitation Act of 1973 (29 USC794d) and applies to U.S. Federal agencies and subcontractors.

Its stated goal is to ensure that employees and the public "with disabilities have access to and use of information and data that is comparable" to that of those without disabilities.

Section 508 consists of several separate sections. E-learning may fall under either of the first two sections, depending on the technology used to construct the e-learning: §1194.21 for content that runs in a plug-in or media player, and §1194.22 for content that appears in Web pages.

Requirements for accessibility

Here are some of the requirements imposed in §1194.22 of Section 508:

(a) A text equivalent for every non-text element shall be provided (e.g., via "alt", "longdesc", or in element content).

(b) Equivalent alternatives for any multimedia presentations shall be synchronized with the presentation.

(c) Web pages shall be designed so that all information conveyed with color is also available without color, for example from context or markup.

(d) Documents shall be organized so they are readable without requiring an associated style sheet.

(e) Redundant text links shall be provided for each active region of a server-side image map.

As you can see, they are quite detailed and prescribe techniques for *building* the e-learning, not specific *design* issues.

Approaches to compliance

Complying with accessibility regulations can be quite difficult and expensive, depending on your approach. Your organization should have a consistent, well-thought-out approach. Here are some possible approaches.

Claim an exemption (to 508)

Most regulations spell out where the regulation applies and where not. For example, Section 508 explicitly exempts projects where:

► "undue burden would be imposed."

► National security, where military and intelligence activities are involved.

► Compliance would require "fundamental alteration in the nature of a product or its components."

► Technology is "incidental to a contract."

Alternative content

One approach approved in most regulations is to provide alternative content. Usually this is phrased as "substantially equivalent or better access." Some forms of alternative content include:

► Alternative formats: "voice, fax, relay service, TTY, Internet posting, captioning, text-to-speech synthesis, and audio description."

► Alternative knowledge product, e.g., accessible e-book, Web site, or text file.

► Human assistance, e.g., e-mail link to ask for help or explanation.

Universal accessibility

Another approach is to make every page accessible to everyone. Every component must follow every particular of the standard. This is called *universal accessibility*. It avoids the difficulty of maintaining multiple versions, but can prove extremely difficult and expensive.

Dynamic customization

The most sophisticated approach stores content in a neutral format and then electronically generates custom versions suited to the abilities of individual learners. This technique is called *dynamic customization*. There are two main approaches, both highly technical.

▶ **Database publishing**. Units of content are stored in a database or in XML. Versions suited for different abilities are generated automatically by formatting the content to match the abilities of the learner.

▶ **On-the-fly formatting**. Like database publishing, but individual pages are generated as requested.

Design issues for accessibility

Having worked on several projects that had to meet Section 508 requirements, I can say that the effect on design is important, but not disruptive. The most common modifications to project requirements were:

▶ Transcripts for all spoken words.

▶ Buttons large enough.

▶ More legible text.

▶ Text descriptions or summaries for all graphics.

▶ Descriptions for all links.

▶ Alternate navigation links.

▶ Link triggers large with good contrast.

▶ HTML layers organized in a logical sequence (in the HTML code) so they made sense when read by screen readers.

Example of "or better" access

Consider those who cannot see. If your authoring tools do not make it easy to build simulations accessible by blind users who rely on screen readers, take a few extra steps to provide an alternative form of the information contained in the simulation.

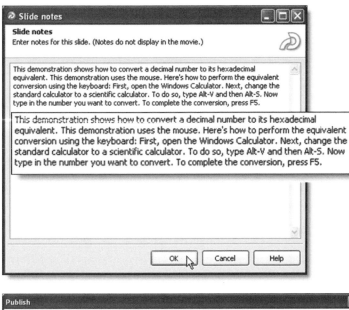

Let's look at how you might do this with Adobe Captivate. For each slide in the simulation, you can enter text in the **Slide notes** dialog box. Notice that here we include the keyboard shortcuts which, for blind users, are easier than mouse actions.

Once we have entered the notes, we can export the simulation to a Microsoft Word document. We make sure the document includes the slide notes.

8

Strategic decisions

Once we have the Microsoft Word document, we can make it available to those who use screen readers. Or we could convert it to a Web page or Adobe Acrobat PDF, which can also be read by screen readers.

SET YOUR OWN TECHNOLOGY STANDARDS

E-learning depends on technology. As such, e-learning designers must take into account their goals and limitations as they lay down some basic rules about what technologies they will rely on. These rules are especially important if the e-learning will be created by separate teams or outside vendors.

Designate target browsers

First decide what browser learners can use to take your course. Limit this list to one or two specific browsers. Be sure to specify the version of your target browsers. For example you might specify your e-learning will run on Internet Explorer 6.0 and Firefox 1.5.

If HTML features are supported by all of your target browsers, use them freely. If features are supported by some of your targeted browsers and ignored cleanly (that is, without causing any error) by the others, use the features for non-essential information, for decorations, and for experiments. If features are not cleanly ignored by some of the target browsers, either do not use the feature or prepare two versions of the page.

Consider requiring a late model browser rather than an earlier one that requires multiple plug-ins. For example, the Dynamic HTML supported in later browsers may be adequate for simple animations that would require a plug-in with Version 3 browsers.

Specify file formats for materials

The choice of allowable file formats has several critical implications for designers. Some file formats will require proprietary plug-ins that learners must download and install. Information in one format may download quicker and display more smoothly than in another. Not all formats can be displayed in all versions of all browsers. The choice of file formats may limit the choice of tools for creating course materials. Pick formats that everyone can display safely.

Favor widely used file formats

So that as many people as possible can take your e-learning with the minimum amount of time spent downloading and installing plug-ins, pick file formats that play in the browsers most people already have.

Start with browser-native formats

Start with formats displayed directly by the browser itself without assistance from other software, such as plug-ins. These formats displayed by the browser are called *browser-native* formats. They depend on the brand and version of browser you have selected. For example, here are browser-native formats for Internet Explorer 6.0:

▶ HTML, including Dynamic HTML, and Cascading Style Sheets (CSS).

▶ Text (ASCII and Unicode).

▶ JavaScript.

▶ GIF, JPEG, and PNG graphics.

▶ XML, including XSL style sheets.

▶ Java.

Next consider platform-independent formats

Platform-independent formats are ones that can be reliably displayed, albeit with plug-ins, in multiple browser versions on multiple operating systems. Although plug-ins are required, they exist for most browsers and are either inexpensive or free. Platform-independent formats are usually industry standards rather than proprietary formats. Some industry-standard formats include:

▶ **Audio**: MP3.

▶ **Music**: MIDI.

▶ **Video**: MPEG.

▶ **Virtual Reality**: VRML.

Then think about popular Web formats

Next consider some proprietary formats that are already widely used and for which technical support is readily available. Many learners will already have the required plug-in installed, and, if they need to install one, help is available. Here are some formats in this category:

▶ **Sound**: WMA, WAV, Real Audio.

▶ **Video**: Shockwave Flash (SWF), Flash Video (FLV), QuickTime, WMV, Real Video.

▶ **Documents**: Adobe Acrobat PDF, Rich Text Format (RTF), FlashPaper.

At this point, consider licensing requirements. Some formats can be distributed freely over the Web from a server but require a license to distribute on CD-ROM.

Finally, consider popular desktop formats

Consider formats common in specific work environments. These might include desktop applications and other tools used by target learners. For example, some businesses have standardized computer set-ups that include a suite of applications such as Microsoft Office. Such a company could include Microsoft PowerPoint, Word, and Excel documents in their courses. Remember to check for licensing restrictions.

Avoid obscure and unsupported formats

I do not recommend using formats that require a rare plug-in or one for which technical support is not readily available—unless you are prepared to provide that support.

Favor virus-proof formats

Favor virus-proof formats. For example, a Java applet is more virus-proof than a Java application. A word-processing document without embedded macros is more virus-proof than one with macros.

Limit file sizes

Unless all learners have high-speed network connections **all the time**, consider suggesting limits for the total file size for each topic, for example the HTML file **and all the files it automatically loads**.

Here are some guidelines that should get most topics down the cable in less than 10 seconds:

If learner's connection speed is:	Limit each topic to a total size of:
14.4 Kbps	10K
28.8 Kbps	20K
56 Kbps	40K
128 Kbps	80K
1 Mbps	640K
Faster	1 Megabyte per Mbps

TITLE COURSES CAREFULLY

Titling your course may seem like a trivial decision. Yet, in e-learning, the name of a course can affect who takes the course.

Often the title is all users see to entice them to click on a link for more information. Name a course so that learners can predict the goals, approach, and subject of the course just by reading the title.

Project management—advanced level simulator

Selling suburban real estate – Self-paced tutorial

Developing your financial plan: Web seminar for individual investors

Think about how a course will be retrieved and sorted in an online catalog. Here are some guidelines in naming your course:

▶ **Put the most important parts first**. That way, the title is predictably situated in an index or alphabetical listing, and learners' rapidly scanning eyes will notice these important words.

▶ **Promise benefits**. Make clear what learners gain by taking the course. Too many titles tell what the teacher wants to talk about rather than how the learner benefits.

▶ **Use terms learners understand**. Use terms meaningful to learners—before taking the course. Avoid esoteric terminology and product names.

▶ **Imply who should take the e-learning**. Use terms like "advanced" or "basic" or name the job categories that benefit from the course.

IN CLOSING ...

Summary

▶ Many types of e-learning courses are possible, depending on a few fundamental choices. Consider where your course should fall along each of these scales:

Pure instructor-led	to	Pure learner-led
Pure synchronous	to	Pure asynchronous
Large class	to	Class of one

▶ Specify where learners should take the course and the devices they will use. Then design it for where and how learners will really take it.

▶ Pure e-learning may not be the best approach to training. Consider mixing different forms of e-learning with different forms of classroom learning.

▶ Specify what technologies can be used in your course. Favor technologies that are reliable, available to many, and fully supported by their vendors.

For more ...

The front line for creating learning objects lies in the design of topics (Chapter 6). You can also learn a lot by searching the Web for the phrase *reusable learning object*.

Complying with standards can be complex. Here are some sources for more information on standards:

▶ **SCORM**: www.adlnet.org.

▶ **Web Content Accessibility Guidelines**: www.w3c.org.

▶ **Section 508**: www.section508.gov.

9 Design for the virtual classroom

Designing and delivering instructor-led e-learning

Virtual classrooms bridge the gap between the medieval classroom and the World Wide Web. Virtual classrooms use collaboration tools to re-create the structure and learning experiences of a physical classroom. When well designed, they preserve the orderly structure and rich interaction of the classroom while removing the requirement for everyone to be in the same location.

Virtual classrooms are a special application of computer and network technologies to the task of education. As in the physical classroom, an instructor leads a class of learners through an explicit syllabus of material on a predetermined schedule. In the virtual classroom, learners and instructors can use e-mail, discussion forums, chat, polls, whiteboards, application sharing, audio- and video-conferencing, and other tools to exchange messages.

While they may include many of the activities in Chapters 2, 3, and 4, they add new possibilities and require additional design and management. This chapter considers the different media and tools used in the virtual classroom and how they may be combined for online presentations, meetings, and entire courses.

CREATE A VIRTUAL CLASSROOM

Why should you use a virtual classroom in your e-learning plans? And how do online presentations and meetings play into the virtual classroom course? Let's see.

Why create a virtual classroom?

Why design e-learning as a virtual classroom? Virtual-classroom courses require an instructor who must be paid. If you have scheduled meetings, are all learners tied to a fixed schedule? Well, virtual classrooms have several advantages:

The instructor can adapt learning to learners. The instructor can directly monitor everything going on in the classroom. The instructor can answer questions and address concerns immediately. The instructor can adjust content and presentation immediately in response to subtle feedback from learners.

The virtual classroom provides the community and discipline some learners need. Being part of a visible group embarked on a common endeavor appeals to a sense of community and tribalism. The requirement to show up at a specific location on a definite schedule enforces a discipline on learners. Face-to-face contact with the instructor and peer pressure combine to keep learners on schedule.

Classroom learning is familiar and proven. Learners are familiar with the procedures, rhythms, and presentation methods used in the classroom. Classroom courses have been the standard in education for 500 years or more.

Learning is flexible and active. The class can combine lecture, question and answer, individual and team activities, reading, and testing. Learners can work directly with fellow learners and gain from meaningful conversations with them.

For more on the advantages and disadvantages of instructor-led e-learning, see Chapter 8.

Courses, meetings, presentations

Virtual-classroom courses may involve three overlapping scopes of interaction and technologies: courses, meetings, and presentations.

▶ **Virtual-classroom courses** are complete programs of learning. They consist of a mixture of synchronous and asynchronous events. Among the synchronous events are online meetings, which may include online presentations.

▶ **Online meetings,** or *Webinars*, are interactive synchronous events. They are possible components of a virtual-classroom course. They may also occur as a standalone e-learning event or as a business meeting used for other purposes.

▶ **Online presentations** provide information, as part of an online meeting or as a separate event altogether. Online presentations are not interactive and may be delivered live or recorded and played back later.

This chapter covers all three. Just keep in mind that you may want to include online presentations and meetings in your e-learning without creating a full virtual-classroom course.

SELECT AND USE COLLABORATION TOOLS

Computer and network technologies provide a wide range of collaboration tools for person-to-person interaction. These range from simple e-mail to complete online-meeting environments. This chapter guides you in selecting among these collaboration tools. It helps you see what each offers and how to use it to educate distant learners.

Select your collaboration tools

Collaboration tools make it possible for distant learners to communicate freely and to work together on tasks common in the virtual classroom. You will need to consider the various tools and how to use them productively. First, you must decide what kind of person-to-person interaction best furthers the objectives of your course. Then, you must implement this interaction in the form and technology appropriate for your situation.

Consider a variety of tools

By incorporating rich communication and collaboration into our e-learning, we can ensure that learners never lack for that human touch, which is often cited as the reason why face-to-face classrooms are necessary for teaching advanced skills.

Collaboration tools can link an instructor and an individual learner, as well as linking groups of learners.

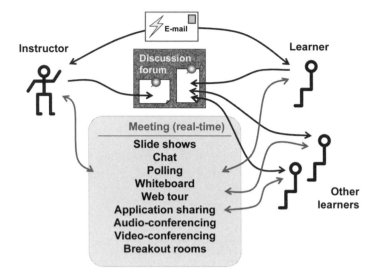

The simplest mechanism is e-mail between the instructor and learner. Often e-mail messages are broadcast, typically from the instructor to announce a change or an event to all learners in a class. Learners can also post messages on a class discussion forum, as can the instructor. Other learners can then read and reply to these messages.

Meeting mechanisms provide real-time exchanges among the instructor and learners. Participants can use chat to exchange text messages—something like instant e-mail. They can use polls to vote on issues and make choices. Through whiteboard or screen-sharing tools, learners can discuss and work together on visual subjects. Learners can use audio-conferencing much as they would a telephone conference-call. Those with fast networks can use video-conferencing to swap video images of one another.

Decide whether you need a live meeting

You need a good reason to require people to work together. You need an even better reason to require them to all log in at the same time. Should you conduct an online meeting?

☹ No	☺ Yes
Teaching explicit knowledge.	Teaching unstructured, implicit knowledge.
Content requires detailed study.	Learners have many questions.
Learners lack language skills.	Isolated learners prefer learning with others.
Learners have unpredictable schedules.	No time to develop standalone materials.

Laziness on the part of the designer is not a good reason for a meeting. Sad to say, many online meetings occur because the instructor lacked the skills or self-discipline necessary to create materials that learners could consume on their own. If information is simple, post it in a well-designed Web page. If your material needs a little interactivity, the computer can provide that interactivity. Require a good reason for an online meeting.

Layer learning activities

Rather than doing everything in one collaboration mode, systematically mix synchronous and asynchronous events as well as solo and group activities. One such plan is shown here.

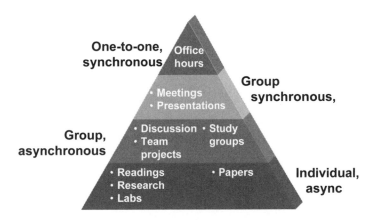

Synchronous exchanges are used sparingly for high-priority tasks such as individual conferences and class meetings. More mundane tasks that do not justify scheduling simultaneous activities or that are best performed individually are lower on the pyramid.

Pick tools to suit learners

Collaboration tools are technology, but they are operated by human beings. The most important factors in your choice of collaboration tools are human factors. Let me list a few.

Language fluency. Some collaboration requires greater language skills than others. Unless learners are all fluent in a language, real-time collaboration mechanisms like chat, audio-conferencing, and video-conferencing may frustrate those who would prefer e-mail or discussion forums, which allow more time to comprehend a message and then compose a response.

Accents. Internet audio quality can exacerbate difficulties in understanding speakers with a distinct accent. I took part in one international audio-conference conducted in English in which the Swedes could not understand the Pakistanis, who could not understand the Texan, who could understand everybody except the British, who thought all the Americans "sounded like bad Hollywood movie characters."

Typing skill. Chat is a spontaneous medium—for touch typists. Unfortunately, many learners are not proficient typists. Nor is it for those embarrassed by their typing mistakes.

Technical expertise. Some learners have been conferencing on the Net for years. Others are still trying to master the double-click. You need to consider how comfortable learners are with computer and network technologies. How much must learners extend themselves to master collaboration tools? If learners already know how to use a whiteboard, then application sharing is not much of a stretch. If they have just learned to use e-mail, expecting them to master chat, whiteboard, and video-conferencing is probably too much.

Also consider what technical support you can offer. If learners must master collaboration tools on their own, they may become discouraged. If you (or the tool's vendor) provide tutorials and phone support, the task is less daunting.

Consider the speed of learners' network connections

What speed network connection will learners use to access your collaborative events? What speed connection do learners have when they access e-learning from a hotel, from a home computer, or over an overloaded network? Remember that different collaboration tools require different network speeds. Here is a rough scale of what real speed most media require.

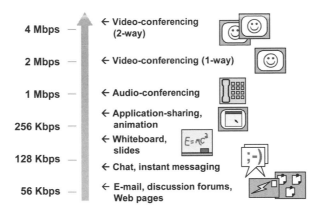

By real speed, I mean the actual, sustained speed of the network at the time of the meeting—not the theoretical speed at 2 AM when no one else is on the network.

Best practice: Consider network latency and gaps

Your learners around the globe are all connected to the Internet with high-speed connections. Yet sound stutters and video skips. I have observed delays like these in collaborative events:

▶ Voice over telephone: 1/10 to 1 seconds.

▶ Voice over network (VoIP): 1 to 4 seconds.

▶ Display of slides and other visuals: 1 to 10 seconds.

I have heard of longer delays, sometimes even minutes long, but suspect these are signs of catastrophic network failures.

Enable interpersonal communication

Consider the nature of the interpersonal communication needed. Different degrees of communication require different media. Consider what you need to communicate your message.

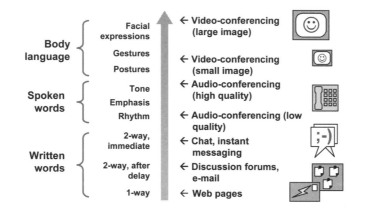

If an exchange of written words is sufficient, you can get by with chat, discussion forum, or just e-mail. On the other hand, if your message involves subtle emotional cues such as gestures, facial expressions, and tone of voice, you may require video-conferencing.

Slide shows

Online slide shows present slides to a distant audience. Instead of watching the slide on a screen at the front of the room, learners watch it on their computer screens.

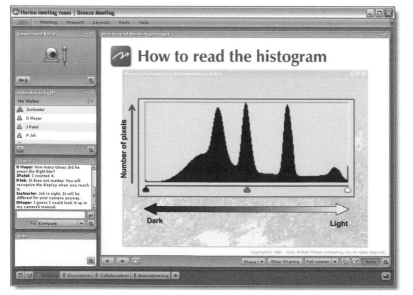

Here we see a slide being presented by an instructor. Learners see the slide and hear the instructor speaking about the slide.

The PowerPoint slide is displayed in Adobe Breeze Meeting.

The slide show feature is among the simplest collaboration mechanisms to use. The instructor creates slides, typically in Microsoft PowerPoint. The instructor may add graphics and animations.

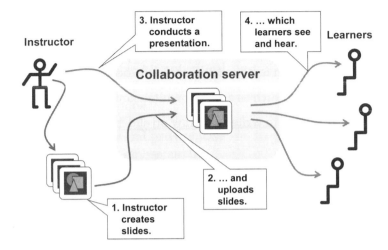

The instructor then uploads the slides to the online-meeting tool. Once the slides are uploaded, the instructor conducts a presentation, which learners see and hear as if in the same room as the instructor.

When to use slide shows

Use online slide shows for:

▶ Content that is changing right up to the last minute. The instructor can customize the presentation based on learners' responses to previous activities.

▶ Efficiently presenting information on spatial, logical, and mathematical subjects.

▶ For showing visual examples, such as photographs, sketches, or diagrams.

▶ When you have proven presentations and capable presenters to give them.

▶ For overviews of a subject area or previews of a collaborative activity.

▶ Briefing learners who have not yet learned to use other collaboration tools or are not ready to collaborate.

Unless you have good reasons to use a live presentation, record the presentation and let learners take it at their convenience (p. 51).

When to use chat

Use chat to let people at different locations on a network carry on a conversation. Use it when e-mail and discussion-forum exchanges are too slow.

Use chat for simple conversations. Some common uses for chat include:

▶ Real-time question-and-answer sessions.

▶ Brainstorming, troubleshooting, and problem-solving sessions.

▶ "Oral" examinations.

▶ Interviews of experts by learners or researchers.

▶ "Study group meetings" among teams of learners.

Use chat as your back channel during presentations. Chat lets learners ask questions while someone is demonstrating an application or drawing on the whiteboard. The questions do not disrupt the person doing the demonstration and do not require a two-way audio channel. The person conducting the demonstration periodically checks the chat window for messages. Or an assistant does, so the presenter is not distracted.

Use chat to personalize learning. Use chat for other than whole-class meetings. Use it for study groups, team meetings, tutoring sessions, and private meetings with the instructor. Provide a procedure for reserving time slots on the class chat server or for setting up a private chat room. Encourage learners to use private chat to communicate to other learners, perhaps to suggest to teammates how the idea being discussed could be implemented in their class project. Keep the chat window available after the official end of the class meeting. And let learners schedule their own chat sessions.

Not for lectures. Chat is for short, spontaneous thoughts. If the ideas are deeper than that, or if you require time to find just the right words, send the ideas as e-mail or discussion-forum messages. Nothing is worse than having to read a sporadically scrolling text narrative—awkwardly composed, inaccurately typed, and saying nothing a textbook does not say better. Using chat to narrate actions in an application sharing or whiteboard session can also be awkward. Having to stop using the visual application to go to the chat window and type a comment or instructions interrupts the flow of the task being demonstrated. Do not ever use chat for lectures, OK?

Not for slow typists. All participants must be good typists. Otherwise the conversation is filled with awkward pauses. By the time a slow typist enters a reply, the conversation has moved on to a completely different subject. Do not rely on chat if all learners must type quickly and accurately or if responses must be complex.

For a small group. Chat can seem painfully slow if only two are chatting. If more than five or seven are chatting, however, it can be difficult to keep up, especially if you are a slow typist. That does not mean you cannot use chat as a back channel in a large meeting provided only a few people are using chat at once. I learned this lesson when I asked a complex question of 60 people in a meeting. For about a minute nothing happened. Then suddenly 5- and 6-line text messages poured into the chat window and the window began scrolling, blurring the responses until they scrolled off the screen.

For whispering to the teacher. Suggest that learners use private chat to ask a question or make a comment without interrupting the whole class. Or to remain anonymous from the rest of the class.

Best practices for using chat effectively

Make sure that learners and instructors use chat in ways that advance learning. Even those who have used chat or instant messaging socially for years may not draw analogies to using it for learning. Here are some ways to use chat for learning:

▶ **Keep it professional**. Learning chat is not social chat. The light banter and heavy flirting that are common late at night on AOL are hardly the kind of conversations you want to foster. Help learners to adopt professional behaviors that lead to learning.

▶ **Prepare spontaneous comments ahead of time**. If you know what questions you will ask or what answers you will give, you can prepare them in a separate text-editor window. At the appropriate moment you can just cut and paste them to the chat window.

▶ **Monitor chat**. In most online meeting systems, the presenter or host sees all messages, even messages sent privately from one learner to another. You might want to warn learners about the instructor's ability to eavesdrop. Or, you might not.

▶ **Save a transcript**. Chat leaves a written transcript. You may want to save the transcript and post it to the class discussion forum so that learners can concentrate on the online meeting without having to make notes of what is said in chat. However, the transcript may seem crude when read later. Some participants may object to seeing their off-the-cuff remarks on display. Warn them ahead of time and ensure that providing transcripts does not inhibit discussion.

Whiteboards

A whiteboard is a collaboration tool that simulates the process that occurs when the instructor draws on a wall-mounted whiteboard and then invites a learner to contribute to the drawing. All participants immediately see everything drawn on the whiteboard. In some online meeting tools, the whiteboard feature can be used as an overlay to annotate slides, Web tours, video clips, and even shared applications. The way the whiteboard looks and works will depend on the meeting tool you use.

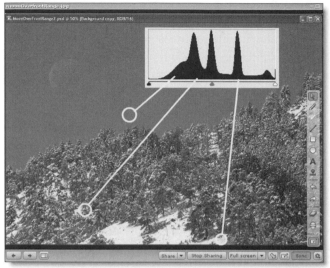

For example, in a course on digital photography, the instructor relates bumps on the histogram to areas in the photograph.

An Adobe Photoshop file is being displayed in Adobe Breeze Meeting.

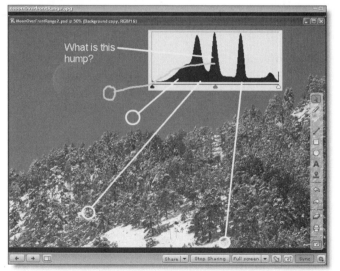

The instructor could pose a question to a learner and then pass control to the learner. The learner would then answer by drawing on the whiteboard.

Use a whiteboard for visual learning

Whiteboards let instructors and learners sketch ideas they cannot express in words. Whiteboards are especially important for courses in science, engineering, mathematics, and other subjects that mix graphics and text. Whiteboards are also important for those with limited English language skills and those who express themselves well visually. Some common subjects include:

▶ **Visual appearance**. The color, layout, shape, or contents of any visual display.

▶ **Arrangement and organization of components** of a system. Participants can draw and edit a diagram.

▶ **Charts and graphs** showing numerical trends and patterns.

▶ **Visual symbols** that the learner must learn to recognize.

Use whiteboards communally

Whiteboards are not limited to one-way presentations to passive viewers. With whiteboards, instructors and learners can interact. Learners can complete a drawing started by the instructor. The instructor or learners can critique a graphic by annotating specific parts. Participants can mark up a slide, photograph, chart, or diagram to suggest improvements.

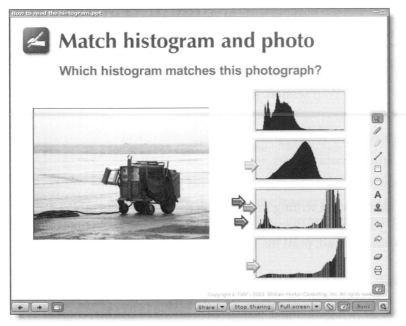

Some systems allow all meeting participants to draw at once. I use this for visual voting where learners can point to their choices. The flurry of arrows adds excitement as learners indicate and revise their choices.

Sounds chaotic, but it can be a productive way for immediate collaboration.

A Microsoft PowerPoint slide is being displayed in Adobe Breeze Meeting.

Here's a list of whiteboard activities you can use to activate your class and get learners accustomed to using the whiteboard:

▶ Vote visually by letting learners indicate their choices on a graphic by pointing with an arrow, placing a checkmark, or highlighting their choices.

▶ Display a map and have students write their names and draw arrows to their locations.

▶ Present a grid with one square for each learner to write answers to a question.

▶ Let learners experience a Web-based game or a simulation.

▶ Point out resources available on the Web, such as publications by professional associations, regulations by government agencies, or tutorials by vendors of products.

Best practices for using Web tours

Web tours are relatively simple ways to use the whole Web as a classroom resource. Just make sure learners accomplish the learning objective.

▶ Allow time for learners to catch up. Not all learners may receive the target page at the same time. If navigating on their own, novices may take longer to find an assigned destination.

▶ Tell learners how long they have to navigate on their own. Remind them of the time remaining before the instructor resumes control.

▶ Do not expect a large group to follow along. "Now everybody click the big blue button at the upper left." If learners must navigate on their own, provide a specific goal and directions learners can refer to.

▶ Use a back channel, such as chat, so learners can report problems and ask for help.

▶ If learners must watch you interact with the Web page, use application sharing (p. 436). I usually conduct such tours in application sharing, as it seems more reliable in most tools.

▶ After the tour, give learners a list of URLs visited in the Web tour so they can re-create the tour themselves.

▶ If learners must investigate sites in detail, provide a list of URLs for them to pursue at their own pace.

Application sharing

Application sharing lets the presenter share programs, windows, or the entire screen with learners. The instructor can demonstrate a procedure or piece of software simply by running it on his or her computer. Learners see exactly what is displayed in the shared window. In some systems, they can take control of the display—with permission of the presenter, of course.

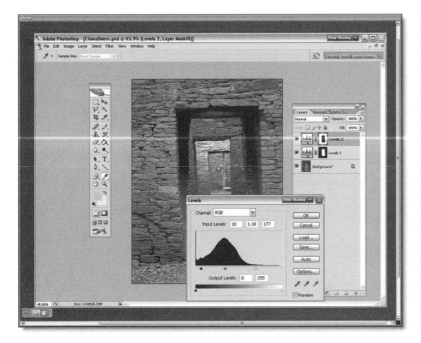

Here is an example of a shared application. It shows the learners' view as the instructor modifies a photograph in Photoshop. The learner's computer does not require Photoshop to view this demonstration. Later the instructor may have a learner perform a similar procedure.

The meeting tool is Adobe Breeze Meeting.

When to use application sharing

Use application sharing to demonstrate computer programs, computer data, pictures, and other material on a computer screen. Use application-sharing sessions to:

▶ Demonstrate computer programs and teach operations skills, especially for programs not released yet or not widely available.

▶ Let learners view data in applications that are not on learners' computers, such as a database not generally accessible.

▶ Let learners try out skills demonstrated by the instructor. Have learners talk aloud as they perform the activity. The instructor can take over if learners fail.

▶ Create collaborative activities involving multiple learners. Periodically call on learners to conduct demonstrations. Have each learner in turn perform one step in a procedure. Share a game to make a multi-player game.

Application sharing is seldom fast enough to show any rapid animation or fluid motions. Use it for demonstrations that require only simple movements.

If your meeting system offers application sharing, you can use it in place of other capabilities that may be missing or inadequate in your tool.

If you lack:	Use application sharing to share:
Chat	A word processor or text editor.
Whiteboard	A slide or drawing program.
Slide show	PowerPoint or another slide program.
Web tour	Web browser.

Best practices for application sharing

Application sharing takes careful preparation and smooth execution. For best effect:

▶ **Rehearse the demonstration** until it flows smoothly. Learners do not enjoy watching the presenter's mistakes. An unrehearsed presentation communicates that the presenter is unprofessional and does not mind wasting the learners' time.

▶ **Share just what you need to share**. Share an individual application or window rather than the whole desktop. Share only one program at a time. Do not let other windows cover the application you are sharing.

▶ **Quit unnecessary programs**. For better reliability and speed, exit other programs that require computer or network resources. Turn off video-conferencing.

▶ **Use audio to narrate**—if bandwidth permits. Continuously explain what you are doing. Let learners hear as well as see the demonstration. Speak slowly and clearly. Allow time for learners to listen and understand.

▶ **Keep security in mind**. If you grant control to others, they can open, modify, and delete files on your system. Do not hand over control and leave the room.

▶ **Move slowly and smoothly and pause frequently** so learners' displays have time to catch up with the presenter's display. Avoid dragging windows on the screen. If you must rearrange the screen, stop application sharing, move and resize windows, and then resume application sharing.

Polls

Polling requires learners to make choices. Also called *virtual voting booths*, *virtual response pads*, or *virtual show of hands*, they let all learners see aggregate totals of how the class voted. Polls are on-screen displays that let learners select among alternatives. The choices are tallied and displayed in a composite view. Polls function like the keypads used by learners in some interactive video courses to indicate their answers to questions posed by the instructor. Online polls, however, require no special hardware.

Types of polls

There are three forms of polls: spontaneous, synchronous, and asynchronous.

Spontaneous polls

Informal Yes/No polls in an online meeting ask participants to indicate their choices by clicking a **raise hand** button or a **Yes** button to indicate yes and a **No** button to indicate a no. Such spontaneous real-time polls get immediate opinions from learners.

Here is an example of a spontaneous poll.

The meeting tool is Adobe Breeze Meeting.

Synchronous polls

Synchronous polls have learners pick from a list of alternatives and then see the results of the aggregate voting. Synchronous polls let members of the class answer informal test questions, make real-time choices, and vote on issues.

Here is an example of a synchronous poll. First, a slide appears to introduce the poll. Learners see the question and possible choices. Then, the voting area is appears, learners vote, and the results are displayed to the class.

The meeting tool is Adobe Breeze Meeting.

Asynchronous polls

Asynchronous polls are available for learners to vote over a period of time, say a week, before their votes are tallied. Asynchronous polls let learners visit and vote on their own schedule. Vote totals may be displayed after a voting period or continuously as they change.

In this example of an asynchronous poll, we ask learners to state how much the objectives for e-learning overlap their objectives for study. It is asynchronous so learners can change their opinions as the course progresses.

Built using Adobe Dreamweaver. View example at horton.com/eld/.

When to use polls

Polls are an effective way to encourage learners to research and think deeply about issues. They are also good to challenge learners to shape the opinions of others, thereby realizing the limitations of their own thinking. They can add a spark of interactivity by polling the class on the point under discussion.

Use polls to force choices, administer surveys, and tally votes. Here are some uses for them in e-learning:

▶ Use spontaneous polls to survey learners instantly on an issue. For example, let learners decide what the instructor should discuss or what the class should consider in greater detail.

▶ Have learners vote yes or no on items in a checklist. Conduct a mock trial and have learners vote on the guilt or innocence of the defendant. Hold a debate and let learners choose the winner.

▶ Use polls to select alternatives in a simulation or game.

▶ Get instant feedback on how well learners feel they understand a concept. Conduct before and after surveys to measure changes of opinion or knowledge.

▶ Vote to narrow choices, discuss the remaining choices, and then vote again to select.

▶ Conduct emotional polls. Ask learners how they feel about an issue. Define emoticons (smileys) they can use to vote.

Best practices for polls

Use polls in ways that let learners naturally express choices.

▶ **Collect opinions at the right time**. Record choices at the most revealing times: after an event, during an event, or both before and after an event. For example, let learners discuss a question before voting. And let them change their votes in response to comments in discussion.

▶ **Make sure learners know how to vote** ("Select your choice and then click **Enter**") and how to refresh their view of others' votes.

▶ **Phrase prompts and choices with extreme care**. Test to make sure learners understand the choices. Explain choices at the beginning of the activity. Test your questions on others to make sure they all interpret the question the way you intended. Refine questions until they are clear.

▶ **Display vote totals only**. Learners may hesitate to vote if they feel others can learn how they individually voted. However, the instructor may want to see how individuals voted. That way the instructor can call on a learner to speak for a particular position.

▶ **Track changes of opinion during an ongoing event**. Such logs can provide a valuable source for research.

▶ **Give learners time to make up their minds**. Do not force them to vote immediately upon receiving the question. Let them turn the question over in their minds, think of an answer, change their minds, figure out how to vote, and do so.

▶ Require research and analysis for asynchronous polls. Use them to provoke research and deeper learning.

▶ **Set up generic polls**. That way you will not have to create a large number of polls or re-create them each time you use a different meeting system. Put the actual questions on your slides. Then prepare polls with choices such as:

  ▪ Yes and No.

  ▪ A, B, and C (keyed to items on the slide).

  ▪ A, B, C, and D.

  ▪ A, B, C, D, and E.

  ▪ More, The Same, and Less.

▶ **Ask open-ended questions**. Let learners give answers not included in the poll. I frequently include a poll choice of "Other (enter in chat)" to encourage learners to think beyond the list of choices I provide.

Audio-conferencing

Audio-conferencing lets participants talk with one another. Audio-conferencing can be conducted by a phone conference call or by using the Internet to communicate speech.

When to use audio-conferencing

Use audio-conferencing when people need to speak. The first question to answer is: When does someone need to hear someone else speak? Use audio-conferencing when:

▶ **Emotions are important.** A tone of voice can tell us whether the speaker is angry, excited, sad, or just joking. A text transcript cannot. "Instructor: How's it going? Learner: Just great."

▶ **Sounds are important.** You want to hear or demonstrate the sound that something makes—a computer disk drive or a healthy human heart, for instance.

▶ **Learners lack writing or typing skills** necessary to collaborate fluently by written media.

▶ **The discussion is complex.** A chat session would require too much typing and have too many delays that break the continuity of the conversation.

Telephone or Voice over IP?

Many online meeting tools offer two ways to transmit voice: over a telephone connection or over the Internet. This second option uses a technology called Voice over Internet Protocol, or VoIP, for short.

Use telephone when	Use Voice Over IP when
You need a reliable, perfected technology, remarkably free of pauses, gaps, and distortion.	A telephone call would be too expensive.
Quality of the voice is critical.	The telephone line is in use or must be kept open for other purposes. Or learners have only one telephone line and it is used for the network connection.
You need to be able to continue the class while the computer reboots after a malfunction.	Setting up a conference call with more than a few people can be complex.

I have had better experiences with telephone connections. I agreed to use the VoIP connection recommended by the conferencing tool vendor. After that decision was made, however, the course enrollment jumped from 15 to 50. During the first session, my state-of-the-art presentation computer crashed repeatedly. I'd switch to my backup computer (I am not that trusting) until it too crashed and I shifted back to my original computer, which had been rebooted. From that point on, we used telephone for voice and had no further problems.

Best practices for audio-conferencing

Audio-conferencing puts strains on your network, your speakers, and your learners. Plan how you will use it within your human and technological limitations.

▶ **Reduce background noise.** Close the window. Turn off the radio. Turn off unnecessary machinery. When not talking, mute the microphone.

▶ **Mute learners' microphones until they need to speak**. Entire classes have had to listen to intra-office gossip, parents disciplining children, and barking dogs because learners did not know how to mute their microphones.

▶ **Put emotion into your voice**. Poor audio connections make everybody sound bored and monotonous. Go a bit overboard. Exaggerate. Emote. Ham it up.

▶ **Speak slowly and distinctly.** Even the best telephone connection is low fidelity. E-nun-ci-ate! Repeat unfamiliar terms. Spell out words learners will not recognize.

stuttering in the sound. Avoid the common practice of showing the presenter in the middle of a room with people walking around in the background. Never pose the presenter outdoors or against an outside window with leaves fluttering in the breeze.

▶ **Frame the scene**. Position the camera so it will capture what is important. Consider the size video window learners will view. You may want to move the camera back to allow the presenter to move back and forth as in a classroom. Or you may want the camera closer to capture gestures or emotions. Make sure the video image shows a glint in the eye of the presenter.

▶ **Steady the camera**. Mount the camera firmly. Use a tripod to reduce shake. Point the camera precisely. If the camera must move to follow the presenter, make sure the tripod has a fluid head that glides smoothly.

Prepare the presenter

▶ **Dress the presenter simply**. Avoid clothing with patterns. Use flat makeup and forego fancy jewelry that flickers and glints.

▶ **Rehearse the presentation**. Practice the presentation with cameras running. Then review the captured video and try again. Presenters may not realize how little is visible in a small video window or how annoying some of their gestures can be. Give them time to learn this new medium.

Prepare learners

▶ **Explain video quality**. Explain to learners why the video quality may be lower than they are used to for broadcast television.

▶ **Tell learners to keep their video cameras off** until requested to turn them on. Too many video streams can clog the network and distract learners. There are few cases in which people need to watch more than 2 or 3 others.

▶ Remind learners to keep their video images simple. Warn against noisy or moving backgrounds.

Conduct the session smoothly

During the video-conference presentation, the presenter and producer must use the medium efficiently and effectively. Here are a few suggestions:

▶ **Keep presentations simple**. Put details in separate Web pages that learners can read at leisure.

▶ **Keep props at hand.** Gather the objects you will show ahead of time. Put them out of camera view but within arm's reach. Practice grabbing and manipulating them.

▶ **Vary camera angle**. If one person must talk for more than a minute or so, periodically shift the camera angle. Have the person walk around. Cut away or pan to an object the person is describing. Insert a reaction shot showing the studio audience listening. Use close-ups to show details.

▶ **Move smoothly and predictably.** Move in slow, smooth, predictable motions. Start and finish movements slowly. Do not inexplicably shift the camera position. Make all movements seem natural and logical. Warn of shifts of locale. "We're now going to the workshop to show how to apply these ideas."

Breakout rooms

Breakout rooms let small groups of learners conduct their own meetings within the main meeting. They are a feature of some online meeting tools. Breakout sessions may be instigated by the instructor or by learners.

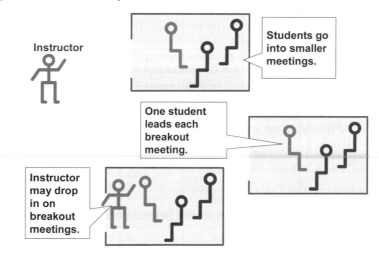

One student leads each meeting. The instructor may drop in on the individual meetings. After a while, the instructor ends the smaller meetings and resumes the original meeting.

When to use breakout rooms

Use breakout rooms for sessions of small-group work. Breakout rooms are especially good when the size of the overall meeting is inhibiting some learners and when activities benefit from a more intimate scale. They are also good for compound activities when part of the activity is done in a large group and part in a small group.

Use breakout rooms for:

▶ Teamwork and small-group projects.

▶ Competitive problem solving. Each group tries to solve a problem quicker or better than others.

Pick the best time of day

Start the meeting at 9:00 AM or later. People are at work, have checked phone messages and e-mails, and consumed the requisite number of caffeinated beverages.

Try to end the meeting before 1:00 PM so that everybody still has time to get lunch. After lunch, learners may be too drowsy to participate fully.

By all means avoid normal sleep time (9 PM to 8 AM) if at all possible.

Set the meeting length

The shortest time for an online meeting is usually 60 minutes. Anything shorter and little of value gets accomplished. Remember that introductions and set-up take time out of that hour.

Try to conclude the meeting within 90 minutes. Longer than that, people fidget and lose concentration. Longer meetings are hard for busy people to fit into their schedules. If you must make the meeting longer, try to keep it to no more than 2 hours and allow a couple of 5- to 10-minute breaks.

Adjust for time-zone compression

Consider where your learners are. It is seldom a problem if learners are spread over a few time zones, say across Europe, within Australia, or within the contiguous United States. Within the contiguous United States, for example, learners may span four time zones. That means you would need to hold your meeting from noon to 1:30 PM Eastern Time, which would be 9:00 to 10:30 Pacific Time.

Whatever you do, try to hold the meeting while everyone is normally awake. And consider whether off-prime learners can log in from home.

Prepare learners for the meeting

Help learners get ready for the meeting—before the meeting. Do not waste meeting time on things that could be done before the meeting.

Inform learners of the meeting

Provide learners the information they need to participate in the meeting. This gives them fair warning and ensures they have time to prepare for the meeting. What should you do before the meeting?

▶ Advise learners of the goals and objectives of the meeting.

▶ Conduct an audience survey to identify who will attend and what they need.

▶ Publish the biography of the instructor and guest speakers.

▶ Tell learners how to set up their computers.

▶ Publish standards of behavior.

Make pre-meeting assignments

One way to make meetings more productive is to give learners an assignment to complete before the live session. Begin the live event with a discussion of the assignment. Reward learners who completed the assignment and prepared well for the opening discussion.

Send related information ahead

If learners must refer to information during an online meeting, send that information ahead of time so that they can review the material and think of questions to ask the presenter. What kinds of materials should you send?

▶ Handouts so learners have a place to take notes.

▶ Reports, white papers, position statements, and other reference documents.

▶ Detailed examples and case studies.

▶ Biographies of the speakers.

At a minimum, provide learners with a copy of the slides in a format that lets them comfortably follow along with the presenter. This way the presenter's slides can use smaller text and more detailed graphics.

Introduce participants

Do not waste time introducing everyone during an online meeting. Have participants send or post biographies before joining the meeting. Include a biography of any guest speaker along with the announcement of the live event. That way the instructor's introduction of the guest speaker can be brief.

Follow up after the meeting

Do not waste valuable meeting time performing closing activities that could be done after the meeting. End the meeting with a strong, memorable activity. Afterwards, perform the routine follow-up work.

▶ Gather learners' feedback with an asynchronous poll.

▶ Post reference materials to a discussion forum along with a transcript or recording of the meeting.

► Publish revised handouts.

Make contingency plans

The best way to prevent problems is to anticipate them. Brainstorm to list things that could go wrong. Plan what you will do if any of these events occur. Here are some not-too-remote possibilities:

► The speaker has laryngitis.

► The speaker's computer crashes.

► Hecklers or nitpickers disrupt the meeting.

► Phone-conferencing or Internet audio fails.

For example, for the case of a computer crashing, we established this procedure:

1. The producer notices that the speaker's computer has dropped out of the attendee list.

2. The producer promotes the presenter's backup computer so the presenter can continue from this backup computer.

3. The speaker switches to the backup computer.

4. The speaker reboots the failed computer and, as time permits, logs it in as a student computer. This computer now becomes the speaker's backup computer.

5. Prepare a "dead-time" graphic. Have an image to broadcast during the "dead time." It might say "We are experiencing technical difficulties. Please stay online." While you are at it, prepare another graphic to display while waiting for the class to begin and immediately after it concludes.

Pack a conversational first-aid kit

Sometimes the best spontaneous comments are the ones you prepare ahead of time. Prepare comments or questions that will start useful conversations or revive flagging ones. Have them ready in case the conversation stalls. Here are some conversation resuscitators:

► Why do you say so?

► Where else might that idea apply?

► Do you have any doubts?

► What if X were different?

► Does the idea have any side effects?

► What else?

► How much would that cost?

► What are the practical applications of this idea?

Prepare for the meeting

Planning the online meeting is not enough. You must still prepare to conduct the meeting. Good planning and preparation almost guarantee a successful live meeting. It certainly lowers the anxiety and blood pressure of the presenter. Expect to spend 5 to 10 hours preparing for each hour of the event. How should the producer and presenter spend their time? As Mark Twain once quipped:

> It usually takes me more than three weeks to prepare a good impromptu speech.

Rehearse completely

About 3 days before the meeting, rehearse the whole presentation and all collaborative activities. Hold the practice session at the same time of day as the real meeting. Test for speed and reliability of the network as well as the ability of learners to participate fully. Make sure the tools work reliably and that the presenter is confident using them.

► Upload materials for the presentation. At the end of the rehearsal, do not delete these materials. More than once, I have been unable to load materials on the day of the actual presentation. The rehearsal materials saved me.

► Practice showing all media. That means all slides, polls, Web sites, and applications. Practice interacting with participants.

► Make a list of things that could go wrong. Write them down on index cards and shuffle the deck. Every 5 minutes during the rehearsal, draw a card and pretend that the problem on the card just occurred. Practice your response.

► Time the rehearsal. The actual class will take 20 to 40% longer than the rehearsal. Learners interrupt to ask questions. Minor technical glitches occur and have to be dealt with on the spot.

► If you discover problems, fix them and repeat the rehearsal again. I like to schedule my first rehearsal 3 days before the actual event. That way I have time to fix problems and conduct another rehearsal or two.

Enlist help

It is difficult for a lone instructor to carry out all the duties of conducting a vibrant online meeting. Get help.

► **Hire a producer**. Have an off-screen producer guide all on-screen activities. The producer can time and pace the event. Using hand signals or earphones, the producer can cue and coach the instructor. If the session is conducted by a guest speaker, the instructor can serve as the producer.

► **Required**? Is attendance mandatory or optional? How much does the event count toward a final grade?

► **Tools to be used**. Will the event use chat, audio, video, application sharing, whiteboard, polling, or other technologies? Learners should learn to use these technologies before the event, not during it.

► **Learning preparation**. What must learners do before the event? What must they read? Are there course topics or pre-tests they should complete?

► **Computer setup**. How should learners configure their hardware and software for best results? Must learners download and install any special software? Are there sample files they need to acquire?

► **Alternative**. What should learners do if technical difficulties prevent them from entering the meeting or force last-minute cancellation? What should they do if they are not available at the specified time?

► **Contact**. Whom should learners contact for more information?

Manage the live portion

It's show time! You have prepared. You have rehearsed. You are ready to go.

Rely on your producer. Have someone other than the instructor, or main presenter, manage the live event. A producer can mind the agenda, call time on long-winded speakers, and handle minor emergencies. An active producer allows the presenter and instructor to concentrate on the needs of learners.

Keep learners active. Make presentations dynamic. Use visuals and multimedia to focus attention on key concepts. Never become a talking head. Or worse, an automatic typewriter. Explain any pauses over 5 seconds.

Interact frequently. Never present for more than 5 minutes without some form of interaction with learners. Spend 40 to 60% of the time interacting with learners. Answer questions every 15 or 20 minutes. Or state that you will do so at the end.

Call on learners by name. In a physical classroom, the instructor can call on people by just pointing to them or just looking their way. In the online event, the instructor must call on people by name. That means the instructor must have a list of the names of all participants, not just the screen names or e-mail addresses displayed by the meeting tool.

Ask more questions than you answer. If you answer a question for a learner, immediately ask the learner a question to test whether he or she understood. Do not give full answers to questions. Clear up any misunderstandings and point learners to resources they can use to answer their own questions.

Be spontaneous. Script out every session, but leave 30 to 40% of the time free to answer unanticipated questions, go into more detail about issues that deeply interest learners, and interject insights that occur to you at the moment.

Keep a back channel open. In face-to-face meetings, we scan the eye gazes, nodding heads, and smiles of meeting participants. And we listen for vocal utterances like "uh-huh" and "OK." In Web collaboration media, instructors must find substitutes to test whether their message is getting through. Keep open an interactive communications channel such as chat available so that learners can interrupt if they do not understand something. Consider pausing after each stage of a presentation to get feedback.

Turn off unused media. Turn off media you are not using at the moment. If you are just talking, turn off the video and leave the audio on.

Maintain control and focus. During online meetings, learners must all be "on the same page." If questions or discussion drift too far, re-establish the subject under discussion. Terminate activities that continually drift off subject. Give learners a chance to explore the limits and fringes of ideas before jerking them back on course.

Attend to all learners. Give attention to all learners, not just those who stand out. Greet participants as they enter the session. Learners who have their microphones turned up will sound louder than others. Those who sit close to their video cameras will seem larger. Learn to ignore these false cues and give equal attention to all learners. Respond to a raised hand in 30 to 60 seconds.

Stay organized. Pause before speaking. Clear raised hands before proceeding. Remember to save polls, markups, and chat. Use available time, such as while learners are filling in a poll or thinking of answers to a question, to relax and gather your thoughts. Run through a mental checklist of what you may want to do next.

Use icebreaker games to get learners started

Getting started in an online meeting can be difficult if learners are strangers or are anxious about the technology. Consider some quick, simple activities to engage learners, relieve anxiety, and introduce fellow learners.

- ▶ Put a world map in a whiteboard and have learners point to where they live.
- ▶ In chat, have learners enter their job titles and the organizations they work for.
- ▶ In whiteboard have learners create a communal painting or graffiti. I put up a picture of myself and invite learners to add beards, horns, and whatever they want.
- ▶ Have participants all say hi in audio or video.
- ▶ Invite learners to upload pictures of their locale, pet, or hobby.

The purpose of such activities is to give learners a non-threatening way to use the collaboration tools while sharing a little information about themselves.

Include make-up activities for missed meetings

Have make-up work for learners who cannot attend meetings. As a minimum, have truant learners play a recording of the live meeting so they can read, hear, and see what they missed. You might also require learners to write a summary of the meeting and post it to the class discussion forum.

Continue the discussion after class

To encourage learners to continue conversations started during a meeting, start a chat session immediately after the class. This gives learners a chance to ask the instructor questions they were too shy to ask in class and enables learners to discuss points that especially interested them during the meeting.

During the meeting, invite participants to contribute to a discussion thread on the subject. Start the thread with transcripts of the meeting and its follow-up chat session.

Evaluate the event

To improve live events, conduct a formal evaluation, something like this:

- ▶ The instructor critiques the meeting, noting what worked well and what could be done better next time.
- ▶ Learners suggest how they could have done better.

▶ The instructor privately comments on participants' behavior, especially if not appropriate. Common problems might include verbally abusing others, dominating the scarce time, and asking questions outside the subject of the meeting.

Thank outside helpers

The instructor (or learners) should write thank-you notes to all those besides staff members who helped them in the meeting. A token gift is appropriate for experts who made presentations or consented to interviews.

GUIDE DISCUSSION ACTIVITIES

Discussion forums evolved from the social and professional exchanges that took place in Internet list-servers and newsgroups. These intellectual watering holes attracted individuals with like interests but distant locations to a free exchange of ideas. And learning took place.

The use of discussion forums in e-learning builds on this informal exchange, but adds an efficient structure. Here's how a discussion activity might be used in formal education:

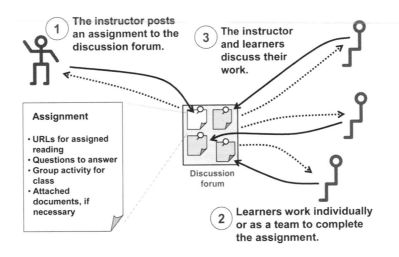

Learning starts as the instructor posts an assignment to the group. The assignment may include URLs or hyperlinks to assigned readings, questions to answer individually, and group activities. Assignments may also include attached reading and other necessary materials.

Allow enough time

Online discussions are not as fast as face-to-face conversations. As a general rule a 10-minute face-to-face conversation in the classroom would require:

- ▶ 20 minutes with audio-conferencing.
- ▶ 30 minutes with chat.
- ▶ 1 to 2 days in a discussion forum.

The same conversation in a 1-hour class meeting may require a week or 10 days in a discussion forum.

Set up needed threads

When learners first arrive at a discussion forum, they should not find an empty warehouse. Put in some walls and a few rooms. Start a few conventional top-level threads, such as:

- ▶ **Introduction.** Tell learners what the whole discussion forum is about in more detail than on the welcome topic. Put any needed instructions here.
- ▶ **Administrative support.** Provide a place where learners can request help with any aspect of the course other than content or technology.
- ▶ **Technical support.** Include a thread for questions about tools and technologies used in the course. Start by posting the technical requirements, instructions for obtaining necessary tools, and a general troubleshooting guide.
- ▶ **General comments.** Plant a general comment thread to collect comments that do not fit any existing thread. The moderator can move these comments to the correct thread or use them to start a new thread.
- ▶ **Student lounge.** Set aside a discussion area where students can talk to one another on any subject—whether related to the course or not.

Ensure learners have necessary skills

Help learners new to your discussion forum learn to interact and to overcome their fear of doing something that makes them look stupid. Teach learners the essential skills for online discussion. Here is a survival kit of discussion skills:

- ▶ **Replying to messages.** Remind learners that they must click the **Reply** button for the specific message they want to reply to.
- ▶ **Posting new messages and starting new threads.** Learners must understand the difference between **New Message** and **Reply**. **New message** adds a message at the

same level as the current message. **Reply** creates a new message beneath the current message. Not heeding this distinction results in tangled threads of messages with no clear context in which to interpret messages.

▶ **Writing a clear subject** for the message. For replies, the default is just to add "Re:" in front of the original subject line. Require learners to replace this with a meaningful subject. Otherwise you have messages that begin "Re: Re: Re: …."

▶ **Editing posts**. Teach learners to correct small errors in their messages. They may not know they can click an **Edit** button to revise the message. Warn learners that it is not polite to make changes after a reply in a way that makes the reply look false or silly. The polite way is to add a message pointing out that the original submission has been revised and perhaps thanking those who suggested improvements.

Moderate discussion activities

In a *moderated* discussion forum the instructor—or someone else—watches over the exchange of messages. The primary duty of the moderator is to ensure that learners have productive discussions with other learners. Moderators perform two main tasks. First, they must set up the discussion forums and threads. Second, they must oversee the conversations that take place there.

Pick the right moderator

Normally, the instructor for the course is also the moderator of the course's discussion forums. However, the requirements for a moderator are different from those for an instructor. And the instructor may be too busy to take on both jobs.

A good moderator is knowledgeable, supportive, and articulate.

▶ **The moderator should be well-informed and on the ball**. The moderator must understand the subject matter, the computer system, and any software used by the discussion forum or other parts of the class. Or have ready access to those who do.

▶ **The moderator must have a caring nature**. The moderator must tactfully endure insults and rude behavior, patiently instruct fumble-fingered technophobes, continually inject enthusiasm into disheartened souls, and repeatedly calm abused and abusive respondents.

▶ **The moderator must be a superb communicator**. The moderator must be able to listen deeply and accurately gauge the knowledge and emotions of others. Not everyone can do this. The moderator must be someone whom others describe as tactful or diplomatic. And the moderator must be able to express complex ideas and subtle emotions in simple, unadorned prose.

Challenge shallow thought

Do not accept mere opinions. Prompt learners to provide the evidence and logical thought behind their opinions. Challenge opinions by responding like this:

> I was intrigued by your answer [Quote it.] Can you explain why you feel so?
> Did particular experiences, research, or other evidence lead you to this opinion?

If everyone else agrees with an opinion, take the opposite opinion. Play devil's advocate. Here are some responses you can use to stir up thought:

▶ OK, then answer me this …

▶ I claim the opposite. Can you prove me wrong?

▶ Throw in a challenging hypothesis.

▶ But what if …?

▶ Suppose just the opposite were true. What then?

Perform message maintenance

Messages dashed off in haste can sometimes go astray. A slight miswording can reverse the intended meaning. To maintain message quality, the moderator should:

▶ Reroute misdirected messages to the correct thread. And inform the poster of the change and the reason for it.

▶ Reword unclear or inaccurate subject headers.

▶ Fix (or have the sender fix) tragic typos or accidental misstatements.

Reject inappropriate postings

The moderator should reject postings that clearly violate course policies. Pacify or expel angry flamers. Remove messages that other learners complain about if you agree they are not appropriate. If you must reject a posting:

▶ Explain exactly why you rejected the posting. Remind the submitter of your standards for postings.

▶ Offer the submitter a chance to re-submit after specific changes are made.

▶ Require an apology if the posting unduly insulted or offended others.

▶ Point out any violations of a broader policy and the consequences of violating it.

If messages are posted immediately ...

In some discussion forums, messages are posted immediately without the moderator seeing them. In this case:

▶ Alert participants to this situation and warn them that some inappropriate messages may slip by.

▶ Read all new messages frequently, and immediately deal with inappropriate ones.

▶ If an offensive message slips by, remove it and post an apology to the group. Also require that the author of the message post an apology.

▶ Make learners responsible for policing discussion. Let them know that you will assist them, but remind them that it is they who decide what is and is not appropriate.

MANAGE VIRTUAL COURSES

Successful virtual-classroom courses usually depend more on human interaction than on technological infrastructure. The secret of success seems to be a carefully orchestrated set of learning experiences and a responsive instructor who attends to the learning needs of all members of the class.

We have already reviewed techniques for two important parts of a virtual course, namely meetings (p. 448) and discussions (p. 463). Now we will look at best practices for the course as a whole.

Select a qualified instructor

The quality of instruction in the virtual classroom depends on the preparation and talent of the instructor. No amount of instructional design can compensate for an unprepared or incompetent instructor. The skills required in the virtual classroom are similar to those used in the physical classroom—but with some crucial differences:

▶ **Learners are not physically present**. The instructor must "read" them not through posture and facial expressions but through tone of voice or even their hastily typewritten words.

▶ **The instructor must communicate through the media available**: displayed words, spoken words, slides, sketches, demonstrations, and video. The instructor must be technically proficient in producing these media and the tools that transmit them. A commanding stage presence may be less effective than a well-modulated voice, swift typing skills, and coordinated operation of multiple computer programs.

▶ **Learners rely less on the instructor**. Lacking direct face-to-face contact with the instructor, learners will communicate among themselves. The instructor must encourage such "talking in class" and make it productive—even if this makes learners less dependent on and attentive to the instructor. The instructor must be willing to move from classroom commander to virtual valet.

What attitudes do instructors need?

Success as an online instructor is as much a matter of attitude as knowledge and skills. What are some necessary attitudes for online instructors?

Egolessness: "I want to help people, not just be a sage on a stage."

Validity: "E-learning is a valuable form of instruction."

Confidence: "I can do this!"

Egotistical instructors are more of a problem than a solution. Be on guard against signs of too much ego, such as statements like these:

▶ "Just point the camera at me."

▶ "I don't need to rehearse. I've taught this 20 times in the classroom."

▶ "I teach in the classroom. That's all I want to do."

▶ "Students want to see and hear me, not some stupid animation."

▶ "I can't teach them if I can't look them in the eye."

▶ "If I'm not there, they do not learn."

What skills are required

The skills of an online instructor are not the same as those of a classroom instructor. Here is a comparison of the main skills of each:

In a physical classroom

▶ Subject-matter knowledge.

▶ Authoritative tone of voice.

▶ Gestures and body language.

▶ Legible handwriting.

▶ Basic PowerPoint skills.

In a virtual classroom

▶ Subject-matter knowledge.

▶ Well-modulated tone of voice (over phone or Internet audio).

▶ Writing and typing.

▶ Ability to operate collaboration tools fluently.

▶ Advanced PowerPoint skills, such as animation.

Require experience first

Teaching in the virtual classroom is a challenge for even experienced instructors. Before letting instructors teach solo, require potential online instructors to:

▶ Experience a dozen online meetings.

▶ Rehearse 3 times with an experienced online instructor.

▶ Assist in 3 online meetings conducted by a proven online instructor.

▶ Teach once with a backup instructor available.

▶ Review their online performance with a proven online instructor.

It can take months before instructors become as capable, fluent, and confident online as in the physical classroom. Start developing your online instructors now. And do not quit. Technologies will continue to develop as fast as instructors can incorporate them into their classes.

Teach the class, don't just let it happen

As the instructor, you must actively lead the class by setting the pace, making sure that learners are participating, and overcoming problems.

Contact learners individually. Call or e-mail learners individually to let them know you view them as individuals and to listen to any concerns they may have. If possible, meet them in person. For one online class, I discovered that half my learners would be at a professional conference I was attending. We spent a few productive hours together.

Help classmates get to know one another. Have learners post their biographies. Then have learners examine the biographies of their classmates to find one common interest or other significant similarity.

Stay on the published schedule. If you publish a schedule, stick to the schedule. Remote learners and those with busy schedules depend on the course schedule to arrange their work and personal calendars to fit the course.

Keep office hours. Make yourself available certain times during the week. Learners may feel reluctant to call you unless you sanction the activity. Unless you set specific hours, calls may come while you are dining or sleeping.

Pace learners. Space out assignments and deadlines. Ensure that the amount of work required of learners is consistent from week to week. Remember that earlier activities may seem more daunting than later ones after learners have become familiar with the course

Provide complete instructions

For many learners, opening an e-mail message is a struggle. Others daily text-message co-workers from their mobile phones or instant message their friends from their computers, listen to podcasts while updating their blogs, attach video clips to their e-mail, use their Webcams to show off their latest digital cameras. Both groups need clear instructions on how to use collaboration tools for learning. Those inexperienced with collaboration tools need simple, explicit instructions and encouragement on getting started. Those fluent in these media need direction on using these tools for learning purposes rather than social exchanges.

Virtual classrooms typically require three main documents to guide learning: Student's guide, Instructor's Guide, and Class Syllabus.

Student's guide

The student's guide provides instructions for learners and team leaders. It consolidates instructions that might otherwise be scattered among FAQs, e-mails, policies, discussion posts, and replies to questions in meetings or forums.

When do you need a student's guide?

A student's guide is especially important when:

▶ Learners are new to the media and collaboration tools of your course.

▶ Learners do not know the conventions and netiquette of e-learning.

▶ Bad student behavior could expose your organization to legal liability, for example, charges of racial bias or sexual harassment.

▶ You lack support staff to coach each learner in the routine tasks of e-learning.

Explain essential actions

Ensure learners can perform all required actions. Make sure learners know how to prepare and send the kinds of messages necessary in the class. Provide step-by-step instructions for each of these actions:

▶ Send a message to an individual or to a whole group.

▶ Reply to messages.

▶ Format the message.

▶ Quote from an original message.

▶ Embed links in messages.

▶ Attach files to messages.

▶ Post a message on a specific thread of a discussion forum.

Provide a complete online manual for the discussion, e-mail, chat, or meeting system used in the course. Unless you have created your own custom system, you can probably link to the online manuals and tutorials provided by the vendors of your tools. I say "probably" because not all vendors have good instructions written for first-time learners.

Make it easy for learners to print out these instructions. Either combine all topics into one file or assemble them into a special printable file. Better still; consolidate all the manuals for all the systems used in the course into one file with a comprehensive table of contents.

Explain how to e-learn

E-learning may be new to some learners, who may not realize the high degree of self-motivation and time-management skills it requires. Point out the specific learning behaviors and attitudes needed and suggest ways to develop them. Tell learners how to:

▶ Verify that their goals can be met in the course.

▶ Set their own objectives and timetables and milestones for achieving them.

▶ Constructively interact with fellow learners.

▶ Actively seek new knowledge and skills rather than waiting to be taught.

▶ Master new technologies like a child. Explore, experiment, and look things up in Help.

Best practices for a syllabus

I have seen courses saved by a revision of the syllabus—it is that important. Give the humble syllabus the attention it deserves.

Make the syllabus comprehensive. List all activities, resources, support contacts, and administrative requirements. Link to mentioned documents and forum threads. Include phone numbers and e-mail addresses of faculty and support staff. And remember to test all links, e-mail addresses, and phone numbers.

Organize the course into bite-sized chunks. If learners are given the complete set of course materials from the start, the very mass of the materials may discourage or overwhelm them. Use the syllabus to divide the mass of course materials into understandable pieces, sort the pieces into logical categories, arrange the pieces into meaningful learning sequences, and set an appropriate schedule for mastering them.

Even if you do not include a formal syllabus, at least suggest a sequence and schedule for consuming the materials—and clearly distinguish high-priority "required" materials from optional ones.

Specify exact dates. When does the week end and begin? Be careful about international differences and time-zone shifts.

> Weeks begin just past midnight Monday morning—GMT!

If practical, fill in actual dates rather than just saying Week 1, Week 2, etc.

Link to everything. Do not require learners to go searching for material mentioned in the syllabus. Link to the materials so that learners can jump to them. For lectures and conferences, link to the meeting site. For activities, link to the form learners must fill in and submit to complete the activity.

Flag required items. Use a distinctive icon for required items. Flag any mandatory or date-specific activities in the syllabus and course announcements. Make crystal clear which items affect the final grade and which do not. If an item is optional, but learners who perform the activity can win extra points, is the activity really optional?

Simplify tasks for learners

Learning is hard under the best circumstances. Make learning as easy as possible. Keep your course simple so learning is productive and efficient.

Keep the class small

Most instructors recommend keeping virtual classes small, say 7 to 10 students. However, small class sizes can thwart economic goals that may best be served by larger classes. You must weigh the immediate revenue of a large class versus the reputation engendered by the quality of learning experiences possible in intimate groupings. Jones International University touts its small class size:

> It's much like being in a traditional classroom, but in many respects more intimate. Many JIU graduates have said they felt closer to their classmates and teachers at JIU than they did in a classroom setting (www.jonesinternational.edu/studentLife/index.php).

If you cannot afford a small class, take steps to ensure that learners are still treated as individuals. Include lots of small-group activity so the scope of the class does not intimidate learners.

Offer a textbook (or equivalent)

One of the most valuable components of an online course can be an old fashioned textbook.

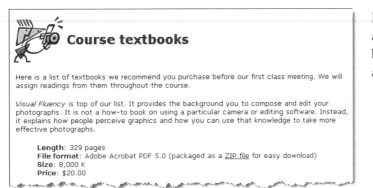

In this example, learners are referred to textbooks to be read for specific assignments.

A textbook is familiar to learners. An electronically accessible textbook helps with accessibility requirements (p. 405). Screen readers for the blind can speak the text aloud. Hearing-disabled can read the textbook to learn what they could not get from voice in the meetings. And, yes, some learners would rather read a well-organized book than struggle with technology.

Problem	Description	Solution
Sloppiness	Learners are lazy and inconsiderate of others. They forget to mute their phones or give meaningful subjects to their messages. They fail to read instructions and write incomprehensible stream-of-consciousness entries. They reply without reading previous posts.	Point out that learners have a responsibility to fellow learners. Show how sloppy learners are wasting the time of others. Institute a neatness-counts policy in grading activities.
Plagiarism	Learners submit the work of others as their own. Typically learners will just copy material from the Web for an activity that should require original work.	Use a Web-based service, such as Turnitin (turnitin.com) to spot plagiarism—and let learners know that you do. For the first offense, explain the policy. Better still: rework the activity so it cannot be answered by simply copying information.
Copyright violations	Learners submit material owned by others. Similar to plagiarism except that learners are violating laws, not just ethics.	Warn learners and require replacing the material and redoing the activity. Also follow the steps for plagiarism.
Latecomers	Some learners join meetings and discussions late and insist that the entire process start all over again.	Start meetings on time. Do not re-start for latecomers. Point out that their tardiness is disruptive. Be prepared for some interesting excuses.
Flaming	Making abusive and emotional attacks on someone else.	If the attack is mild, let the group deal with it first. Step in as necessary. Require an apology and warn the sender.
Dominating	Some learners may try to dominate the conversation by intimidating others or by trying to answer every question.	In private e-mail ask the sender to post questions for others to answer. At the same time, encourage others to join in.

Adapt collaboration for small and asynchronous classes

For some courses you may not have enough learners to form frequent classes. In this case you may let learners move through the course at their own pace. Although this has advantages, it can create problems. Collaborative activities can be difficult if learners are not at the same level of knowledge or are not focused on the same issues at the same time.

Modify for nearly synchronous courses

You can modify collaborative activities to make them work better in classes in which not everyone is on the same page. Here's how:

▶ Design courses as a cycle of modules so that learners can take any module first. Learners start when they are ready and quit when they have completed the cycle.

▶ Make real-time activities optional. Rely more on discussion forums and other asynchronous activities than on synchronous ones.

▶ Allow learners to play back recorded meetings from earlier classes.

▶ Design activities so all levels of learners may participate.

▶ Have learners in later phases of the course assist and tutor those in earlier phases of the course.

Use public chat and discussion forums

If you do not have enough synchronized learners to ensure a vigorous chat or discussion forum, you can still use these mechanisms. Have learners participate in public chat rooms and discussion forums in the general area of your course.

▶ Have learners locate chat rooms, discussion forums, and newsgroups on the subject of the course. Have them investigate them to decide which best suit their needs and best match the goals of the course.

▶ Require learners to use chat and discussion forums. For example, ask them to use a chat or discussion forum to obtain the answers to 3 questions that you pose.

▶ Have learners use chat and discussion forums to obtain the answer to questions they propose.

Consider related decisions

If you cover the screen, you must know the display size or at least the minimum display size among your learners. And you must design everything to fit that size. You may also want to allow some secondary windows on top of your screen-hogging main window. This, however, can defeat the purposes for which you chose to cover the screen. If you go with a floating window, you must decide its size and other characteristics. Thus, each decision you make will affect others.

NUMBER OF WINDOWS

Another critical design decision is the number of windows to use in your e-learning.

Use separate windows sparingly

Most e-learning uses separate windows sparingly. Here is an example that illustrates that trend. The primary window is divided into two areas: the menu on the left and the content area on the right. Within each of these two areas are secondary areas, navigation buttons, titles, and other minor items. This one window contains most of the content of the course.

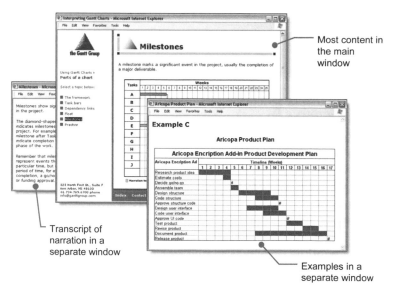

There were few exceptions. One was for the text transcript of voice narration. A second was for examples that were the subject of practice activities. These appeared in their own windows so they were not confused with the main content of the course itself.

As a designer, you must decide when to violate the one-window policy. You will need a consistent rule about when to display content in a window separate from the main display.

When to display in the same window

When should you display all your course content in the same window? Displaying all content in a single window minimizes the distractions caused by windows popping up in the learner's field of view. Displaying content in this main window lets you control that display. Learners cannot resize, reshape, or move content.

Another time to display everything in one window is when you cannot disable learners' pop-up blockers. Pop-up blockers prevent Web browsers from displaying additional windows. Pop-up blockers are commonly used to prevent the display of advertisements from Web sites the user is visiting. If your users have pop-up blockers enabled, you must either instruct them to turn off the pop-up blockers while taking your course or you must avoid displaying additional windows. Keep in mind that some users may not know how to turn off their pop-up blockers, especially if someone else installed them.

Displaying in a single window is helpful during a test to ensure that learners cannot view other parts of the course while answering the test questions. Although displaying everything in one window cannot prevent a clever learner from accessing related information, it can make it clear that such access is not approved.

When to display a new window

When should you display content in a separate window? Let's consider some conditions under which it is appropriate to launch a new window in the middle of a course.

You may need a new window for material that requires a larger or differently shaped window. One place where this occurs is when you need to launch a simulation to teach someone to use a computer program that itself needs most of the screen space. The simulation may require more space than is available within your course window.

Another use for a separate window is for a graphic or other material learners must refer to repeatedly. Putting the material in the main window could cause it to scroll out of view or get replaced as new content is introduced. Separate windows allow learners to make side-by-side comparisons of separate pieces of content in the way most convenient for them.

There are also technical reasons for using a separate window. Sometimes material uses a frameset to format the display or contains scripts for interactivity. Sometimes these framesets or scripts will not work correctly unless the content appears in its own independent window.

You will also need a separate window to display material owned by someone else whose terms of usage require a separate window. Copyright owners often require independent displays to make clear that their content is from a separate source and is not an integral part of your course. Putting the content in the main window could create the impression that you own or endorse the content displayed.

WINDOW CHARACTERISTICS

When we display e-learning, we must be concerned with the characteristics of the windows where the e-learning appears. We must carefully specify the size, shape, and configuration of the windows. Start with your main window and then consider any secondary windows you need.

Window size

One of the first decisions we need to make is the target window size. That is, how large should you make your display window?

Calculate your window size

To specify your window size, you need a systematic process. That process must account for constraints you face and requirements that your e-learning must meet.

Calculate the maximum size

Start by calculating the maximum size you can make the window for your e-learning.

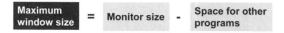

First, consider the size of the smallest monitor you will target. This monitor size provides an absolute upper limit on the size of your e-learning window. How many pixels vertically and horizontally does it display? For example, the monitor may display 1024 by 768 pixels, meaning it displays 1024 columns of pixels by 768 rows of pixels. Remember, it is the pixel dimensions, not the linear size that is important here. A 30-cm monitor may display more than a 35-cm monitor.

Next you must consider the space required for other programs that must be visible at the same time as your e-learning window. These might include a task bar for switching to other programs and an instant messaging window. It might also include a Notepad window for taking notes or another Web browser window for conducting research or viewing examples.

Once you subtract the space required for other programs from the size of the monitor you have the space available for your e-learning. This gives you a maximum size for your window.

Calculate minimum size

The next step is to calculate the smallest size you can make the window displaying your e-learning.

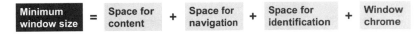

Start with the minimum content you must display at once. What is the smallest area of content before the content becomes confusing? To this, you need to add area for course navigation, such as navigation buttons and a menu of topics. Next, you need to add areas for course identification, such as the logo of the course sponsor or a contact address. Finally, you need to add area for window "chrome," such as a window title, window menus, scroll bar, and status area. Adding up all these areas gives you your minimum window size.

If your minimum window size is larger than the space available, you have some hard compromises to make. At least you know about these requirements before you design your e-learning and its media.

Small or large window?

Do you design for a small or a large window? What are the tradeoffs and constraints of this choice? Let's consider a range from a small window to a large window. At the small end of the scale we might have a window less than 640 by 480 pixels. Along the scale, we might have displays of 800 by 600 pixels, 1024 by 768 pixels, or larger.

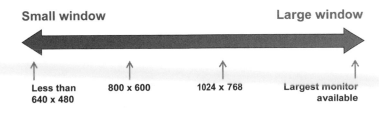

Designing for a smaller display means that more learners will be able to display our e-learning and to take it without extensive scrolling. Courses designed for a small window can be deployed more widely, without undue concern for the size of learners' monitors. You do not need to worry whether learners take the course on a desktop computer or a laptop or whether learners take it on work or home computers. A small window leaves space so learners can see other windows while taking e-learning, making it easier to consult reference materials, take notes, and perform other tasks.

In a large window, you can make text more legible. And you do not have to squeeze text. You can enlarge graphics so small details show clearly. Because more content can fit in the main display, you will need fewer separate windows that can startle learners and trigger pop-up blockers. Large windows allow a more sophisticated layout. You can permanently display a table of contents to enable rapid and fluid navigation. You can put related graphics side by side and use large tables where needed.

Design for the future

In selecting your window size, consider where you will display learning in the future. During the life of your e-learning, display sizes may change. Display technologies and display devices are evolving. Large high-resolution monitors are dropping in cost and small-screen mobile devices are becoming more common, as is the desire to move to mobile learning. Let's look at some places where e-learning is being displayed in the present time and where even more e-learning will need to appear soon.

A desktop computer can have a monitor displaying many times what a similar computer did just a few years ago. For example, Apple's HD Cinema screen can display up to 2580 pixels by 1600 pixels. A modern laptop computer can display 1400 by 1280 pixels. Most tablet computers display on a screen 768 by 1024 pixels. Tablet displays can be portrait or landscape orientation. The latest personal digital assistants (or PDAs) have displays of 640 by 480 pixels. This size screen is called a VGA size and is four times the size of the previous-generation PDA displays. Smart phones have a display of 240 by 320 pixels. Conventional mobile phones have displays of typically 120 by 150 pixels. The difference from largest to smallest area is a factor of well over 200 to 1!

On the next image, devices are scaled to a consistent pixel size so you can see the relative amount of information each device can display.

**Wide-screen monitor
2560 x 1600**

**Mobile
phone
120 x
150**

**Smart
phone
240 x
320**

**VGA
PocketPC
640 x 480**

**Laptop
1400 x 1280**

**Tablet
786 x 1024**

Before you design for one screen size, consider whether there are other sizes in your future. And remember, it is easier to move from a smaller display to a larger display than vice versa.

Window shape

You must design your content to fit your display area. Or shape your window to fit your content. So what shape do you make your window? Is it tall or wide or square? Or do you fit the shape to its purpose? Or do you just fill the screen and take on the shape of the monitor?

Match layout and window shape

Do not waste space and force unnecessary scrolling.

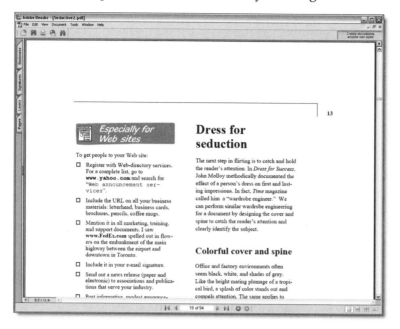

This example of an online reference work was designed for a vertical shape but displayed in a horizontal shape—it was dumped online. The signs of the mismatch are the necessity to scroll to see a complete page and the excessive blank space. And even worse, learners must scroll back to the top to continue reading after the first column.

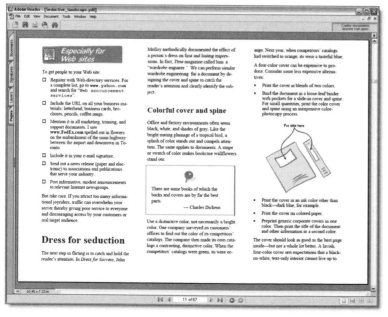

The second example shows the page reformatted to fit a horizontal window. Now all of the content fits without scrolling and the space is used more efficiently.

My point is not that horizontal displays are better or that scrolling is bad, but that the layout of the content must match the shape of the window and vice versa. In selecting a window shape, you are constraining your layout. Consider the content of your course when you decide on window shape.

What shape is best?

Is a vertical *portrait* shape better than a horizontal *landscape* shape? Let's look at some historically common shapes of information displays and see what their popularity tells us.

Paper sizes have traditionally been portrait shaped. Consider both A4 and U.S. letter size pages.

Formats for still and moving pictures have taken a landscape orientation. Although the exact proportions vary, HDTV, U.S. television, and 35 mm film all use a wide shape.

Well, which is better? Several research projects attempted to determine the answer by letting test subjects reshape display areas to suit their preferences. Most test subjects chose a shape wider than tall. (The proportions chosen were 1.6 times as wide as tall, which is close to a golden rectangle.)

Why was the wider-than-tall shape consistently preferred by test subjects? Probably because it corresponds closely to the human field of vision, which is wider than tall by about the same proportions.

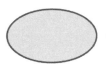

Why then are paper pages taller than wide? The answer is that they are not really. When we read a book, we typically look at a two-page spread, which is wider than tall by about the same proportions as the human field of view.

The answer to our question of what shape is better seems to be a horizontal golden rectangle. At least in theory.

Exception: Hands-on tutorials

One exception to the horizontal-is-best rule is in hands-on computer tutorials.

This example instructs learners on how to capture a simulation using the program Adobe Captivate, whose window appears at the bottom right of the screen. Above it a red rectangle surrounds the area to be captured.

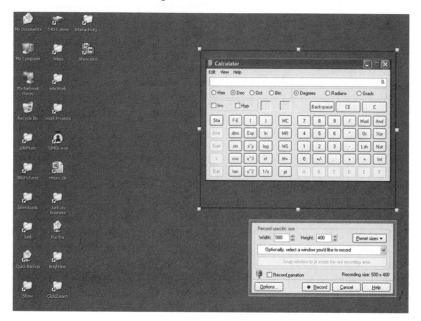

Displaying the tutorial reveals the problem with a wide display. Because instructions are beside graphics, the display must be so wide that it intrudes into the area we want to capture, a serious inconvenience.

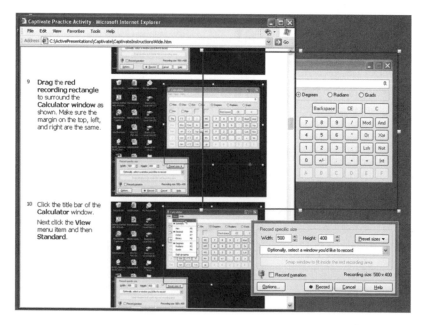

This example shows the tutorial formatted vertically. Now it fits on the screen beside the Captivate window and the area I need to record.

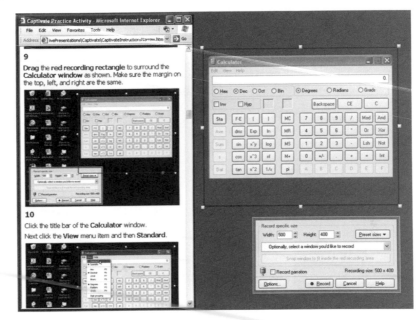

This example shows that when the learner must attend to something other than just our e-learning, we must consider the overall display, not just the e-learning display. The overall display is a horizontal rectangle. The e-learning must be designed to share the rectangular space.

Scrolling or non-scrolling display

Do you use scrolling or non-scrolling displays? That is, do you fit content to the window or let learners scroll to see more? We are talking about vertical scrolling. Horizontal scrolling is almost always bad and should be avoided, except where it is used to allow access to a horizontally oriented graphic, such as a wide timeline.

Non-scrolling display

What then is a non-scrolling display? Obviously it is one that does not scroll. What does that look like in practice?

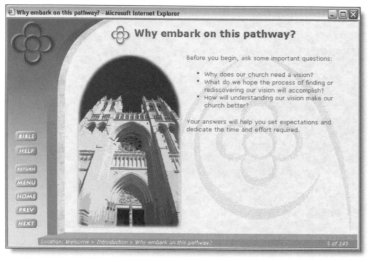

Here is an example. I used a fixed-size, non-scrolling display for the course *Vision and the Church*.

Built using Adobe Dreamweaver, Active Server Pages, custom JavaScript, and Adobe Flash. View example at horton.com/eld/.

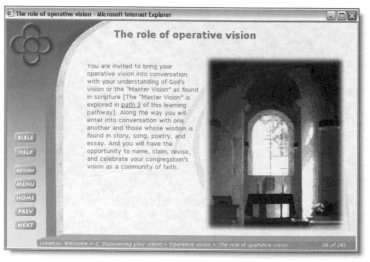

Content was selected and sized to fit entirely within the fixed size of the window so that no scrolling was required. This meant that a single aspect of the subject might require several pages.

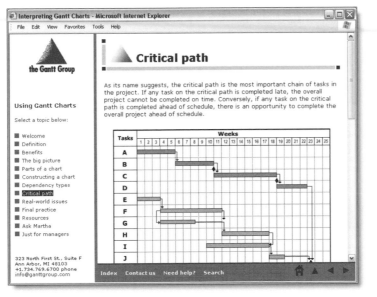

This non-scrolling display gave the course a card metaphor whereby content appeared as if on a deck of cards all of the same shape and size.

Scrolling display

What do we mean by a scrolling display? It is one that can move vertically in the window to reveal more content.

Here's an example. I used a scrolling display for the course *Using Gantt Charts*.

Built using Adobe Dreamweaver, custom JavaScript, and Flash. View example at horton.com/eld/.

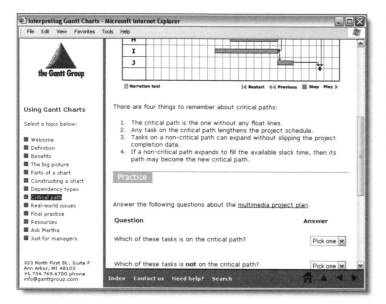

The learners could scroll downward to see the part of the display not initially visible and to center an interesting part of content in the display. In this example, most topics fit in three scrolling zones.

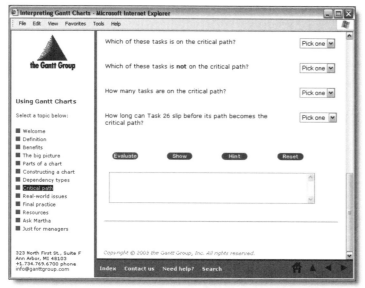

The space afforded by the scrolling display allowed me to put an entire learning object on a single page. That is, the introduction, learning activities, and assessment appeared together on one page. It also meant that the course had no fixed topic length and that the length was determined by the content necessary to accomplish the objective.

Non-scrolling or scrolling display?

Should you use a non-scrolling display or a scrolling display for your e-learning? Rigid rules may have been appropriate when the Web was new and learners had never sent e-mail or ordered merchandise online. Today the decision requires more thought.

The non-scrolling display is generally better for novice users who might not know how to use a scroll bar or might not notice it if it does not appear for every page in the course. Remember that many highly educated professionals are nonetheless novice computer users. A non-scrolling display is also good to focus on one issue at a time. It ensures that all the content about a topic is displayed at once. Nothing is hidden, and no half-visible content beckons the learner's attention away from the first pieces of content. A non-scrolling display gives you more control of the layout of the display. You can control exactly what the learner sees. You decide what is in the upper-left corner and the lower-right corner.

A scrolling display is usually best for complex content. Such content does not come in simple units that are all the same small size. Complex content can also suffer if related concepts are put into physically separate displays. A scrolling display can avoid the fragmentation that occurs when a topic must be split into separate displays. Learners are less likely to miss related concepts when they are in the same physical page. And scrolling makes it easier to combine presentation and practice right in the same page, thus completing the learning cycle more quickly. If learners will print out pages of your course, scrolling pages make the task easier. With larger scrolling pages, learners have fewer pages to print.

Sometimes designers opt for non-scrolling displays based on outdated research. Yes, research done in 1995 with small numbers of clerical workers who had about 10 minutes' experience using a Web browser indicated scrolling was confusing. Consider that today most popular Web sites such as Google, Amazon.com, and CNN.com all use scrolling as a matter of course.

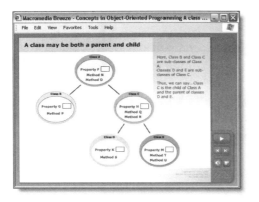

Shrink the window and the text and graphics contract. Notice that the display shows the same material at a smaller size.

With a variable-sized display, the learner can stretch or shrink the window. Content grows or shrinks to fit the resized window. The size of the display is not limited to the screen resolution. To make text more legible, learners can stretch the window.

Fixed- or variable-sized display?

Should you use a fixed- or variable-sized display for your e-learning? Where would you use each?

A fixed-size display is good for simplicity and uniformity. Every display is the same size and shape. Controls and other recurring parts of the display always appear the same size and at the same location. This simplicity and uniformity make a fixed-size display the best choice for novice computer users, who may be bewildered by a resizing display or may not even know that they can resize the display. The fixed size is good when implementing a page or card metaphor to indicate that units of display are comparable in size and scope.

On the other hand, a variable-sized display may be best when you have no fixed monitor size. Perhaps you have a widely varied audience or learners will take e-learning on different generations and types of equipment. Perhaps some will want to take your e-learning on some of the newer mobile devices with small displays. A variable-sized display may be necessary if learners need access to other parts of the screen while taking e-learning. The learner can resize or reshape the display to gain access to other information without losing sight of e-learning content. A variable-sized display can help with learners of varying visual acuity—provided the content enlarges when the window is enlarged. Learners with less-than-perfect vision can stretch the window to enlarge the text and graphics.

LEGIBILITY

Legibility refers to the ability of learners to read text and recognize graphics. For legibility, we must make content clear, crisp, and easy to read.

Keep text legible

For successful e-learning, we must ensure that readers can actually read the text. Sounds simple, right? It is, provided you follow a few guidelines.

Design text for easy reading

For legibility, we must design text for easy reading. A half-century of research on legibility of displayed text has left us some fairly simple guidelines to ensure that even learners without perfect eyesight can read the text we display.

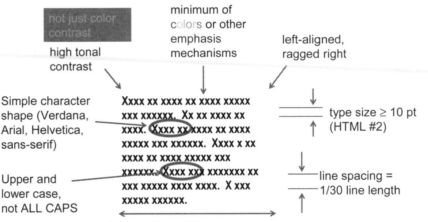

Our first guideline is to display text in high contrast with its background. That means not just color contrast, but high tonal contrast, such as black on white. Tonal contrast requires a difference in inherent lightness. Black and white is not the only legible combination, but using any other colors gives up some contrast and potentially some legibility.

Within the body of text, use a minimum of colors or other emphasis mechanisms. That does not mean you cannot occasionally highlight an individual word. Just do not make every third word a bright, bold color. Remember, you can never emphasize more than about 15% of the content in any display.

Align the lines of text of a paragraph along the left edge and leave the right edge ragged. It is OK to center the lines of a label, provided there are no more than three lines. Do not fully justify the lines of text. Doing so inserts spaces between words that encourage the eye to skip to the following line rather than jump the gap to the next word of the current line.

Make the text an adequate size, typically at least 10 points or HTML #2 size. Remember that font sizes on computer displays depend on the resolution of the learner's display, which may be adjustable by a factor of two or more. Font sizes may also be affected by any conversion or scaling process through which your content passes. Evaluate the type size as it appears on the learner's screen.

The next factor is often ignored but is almost as important as type size. Make line spacing one thirtieth of the line length. That ensures enough space between lines that the eye can reliably find the beginning of the next line. With too little line spacing, the eye is prone to repeat the current line or skip the following line.

Speaking of lines, make lines of text in a paragraph 40 to 60 characters long. Shorter lines may waste a bit of space but are seldom a problem for legibility. Longer lines can reduce legibility, especially if the guideline about line spacing is violated.

Write text in upper and lower case, NOT ALL CAPITAL LETTERS. Although capital letters look larger, they are actually harder to read because the shapes of letters are less distinctive than for lower-case letters.

Pick a font with a simple character shape. Legible fonts include Verdana, Arial, Helvetica, and the generic san-serif face available in Web browsers and Adobe Flash. Avoid highly stylized fonts, especially for small type sizes.

Beware the Picasso effect

One common mistake made by novice screen designers is playfully called the *Picasso effect*. It occurs when designers use so many colors and emphasis mechanisms within text that the eye treats the display, not as text to be read, but as a beautiful abstract composition to be admired. Rather than moving along lines of text, the eye drifts from one bright area to the next. Try reading the text of this display and you will experience the Picasso effect directly. It is available in living color at horton.com/eld/.

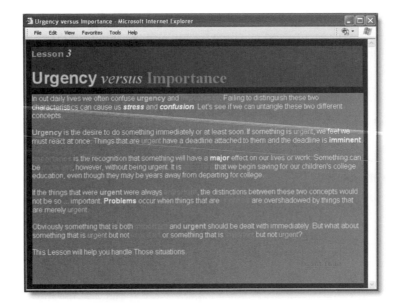

Ensure foreground-background contrast

Rule zero of legibility is to ensure foreground-background contrast. It is Rule zero because if text and graphics do not stand out from the background, they are invisible.

Ensure tonal contrast

Let's consider foreground-background contrast for text.

ABCDEFGHIJKLMNOPQRSTUVWXY
ABCDEFGHIJKLMNOPQRSTUVWX Z
ABCDEFGHIJKLMNOPQRSTUVW XYZ
ABCDEFGHIJKLMNOPQRST U WXYZ
ABCDEFGHIJKLMNOPQR UVWXYZ
ABCDEFGHIJKLMN QRSTUVWXYZ
ABCDEFGHIJK NOPQRSTUVWXYZ
ABCDE KLMNOPQRSTUVWXYZ
AB HIJKLMNOPQRSTUVWXYZ

Which letters stand out in each row?

First against a white background, which letters are most legible?

Now how about a middle gray background?

And finally, against a black background.

The answer is that the legibility of the text depends on its tonal contrast with its background. For this reason, never specify a foreground color without also specifying the background color at the same time.

Light or dark background?

As long as there is tonal contrast between foreground and background, text and graphics can be legible. So which is better, light text on a dark background or dark text on a light background? Twenty-five years ago when displays were dimmer than today and people kept computers in partially darkened rooms, light text on a dark background was regarded as more legible.

However, today, with bright displays and equally bright illumination of offices, most experts opt for the dark text on a light background. Such a combination makes it easier to switch back and forth between reading paper documents and screen displays. And it lessens the glare from light reflecting off the screen. It also has a big practical benefit. Graphics that work on the computer screen remain legible when printed out on white paper.

One exception may be when the color of fine lines and small images is critical, as in interpreting CAD drawings.

Keep the background quiet

One common practice is to use a texture or pattern as a background. Usually this is done to add visual variety or to achieve a richer look.

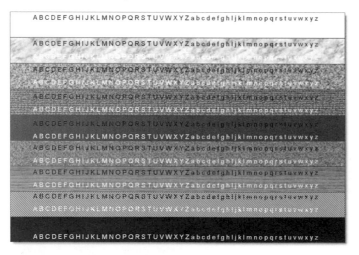

Before you use a textured background, look at this example and see which textures make text easier to read. On each texture are samples of text in black and in white.

Most people report that the simpler the texture, the easier it is to read small text. And, as always, higher contrast helps legibility.

Do not sacrifice legibility for supposed visual appeal. Nothing illegible is beautiful.

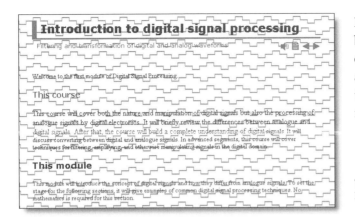

Here is another bad background. It replicates a real example. The waveforms slide across the screen. Do you think the effect makes the text easy to read?

This example is available in color at horton.com/eld/.

Start with a simple, solid background

Start your display design with a simple, solid background. Use a neutral or cool color.

Pick a background color that will contrast with the color of your text and graphics. Use areas of solid color to zone your display, that is, to divide it into functional areas.

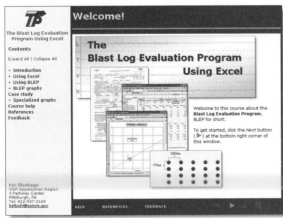

Use bits of color to draw attention to small items. Reserve bright colors for use within primary elements of content.

This screen is available in color at horton.com/eld/.

LAYOUT

Layout concerns how you arrange content predictably within the display window. There are many schools of design, and even more rules and fads. In the end, though, the most important characteristic of a layout is that learners find it predictable. That is, they can find the information and controls they seek in the display.

Zone the display

A display can be complex and densely packed and still be predictable. The key is that each area must have a distinct role and learners must be able to infer that role. Here is a test of the basic layout of an e-learning display. It asks potential learners to identify the areas of the display by matching them to the names of the areas.

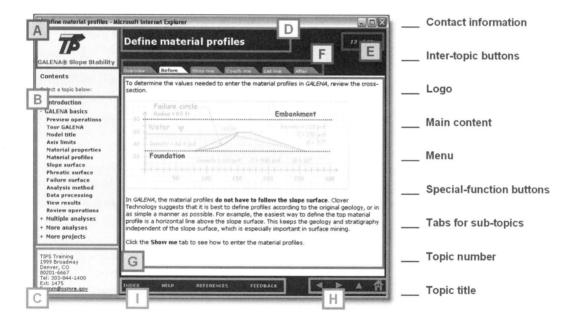

_____ Contact information

_____ Inter-topic buttons

_____ Logo

_____ Main content

_____ Menu

_____ Special-function buttons

_____ Tabs for sub-topics

_____ Topic number

_____ Topic title

Simple tests like this help you quickly refine your layout. By the way, the answers are, in order, C, H, A, G, B, I, F, E, and D.

Define a flexible scheme

In designing the layout of your display, use a flexible scheme that can handle different kinds of content and allows for appropriate variations. Here is an example of such a design. It is the layout for the course *Using Gantt Charts*. Notice that it defines several main areas or zones in the display and designates what they will be used for.

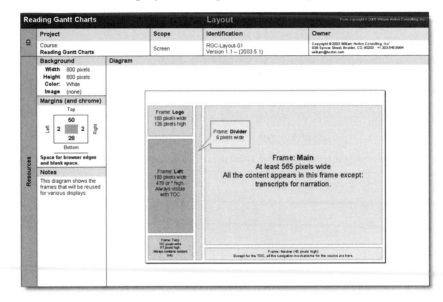

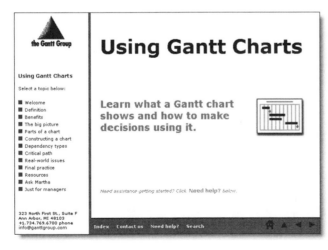

Here you see how the layout was used for the title screen.

Built using Adobe Dreamweaver, custom JavaScript, and Flash. View example at horton.com/eld/.

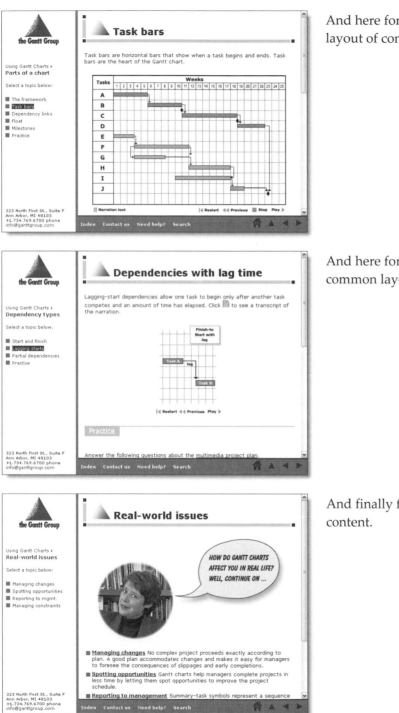

And here for the most common layout of content.

And here for a variant on that common layout.

And finally for a special type of content.

One flexible layout accommodated a variety of types and variations of content.

Focus attention on content

Unless learners attend to content, they learn little from it. So use layout to direct learners' attention to the most important parts of your content and away from incidental matter that could distract or confuse.

Visually feature content

Often organizational-identity standards require cluttering screens with logos, emblems, and legal gobbledygook. This is a problem even on large displays where we can use zoning and color to separate essential from incidental. It is a crisis on small displays where noisy gewgaw crowds out crucial content.

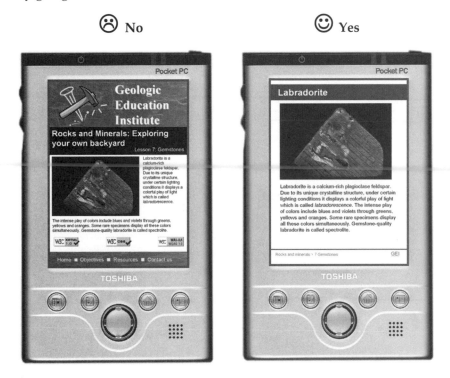

Put such secondary material on an *about* or *information* page and just include a link to the page throughout your e-learning.

Show only the essential part

One way to focus attention is to display only what you want learners to attend to. Most graphics, in my experience, are too large, complex, and detailed.

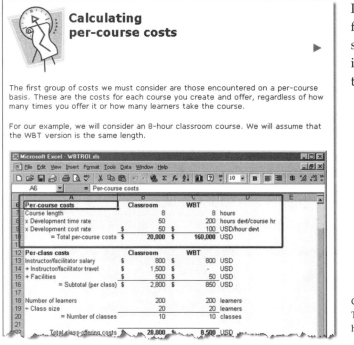

In this first-draft, only the first five rows of the spreadsheet are important, as indicated by the box around them.

Created using Adobe Dreamweaver and TechSmith SnagIt. View example at horton.com/eld/.

The second draft fixed that problem. The display is simpler and less distracting.

Highlight the item under discussion

Help learners notice what is important. In visual displays, draw the eye to the item under discussion.

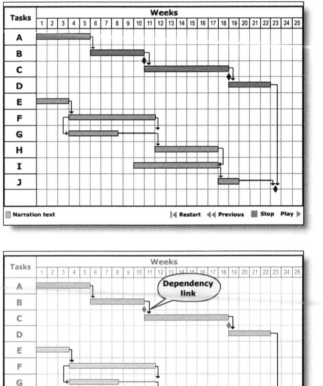

In the *Using Gantt Charts* course, a voice narrator commented on simple Gantt charts.

Created using Adobe Flash. View example at horton.com/eld/.

When a particular item was under discussion, other items were dimmed down and a label pointed to the item being discussed.

Beware information overload

Often you will want to include more information than will fit comfortably in e-learning displays. The solution is to first *edit* the text, and then move some of the remaining information to the narration track. Finally, display just key phrases that are synched to the narration.

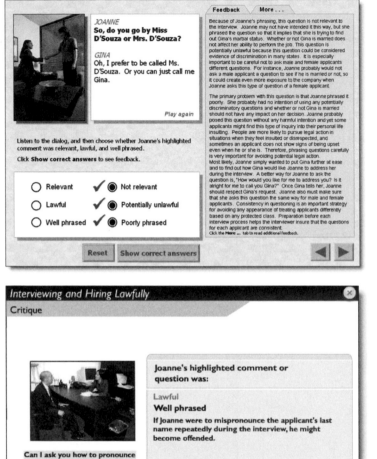

Here is an example of a prototype that revealed the difficulty of combining too much information in one display.

Created in Microsoft PowerPoint.

And here is the resulting display from the final course from Brightline Compliance (www.brightline compliance.com). It shows the value of prototyping your displays with actual content.

Built using Adobe Flash by Brightline Compliance.

UNITY

Your e-learning should appear coherent and pleasant. For that to happen, you must ensure a consistent and high-quality look and feel that unifies the entire course or curriculum. If you have been wondering where design considers aesthetics, you will find your answer here.

Case study in unity

Let's look at some of the displays of a course and see some of the steps taken to ensure that learners perceive them as coherent and attractive.

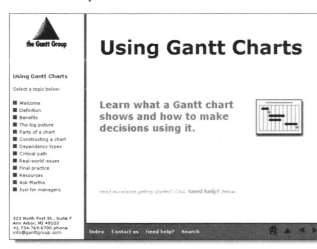

These pages are all from the course *Using Gantt Charts*. Starting with the title screen, you notice some design themes.

Built using Adobe Dreamweaver, custom JavaScript, and Flash. View example in color at horton.com/eld/.

The simple white background and relatively sparse layout were chosen to avoid noise and clutter. The dark red color used for the title and accents was taken from the client's logo. Normally I would not use red this way, but the course was being offered for free to promote the company offering it. Tying the course to the company was a business objective. Notice that the red chosen was just a shade darker than that of the logo. That was done to increase legibility and to reduce the "aggressiveness" of the color. The only other color was gray. I chose gray so as not to compete with the red. A couple of shades of gray gave me a convenient way to control the relative prominence of text and graphics.

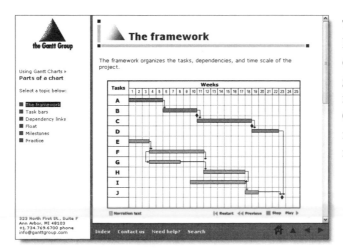

This example shows a typical lesson. Notice the continued use of the dark red for emphasis and grays for secondary matter. The rectangular shape of the sample Gantt chart shows one of the reasons for basing the design on rectangular forms.

Overcome the one-path-for-all syndrome

One of the relics of classroom learning haunts the design of e-learning. It is the one-path-for-all syndrome. Let me explain it in architectural terms. Imagine that you are in a building of five floors. You are on the second floor and want to go to the fourth floor.

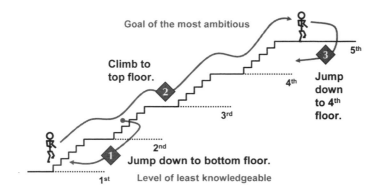

To go from the second floor to the fourth floor, you have to first jump down to the bottom floor. Then you have to climb the stairs all the way up to the top floor, bypassing your goal of the fourth floor. Once you reach the top floor, you must then jump down to your destination, the fourth floor. How would you rate the architect of such a building?

Now consider the building as a metaphor for course design, where the first floor represents the level of the least knowledgeable learner being educated. And the top floor represents the goal of the most ambitious learner.

It is common for classroom courses to adopt such a design, requiring all learners to span the entire distance from lowest common denominator to highest aspiration. But in e-learning, at least that which is taken individually rather than as part of a class, there seems to be little excuse for forcing all learners to start and end at the same point.

In e-learning all learners can have a direct path from their current levels of knowledge and skill to their desired levels. Provided we designers supply the necessary navigation mechanisms.

Sparse or rich navigation?

Do you want to guide learners through your e-learning along a specific path, or do you want to let them blaze their own trails? That is, do you want to implement sparse navigation or rich navigation?

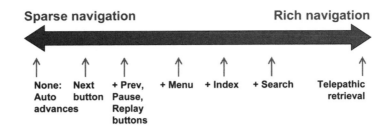

Options range from almost no control to complete control. We might conduct a live presentation or play a recorded presentation without letting learners affect the playback. That would give learners no control other than to quit. Or we might give learners a **Next** button to click to advance to the next segment. For a bit more control, we might give learners standard playback buttons, such as **Previous** to go to the preceding segment, **Pause** to temporarily stop the display, or **Replay** to begin the presentation again from the start. For even more control, we might include a menu or table of contents from which learners could pick individual topics. We might go further to include an alphabetical index or a search facility so learners could find topics regardless of where they occur in the organization of the course. Now learners are really in control. Who knows what lies beyond? Perhaps we will have read-my-mind interfaces that will locate topics a few milliseconds after learners think of them. So how much control do we give learners?

Sparse navigation	Rich navigation
Best for simple tutorials taken by novices.	Best for just-in-time learning by Google-addicted Web-surfers.
Protects learners.	Empowers learners.
Makes the experience more predictable.	Makes e-learning more flexible.
Simplifies the user-interface. Learners have fewer buttons to click and display areas to watch.	Enriches the experience by providing learners with access to more resources and learning experiences.
Can restrict access to particular parts of the course, for example, requiring learners to complete the core of the course before attempting the final exam.	Can accommodate more groups of learners trying to accomplish different purposes under different circumstances.

In the *Using Gantt Charts* course, I chose a moderately rich navigation scheme. Why? Learners were generally experienced computer users. They would be using the Web to access the course and would expect the same degree of navigation offered by Amazon.com, CNN.com, horton.com, and other popular Web sites.

I knew that these learners were impatient. They were mid-level managers and accustomed to making their own decisions to get things done quickly. They wanted to learn what they wanted to learn when they wanted to learn it.

The course would be taken as a refresher for many and would continue to serve as a reference for others. They needed to look up things without having to plod all the way from the beginning.

NAVIGATION MECHANISMS

Learners today are used to the freedom and "searchability" of the Web. "Don't fence me in!" they shout. The trend today is to include more and more ways to move through a body of online material. This graphic summarizes all the common methods. You will seldom need all of these, but you may need several.

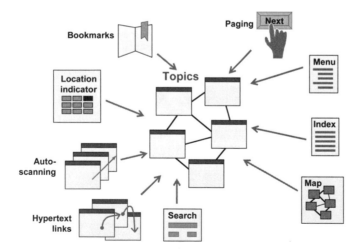

Some of these mechanisms are common within courses. Others are more often found in other forms of e-learning, such as knowledge bases and repositories of learning objects.

Your course or document or Web site consists of a large number of linked topics or pages. How can learners find the one they want?

The simplest method, **paging** (p. 535), merely requires learners to repeatedly press or click a **Next** button as if following a guided tour.

Another class of access mechanisms lets learners consult some kind of a directory to find the location of needed information. The most familiar kind of directory is a table of contents or **menu** (p. 537) to let users find topics by subject category. Another directory of locations is an **index** (p. 549), that is, an alphabetical list of topics. A **map** (p. 550) can show the organization of the topics as well as serve as a visual menu.

Most large Web sites include a **search** (p. 555) facility whereby visitors can specify the characteristics of the knowledge they seek and be transported to the topic containing that knowledge. Large courses are adding search as a navigation option.

For local navigation or references to external material, you may include **hypertext links** (p. 557), like those common on Web pages.

Some sites, for example virtual museums, include a grazing or **autoscanning** (p. 561) mode that automatically advances through the material at a rapid pace until the learner presses a **Stop** button.

To aid navigation, learners may consult a you-are-here sign to learn where they are. Such a **location indicator** (p. 563) in e-learning can also let learners navigate to related topics.

Bookmarks (p. 565) let users construct private lists of topics to which they will want to return later. A history mechanism may list topics visited recently.

Let's consider each of these navigation mechanisms in turn.

Paging

Paging provides a logical path through the e-learning. It lets learners flip through content just as they have with books for five centuries. It is the simplest access mechanism for learners. Typically a button takes the learner through topics in the order they are listed in the menu or table-of-contents, from top-to-bottom.

Include next and previous buttons

Next and **Previous** buttons take learners to the subsequent and preceding topic in a logical sequence.

Learners are familiar with using a table of contents from books. It lets learners drill down to specific topics through a series of simple decisions. The table of contents can also serve as a map, revealing how the e-learning is organized.

Designing menus requires some important decisions about how the menu is displayed and formatted and how your e-learning is organized.

Constantly displayed menu vs. menu-on-demand

Are menus always visible on the screen or do they appear only when summoned by the pressing of a **Menu** button?

Constantly displayed menu

A constantly displayed menu is a permanent part of the display. It is never hidden and remains immediately available.

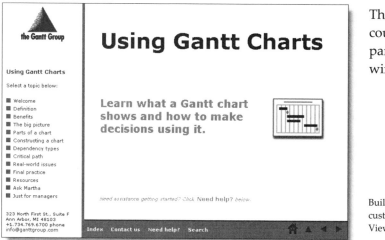

The *Using Gantt Charts* course included a menu panel at the left of its window.

Built using Adobe Dreamweaver, custom JavaScript, and Adobe Flash. View example at horton.com/eld/.

A constantly displayed menu is always available. It invites navigation and reminds learners of how the course is organized. It does take up space and can distract learners from the current topic. For a constantly displayed menu, entries must be short. Sometimes it is hard to write meaningful entries in the space available.

Menu-on-demand

With a menu-on-demand, learners must click a button to make the menu appear.

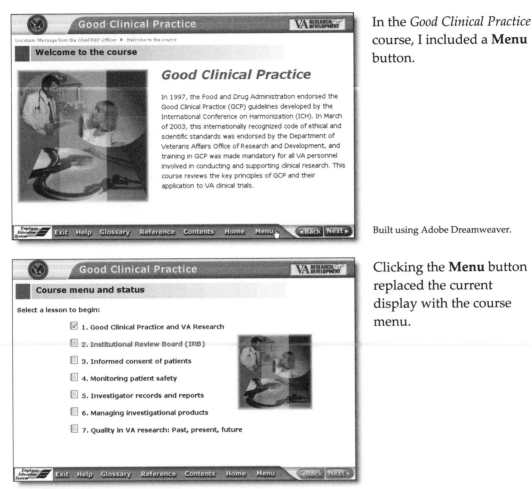

In the *Good Clinical Practice* course, I included a **Menu** button.

Built using Adobe Dreamweaver.

Clicking the **Menu** button replaced the current display with the course menu.

A menu-on-demand conserves space. When the menu does appear, it has adequate space. Thus, titles can be complete and easier to understand. However, learners may find it distracting to have the menu replace the current display.

With a menu-on-demand, you will have to provide a way for learners to get back to where they were before they summoned the menu. Notice that the *Vision and the Church* course has a **Return** button that restores the previously displayed page. Experienced Web browsers may know that the browser's **Back** button will take them back where they were, but not all e-learners are that knowledgeable.

Multi-level vs. expanding menu

If the entire menu will not fit in the available space, you may want to divide the menu into multiple levels or else employ a menu that expands in place to reveal lower-level components of selected entries.

Multi-level menu

In a multi-level menu, selecting an entry replaces the current list of choices with a list of choices for the entry chosen. Each menu display contains only sibling entries.

Selecting items in the menu for the *Using Gantt Charts* course revealed lower-level menus.

Selecting **Parts of a chart** here, …   reveals the sub-menu for Parts of a chart. Selecting **Dependency links** here, …   reveals that topic and highlights the item in the menu.

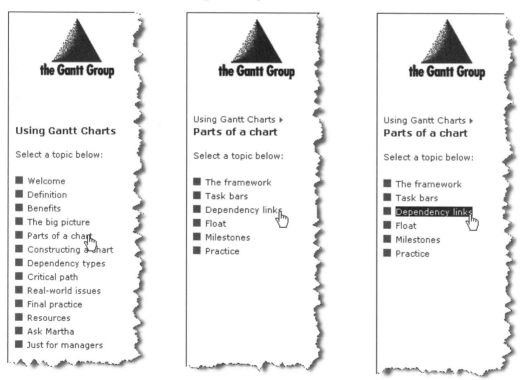

Multi-level menus reduce clutter because learners have to examine only one set of choices at a time. However, multi-level menus can cause tunnel vision as learners are looking at only a small area of the whole menu system at a time.

Expanding menu

An expanding menu displays sub-entries in place, indented below the main entry. For example, in the *GALENA Slope Stability Analysis* course menu entries expand as selected.

Selecting **GALENA basics** here, …

reveals the sub-menu for GALENA Basics. Selecting **Material properties** here, …

reveals that topic and highlights the item in the menu.

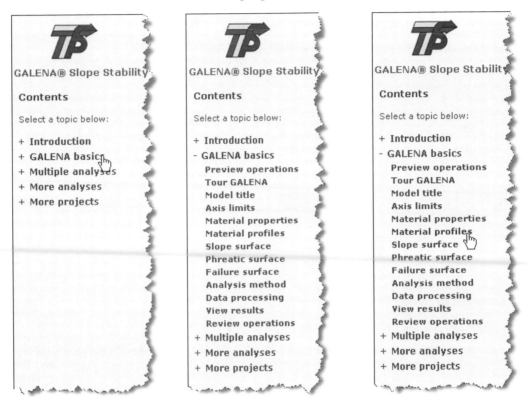

An expanding menu like this shows context of entries. Learners can always trace the path from the top of the menu down to an individual topic. Expanding menus can, however, result in a somewhat cluttered display that takes more time to search.

Depth versus breadth tradeoff

Menus can be deep or broad. *Depth* refers to the number of choices required to descend the menu from the top to a specific topic. *Breadth* refers to the number of choices on each level of the menu. This is not just a choice of how menus are organized but how your e-learning is structured into lessons (Chapter 7).

Deep menus

Deeper menus simplify the choices at each level but require more decisions. As a general rule, require no more than 3 decisions to get to a menu choice.

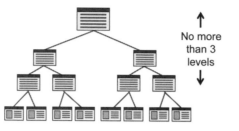

No more than 3 levels

Broad menus

Broader menus reduce the number of choices learners must make to get to a topic. However, the individual choices are harder, as there are more items to pick from at each level. In general, try to limit the number of choices to no more than 7 per level of the menu.

No more than 7 choices per level

Better broad than deep

Sticking with our guidelines of only 3 levels and only 7 choices at each level, we could ideally accommodate a course with 343 topics (7 x 7 x 7 = 343). That should be enough for most simple courses. Courses are not so regular in real life, and compromises are necessary.

Research on computer menus suggests that wide menus are better than deep ones. It is easier to re-read a long menu than to have to click back and forth between levels of a menu system. Also, it is easier to find entries by moving the eyes than by moving the mouse.

Compromise by organizing menus

One solution to the depth-breadth tradeoff is to present lots of choices in one display, but to group them into a few categories.

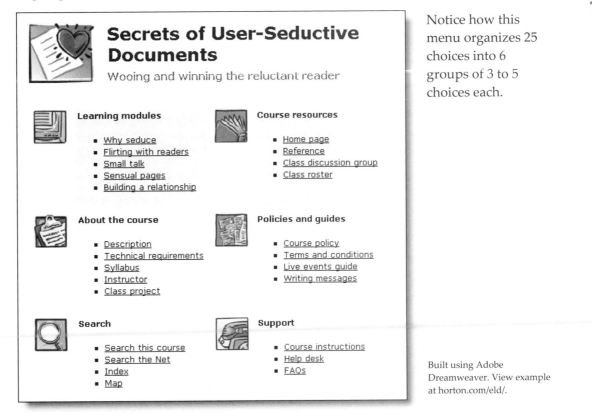

Notice how this menu organizes 25 choices into 6 groups of 3 to 5 choices each.

Built using Adobe Dreamweaver. View example at horton.com/eld/.

Exception: Content for children

Children may be easily distracted or overwhelmed by menus with too many choices but sufficiently motivated by curiosity to pursue their interests through several menu levels. For children, keep individual menu displays short and simple. Use graphics, animation, and other techniques to keep children interested and to give them a sense of progress as they select through a series of menus. Make selecting from the menus like playing a game.

11

Navigation

Designing better menus

Create menus that show the organization of the course and guide learners to the specific topics they need.

Avoid dump-truck menus

Avoid the "dump-truck" menu, which occurs when all topics appear at the same level in the menu without regard for how they are related.

😞 No   😊 Yes

No	Yes
Taking pictures with a digital camera	Taking pictures with a digital camera
Setting exposure mode - digital	Setting exposure mode
Setting speed - digital	Setting speed
Composing the shot - digital	Composing the shot
Focusing - digital	Focusing
Taking pictures with a film camera	Taking pictures with a film camera
Setting exposure mode - film	Setting exposure mode
Setting speed - film	Setting speed
Composing the shot - film	Composing the shot
Focusing - film	Focusing
Uploading from a digital camera	Uploading from a digital camera
Connecting the digital camera	Connecting the digital camera
Completing the upload	Completing the upload
Scanning film pictures	Scanning film pictures
Starting the film scanner	Starting the scanner
Importing scanned pictures	Importing the pictures
Editing pictures in the computer	Editing pictures in the computer
Adjusting brightness	Adjusting brightness
Adjusting contrast	Adjusting contrast
Adjusting saturation	Adjusting saturation
Cropping the picture	Adjusting hue
Rotating the picture	Cropping the picture
Adjusting hue	Rotating the picture
Printing your photographs	Printing your photographs
Calibrating the monitor	Calibrating the monitor
Calibrating the printer	Calibrating the printer
Printing photographs	Printing photographs

Front-load menu entries

Make sure the most important words in the menu entry appear at the beginning of the entry. Impatient learners may not scan past the first few words. If the menu must appear in a narrow panel, only the first few words may be visible.

No

No	Yes

Lesson 1: How to take pictures with a digital camera
Lesson 2: How to take pictures with a film camera
Lesson 3: How to upload from a digital camera
Lesson 4: How to scan film pictures
Lesson 5: How to edit pictures in the computer
Lesson 6: How to print your photographs

Taking pictures with a digital camera
Taking pictures with a film camera
Uploading from a digital camera
Scanning film pictures
Editing pictures in the computer
Printing your photographs

Speak the language of learners

In menu entries, use terms learners will understand and value. Replace esoteric terminology that learners can appreciate only after completing your e-learning with simple, everyday language they will already recognize.

 No   Yes

MERCHECK Program
CHARGNET Network
FraudAlert page
OverLim page
Reissue DB
FastHold program
RePortal Site

Reduce merchant fraud
Verify card charges
Spot fraud
Check credit limits
Accept reissued cards
Hold dubious charges
Get up-to-date info

Stick with one or two menu styles

As a consultant, I once encountered a suite of courses that included 6 distinct styles of menus: textual and graphical; items arranged in one column, two columns, a grid, and a diagram; menu on the left, center, and right of the page; and sub-menus on subsequent displays and sub-menus in pop-up areas. In some cases to get to a single topic, the learner had to select from four different styles of menus. Please, pick 1 or 2 styles of menus and stick with them.

Use the home page as a starting menu

You can use your course home page as a special menu to some of the high-priority topics. What's the difference between a menu and a home page? A good home page:

▶ Welcomes learners.

▶ Orients learners.

▶ Reveals top-level organization.

▶ Supplies one-click access to featured items.

A home page prepares learners to navigate to high-priority topics. It may not be complete, but it is informative and convenient.

Reveal the full title

Often menu displays that appear in a narrow panel do not have room for a complete title. Here are some ways to work around this limitation:

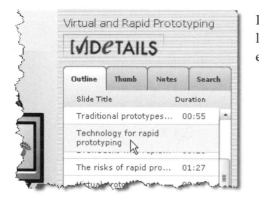

In *Virtual and Rapid Prototyping*, when the learner points to a menu item, the menu item expands to reveal the complete title.

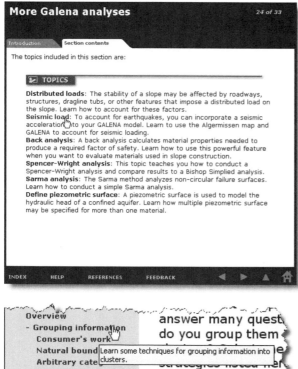

In the *GALENA Slope Stability Analysis* course, there is a lesson-overview page for each top-level selection in the menu. This page gives more details about the topics within that part of the menu.

In *Designing Knowledge Products*, when the learner points to a menu item, an explanation of it appears in a tool tip.

Visual menus

Visual menus indicate choices with visual images rather than just word labels. They work well when learners know what something looks like but may not be able to recognize its name.

Here is an example of a menu of simulations for learners to select from as part of the *GALENA Slope Stability Analysis* course.

Built using Adobe Dreamweaver and custom JavaScript.

And here is an example from the *Mineral Museum* project. Miniature images preview the appearance of the topic or its subject.

Built using Adobe Dreamweaver, Active Server Pages, and custom JavaScript. View example at horton.com/eld/.

Visual menus are also provided automatically in some tools. Adobe Acrobat includes thumbnails of pages, and Articulate Presenter and Adobe Breeze Presenter include small images of slides converted from PowerPoint to Flash.

A visual menu may be useful in subjects for which visual appearances are important, for example, architecture, astronomy, art, archaeology, geology, and biology.

If you are considering a visual menu, think about maps (p. 550), which extend the idea of a visual menu by organizing the items into a composite visual display.

Help menu

Computer programs often let users access tutorials, simulations, and demonstrations from the same menu used to access Help topics. Such access provides shortcuts for people impatient to learn the product.

For example, in the *Horton Timer-Picker*, clicking on the **Help** menu reveals not only conventional help, but also a list of tutorials. For example, selecting **Help → Touring the interface** …

… reveals a short tutorial on how to use the most common features of the program.

Built with Adobe Captivate. View example at horton.com/eld/.

Should you use a menu?

Should you include a menu in your e-learning project? With few exceptions, yes. A good menu is essential if learners need to zero in on specific subjects, for example, when taking e-learning as a refresher or using it as a reference.

The few exceptions for which a menu is not warranted include these:

▶ You do not want to let learners skip ahead.

▶ No hierarchical organization of the subject is meaningful.

Indexes

The index for the course, like an index for a traditional book, presents an alphabetical list of topics for learners to pick from.

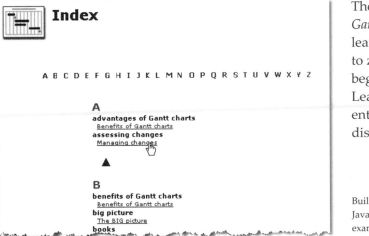

The index for the *Using Gantt Charts* course let learners select a letter button to zip to the entries beginning with that letter. Learners could then select an entry and see its topic displayed.

Built using Adobe Dreamweaver, custom JavaScript, and Adobe Flash. View example at horton.com/eld/.

Should you use an index?

An index is usually a good idea that takes lots of work to create. The index has an advantage over menus or a table of contents. The index can include synonyms that anticipate what words learners may use to describe a concept. An index may be especially useful in helping learners find a specific concept, whose name may not appear in the title of any topic. An index is doubly important if e-learning does not include a search facility.

But creating an index is time-consuming and difficult. It requires a good understanding of both the subject and learners' vocabulary.

An index may not be appropriate if it encourages learners to experience topics out of context and out of sequence. If you include an index, make sure that your topics are not confusing or misleading when accessed in almost random order.

Design better indexes

For several years, I purchased the Cinemania CD-ROM because it contained reviews, biographies, photographs, sound and video clips, and other information about movies. One day I wanted to find a picture of the director Alfred Hitchcock, so I began looking in the media index under the letter H.

I could not find Hitchcock, but I did notice a few other entries that seemed to be listed by first name. So I looked under the A's. No Alfred Hitchcock. Can you guess where I had to look? To find Alfred Hitchcock, I had to look in the S's for Sir Alfred Hitchcock. A convenient way for the computer to sort items, but hardly the way human beings do it. I do not think Sir Alfred would have been amused.

So index by the way people call things—even those ignorant souls who have not learned the correct names by completing your course.

In compiling your index, use terms your learners already know and understand. Use terms they would use to describe what they want to learn. For some guidelines on indexing topics, see page 309 in Chapter 6 on Topics.

Maps

A map is a visual menu that shows how e-learning or its subject is organized. A map displays the logical or navigational organization of e-learning. A map provides shortcuts to the main topics and helps learners form a mental model of the course so they can navigate more reliably on their own.

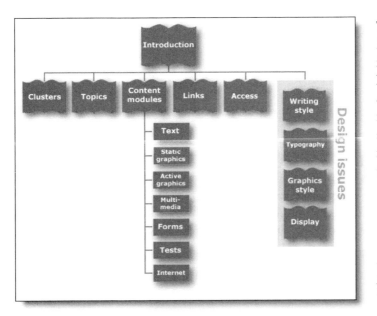

The course *Designing Effective Electronic Courses* features a map showing how content is organized and indicating important relationships within the subject. Clicking on an item in the map displays that topic or lesson.

Built using HTML and custom JavaScript. View example at horton.com/eld/.

If the course contains a separate menu, the map need not be complete. In fact, a single course can contain multiple maps, each emphasizing a different aspect of the subject.

Logical maps

A logical map shows the logical relationships among the lessons and topics of the course.

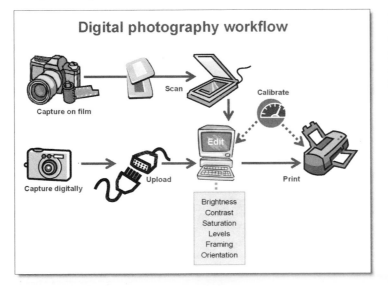

For example, this map shows the processes involved in digital photography. It shows logical dependencies among tasks, alternative paths through the process, and optional steps—all in a way that provides a conceptual overview and lets learners select the part of the process they want to learn about.

Schematic maps

A schematic map invites learners on a figurative journey. It recommends sequences of topics and offers side excursions.

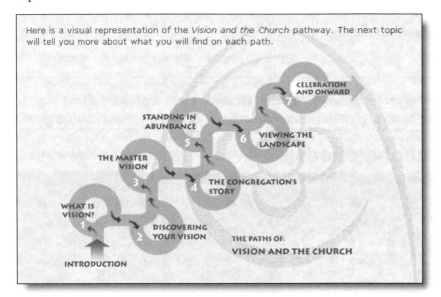

The pathway map from *Vision and the Church* shows the sequence of lessons in the course but indicates that each represents an exploration along the way to the ultimate goal.

Built using Adobe Dreamweaver, Active Server Pages, custom JavaScript, and Adobe Flash. View example at horton.com/eld/.

Use a schematic map when none of the other types of map captures the relationships you want to communicate. It is especially appropriate when you want to suggest relationships to learners, even though the relationships do not exist in a physical sense.

Should you use a map?

Should you include a map in your e-learning projects? A map is seldom an absolute requirement, but it is a valuable addition for visual subjects and for visual learners. If you are teaching art history to architects, a map will be appreciated and understood.

A map is also a good idea when you need to teach how the subject and the course are organized. If the organization is a simple linear sequence or a regular hierarchy, a map may not be so critical because learners can pick up the organization from the menu. A map may not be necessary when it would just duplicate the menu. If the menu captures the organization of the subject and the course, save the space and forego the map. However, if the organization is complex or critical relationships exist among units of content, include a map to make those relationships clear.

Search facilities

A search page might seem an odd idea for a course. Yet many learners, whose models of online information and knowledge are shaped more by Internet search engines than by books, may expect or even demand a search facility.

Several years ago I confused and enraged a group of instructional designers by suggesting they include search mechanisms in their courses. Half had no idea what I was talking about and the others thought it was the worst idea since junk mail. Today, most designers have used Google, Yahoo, Alta Vista, MSN Search, or some other search engine and recognize the value of being able to search for learning. If they do not see the value, their younger learners will be glad to explain it to them.

How search works

In e-learning, we let learners search for courses or within courses.

For example, in the *Using Gantt Charts*, course, clicking the **Search** button brings up a simple search screen.

Built using Adobe Dreamweaver, Active Server Pages, and custom JavaScript. View example at horton.com/eld/.

The learner enters a search term and clicks the **Submit** button. The system then displays a list of topics that match the search term. Matches are listed by rank, that is, by how closely the topic matched the search terms. Clicking on the name of one of the topics displays that topic.

A more advanced search mechanism might let learners search for words or phrases, specify where the match must be found, and how the resulting matches are displayed.

Built using Adobe Dreamweaver, Active Server Pages, and custom JavaScript.

An even more advanced search mechanism may let learners search for learning resources on a particular subject, in a particular medium (book, course, presentation, person), of a specified length, in a certain language, or of a particular file format.

Built using HTML, Active Server Pages, and custom JavaScript

Still another kind of search lets learners locate topics by subject characteristics. For example, the *Mineral Museum* lets learners search for minerals by color, hardness, source locations, and other characteristics.

Built using Adobe Dreamweaver and Active Server Pages. View example at horton.com/eld/.

11

Navigation

The advantage of a search facility is that it allows learners to describe in precise terms the knowledge they seek and then zip right to the topic that best provides just that knowledge. With an effective search facility, the size and organizational complexity of the course are no barrier to finding the needed knowledge.

Should you use search?

Should you allow search in your e-learning projects? If impatient learners will use the course for reference or a refresher, include a search mechanism—especially if learners are accustomed to using Google, Yahoo, and other Internet search services. A search mechanism is also good if you cannot include an index.

Realize though that a search mechanism can subvert your course organization by making it easy for learners to jump directly into the middle of your course. If you include a search mechanism, make sure your topics are self-contained enough to be understood out of context (p. 312).

How to improve search

What can you do to make search work better for your learners. Here are some suggestions:

▶ Explain how to conduct complex searches. Provide instructions on how to search for individual words, combinations of words, and specific phrases.

▶ Edit the text throughout your e-learning so it uses terms that searchers use. Write your content in the vocabulary that learners use. Doing so makes your content easy to search and easy to understand.

▶ Include keywords in metadata (p. 400) to provide synonyms for words used in text.

Hypertext links

Hypertext links, or hyperlinks for short, let learners select information to display. Clicking on an icon or area of text on the screen jumps to a new location in the document or course and displays the content found there.

What are hyperlinks?

Hyperlinks invite learners to stop reading in one place and continue elsewhere. They also express relationships between topics. Links are nothing new. They have existed in books for centuries as cross-references, tables of contents, index entries, footnotes, bibliographies, figure citations, and thumb tabs.

In e-learning, a hyperlink is a sacred contract with the learner that says, "If you take the trouble to click this link, you will experience something of value."

Label hyperlinks clearly

Ensure that learners can predict the destination of every link they encounter.

Anatomy of a hyperlink trigger

A well labeled hyperlink communicates three vital pieces of information: the promise, the trigger, and requirements.

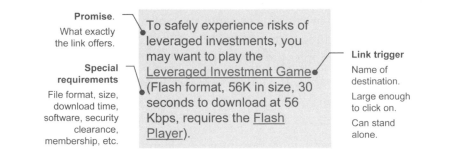

Make a clear promise

Tell learners what they will experience after clicking on the link. A single, precise phrase is usually sufficient.

Show where to click

Visually indicate where learners should click. Do not require learners to mouse all over the screen looking for the cursor to change indicating something to click on.

No

Would you like to continue the course or return to the simulation?

 Yes

Would you like to <u>continue the course</u> or <u>return to the simulation?</u>

Leave text legible

Links should not degrade the legibility of text. Choose link colors and styles that leave text legible. Make link triggers large enough to click, but do not turn whole paragraphs into links.

 No

<u>You may want to see a detailed drawing showing the overall plan for the project and the main phases of work it requires.</u>

 Yes

You may want to see a <u>detailed drawing</u> showing the overall plan for the project and the main phases of work it requires.

Integrate hyperlink triggers into text

Do not disrupt continuous reading. Place link triggers at the end of sentences and paragraphs.

 No

Try the <u>advanced procedure</u> only after you have mastered the simple procedure.

The most valuable form of the mineral beryl is the gemstone emerald. <u>Click here,</u> to learn more about emeralds.

Yes

If you have mastered the simple procedure, try the <u>advanced procedure</u>.

The most valuable form of the mineral beryl is the gemstone <u>emerald</u>.

Display new content appropriately

You often have a choice of where the destination content should appear. Should it replace the content you clicked on or appear in an entirely new window? Or somewhere else? Let's review your choices and their pros and cons.

Where content appears	Advantages	Disadvantages
Replaces the current window's content.	No separate windows to manage. Learners have only one thing to view at a time.	Learners cannot refer to the original display. A novice may not know how to get back.
In an additional window.	Learners can compare the new display to the one containing the link. The new display is self-contained and clearly separate.	The new display may cover up other windows and clutter the screen.
In another frame or area in the same window.	The display remains stable. The context of the new information is clear.	The new content still replaces the previous content of the target area. Can make text more difficult for screen readers for the blind.
In line with the text of the link.	Information appears where the learner is looking. The surrounding information provides context. Good for definitions of terms, for example.	Limited to small amounts of new information, not for navigation between topics.

Pick persistent Web links

Links to external Web content can create a problem if the content is removed or relocated. Some solutions include:

▶ **Link to providers not likely to go out of business**. The university-based Web site of a student is likely to change once the student graduates.

▶ **Link to stable sites**. Prefer sources that do not reorganize their Web sites every few months. Trendy subjects rarely occasion stable sites.

▶ **Link to highly cited resources**. The provider may feel a community duty to keep the material available.

▶ **Provide multiple links for each type of information** you want to make available. At any moment, some of them will be available.

▶ **Check your links frequently** to identify problems. Find replacements for dead links.

▶ **Give search terms** instead of links to find resources. For example, "Conduct a Web search for the terms: **gastroenterology seminar.**"

Autoscanning

Autoscanning lets learners flip through topics rapidly until they spot the one they want. Why, you ask, would anyone ever want to access e-learning that way? Well, did you ever flip through the pages of a new book just to see what was there? Later, did you ever return to the book to find something you read by flipping, looking for the page where you remember the information was located? Do you, or perhaps someone in your family, ever flip through TV channels looking for something to watch?

How autoscanning works

Autoscanning automatically advances through pages, screens, or topics of e-learning at a fixed rate of so many displays per minute until the learner signals it to stop.

The *Mineral Museum* includes an autoscanning mechanism.

Built using Adobe Dreamweaver and Active Server Pages. View example at horton.com/eld/.

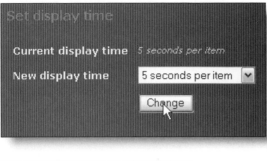

Clicking the pocket watch icon in the upper right displays the **Set display time** window, where the learner can specify how long to display each page.

Then, if the learner clicks the **fast forward** icon (double right-pointing triangles) on the main display, the virtual tour begins, showing mineral specimens at the rate specified.

Upon spotting a mineral of interest, the learner clicks the **stop** icon.

Should you use autoscanning?

Should you use autoscanning in your e-learning project? Autoscanning is a special-purpose tool. Do not use it for general access to learning but for specific occasions, such as:

► Previews and introductions.

► Unattended demonstrations.

► Teaching basic navigation skills.

► Getting learners' full attention.

► Controlling the pace.

Autoscanning is a good addition for visual subjects such as art and architecture. It also helps when learners can recognize something but cannot recall its name, such as a distinctive photograph, drawing, diagram, or chart. Or when learners can search for a particular title, banner, heading, bullet list, table, or other visually distinct topic component.

Autoscanning is not effective, however, when objects all look the same or when slow-speed connections make updating the display erratic.

Location indicators

In large, complex courses, it is easy for learners to get lost. Or be unable to find a topic they visited earlier. One way to alleviate this confusion is to include signposts and "you-are-here" maps. Dictionaries tell you where you are by putting the range of words defined at the top of the page in a page header. This book does a similar thing with its page headers. In an amusement park or sports stadium, it is common to find "You are here" signs that include a map with an arrow showing your location.

How location indicators work

In e-learning, location indicators visually show how the current topic is related to other topics. They may show its place in the organizational scheme. Location indicators help learners develop a mental model of how the course is organized.

One common approach in hierarchically organized courses is to show the path from the home page or main menu down to the current page. *Basic Training in Protecting Human Subjects* displays such a "breadcrumb trail." Clicking on one of the items on the path, displays that item.

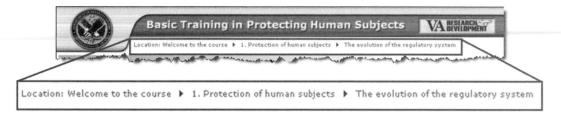

Another form embeds the location indicator at the top of the menu.

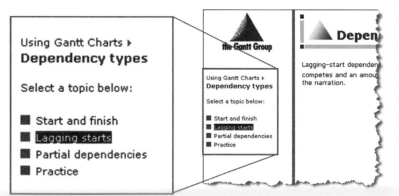

In the *Using Gantt Charts* course, the location of the current menu is indicated at the top of the menu. The current topic is highlighted within that menu.

In courses with a more complex organization, additional organizational clues may be required.

In a grid organization it may be necessary to show the position in the grid as well as the names of the current row and column.

Built using Adobe Dreamweaver and custom JavaScript. View example at horton.com/eld/.

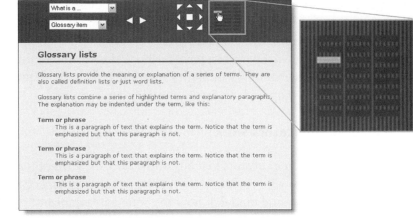

Should you use location indicators?

Should you use location indicators in your e-learning projects? I have found them valuable when the course is more than two levels deep. It also helps when learners frequently need to backtrack and start down a new path, as in simulations and exploratory learning.

Location indicators are especially important when learners must follow long paths, for instance, in simulations or troubleshooting procedures. Location indicators simplify reversing direction or undoing recent choices and starting down another path.

The top of each page in this troubleshooting procedure shows the diagnostic trail taken to get to this page.

A location indicator may not be of much benefit if the course is not organized in a regular structure, such as a linear sequence, a hierarchy, or a grid. And a location indicator may require valuable space better used for other purposes.

Bookmarks

Bookmarks flag the location where we left off so we can easily return there. When reading a book, we may dog-ear a page or insert a slip of paper to mark our location. In e-learning, we do the same with electronic bookmarks.

How bookmarks work

In e-learning, bookmarks serve the same function as in paper books, but they work differently. In e-learning, a bookmark may record where the learner was when exiting and offer to return the learner to that location the next time the learner begins the e-learning.

When learners log into *GALENA Slope Stability Analysis,* they can choose to resume learning where they left off last time.

Or the learner can manually define a bookmark.

In courses converted from PowerPoint with Articulate Presenter, the learner can click a Bookmark button.

Created in Microsoft PowerPoint and converted for Web delivery using Articulate Presenter. View example at horton.com/eld/.

The learner can then create a bookmark to the module or to the current location within the module.

For courses that play in a Web browser, the learner can use the **Bookmark** or **Favorites** feature to define a shortcut to the current page.

And some learning management systems, such as The Learning Manager, can display a history of recently displayed topics.

Should you use bookmarking?

Should you use bookmarking as a navigation aid in your e-learning project? Bookmarking is valuable if segments of the course are longer than learners can take at one time or if learners are frequently interrupted. They have less value for short courses. They can be difficult to create unless your tools automate the process.

BALANCE NAVIGATION MECHANISMS

By adding navigation mechanisms to your e-learning, you turn them into efficient reference works as well. If learners can quickly find an individual explanation, fact, or sequence, they can look up knowledge when they need it—without having to take the entire course. If learners can quickly find the part of the course on a single subject, they can use it for just-in-time learning, right when they need specific skills or knowledge.

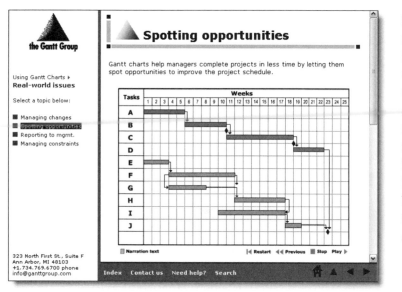

Several navigation mechanisms are built into the *Using Gant Charts* course. First there is a constantly displayed **menu** to the left. As part of the menu is a **location indicator**. At the lower-right are buttons for **paging** through the course one topic at a time.

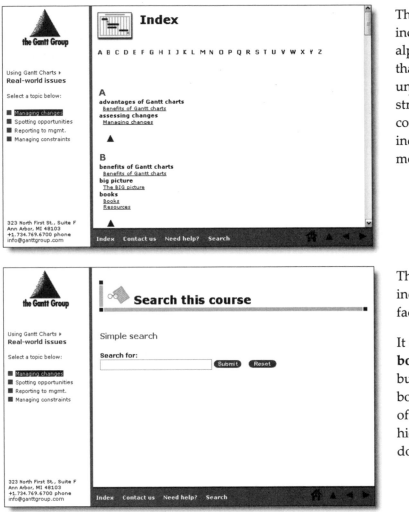

The course also includes an alphabetical **index** so that learners, unfamiliar with the structure of the course, can find the individual topics or modules they want.

The course also includes a **search** facility.

It does not contain a **bookmarking** feature but relies on the bookmarking feature of the browser. The hierarchical **menu** doubles as a **map**.

Built using Adobe Dreamweaver, Active Server Pages, custom JavaScript, and Adobe Flash.
View example at horton.com/eld/.

The course does contain a couple of other navigation aids: a **Home** button to return to the starting topic of the course and an **Up** button to move up one level in the menus.

IMPLEMENT NAVIGATION MECHANISMS

There are three ways to provide the access mechanisms mentioned in this chapter:

▶ Run the course in a learning management system (LMS) or learning content management system (LCMS) that provides access mechanisms.

▶ Build the course in authoring tools that automatically create access mechanisms.

▶ Manually construct the mechanisms using custom programming or scripting and custom-created buttons.

Let your LMS/LCMS provide a framework

Learning management systems launch and track completion of courses. Learning content management systems consolidate the modules or objects of a course and provide navigation among them. As such, these tools can provide some of the navigation mechanisms you need.

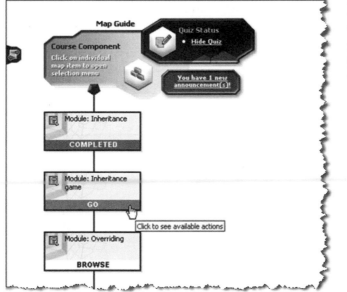

For example, here is a course map generated for a course managed by an LMS called The Learning Manager.

Management systems vary in the mechanisms they implement. Some pure LMSs merely launch the course. Those that combine some features of LCMSs automatically generate menus, maps, paging buttons, bookmarks, location indicators, search facility, and other navigation aids. Check the technical documentation of the LMS or LCMS before you depend on it for your navigation.

The advantage of using a management system to provide navigation is that the navigation is automatic and is consistent among all the courses managed by the system. With some systems all you need to do is to create the individual learning objects, import them into the system, and define a menu. The designer selects the desired navigation tools from a dialog box and the system takes care of the details.

A disadvantage of relying on the management system is that your course is totally dependent on the management system. If you need to move your course to another LMS, it may not have the same navigation mechanisms. If your course needs to run outside a management system, you are out of luck.

Use your authoring tool for standard features

Some authoring tools for e-learning can automatically create navigation aids, or at least simplify the process for the author. For example, let's consider the navigation provided by Articulate Presenter. It is a tool for converting PowerPoint presentations into e-learning. Articulate provides several navigation mechanisms. In a panel to the left of the content, Articulate creates an **Outline** tab which displays a multi-level menu of slides and assessments. A **Thumbnails** tab offers a visual menu where learners can select from miniature images of slides. A **Search** tab provides a simple search facility.

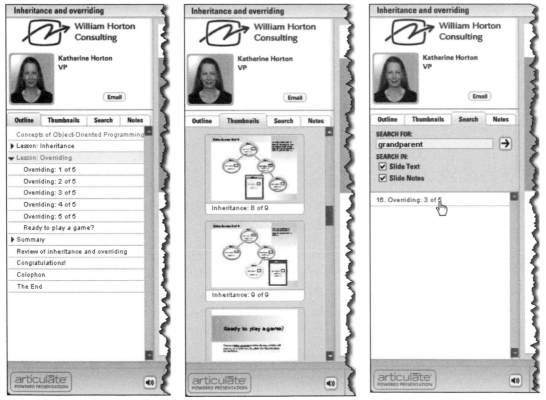

Created in Microsoft PowerPoint and converted for Web delivery using Articulate Presenter. View example at horton.com/eld/.

Articulate also includes buttons to page through the course and to create bookmarks. It also creates links to related documents and can display text notes or a transcript of narration.

If your authoring tool can create navigation mechanisms, by all means consider using them. They will save you a lot of time over creating the navigation manually. However, do not let the authoring tool dictate the navigation. If an authoring tool does not provide adequate navigation or does so in an awkward way, consider hand-building custom navigation.

Hand-build custom navigation

Sometimes, you just have to manually build navigation into content. Perhaps you cannot depend on the presence of a management system and your authoring tool cannot provide the specific type navigation you need.

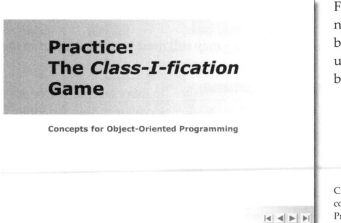

For the *Class-I-fication game*, I needed to construct navigation buttons keyed to this particular unit of content. Those are the buttons at the bottom right.

Created in Microsoft PowerPoint and converted for Web delivery using Articulate Presenter. View example at horton.com/eld/.

When is it worth the effort to break out the manuals, roll up your sleeves, and custom-code a navigation scheme? Here are some cases for which lazy (that is, time-efficient) developers resort to manual means:

▶ You need a custom pathway through the course or you need to customize navigation to local areas of your course.

▶ You need navigation that is specific to the subject matter. A management system would thwart subject-specific navigation, such as in highly-branching simulations.

▶ Your course needs to run independent of any management system.

▶ Your course does not have a simple organization.

Shorten pathways

When learners want to learn, they want to learn. They do not want to rummage around in your e-learning hoping to find something useful. As a standard, I suggest this rule:

> Require no more than 3 to 5 decisions to get to any component of the course or to answer any question.

Anything more than that and learners will give up before they get to the component they need.

IN CLOSING ...

Unless learners can find the content they need, e-learning is for naught. Navigation mechanisms ensure that learners can move through e-learning in ways that help them accomplish learning objectives—their own and those of the provider of e-learning.

Summary

E-learning benefits from an appropriate mixture of navigation mechanisms, selected with the needs of learners in mind. Some of these mechanisms are familiar from their use in paper books while others are creations of the electronic era. Pick wisely from this list:

Navigation mechanism	Description	When to use it
Paging	The learner repeatedly clicks a **Next** button to move through the content in a logical sequence.	Almost always, especially for novices who lack skills required by more sophisticated navigation mechanisms. Also when you want to restrict access to a single path.
Menu	Learners pick lessons and topics from a hierarchical list organized by logical categories.	To allow learners to drill down to a specific topic. To reinforce the organization of the course.

Navigation mechanism	Description	When to use it
Index	Learners pick from an alphabetical list of topics.	To enable just-in-time learning by letting learners directly access specific topics, regardless of where they occur in the course.
Map	Learners pick lessons or topics from a visual representation of the organization of the course.	To communicate a complex organization of a visual subject to visual learners.
Search	Learners search for words and phrases in the course.	Learners familiar with Web search engines need to go directly to individual topics.
Hypertext links	Learners click highlighted words or phrases to jump to related content.	Not everything fits in the formal organization or learners need access to auxiliary materials.
Location indicators	Learners see visual indications of their current locations in the course.	When learners need to learn how the course is organized so they can navigate more reliably.
Auto-scanning	Learners watch as displays appear in sequence. Learners signal when they want to stop and examine a display.	Learners recognize what something looks like but do not know its name.
Bookmarks	Learners return to topics they visited earlier.	Learners need to return to topics they visited earlier or just to resume where they left off.

For more ...

The navigation needed for a course depends on how the course is organized. Chapter 7 suggests ways to organize topics into lessons. Navigation mechanisms typically require buttons, text items, and other gadgets that must be displayed. Chapter 10 suggests how to design the visual display.

Implementing navigation mechanisms will require tools. Of first importance are tools for authoring e-learning. Also important are *learning management systems* and *learning content management systems*. Web searches using these terms will guide you to specific tools.

Conclusion

The future of e-learning

E-learning is not just a change of technology. It is part of a redefinition of how we as a species transmit knowledge, skills, and values to younger generations of workers and students. I will end this book by daring to make a few predictions of how e-learning and the functions it serves will continue to develop.

THE NEW MODEL OF LEARNING

E-learning is enabling a new model of learning that is replacing the one in effect for the past 500 years.

The publishing model is our past

For 500 years most academic education and industrial training has relied on the publishing model. The publishing model—or broadcast model as it is sometimes known—gathers knowledge from the enlightened few and distributes it to the ignorant masses.

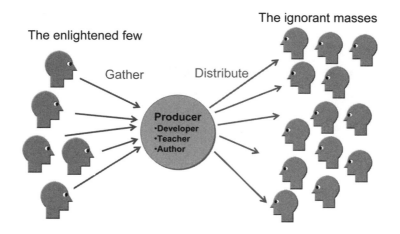

At the center of the publishing model is the producer. The producer may be a developer of training, a teacher in the classroom, or author of books and manuals. The producer works by consulting the enlightened few. These are the people who have the knowledge needed by others. The producer gathers this knowledge, organizes it, and expresses it. The producer then distributes or publishes the information to the "ignorant masses."

This model arose when only a small percentage of the population was educated, and entire classes of people had little access to education. It has succeeded phenomenally well. Universal education is an accepted goal, if not the norm. And everybody has knowledge to share and needs more knowledge.

The catalyst model is our future

The catalyst model of education is more sophisticated—and considerably messier.

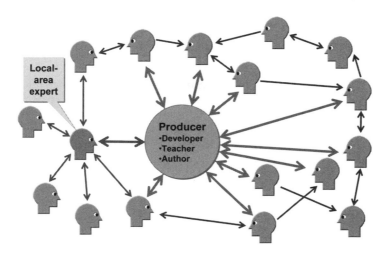

We still have a knowledge producer. And we have those who need the knowledge. But now, the exchange with knowledge consumers is a two-way exchange. Consumers can ask questions and may even contribute ideas themselves. Every student is a teacher; and every teacher, a student.

Some knowledge consumers also become knowledge producers themselves. I call them local-area experts. Local-area experts exchange information with a subset of the knowledge consumers. This subset may be those interested in an esoteric issue of the overall subject. Or they may be experts in how one particular department or company is applying the knowledge.

Knowledge consumers are no longer isolated. They discuss, they chat, and they exchange e-mail furiously. These circumferential exchanges complement the radial exchanges centered upon the producer.

What does this new model imply for us, the producers? We must conduct dialogs with our consumers, not merely broadcast information. We must develop materials to foster and support local-area experts. We must put in place communications mechanisms that allow consumers to communicate with one another, with local-area experts, and with us.

HOW WE WILL LEARN

The new models lead us to some interesting new visions of how education will be acquired in the future. One scenario goes like this.

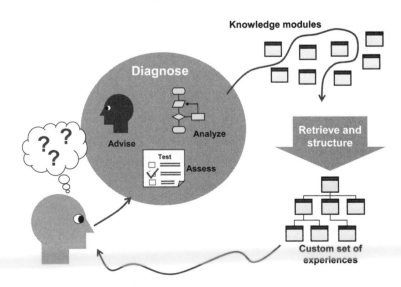

Learners will have access to millions or billions of knowledge modules. Some will be Web-pages with simple text and graphics. Others may include multimedia simulations. Some may consist of coupons for a video-conference with a human expert.

When learners have a need for knowledge, they will engage a diagnostic procedure. This diagnosis may be performed in a few nanoseconds by an algorithm in their computers. Or this diagnosis may involve taking an exam or filling out a questionnaire to assess their current knowledge level relative to their needed level. It may involve working with a counselor or advisor over a period of days.

The result of this diagnosis will be a request to a database containing millions or billions of knowledge modules. The needed modules will be rounded up and herded into a structure comprising a lesson or document custom tailored to the needs of the individual who requested it.

This cycle of requesting and receiving knowledge may take place dozens of times a day. The custom set of experiences may take minutes or months to consume. The result, though, will be a shift from mass-manufactured to handcrafted education.

JUST THE BEGINNING

We are just at the beginning of e-learning. We are using Version 1, 364, 287.4.6 of classroom learning. It is highly refined and efficient. We are only on Version 2.0 of e-learning. It is crude, buggy, and full of limitations. But every day it gets better. Creative designers are just now warming up.

I can't wait to see what you do.

Index

Index

Pfeiffer Publications Guide

This guide is designed to familiarize you with the various types of Pfeiffer publications. The formats section describes the various types of products that we publish; the methodologies section describes the many different ways that content might be provided within a product. We also provide a list of the topic areas in which we publish.

FORMATS

In addition to its extensive book-publishing program, Pfeiffer offers content in an array of formats, from fieldbooks for the practitioner to complete, ready-to-use training packages that support group learning.

FIELDBOOK Designed to provide information and guidance to practitioners in the midst of action. Most fieldbooks are companions to another, sometimes earlier, work, from which its ideas are derived; the fieldbook makes practical what was theoretical in the original text. Fieldbooks can certainly be read from cover to cover. More likely, though, you'll find yourself bouncing around following a particular theme, or dipping in as the mood, and the situation, dictate.

HANDBOOK A contributed volume of work on a single topic, comprising an eclectic mix of ideas, case studies, and best practices sourced by practitioners and experts in the field.

An editor or team of editors usually is appointed to seek out contributors and to evaluate content for relevance to the topic. Think of a handbook not as a ready-to-eat meal, but as a cookbook of ingredients that enables you to create the most fitting experience for the occasion.

RESOURCE Materials designed to support group learning. They come in many forms: a complete, ready-to-use exercise (such as a game); a comprehensive resource on one topic (such as conflict management) containing a variety of methods and approaches; or a collection of like-minded activities (such as icebreakers) on multiple subjects and situations.

TRAINING PACKAGE An entire, ready-to-use learning program that focuses on a particular topic or skill. All packages comprise a guide for the facilitator/trainer and a workbook for the participants. Some packages are supported with additional media—such as video—or learning aids, instruments, or other devices to help participants understand concepts or practice and develop skills.

- *Facilitator/trainer's guide* Contains an introduction to the program, advice on how to organize and facilitate the learning event, and step-by-step instructor notes. The guide also contains copies of presentation materials—handouts, presentations, and overhead designs, for example—used in the program.

• *Participant's workbook* Contains exercises and reading materials that support the learning goal and serves as a valuable reference and support guide for participants in the weeks and months that follow the learning event. Typically, each participant will require his or her own workbook.

ELECTRONIC CD-ROMs and web-based products transform static Pfeiffer content into dynamic, interactive experiences. Designed to take advantage of the searchability, automation, and ease-of-use that technology provides, our e-products bring convenience and immediate accessibility to your workspace.

METHODOLOGIES

CASE STUDY A presentation, in narrative form, of an actual event that has occurred inside an organization. Case studies are not prescriptive, nor are they used to prove a point; they are designed to develop critical analysis and decision-making skills. A case study has a specific time frame, specifies a sequence of events, is narrative in structure, and contains a plot structure—an issue (what should be/have been done?). Use case studies when the goal is to enable participants to apply previously learned theories to the circumstances in the case, decide what is pertinent, identify the real issues, decide what should have been done, and develop a plan of action.

ENERGIZER A short activity that develops readiness for the next session or learning event. Energizers are most commonly used after a break or lunch to stimulate or refocus the group. Many involve some form of physical activity, so they are a useful way to counter post-lunch lethargy. Other uses include transitioning from one topic to another, where "mental" distancing is important.

EXPERIENTIAL LEARNING ACTIVITY (ELA) A facilitator-led intervention that moves participants through the learning cycle from experience to application (also known as a Structured Experience). ELAs are carefully thought-out designs in which there is a definite learning purpose and intended outcome. Each step—everything that participants do during the activity—facilitates the accomplishment of the stated goal. Each ELA includes complete instructions for facilitating the intervention and a clear statement of goals, suggested group size and timing, materials required, an explanation of the process, and, where appropriate, possible variations to the activity. (For more detail on Experiential Learning Activities, see the Introduction to the *Reference Guide to Handbooks and Annuals*, 1999 edition, Pfeiffer, San Francisco.)

GAME A group activity that has the purpose of fostering team spirit and togetherness in addition to the achievement of a pre-stated goal. Usually contrived—undertaking a desert expedition, for example—this type of learning method offers an engaging means for participants to demonstrate and practice business and interpersonal skills. Games are effective for team building and personal development mainly because the goal is subordinate to the process—the means through which participants reach decisions, collaborate, communicate, and generate trust and understanding. Games often engage teams in "friendly" competition.

ICEBREAKER A (usually) short activity designed to help participants overcome initial anxiety in a training session and/or to acquaint the participants with one another. An icebreaker can be a fun activity or can be tied to specific topics or training goals. While a useful tool in itself, the icebreaker comes into its own in situations where tension or resistance exists within a group.

INSTRUMENT A device used to assess, appraise, evaluate, describe, classify, and summarize various aspects of human behavior. The term used to describe an instrument depends primarily on its format and purpose. These terms include survey, questionnaire, inventory, diagnostic, survey, and poll. Some uses of instruments include providing instrumental feedback to group members, studying here-and-now processes or functioning within a group, manipulating group composition, and evaluating outcomes of training and other interventions.

Instruments are popular in the training and HR field because, in general, more growth can occur if an individual is provided with a method for focusing specifically on his or her own behavior. Instruments also are used to obtain information that will serve as a basis for change and to assist in workforce planning efforts.

Paper-and-pencil tests still dominate the instrument landscape with a typical package comprising a facilitator's guide, which offers advice on administering the instrument and interpreting the collected data, and an initial set of instruments. Additional instruments are available separately. Pfeiffer, though, is investing heavily in e-instruments. Electronic instrumentation provides effortless distribution and, for larger groups particularly, offers advantages over paper-and-pencil tests in the time it takes to analyze data and provide feedback.

LECTURETTE A short talk that provides an explanation of a principle, model, or process that is pertinent to the participants' current learning needs. A lecturette is intended to establish a common language bond between the trainer and the participants by providing a mutual frame of reference. Use a lecturette as an introduction to a group activity or event, as an interjection during an event, or as a handout.

MODEL A graphic depiction of a system or process and the relationship among its elements. Models provide a frame of reference and something more tangible, and more easily remembered, than a verbal explanation. They also give participants something to "go on," enabling them to track their own progress as they experience the dynamics, processes, and relationships being depicted in the model.

ROLE PLAY A technique in which people assume a role in a situation/scenario: a customer service rep in an angry-customer exchange, for example. The way in which the role is approached is then discussed and feedback is offered. The role play is often repeated using a different approach and/or incorporating changes made based on feedback received. In other words, role playing is a spontaneous interaction involving realistic behavior under artificial (and safe) conditions.

SIMULATION A methodology for understanding the interrelationships among components of a system or process. Simulations differ from games in that they test or use a model that depicts or mirrors some aspect of reality in form, if not necessarily in content. Learning occurs by studying the effects of change on one or more factors of the model. Simulations are commonly used to test hypotheses about what happens in a system—often referred to as "what if?" analysis—or to examine best-case/worst-case scenarios.

THEORY A presentation of an idea from a conjectural perspective. Theories are useful because they encourage us to examine behavior and phenomena through a different lens.

TOPICS

The twin goals of providing effective and practical solutions for workforce training and organization development and meeting the educational needs of training and human resource professionals shape Pfeiffer's publishing program. Core topics include the following:

Leadership & Management

Communication & Presentation

Coaching & Mentoring

Training & Development

E-Learning

Teams & Collaboration

OD & Strategic Planning

Human Resources

Consulting

What will you find on pfeiffer.com?

• The best in workplace performance solutions for training and HR professionals

• Downloadable training tools, exercises, and content

• Web-exclusive offers

• Training tips, articles, and news

• Seamless on-line ordering

• Author guidelines, information on becoming a Pfeiffer Affiliate, and much more

Discover more at www.pfeiffer.com